LIFE, DEATH AND GROWING UP ON THE WESTERN FRONT

LIFE, DEATH AND GROWING UP ON THE WESTERN FRONT

ANTHONY FLETCHER

YALE UNIVERSITY PRESS
NEW HAVEN AND LONDON

For information about this and other Yale University Press publications, please contact:
U.S. Office: sales.press@yale.edu   www.yalebooks.com
Europe Office: sales@yaleup.co.uk   www.yalebooks.co.uk

Set in Minion Pro by IDSUK (DataConnection) Ltd
Printed in Great Britain by TJ International Ltd, Padstow, Cornwall

Library of Congress Cataloging-in-Publication Data
Fletcher, Anthony.
   Life, death and growing up on the western front/Anthony Fletcher.
      pages cm
   ISBN 978-0-300-19553-8 (cl: alk. paper)
1. Great Britain. Army—History—World War, 1914–1918. 2. World War, 1914–1918—
Social aspects—Great Britain. 3. World War, 1914–1918—Social aspects—Europe,
Western. 4. Great Britain. Army—Military life—History—20th century. 5. World War,
1914–1918—Personal narratives, British. 6. Great Britain. Army. British Expeditionary
Force. 7. Soldiers—Great Britain—Correspondence. I. Title.
   D546.F54 2013
   940.4'8141—dc23

                                                                              2013010439

A catalogue record for this book is available from the British Library.

10 9 8 7 6 5 4 3 2 1

In Memory of Reggie, Clare and Delle

Chanctonbury Ring

I can't forget the lane that goes from Steyning to the Ring
In summer time, and o'er the Downs how larks and linnets sing
High in the air. The wind comes off the sea and oh! the air
I never knew till now that life in old days was so fair
But now I know it in this filthy rat infested ditch
Where every shell must kill or spare and god knows which
And I am made a beast of prey and this trench is my lair
My God I never knew till now those days were so fair
And we assault in half an hour and it's a silly thing
I cannot forget the lane that goes from Steyning to the Ring

JOHN STANLEY PURVIS, 5th Battalion the Yorkshire Regiment,
2 December 1915

A stone with these words was placed in Mouse Lane by the people of Steyning in the year 2000, in celebration of their inheritance.

Contents

Part III: Sacrifice

List of Main Characters

Letter Writers

Second Lieutenant Yvo Charteris (1896–1915), Grenadier Guards
Lieutenant-Colonel Rowland Feilding (1871–1945), Coldstream Guards, Connaught Rangers, London Regiment
Captain Graham Greenwell (1896–1970), Oxfordshire and Buckinghamshire Light Infantry
Captain Julian Grenfell (1886–1915), Royal Dragoons
Lieutenant-Colonel Robert Hermon (1878–1917), King Edward's Horse, Northumberland Fusiliers
Private Peter McGregor (1871–1916), Argyll and Sutherland Highlanders
Captain Billie Nevill (1894–1916), East Surrey Regiment
Lance Corporal Cyril Newman (1893–1978), Queen Victoria's Rifles, London Regiment
Private Alec Reader (1897–1916), Civil Service Rifles, London Regiment
Second Lieutenant Ernest Kennedy Smith (1892–1915), Artists Rifles, The Buffs
Lieutenant Wilbert Spencer (1897–1915), Wiltshire Regiment
Captain Lance Spicer (1893–1980), King's Own Yorkshire Light Infantry
Sergeant Will Streets (1885–1916), York and Lancaster Regiment
Private Jack Sweeney (1889–1961), Lincolnshire Regiment
Lieutenant Herbert Trench (1892–1971), Honourable Artillery Company, Army Service Corps
Major Reggie Trench (1888–1918), Inns of Court OTC, Sherwood Foresters

Diarist

Captain Charlie May (1889–1916), Manchester Regiment

Illustrations and Maps

Figures

Plates

1. Reggie Trench, Lafayette, 1915. Trench Archive.
2, 3. Members of the Inns of Court Officers Training Corps in Ashridge Park, Berkhamsted, 1915. Trench Archive.
4. Sheffield Pals Battalion at Bramall Lane Football Ground, September 1914. Victor Piuk, *A Dream within the Dark*, Derbyshire County Council, 2003.
5. Lieutenant Herbert Trench with Army Service Corps 363 company, Ypres Depot, 1916. Trench Archive.
6. Private Alec Reader and his family. Reproduced by permission of Doug Goodman.
7. Private Jack Sweeney. Reproduced by permission of the Imperial War Museum, DOC 842.
8. Sergeant Will Streets. Reproduced by permission of Harold Streets.
9. The Wedding of Reggie and Clare Trench, 28 January 1915. Trench Archive.
10. Lance Corporal Cyril Newman in the trenches. Reproduced by permission of the Reverend David Newman.
11. Captain Graham Greenwell. G.H. Greenwell, *An Infant in Arms*, Allen Lane, 1972.
12. Julian Grenfell by Violet Rutland, 1909. Nicholas Mosley, *Julian Grenfell: His Life and the Times of his Death*, Holt, Rinehart and Winston, 1976.
13. Captain Lance Spicer. Reproduced by permission of Sir Nicholas Spicer.
14. Captain Billie Nevill. Ruth Harris, *Billie: The Nevill Letters 1914–1916*, Naval and Military Press, 2003.
15. Lieutenant Colonel Rowland Feilding. Reproduced by permission of Caroline Gordon-Duff.
16. Lieutenant Colonel Robert Hermon. Reproduced by permission of Anne Nason.
17. Lieutenant Colonel Robert Hermon with his children and dogs, 1915. Reproduced by permission of Anne Nason.
18. Lance Corporal Gordon Buxton. Reproduced by permission of Anne Nason.
19. Captain Ernest Smith. Reproduced by permission of Benjamin Cobb.
20. Captain Charlie May with his wife Maud and daughter Pauline. Reproduced by permission of Gerry Harrison.
21. Private Arthur Bunting. Reproduced by permission of Lieutenant Colonel Adrian Bunting.
22. Janet McGregor. Reproduced by permission of the Imperial War Museum, HU 38371.
23. Private Peter McGregor. Reproduced by permission of the Imperial War Museum, DOC 840.
24. Yvo Charteris. Reproduced by permission of the Earl of Wemyss.

Maps

Preface and Acknowledgements

Venturing into a new field, I have enjoyed friendly advice and support over the past ten years or so from a number of military historians of the Great War. Gary Sheffield, in particular, generously gave time to reading and commenting upon some early draft material.

I have turned to two of my undergraduate colleagues at Merton College, Oxford for detailed scrutiny of draft chapters. Malcolm Kitch has taken a benignly quizzical interest in the project from the start and offered numerous helpful suggestions, some of them informed by his own National Service experience. Niall Campbell has contributed astute and thoughtful commentaries chapter by chapter, returning my scripts with remarkable speed together with his neatly handwritten notes. Jim Honeybone, a more recent friend, guided my first steps in writing this kind of history for a general audience with some trenchant advice.

I had many stimulating conversations with Michael Roper when he was working on his book *The Secret Battle: Emotional Survival in the Great War*, published in 2009, and with Jessica Meyer, about her book *Men of War: Masculinity and the First World War in Britain*, which was published in the same year.

I am grateful for help from the staff of the Imperial War Museum as I explored their very extensive collections. They have answered numerous questions about the archives they hold, especially those relating to the war experience of eight of my leading characters. Roderick Suddaby, Keeper of the Department of Documents, and Anthony Richards have been particularly supportive. I am very grateful indeed for the generosity of families in giving me permission to reproduce extracts from papers in the Imperial War Museum to which they hold the copyright. I would like to thank Gerry Harrison for the papers of C.C. May, Reverend David Newman for the papers of C. Newman, Doug Goodman for the papers of B.A. Reader, Benjamin Cobb for the papers of E.K. Smith, Nicola Kent for the papers of W.P.B. Spencer, Harold Streets for the papers of J.W. Streets. Efforts have been made without success to trace the copyright holders of the papers of P. McGregor, W.P. Nevill and P.J. Sweeney. The author and the Imperial War Museum would be grateful for information, which might help to trace their identities and addresses.

I was fortunate in the affectionate interest shown in my life as a boy by my great-uncle, Herbert Trench, the only shell shock victim among my cast of leading figures. Sadly, he never felt able to tell me anything about his experience on the Western Front, though he did talk occasionally in his later years to his daughters, Robina Lockyer and Valerie Kerslake. They have taught me a great deal about his life. I owe both of them a particular debt of gratitude, for the sensitive but open way they have encouraged me to explore some very intimate aspects of their father's military life using documentation about which they had not previously known.

It has been rewarding hearing actual reminiscences or family lore about others among my leading characters. Nicola Kent has helped me to work out how her uncle Wilbert Spencer got to Sandhurst so very rapidly in August 1914. Sir Nicholas Spicer told me of his memories of spending time with his great-uncle Lance Spicer in his youth. Caroline Gordon-Duff, daughter of Prunella Feilding who appears as a child in this book, kindly lent me the portrait of her grandfather, Rowland Feilding. Amanda, Countess of Wemyss, another granddaughter of Rowland's, also contributed family memories of the fine soldier everyone knew as 'Snowball'. I enjoyed talking with Harold Streets, a great-nephew of Will Streets, about 'Uncle Will', as he was known in the family. David Newman offered a fund of reminiscence and information about his father, Cyril Newman. James, Earl of Wemyss shared family knowledge of his great-uncle, Yvo Charteris.

I was able in two cases to use exceptional family archives now in private possession. I am extremely grateful to the Earl of Wemyss for allowing me to consult the Charteris papers and family photographic collection at Stanway. I greatly appreciated his hospitality there. David and Ann Newman were welcoming at their home in Daventry when I consulted his father's remarkable and meticulously created archive. David also lent me his father's typescripts to work from.

I have been privileged to talk to several descendants who have made themselves experts on the roles that their family members played on the Western Front. Anne Nason, editor of the letters of her grandfather Robert Hermon, has been informative about the family's close and lasting connection with the Buxton family. She introduced me to Jessica Hawes, daughter of Gordon Buxton, who was Robert Hermon's batman at the Front. Gerry Harrison, his great-nephew, told me about Charlie May's early background and helped me to understand the puzzle of how his papers ended up in both the Imperial War Museum and Tameside Local Studies and Archives Centre. Adrian Bunting has enabled me to give a much fuller account of the relationship between Charlie May and his grandfather Arthur Bunting, Charlie's batman, than would otherwise have been possible. Doug Goodman kindly referred me to published work on his great-uncle, Alec Reader's war service. He provided family papers, relating the story of their discovery and his family's subsequent dedication to commemoration of Alec at High Wood.

Peter Robinson, a pillar of the history publishing world, was generous with his time in giving advice and encouragement. This is my fourth book published with Yale University Press. My editor there, Robert Baldock, has been, as usual, the most patient, inspirational and constructively attentive of publishers.

My sister-in-law, Diana Fletcher, has been unsparing with her time and expertise in helping me trace genealogical leads regarding Great War soldiers. She also provided important material on an area of special interest to her, the Voluntary Aid Detachment scheme in Red Cross nursing. Delle Fletcher read and commented on much of the book in various drafts. It is appropriate that she should share the dedication of the book with her father and mother, Reggie and Clare Trench, for it was Reggie's wonderful letters from the Western Front that prompted me to think of writing it in the first place. Finally, my profound thanks to my wife Brenda for living with this book so selflessly for so long.

A.J.F.
South Newington, November 2012

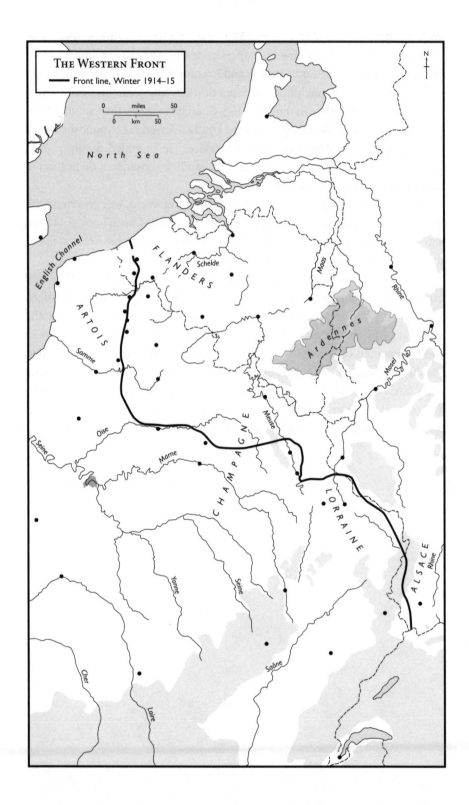

THE WESTERN FRONT

Front line, Winter 1914–15

North Sea

English Channel

FLANDERS

Schelde

ARTOIS

Somme

Oise

Marne

CHAMPAGNE

Meuse

Maas

Ardennes

Rhine

Mosel

LORRAINE

ALSACE

Rhine

Seine

Yonne

Seine

Cher

Loire

Saône

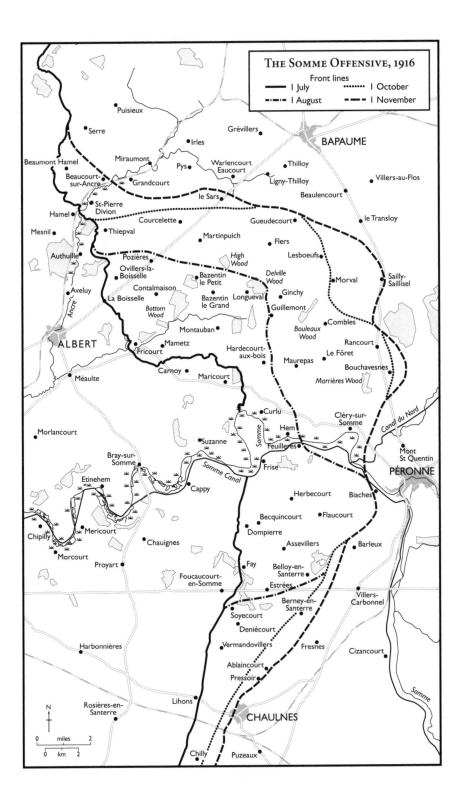

THE SOMME OFFENSIVE, 1916

Front lines
I July   I October
I August   I November

Puisieux
Serre
Grévillers
Irles
BAPAUME
Beaumont Hamel
Miraumont
Pys
Warlencourt
Eaucourt
Thilloy
Villers-au-Flos
Beaucourt-
sur-Ancre
Grandcourt
Ligny-Thilloy
le Sars
Beaulencourt
St-Pierre
Divion
le Transloy
Hamel
Courcelette
Gueudecourt
Mesnil
Thiepval
Martinpuich
Flers
Authuille
Pozières
High
Wood
Lesbœufs
Ovillers-la-
Boisselle
Bazentin
le Petit
Delville
Wood
Morval
Sailly-
Saillisel
Aveluy
Contalmaison
Ginchy
La Boisselle
Bazentin
le Grand
Longueval
Guillemont
Combles
Bottom
Wood
Montauban
Bouleaux
Wood
Rancourt
ALBERT
Mametz
Hardecourt-
aux-bois
Le Fôret
Fricourt
Bouchavesnes
Méaulte
Carnoy
Maricourt
Maurepas
Marrières Wood
Curlu
Cléry-sur-
Somme
Morlancourt
Hem
Suzanne
Feuillères
Mont
St Quentin
Bray-sur-
Somme
Frise
PÉRONNE
Etinehem
Somme Canal
Cappy
Herbecourt
Biaches
Chipilly
Mericourt
Becquincourt
Flaucourt
Chauignes
Dompierre
Morcourt
Proyart
Assevillers
Barleux
Fay
Belloy-en-
Santerre
Foucaucourt-
en-Somme
Estrées
Villers-
Carbonnel
Berney-en-
Santerre
Harbonnières
Soyecourt
Deniécourt
Vermandovillers
Fresnes
Cizancourt
Somme
Ablaincourt
Pressoir
Rosières-en-
Santerre
Lihons
N
CHAULNES
0   miles   2
0   km   2
Chilly
Puzeaux

Prologue

My interest in the Great War began when I found a tin trunk among my grandmother's possessions after she died in 1989. I soon realised that this was a treasure trove.[1] There were 243 letters written in indelible pencil on exercise book paper sent by my grandfather Major Reggie Trench to his wife Clare from the Western Front. There were also another 35 of his letters to his mother, Isabel Trench. Every pencilled word in the letters to his mother had been carefully written over by her in ink, as she sought solace following his death in battle in 1918. Reggie was not a professional soldier. When the war broke out in 1914 he was training to be an accountant. But, reading the letters, I became fascinated by the account they give of how, as a keen Territorial officer accustomed to no more than an annual fortnight's camp, he rapidly became engrossed in the full-time business of what he called 'practical soldiering'.

The origins of this book lie in my exploration of the stories which he and other young men told in letters about their experience of war in France. Letters, I discovered, have been much used to illustrate general accounts of campaigns, battles and trench warfare but often in an anecdotal way. They can seem remote from the conditions in which men lived and the personal stories of family lives. The authenticity of letters lies in their freedom from constraints other than the permanent problem of what to tell and what to conceal. I am not a military historian and have spent my professional career in earlier periods of history and other fields, especially British politics, government, society and gender. But the potential of war letters, I felt, might be more fully exploited. Here was an opportunity to throw fresh light on a cataclysmic event that shaped our world. This avenue of research quickly became compulsive and absorbing.

Letters project the myriad voices of soldiers at war. They were written for a very particular kind of audience, overwhelmingly one that craved reassurance. Letters confided both information and the feelings of soldiers, vividly revealing preoccupations and fears or even telling of survival in battle. They have an immediacy unlike any other source. Yet what a man felt comfortable with saying to a wife, mother, father or brothers always reflected his state of mind at a specific time. Every letter crossed a gulf of incomprehension between those at home, fed on wartime propaganda characterised by 'chaos and lack of direction', and the accounts of men who had learnt what trench warfare was really like.[2] It has been said that that gulf between the Home Front and the Western Front was always wide. But it has come to seem to me that civilians had a better idea of conditions at the Front than some have suggested. Letters like the ones I have used must surely be a principal reason for this.

Every letter was an exercise in shaping a military experience, in structuring sentences to inform yet protect loved ones, in taking into account domestic worries and preoccupations. Yet these were men, mostly very young, whose adult civilian personalities had hardly been formed. Many were raw from school or the workplace. I have come to think there is a problem in the massive historiography of the Great War that has not been fully tackled. How did young men create a personal identity as soldiers before they had properly found themselves as professional and working men at home? How, on short periods of leave and in writing home, did they cope with the demands of these two very different identities?

A book which attempts to answer questions of this kind has to focus on the experience of a small group of soldiers in some depth. In this respect, as in others, I have followed the example of Michael Roper in *The Secret Battle*, a pioneering study published in 2009 of emotional survival in the Great War. Writing about men's relationships with their mothers, he used letters from Reggie Trench to his mother Isabel which I lent him. There is a small further overlap in our source material. However, by and large, I have been asking some of the same questions as he did but with a different set of subjects and on the wider canvas of men's correspondence with their whole families. For balance, I have included three middle-aged family men as well as unmarried or just-married ones.

By 1917 the British Expeditionary Force was sending home eight million letters a week. Soldiers were then receiving even more letters than they sent.[3] These letters sent to men at the Front were a cumulative and untiring act of love and care on a scale never before known in the nation's history. The essence of men's letters home, on the other hand, was that they were cathartic and private.[4] Some men numbered their letters and had their wives number the replies, a way of checking for losses in the post. But the post was generally both fast and reliable. Reading these letters has been an enormous privilege and an imaginative challenge. No amount of background reading can prepare one fully for the task of empathy that handling material of this kind demands. Yet handling the paper these men wrote upon – including in some cases the envelopes in which they posted letters to England, the photographs of pals in the trenches, the mementos and scraps like treasured leave tickets – is extraordinarily moving. This historical research has given me every bit as much of a thrill as any of my earlier archival ventures.

The dominant impression left by the mass of correspondence from the Western Front that I have read has been of men's strong ties with home. Their powerful need to express a nostalgia which drew upon memories of a shared past, created a shared present and dwelt upon hopes for a shared future marked the letters. Of course, home meant very different things to different people. For middle-class men it was a respectable house and garden, for the agricultural labourer a cottage, for the urban dweller a back-to-back street. But it was Sunday dinner, smiling family faces, that mattered, whether home was a manor house or a semi-detached.[5] Ernest Smith ended a long, rambling letter to his mother on 6 October 1915 by imagining his parental household that evening: 'I am running on too far into the night now, everyone else has turned in, it is just the time when I expect you will be dozing by the fire and Father perhaps walking in and out of the bathroom in scanty attire! Give him very special love and all the others.'[6]

1. 'Our billet at Bailleul'. Sketch by Ernest Smith, undated.

'We have to live on memories and anticipations,' Cyril Newman told his sweetheart Winnie. Meanwhile it was a kind of therapy for him to spend hours imagining Winnie going about her daily routines. Sometimes he spelt out these thoughts. This came most easily when he wrote one of the uncensored 'green envelope' letters which were made available to the Tommies from time to time. 'I often think of you Dear,' he wrote once, 'in your business life – the crowded railway journey from Muswell Hill – the almost suffocating closeness of the carriages.' He pictured her 'close-aired' office room. Fantasy took hold: 'she is sitting neatly by the desk – her head bent slightly over her ledger . . . for a moment her brow is furrowed. How I should love to kiss that furrow away! . . . Does she know how her boy longs to take her into his arms, longs for even an hour's talk?' Cyril and Winnie spent pages planning the home they would make as man and wife after the war was over.[7]

Back at the Front after his leave in the autumn of 1917, an overwhelming spate of nostalgia was provoked in Reggie Trench by Clare's request to use his tennis racket: 'isn't it a little heavy for you?' They had fallen in love at house parties in 1911 and 1912. 'I can see you clearly darling,' he wrote, 'at Bark Hart coming down the lawn swinging your tennis racket and sometimes smiling at me just a little – that was before we were even engaged between ourselves – though that was such a short time really wasn't it?' The tennis racket had summoned up memories of his romantic quest, his wife, his daughter, his patriotic service for his country, his whole young adult life.

Imagining home and imagining the Front, for those intimate with each other, involved recalling activities. Detail mattered; letters joined up separated lives. 'You ask what I was doing on Easter Day,' Reggie replied to his mother on 13 April 1917: 'well I was up and about all the night before and got to sleep about 7 a.m. after a breakfast of tea (with rum) sardines and army biscuits. I slept till about 10 a.m. when I regret to say the General found me.' He repeated this story to Clare later, glad to know she had received two of his letters on Easter Day: 'you must have been reading them as I slept.'[8]

This book has been made possible by the dedication of the staff of the Imperial War Museum, who have listed, catalogued and cared for hundreds of collections of letters, just eight of which I have used in detail. Relatives of some soldiers and historians edited and annotated several of the published collections I draw upon. I have read and pondered more than 2,000 letters in all. Yet this is a minute sample of the correspondence of a massive citizen army, for during the Great War the British Expeditionary Force grew to over five million men.

The criteria I applied in choosing the characters of my book have been simple. I looked for letters that are explicit about the lives men lived at the Front, that reveal their emotional experience, that relate vividly their ups and downs, their excitements and frustrations. I sought throughout to know what it was really like to be there and to fight, to live behind the lines and to go home on leave. I have tried to choose collections of letters which have a quality that makes them truly revealing. This may also, of course, make my soldiers distinctive, more deeply engaged than some others, more alert to the nuances of army life. No small group of soldiers extracted from a huge army is likely to be representative or typical of the whole British Expeditionary Force. This book can only present one view, based on lives at the Front lived out by thoughtful men, by and large from close families, whose performance as soldiers was in some cases exemplary and was always competent.

In deciding whom to include as a leading figure in the book I paid no attention to whether a man was killed or survived. Having drawn upon a large range of sources which introduce many minor characters to the book, I ended up with the seventeen men, sixteen letter writers and one diarist, who constantly bestride my stage. They are listed on p. ix. Eleven of them were killed and six survived. This is not in proportion to the actual war, since, of about 715,000 men in all who fought on the Western Front, only around 12 per cent were killed.

In creating this artificial band of brothers, which includes two men from my own family, I have been deliberately diverse. They did not know each other, they came from different regiments, different parts of England, different schools, professions and kinds of employment. There is one Scot, but no Welsh or Irish men. They span the aristocracy, middle class and working class. Most fought as infantrymen in the front line. I am aware of the omission of artillerymen and engineers. I have been concerned to include letters from all ranks, although the nature of the material available has led to my using proportionately more letters from officers than from NCOs and Tommies. The leading characters of the book are two lieutenant-colonels, one major, five captains, four subalterns, one sergeant, one lance corporal but only three privates. Yet every one of the soldiers I have chosen, I believe, establishes himself through his letters as a man of character, commitment and, within his lights, of determination.

The men who fought on the Western Front were by and large incredibly young. About 500,000 of those who were killed in the Great War were under thirty at their death. Two of my soldiers, at the outbreak of war in 1914, were in their forties, one was in his thirties, ten were in their twenties and four were only seventeen or eighteen. Two of them were regular soldiers, two came out of early retirement from the army, the rest were volunteers. There are no conscripts in my sample or men who joined the army after 1916.

The structure of the book, in three parts, is straightforward. The first three chapters, on 'Going to War', describe British entry into the conflict, the nature of the national cause and the patriotic idealism that inspired so many to take up arms. A new moral order, it is argued, was created by the outbreak of the war in 1914. An account of training covers commissioning and enlistment, inculcation of martial discipline, the Channel crossing and the journey to the Front.

The core of the book is Part II, 'At the Front', which employs a thematic as well as a chronological approach to the realities and trials of war in eleven chapters. This begins with an account of how letters and parcels sustained men through months and years of service overseas. Chapter 5 discusses fear and shell shock, Chapters 6 and 7 the leadership of officers and the care they gave their men in this age of unquestioned social hierarchy. Chapter 8 stresses that for most soldiers it was the loss and injury of close colleagues which caused the most searing distress, rather than the daily irritations of mud, cold and lice. Horror, it is shown, could stalk the trenches at any moment.

Chapter 9 assesses how the British Expeditionary Force held together during a war that it seemed would never end and which finally yielded victory to the Allies through the BEF's extraordinary spirit and resilience. Several of the key ingredients of morale, like caring leadership and sustained contact with home, have already been established. The exercise of discipline, it is argued, was more flexible and shot through with more consideration for the strains on the Tommies than some have suggested. Incentives to performance at battalion and company levels are set out. The aggressive and hostile attitude to the German enemy of a minority of British soldiers is put in context.

The deaths at the Front of eleven of our soldiers are treated in three narrative sections which appear in Chapters 10, 12 and 13. The letters of senior officers reporting what actually happened provide crucial testimony about how these individuals fell in battle. Blighty leave, treated in Chapter 11, was a shot in the arm for soldiers. It always seemed too slow to come round but was then usually uplifting in its impact. Morale constantly ebbed and flowed. But in the long perspective the turning point of the Great War, William Philpott has argued convincingly, was the Somme, the 'pivotal clash' in 140 days of battle which 'shaped our world and is with us still'.[9] Chapters 13 and 14 explore how the road from 1 July 1916 to the Armistice on 11 November 1918 was by no means smooth but in the end was inexorable. Allied morale during these last twenty-eight months was on a steadily rising curve.

The final section of the book, 'Sacrifice', deals first with the establishment of Remembrance Day and the process of commemoration of soldiers who died from 1919 to the present day. Chapter 16 is concerned with the rhetoric and ideology of sacrifice, recalling the argument about patriotic idealism set out in Chapter 1. The later lives of the survivors, meanwhile, illustrates in Chapter 17 how the Great War was a stage in many different kinds of lives. The Epilogue considers the Great War in the perspective of the century that followed.

PART I

GOING TO WAR

'Quiet Earnest Faces'

The National Cause

The catastrophe that led during July and August 1914 to the outbreak of the Great War is very well known. The Archduke Franz Ferdinand, heir to the throne of Austria–Hungary, was assassinated at Sarajevo on 28 June by a Bosnian Serb. Austria, confident of German support, sought to punish the Serbs. The international crisis developed over eight days in July. Austria's declaration of war on Serbia came on the 28th. In the next four days Germany mobilised its navy, Russia began to mobilise and Germany declared war on Russia.

The British government began to assemble its home fleet at Scapa Flow on 28 July, enabling it to dominate the North Sea. On the 30th, the Prime Minister, Herbert Asquith, bundled the problem of Irish Home Rule into cold storage and turned his attention to Europe.[1] He found 'depression and paralysis' in the City, combined with a very general and desperate desire to keep out of the European conflict. But Britain's ultimatum to Germany, after the news that German troops had entered Belgium, expired on the night of 4 August.[2]

On 30 July, Reggie Trench, an alert young man with his ear to the ground, was preparing for his annual Territorial camp on Salisbury Plain. He reflected to Clare Howard on whether Britain would 'come out of the fog alright'. Reggie considered Asquith's change of focus 'excellent'. He guessed it depended upon Germany's 'preparedness for war whether they will go in or not'. 'If they come in we do inevitably I think,' he declared, 'and one must remember that we would not then be fighting for any abstract "Serbian" reason but rather to prevent France being overwhelmed and to protect the neutrality of Belgium and Holland, which are of enormous importance to us as regards Germany.'[3]

Reggie was stating the argument with which on 2 August Sir Edward Grey, the Foreign Secretary, swayed the Cabinet. He insisted, before the German ultimatum to Belgium, on the dangers to Britain if Belgium and France fell. The risks for Britain of non-intervention outweighed the risks of intervention. This was the centuries-old balance of power argument. 'We cannot allow Germany to use the Channel as a hostile base,' Prime Minister Herbert Asquith wrote to Venetia Stanley that night. The Liberal government's case would have been instantly recognisable to Palmerston, to Castlereagh, even, before the Spanish Armada, to Queen Elizabeth.[4]

Mary, Countess of Wemyss, mother of three Charteris boys, was the confidante of Arthur Balfour, the Conservative leader.[5] Her diary for the first weekend in August 1914, full of cricket, tennis and entertaining grandchildren, records the routines of country house life. But in her upper-class circle in Gloucestershire, she noted, 'everyone talks of war': 'I heard trains rumbling in the night which brought home the facts,' she recorded. She came up to London with her youngest son, Yvo, on the morning of Monday, 3 August. 'One saw in his face how much he was going through,' she wrote, after meeting Balfour that day. Balfour was urging the despatch of an Expeditionary Force to France. 'Mobilise and Embark' was the Conservative Party's message. Between 2 and 4 August Asquith pulled together a divided Cabinet. Hearing the story from Balfour, Mary Wemyss concluded, 'I think Asquith has done well.' Lloyd George, Chancellor of the Exchequer, difficult at first, was now 'full of zeal'.[6]

There was no frenzy of war enthusiasm in August 1914.[7] Catriona Pennell has recently demolished myths about the outbreak of the war which have long stood in for the meticulous investigation into popular responses to the outbreak of war in Britain and Ireland that her prodigious research has now provided. An image of rampant jingoism has to be replaced with a more complex picture, as Britain became engaged in a war seen as one of national defence. A mood of sober commitment quickly united the nation. A Tory evening paper The Globe on 3 August described a normal Bank Holiday crowd 'bent on enjoying themselves'. It was only when military music was heard that 'fathers picked up their children, mothers gathered the bottles of milk, bags of cake and fruit and there was a general rush in the direction of the Palace.'[8] A famous photograph of crowds outside Buckingham Palace the next night shows mainly middle-class young men in straw hats, cheering the Royal Family on the balcony. As an icon of going to war this is deeply misleading.[9]

One of those young men outside Buckingham Palace was the seventeen-year-old Yvo Charteris. Mary Wemyss left him a note at midnight saying he was very late and she hoped he was 'not Mafeking'.[10] The press in August 1914 used reports of that night as a yardstick to remind people that the hysteria of Mafeking Night in 1900 was by no means appropriate in this national crisis. There was some rowdyism, admitted the Cambridge Daily News, 'but it was not by any means of the same character' as the orgy of rejoicing when news came through that Baden-Powell's force had been relieved in far-off Africa. The mood now, reported H.A. Gwynne to his *Morning Post* correspondent in St Petersburg, was 'England at its very best, silent, undemonstrative but absolutely determined'. There was some concern that young men's behaviour should not get out of control.[11] There were also fears, among both Liberals and Conservatives, about the general excitability of mass society.[12]

Everyone was taken aback by the declaration of war. The language in early August 1914 was one of surprise: 'shock', 'thunderbolt', 'whirlwind' and 'bomb-shell' were typical words used. Dread, anxiety and fear were the keynotes of the public mood. Reggie Trench, soberly recounting daily developments to Clare, whom he expected to marry that summer, met her panic with an attempt at reassurance. 'My darling I cannot bear to think of you getting unhappy on my account,' he began his letter of 1 August. 'I was clumsy in my explanation of what I might have to do. I really think I shall not have to fight at all.' His administrative record in the Inns of Court OTC meant he was 'pretty certain' to be employed on clerical work in England or abroad. She trusted he would be kept to 'drill and instruct recruits'; Clare asked: 'is it very cowardly of me?' She confessed how difficult she was finding it to reconcile herself to the idea of her man in danger.[13]

On 4 August Mary Wemyss went to see her lifelong friend Lady Ettie Desborough, back in London from a house party and trying to 'keep quiet and calm'.[14] They had a 'sad and serious confab' since both of them had three boys grown up or almost so.[15] Then, back home at Stanway, she saw her eldest, Ego ride off to join his territorial brigade, the Gloucestershire Hussars. Having begun a legal career, he had been immediately called up. Watching the parade at Gloucester Cathedral on 9 August, Mary found it 'very moving'. Years later, she recalled how this was the moment, surveying the 'quiet earnest faces' of her son and his troop praying, that 'it sank into my heart for the first time that they were going to fight'.

No wonder that the stress caused Mary Wemyss to go to pieces. For now, the first time this had happened since the age of sixteen, she briefly abandoned her diary keeping: 'shall we put it on the war which has caused so much misery and infinite sorrow and loss to many, nothing seems to matter when so much is amiss'. Balfour had written to her to say that the Expeditionary Force had sailed. The only solace lay in early morning rides with Yvo. The Cotswolds looked 'magically silent, waving corn and misty distances; the world had a strange unreal look'.[16]

It was possible, at least for a while, to ignore the war. The diarist Miss E. Barkworth in Devon barely mentioned it in August, recording trips to the beach and reading Dickens. What is certain is that, in both their emotions and motivations, people felt huge ambivalence; their mood could shift rapidly between foreboding and excitement. Mrs Eustace Miles, running a London restaurant, noticed people in the streets singing the Marseillaise and 'Rule, Britannia'. Children, she said, were marching instead of walking and carrying bits of stick as bayonets. Yet losing some of their most valued employees who quickly joined up felt 'like parting with members of our own family'. Ada Reece, also in London, stressed the end of suspense on 5 August. It was 'glorious' news that Britain had declared war, 'although we undertake hostilities very gravely and reluctantly'.[17]

Some only discovered that Britain was at war very slowly. In towns the shouts of newsboys were the principal channel of communication. In rural areas, on government orders, every post office ensured that regular bulletins of war news were posted.[18] People gathered to discuss the scraps of information they picked up. 'Every night there is a rush for the evening papers which arrive at 9.p.m,' recounted Robert Saunders, the schoolmaster at Fletching in Sussex, 'then the doctor and his wife come in to compare notes and discuss the war generally.' Rudyard Kipling, on holiday in Suffolk, noted on 7 August how calmly the local people were reacting: 'they don't howl or grouse, or get together and jaw but go about their job like large horses . . . the simple Suffolker doesn't panic . . . he just carries on all serene'. There was an immediate negative impact on trade and employment, yet there were very few opponents of the war. The most striking impression left by a mass of documentation is that everyone quickly felt part of a national struggle.[19]

Those who obtained copies of *The Times* in the first weeks of August could not fail to learn, day by day, what it meant to be drawn into a world war. The normal summer events, cricket and the Henley Royal Regatta, suddenly seemed another world. The edition on Friday 7 August is illuminating. Boldly dominating a centre page was Kitchener's 'Call to Arms' under the royal crest. The famous words 'Your King & Country need you' had begun to be burned into the minds of all men between the ages of nineteen and thirty. The 'Terms of Service' were baldly stated as 'three years or until the war is ended'. The Kaiser's parallel appeal, invoking 'the warlike spirit of Germany', was reported close by on the same page. International reports of 'emotional exaltation' in France, the 'sacrifices of Russia', 'Canada preparing for the issue', 'New Zealand's expeditionary force', 'India to send two divisions', and the 'Demand for action' against German South-West Africa all appeared in this edition. 'If your horses are commandeered,' announced a large advertisement by the Standard Motor Company, 'why not use a light motor vehicle?' Their 9.5 light van was available for hire at £185.

Fourteen West End theatres, meanwhile, continued to do good business. The choice included *When Knights Were Bold* at the Apollo and a comedy by Arnold Bennett, *The Great Adventure*, at the Kingsway. The variety theatres offered the last weeks of *Vive L'Amour* at the New Middlesex, seats from six pence to seven shillings and six pence, and Leslie Stiles singing patriotic songs at the Empire. His programme was entitled *Stick to your Guns*. An appeal by the Prince of Wales who was setting up a National Fund was given prominence.

But the substance of *The Times* centre pages on 7 August was a very long parliamentary report from Westminster together with a powerfully argued leading article headed 'In Battle Array'. Mr Asquith's speech the previous day, declared the editor, would 'live in history'. The country had rallied to him; 'the young manhood of the nation' would respond eagerly to Kitchener's appeal. 'The spirit of the country has already amazed all beholders,' insisted *The Times*, 'it is distinguished by a quiet, dogged calmness and is reflected with absolute accuracy in the House of Commons.' 'Stern determination' was identified as the keynote of a national mood. War enthusiasm was not the issue: a new moral order was being created.

The Miles family spent the Bank Holiday weekend at Westgate-on-Sea. Back in London on Tuesday the 4th, Mrs Miles wrote in her diary, 'we already seem to be in a new world ... in the short time we have been away everything seems to have changed ... awful as it is – it is very thrilling'.[20] This was what Rupert Brooke meant in now famous lines penned at this time:

Now, God be thanked Who has matched us with His hour
And caught our youth, and wakened us from sleeping,
With hand made sure, clear eye, and sharpened power,
To turn, as swimmers into cleanness leaping,
Glad from a world grown old and cold and weary.[21]

Five days previously the Cabinet had been utterly divided, recorded Neville Chamberlain on 6 August; 'now the spirit of the country could not be better'. There was a significant decrease in serious crime during the first months of the war. Everybody started helping other people. Solidarity, with the soldiers who went to war, the wounded coming home, refugees from Belgium, became universal. Money poured in to the national relief funds under royal patronage. Women knitted furiously. Patriotic flag days and fund-raising events were held across Britain. 'We're in a horrid mess and huddle closer,' wrote Walter Scott to a friend on 10 August. But 'it's more than that', he confessed: 'death's in the air and we begin to realise in its bare elements the astonishing fact of life'.[22]

On the morning of the 22nd, near Mons, the first shots were fired in battle by British soldiers on the continent of Europe, other than in the Crimea, for almost one hundred years. In the previous ten days more than 80,000 men had been transported in the utmost secrecy across the English Channel without the loss of a single man or ship.[23] At the summit of the new moral order was the soldier, suddenly prized beyond measure. For everyone was bound together in a common purpose. But those in uniform were the heroes, symbolising honour and bravery, embodying all that the nation was fighting both for and against.

Reggie Trench was growing the moustache he had begun, almost in premonition, in late July (plate 1). He spent August recruiting at the Inns of Court Officers' Training Corps and training volunteers in Richmond Park. A weekend visiting Clare's home in the village of Orpington was a heavenly break. Tennis provided a semblance of normality. Hammond, the chauffeur, Clare told him later, had accosted her to ask 'if I would give him a photograph of you in uniform'. Lafayette, the society photographer, was run off its feet with business as young men queued for the studio portraits that their families demanded. Hammond told Clare how impressed he was with Reggie's 'martial bearing', saying he was of 'the right soldier stamp'. His wife, he admitted, 'had also seen and admired from her window'.[24] A sister might confess to a brother to being head over heels about males in khaki: 'I am sorry you have got khaki fever – you seem to have got it badly', Yvo Charteris told Mary after an emotional letter from her.[25]

Sacrifices had to be made that were respected and equal. Much was expected of women – devotion, sobriety, deference – while their men were away. Women and girls, noted Violet Clutton in her diary, could 'serve their country best by leading quiet lives, thus setting an example of self-restraint and uprightness at home'. Failure in their national duty, such as drinking too much on their own while enjoying a separation allowance, was seen as slighting male sacrifice.[26]

Reggie Trench and Clare Howard were in constant, almost daily, correspondence between August and December. Their letters provide a fascinating commentary on the worlds of young men preparing for the Western Front and of an upper-class family immersed in the work of the Home Front. From October, Reggie was at Ashridge Park at Berkhamsted with the Inns of Court OTC.[27] Clare was keenly aware how tired his work made him, as she observed the impact of events on soldiers in her own locality. On 6 August the village's Territorials returned to Orpington from their summer camp on Salisbury Plain, 'absolutely done [sic] not having taken off their clothes for three nights'. Clare and her sisters fed them on tea and biscuits in the village hall, before they went off, on new orders with two days' rations, to Sevenoaks and Dover. Her brother Edgar, volunteering for active service, went into the ranks with them: 'there was a large crowd at the station to cheer them off'.[28]

Clare's letters reveal how quickly this became a family war. Children learnt that grown-ups had taken on new roles and were suddenly very busy. Their games copied the new moral order of commitment and duty. Little Nigel, her nephew, harassed Clare's letter writing with his noisy play one day in December 1914, 'stumping round in full armour, varied by shouting "stand at ease", "shun" in most approved manner'. Another day, Clare described Nigel's 'great game' with his baby sister Margaret: 'Nigel shoots the soldiers and Margaret conveys them in an ambulance to the Red Cross hospital, they've just got Sir John French in bed'.[29] Margaret was replicating the Voluntary Aid Detachment work with the Red Cross which Clare and her sisters, Violet and Amy, maintained throughout the autumn. But Margaret knowingly also understood about censorship, writing a childish censored letter 'from the Front', which she delivered into her aunt's hands.

Reggie was glad to hear of plans for a hospital with fifty beds at Orpington, after Clare reported 'measuring the village hall with the church rooms adjoining'. His realism was shrewd: 'we shall have a good deal of casualties before we are through with this show I'm afraid'. Within a few days wounded Belgian soldiers were being accommodated and cared for. On 13 August Clare described a full day of making beds, dusting the ward, inspecting the impro-vised operating theatre and serving meals. She had to steel herself for 'the part I rather disliked – watching wounds being dressed'. But her sister Amy quickly discovered 'a natural bent' for nursing, doing dressings and bandaging as well as taking temperatures and pulses. When they were not at the hospital, the Howard girls held working parties for local women at their home, Bark Hart, cutting out garments. Her friend Mary Waring managed eighteen vests in a single session. Clare's counselling skills were also in demand, when she visited Orpington villagers for the Soldiers' and Sailors' Families Association. One man, father of the 'scamp' in her brother Edgar's Territorial company, told with 'many tears' of his son's being confined to barracks for a fortnight.[30]

In Reggie's eyes, a man with neither a commission nor enlisted for the Front inevitably became frustrated by kicking his heels. He portrayed his Oxford friend Eddy Burney and his brother Herbert as 'rather fed up with life', when on 19 August their motorcycle dash to assist the French army proved abortive: 'of course they will get something if they hang about long enough but it is rather trying'.[31] He believed everyone must expect weeks of routine to fit them for their duty to the nation. Clare's brother Walter, hampered in leadership by a bad stammer, found a night-time special constable job, using the family car to oversee a stretch of road into London, which was very boring. Agreeing it must be 'dull and pretty hard hours', Reggie commented philosophically, 'but perhaps it is the same as the rest of us'. At least Walter could feel he was doing his bit.[32]

In an atmosphere of such high seriousness consciences were unsteady. Clare confessed to a 'very frivolous' day on 19 August, when she went off to play tennis, leaving a working party, crammed with women who declared they were 'longing to do something', busy at Bark Hart. They were engrossed in padding splints. Five days later, after news that Namur had fallen, the lure of the tennis court perturbed Reggie's sense of equilibrium: 'and think of it our men were fighting all yesterday when I was slacking at Bark Hart – and fighting for their lives too'. But it was 'no good being perturbed', said Clare, placating him, after 'slaving for the very same army all the week' by training officers for the Front.[33]

Reggie's most constant correspondent from the Western Front was his close Oxford friend Eddy Burney. 'Quite safe so far', his first report read: 'he has a job as an orderly dispatch rider which he wanted'. 'I had a ripping letter from Eddy', Reggie related on 14 October: 'he has not had any great adventures yet'. A candid account of his work with the intelligence section of the Fourth Army Corps later that month did not dent Reggie's own fervour. Eddy confessed to 'several baptisms of fire', motorcycling through villages with 'bullets whizzing past me several times in quite sufficient numbers to make me uncomfortable'.

Eddy had been shocked to encounter a group of Germans dead and wounded in a hole in the ground beside a roadside: 'two or three of the poor men groaned to me for water and said they had been lying there three days'. Eddy gave them some morphine. He headed his letter in capital letters 'WAR IS AN ABOMINATION'.[34] This was the Western Front in the raw. 'He seems to be having an exciting time lucky devil', was Reggie's insouciant summary to Clare.[35]

Reggie wrote his brother Herbert a cheerful and positive letter on 18 November.[36] The reply was full of what he hoped for, a younger brother's bravado, contradicting the much less happy story Herbert, now at the Front, was currently telling his sisters. 'Yes, I'm having a topping time', he announced: 'I'm awfully sorry you are in such a dull job. It must be bloody awful training glorified schoolboys.' Herbert could not bear to seek to dampen his older brother Reggie's ardour by confessing his insomnia or his fragile state of mind.[37]

The next missive from Eddy in December had a quieter tone: Reggie summarised it by saying Eddy was 'quite safe he says and no hardships at all'. 'Do wish him the best of luck from me', Clare wrote, when he was home on six days' leave that month and the Oxford friends met up.[38] Only five years before, Eddy and Reggie had been punting together on the Cherwell and enjoying themselves as undergraduates at Merton. Both had needed to grow up very fast. For the moment, though, it was Eddy who was the one for whom the war had become traumatic. Five years previously Herbert Trench, also in France, and finding it equally traumatic, had still been at school.

Twice in these months Reggie showed some of the emotions he felt when absorbing the growing lists of casualties. On 9 November he told Clare about the first death in the immediate family. His cousin Max Trench has been 'knocked out . . . I'm awfully sorry . . . you remember he stayed in my digs the night before he was married . . . he had just been gazetted a major . . . I must write to his wife'. Later that month the deep distress of the commanding officer at Berkhamsted Lieutenant-Colonel Francis Errington moved him. 'The poor old C.O. His son is reported wounded and missing and he hardly says a word but stares in front of him all day and at Mess'.[39]

It was ironic that, working with wounded men home from the Front, Clare, eagerly joining a Voluntary Aid Detachment of the Red Cross, learnt more quickly about the emotional realities of warfare than Reggie. While he was being schooled in the technology of arms and in trench digging, Clare's nursing skills advanced rapidly, despite an early reprimand 'for touching and handling some sterilized gauze with my fingers instead of scissors'. In October, she was helping the village hall commandant 'preparing fomentations and bandaging' and had become matter of fact about chatting with a soldier who had had 'two fingers recently amputated'. Clare enjoyed the task of collecting the details of men's names, regiments, ages, and the battles they had fought in. Many had been at Louvain and Malines. Her French came in useful. The Belgians, she told Reggie, 'insisted on the uselessness of their own officers, except for purposes of "parade"'. The German artillery, a man at the siege of Namur declared, 'far outranged theirs'. One Belgian wounded, a good linguist fortunately, managed to get his wife to visit and she was accommodated by 'one of our Red Cross people' in Orpington. Clare spotted them writing letters together and was thrilled 'they are so happy'.[40]

The opening of a second hospital at St Mary Cray, with twenty-five beds, in October increased Clare's workload. She became used to long nights on duty, giving lozenges to men who coughed and water to men who did not sleep. Not yet twenty-two and accustomed to a boarding-school life, balls and tennis parties, Clare found this a rude awakening into adulthood.[41] On 24 October she encountered her first case of nervous breakdown. A soldier was crying out in his sleep: woken by Clare and two others he was able to explain a dream 'that the Prussians were trying to cut his throat, having already done so to two of the men, and he was struggling with his would-be slayers'. 'Poor man,' she noted, 'it shows what they must have been through'. Clare was innocently handling battle stress of a kind that had not yet even been named and diagnosed.[42]

The Red Cross work became less strenuous as the friendship of the soldiers with nurses blossomed: the Belgians were persuaded to make their own beds and help the incapacitated. Visiting two Bromley hospitals, with 'good discipline' and men and nurses 'who stood up when the commandant walked through the ward', Clare noted how different this atmosphere was from the rather chaotic Orpington beginnings. Men improving were sent on to convalescent homes in Llandudno or Aberdeen and new wounded arrived. Visiting the village hall men on 2 November, Clare was 'astonished' at how wounds had healed.

But there was acceptance when VAD nurses were out of their depth. When a sergeant major broke down with shell shock he was moved to a Woolwich hospital: 'his mind is quite unhinged and he has a constable in plain clothes with him'. The following week, Dr Smith, in charge at Orpington, addressed the nurses en masse about 'loyalty, esprit de corps etc.' There was the constant possibility of new responsibilities. 'Ten English with frostbite have arrived for our hospital from Woolwich,' Clare reported on 8 December; 'it is v. painful and they are kept in bed.'[43]

VAD work, furthermore, had its lighter side. Two Belgians were packed off to the Woolwich hospital for drunkenness. 'One returned on foot the next day!' Clare commented, 'and possibly we shall keep him if he reforms'. On Christmas Eve, she related the tale of a 'bilious Belgian' who refused to swallow a pill. He secreted it in his mouth, 'declaring continuously "il est parti" then ejected it'. When she gave him a second pill, Clare had to stand 'for ten minutes with my flash lamp turned on him, prepared to wait half an hour . . . the other men were highly entertained and one offered me a chair for the session'.

The Howard girls welcomed the Belgians into their home and took them for outings. Twenty-seven wounded visited Bark Hart on 8 November. There was tea first then a concert, featuring Amy Howard as a soloist and a group of children acting a French play with their Mademoiselle. At first embarrassingly silent, the soldiers 'were quite noisy over the chorus of Tipperary'. By December, Clare was ready for a break, but conscience would not let her ask for more than four days' leave when Reggie wanted to take her to see his mother in Dublin. 'I shouldn't have the face to ask for a longer holiday as there are not a great number of nurses and it only means the others have more work,' she told him.[44] Her marriage, delayed by the outbreak of war, had been arranged for 28 January. Her resignation at the hospital was imminent so she could join Reggie at Berkhamsted.

His drive and energy emerge constantly from Reggie's autumn letters. 'Like all of us he is mad to do something immediately,' he noted, reporting a letter from an Oxford friend. He found it invidious selecting from his company those to be commissioned at once; 'the others left looked so miserable'. He was thrilled to see Clare's eldest brother Hal, in one of the new public school battalions, 'marching along in a very soldierly way'. He made light of the wound of a next-door neighbour at his London home, 'a bullet in his head just where the hair starts', when the man returned there on a week's leave.

'A near thing,' he commented, emphasising the 'great excitement' this brief heroic visit brought to the inhabitants of Tedworth Gardens in Chelsea. Everyone had begun to scan the lists of wounded. 'He is such a ripper I hope he comes out alright,' Reggie told Clare on 20 September, noting the name of a particular friend who was 'seriously' hurt. There was one entry indicating more grievous wounding than 'seriously', which they called 'dangerously', he explained to Clare.[45]

In the first months of the war, people were totally unable to comprehend what lay in store because trench warfare had not yet been invented. Clare Howard, reading about Waterloo, with 72,000 English men on a two-and-a-half-mile line of battle, understood how entirely different the situation was from a million men, as she believed, now massed along a 220-mile front in Europe. Yet she could not conceive of the outcome except in terms of a single pitched battle: 'I suppose this battle will begin at any time now,' she reflected on 14 August.[46] There was a brief flurry of optimism in mid-September yet those who pondered what Lord Kitchener was saying began to realise that Britain was in for a long haul. How at that moment could anyone's mental horizons extend to 1916, when two great armies would encounter each other on the Somme?[47]

The British Expeditionary Force (BEF) in August 1914 was pitifully small. It contributed four infantry divisions and one cavalry division in an armed conflict where Germany was fielding 100 infantry and 22 cavalry divisions and France 62 infantry and 10 cavalry divisions.[48] Yet the BEF's performance in the first months established Britain's formidable role in battle and presaged its massive contribution to the war on the Western Front. There were heavy British casualties on 23 August, when 1,600 were killed or wounded. Some ground was lost. The BEF began to retreat southwards, fighting another fearsome battle, at Le Cateau.

The Times broke the story on the 25th, following it with an eyewitness account on the 30th of 'broken bits of many regiments' battered by retreat. The British public was shocked. Thousands anticipating a quick and decisive battle had not expected this. But the Battle of the Marne from 5 to 8 September brought some relief. It marked the destruction of the plan for a rapid German victory over the French. On 9 September the Germans retreated on the Marne. They had been denied their triumphal entry to Paris.[49]

The agreement on 5 August by Field Marshal Earl Kitchener of Khartoum to join the Cabinet as War Minister had been a tonic to public confidence. Its impact was noted as 'instantaneous and overwhelming'.[50] Memories of his achievements in the Sudan and South Africa were enduring. Moving in the highest social circles, he had long been a close friend of the Desborough family at Taplow Court. Julian Grenfell modelled himself on Kitchener as on no one else apart from his sportsman father. 'He looked a soldier from head to foot,' Julian wrote at fourteen in 1902, 'and there was something about his manner that showed me he was no ordinary man . . . it was easy to see that he was used to being obeyed.'[51]

Julian's father Lord Desborough was hard to emulate. He boasted sporting feats which amazed Edwardian society: horseman, big-game hunter and fisherman, he had swum Niagara Falls and climbed the Matterhorn by three different routes. Holidays in Sutherland, with long days out fishing and later deer stalking, tested the Grenfell boys, Julian and his brother Billy, harshly. Growing up to be like Kitchener was an exercise in manly self-control. Julian was sick several times on his first journey to his prep school Summerfields in Oxford. His schoolboy letters were factual, a catalogue of achievement. He learnt not to discuss his feelings.[52]

Kitchener at once dominated the Cabinet, replacing Lloyd George as Asquith's principal lieutenant. Cabinet members were intimidated by this famous soldier in their midst, Lloyd George admitted, because of his repute and his influence in the country. Kitchener stressed that the war would last at least three years. Britain's full military strength could not be deployed until 1917. His first call to arms came on 7 August 1914. Waving aside the Territorial force, he was soon raising four new armies.[53]

The British army was led by gentlemen. Social standing had long been the foundation of military leadership. Kitchener believed that education, still largely an upper- and middle-class preserve, really mattered. But he knew there was a massive problem in providing his New Armies with enough good company commanders and subalterns. On 10 September, he grasped this nettle. Two thousand junior officers were needed, the newspapers announced, with OTC experience as the main requirement.

The Officers' Training Corps had been founded in 1908. By 1914 it was flourishing in the universities, at the Inns of Court and at 166 of the public and grammar schools. The basic military training it had provided to thousands of teenage boys was of inestimable importance when the army was suddenly plunged into creating from scratch a huge new officer corps.[54] 'Recruiting apace,' Reggie wrote to Clare on the evening of 4 August: '50 turned away today: men who have not had any previous training.'[55] Kitchener's tactic ensured that there was no radical change in the social composition of the officer corps at the start of the war: 20,577 men with some kind of military experience across the country in an OTC were commissioned between August 1914 and March 1915.

Time and again it was the name and standing of a school that mattered. Three hundred and fifty men were gazetted from Eton whereas only thirteen joined from there as privates or NCOs. Wellington and Rugby provided contingents of 403 and 291 officers respectively, but no one appears to have enlisted in the ranks from these schools up to March 1915.[56] R.C. Sherriff's well-known story of his initial failure to obtain a commission is about OTCs at the major public schools and the training this provided. '" School?", enquired the adjutant, 'His face fell. He took up a printed list and searched through it . . . I was mystified. I told him my school was a very old and good one – founded, I said by Queen Elizabeth in 1567. The adjutant was not impressed'. But it was the fact that he had not even been in the OTC at his school, as he himself stresses, which was decisive. He had 'a long hard pull' before he was accepted as an officer. The major public schools dominated officer recruitment. Few from the smaller ones and from grammar schools, though many of these did have OTCs, were commissioned. Most of those who had attended these schools went into the ranks.[57]

The Mons Despatch in *The Times* on 25 August 1914 accelerated the recruiting boom. Daily enlistment during the next four days exceeded the total for the first week of the war. In early August the existing recruiting offices had been overwhelmed. Many were sent away and told to come back later. The Amiens Despatch which appeared in *The Times* on 30 August, a highly coloured and rather inaccurate account of the retreat from Mons, was a further shock. Men began to turn up at recruiting offices in their hordes. On 3 September, 33,304 men joined the army, the highest enlistment for any day of the whole war. So it was not when war broke out but nearly a month later that the main rush to the colours occurred. This was the month that saw the highest rate of recruitment between August and January 1915. People were becoming aware of the violence and horror of the war.

It was much easier to recruit in industrial areas than rural ones. Scotland is a good example. While the most agricultural areas, Aberdeen, Forfar and Inverness, provided nearly 3 per cent of the recruits in the September surge, the industrial areas of Lanark and Ayr provided more than 56 per cent. There was an obvious connection with unemployment. Coal mining, engineering, shipbuilding and iron and steel in this region all suffered contraction in trade. Conversely, Cornwall, Cheshire, Devon and rural North Wales had levels of recruitment well below the national average in the period up to mid-November 1914. But it was a sense of detachment in remote areas rather than opposition to the war which explains this. 'People have not the remotest conception of what their war is or signifies,' wrote a Devon commentator on 1 September.[58]

This was the first mass army in Britain's history. Lieutenant Colonel Cobb recalled the broad pattern of recruiting to the 5th Oxfordshire and Buckinghamshire Light Infantry. There were 'gentlemen, many indoor servants, grooms, gardeners, chauffeurs, gamekeepers, well-to-do tradesmen, hotel keepers, clerks, to say nothing of the engineers, fitters and hands from the great works in Birmingham and Coventry'. They had all, Cobb emphasised, 'left good, comfortable homes, with good wages, and had come voluntarily out of a sheer sense of duty'.[59] The young were everywhere in the forefront. Reading the stories in the newspapers, men joined Kitchener's Army soberly and responsibly, having come to expect a desperate fight to defend the nation. By 12 September 1914, 478,893 recruits had come in.[60]

How did the British people define the national cause in the summer and autumn of 1914? They did so by making explicit deeply ingrained values in Victorian and Edwardian culture. It was the Liberal Party, elected in 1910 on a manifesto to reduce military spending, that had to make the case. There was suspicion in the party of Conservative jingoism. Yet this was, from the start, a war for idealistic aims such as freedom, liberty and justice. In his crucial speech on 6 August, Asquith announced that Britain was fighting 'to fulfil a solemn national obligation . . . not only of law but of honour' and to 'vindicate the principle that small nationalities are not to be crushed in defiance of international good faith, by the arbitrary will of a strong and overmastering power'. This was a war, he declared, 'to defend civilisation', a war, he insisted, he himself entered with a clear conscience. 'Poor little Belgium' was on everyone's lips.

The recruitment campaign became a forceful propagandist effort that stressed the positive values which Britain stood for. Much was made of Elgar's 1902 hymn 'Land of Hope and Glory'. The mainstay was public recruiting meetings. At one in Brighton on 7 September, Rudyard Kipling insisted that, since Germany was fighting to overthrow the civilised world, more British men should come forward to 'check this onrush of organised barbarism'.[61] Such appeals were often printed in newspapers; this one appeared next day in The Times. People's diaries and letters chimed with official speeches and pamphlets, proving that the government was in tune with the people. The government spoke to a public mood rather than dictating it, even if that mood was more immediately and powerfully realised in Kent and London than, for instance, in Cornwall or North Wales.

Thus the reasons that Britain was at war soon permeated the nation regardless of class or region.[62] Lord Moran wrote much later that, while 'pride in arms . . . was of course an abiding source of strength in the regular army', it never took root 'in the citizen force upon which the burden of the struggle fell'. These were men answering a national emergency.[63] The editor of Edinburgh University's student newspaper declared that August 1914 would be 'hailed as a great month in our nation's great history', since the British people as a whole were now 'knit together in a great project of sacrifice'. 'It ought to do people a world of good . . . people were getting too silly', wrote the artist Augustus John. Ada McGuire told her sister in a letter on 28 August that 'the war would awake England from the pursuit of pleasure and selfishness'.[64] In Rupert Brooke's words, it was now that God 'matched us with His hour'.

Because the sense of duty to France and Belgium was a major reason for Britain entering the war, solidarity with these two countries was central to how the nation understood the struggle. Vera Brittain wrote of the sense of strength and comfort fighting for the Allies gave her. Others found strength in the support of the Empire. 'They must see we are in the right in declaring war,' Beatrice Trefusis wrote in her diary on 11 August, noting the offer of a million bags of flour from Canada.[65] The image of the enemy naturally had to be constructed as the reverse side of the values that Britain and the Allies espoused. Germany's militarism was understood to have caused the war. Atrocities by the German armies reported in Belgium and France confirmed British opinion that this militarism was both barbaric and bloodthirsty. Humour and satire were used to humiliate and ridicule the enemy. Cartoons, especially in *Punch*, fed hatred of Germany.

There had to be an internal enemy as well: the figures of the enemy alien and the spy already had deep roots. It is appropriate to speak of spy fever in the years 1900 to 1915 because the term refers to the imagined spies who, it was believed, could subvert national strength and unity by their activities within Britain.[66] There were five major outbreaks of anti-German violence in Britain between August and December 1914. They have a similar pattern: crowds built up around a victim, usually a shopkeeper, leading to cheering, booing, stone throwing, the smashing of windows, and looting. During the war British citizenship became defined more by blood and ethnicity than by character. Friends and neighbours could become enemies and outsiders. Scattered incidents of violence in the localities exacerbated growing hatred of the German people.[67]

Atrocity propaganda between August 1914 and May 1915 did much to enhance popular patriotism. Lord Northcliffe's *Daily Mail*, the country's best-selling newspaper, got into its stride on 6 August 1914, with editorial comment on the destruction of a Belgian village as 'a monstrous crime against the laws of nations'. There were instances both of cold-blooded executions of hostages and of German military units that went on the rampage. Around 4,000 Belgian citizens were deliberately killed. Throughout August the *Daily Mail* used all the factual copy it could lay its hands on to promote the story of German brutality. The sack of Louvain, at the end of the month, became the outstanding atrocity tale of this period. The cultural damage caused by the burning of the Old Market, the Cloth Hall and the eighteenth-century University Library caused great shock.[68]

Long before Kitchener's Army reached Belgium and France, there was unprecedented violence on the Continent. There were huge losses in the opening stages of the war: 260,000 French casualties occurred in the first month. Around 6,500 Belgian and French civilians were killed between August and October 1914. The BEF's own experience was of bloody fighting between the Battle of Mons in August and the First Battle of Ypres in October. A conservative estimate has put British casualties at over 89,000 in the period from August to November.[69] So what did the people know about all this? By and large the press bureau was efficient in preventing information that could be useful to the enemy being published. Moreover the patriotic press passed over or delayed unfavourable news. Journalists at the Front had difficulty in witnessing actual fighting and relied a great deal on the accounts of eyewitnesses after a battle. Articles in *The Times* in late August and early September emphasised higher German losses and played down defeat and retreat.

Yet there is evidence that men at the Front wrote graphically about their experience and that censorship of letters was often ineffective. Officers themselves revealed a good deal of the truth. On 8 November, Ralph Verney, with the Rifle Brigade in France, told of German infantry within 200 yards of their recently constructed trenches: 'we open up on them with rapid fire and machine guns, and simply mow them down till it is quite sickening'. As Edward Hulse explained to his mother that month, 'far and away the worst part is the cold in one's feet at night, which makes sleep impossible'. Local newspapers contained masses of front-line correspondence, handed in by people prepared and even eager to share their news. Everyone relied largely upon rumour.

The correspondence between Reggie Trench and Clare Howard made less and less mention of events abroad during the autumn. When Clare commented on newspaper reports it was usually in puzzlement: 'I'm sure some of them will fight their way out,' she speculated on the news of Lodz; maybe her brother Edgar was in action when the Turks were within twenty-five miles of the Suez Canal; would the Kaiser's operation influence the war for good or ill? When the *Emden* was sunk she rejoiced, reflecting that the captain and crew had 'played a very sporting and clever game'.[70] As Beatrice Trefusis put it in London, 'one has so little news from authentic sources that one seizes any odd rumours'. These were 'crumbs to live on'. Those who first saw wounded men exhibited the kind of empathy which, over four years, would bind the British at home to those who were fighting for them abroad. As early as 29 August, Annie Brunton saw two invalided soldiers at Victoria Station: 'one with his arm bound up and the other a boy of about eighteen with cotton wool and bandages over his eye'. King George V and Queen Mary visited wounded officers in hospital on 1 October, commenting, 'we saw each of the thirty there, some of them are rather bad'.[71]

In December fears of invasion turned to a story of invasion, when the nation's traditionally impenetrable island fortress was briefly violated by the shelling of Scarborough, Hartlepool and Whitby by eight enemy craft. Nine soldiers, 97 civilians and 37 children were killed; there were 592 civilian casualties. Around 600 houses there were destroyed.[72] 'Over the town hung a mantle of heavy smoke,' wrote the schoolgirl Winifred Holtby in Hartlepool, 'yellow, unreal which made the place look like a dream city, far, far away'. Rumours that the Germans had actually landed proved false.[73] But this attack aroused more universal horror than events in Belgium, fixing the image of German barbarity in British minds. Ellen Bilsborough clipped two pages of newspaper pictures into her diary, adding the comment: 'house in Scarborough where dead babies were found'.[74]

Reporting a Zeppelin air raid on Yarmouth in January 1915 the *Daily Mail* castigated Germany for taking its first toll of non-combatant British blood.[75] The greatest single atrocity of the war was the sinking of the *Lusitania* in May 1915: 94 of the 1,200 non-combatant victims were children. By then the iniquity of Germany in British eyes could largely be taken for granted. Propaganda constantly reiterated that the war was to protect Britain from an enemy that had first shown its true colours in August 1914 in its treacherous invasion of Belgium.[76]

Rumour constantly created new fears and anxieties. The British people, hungering for reassurance in the latter months of 1914, found it in the circulation of two rumours which were overtly positive. The first one, that a group of angels had protected British soldiers at the Battle of Mons, reached England in numerous letters from servicemen written in late August and early September 1914. On 29 September the *Evening News* carried a short story with the title 'The Bowmen' by Arthur Machen. This rumour did not appear in the diaries or letters of ordinary people on the Home Front but it caused a flurry of similar stories, which were published in 1915.[77]

The colourful story that Russians 'with snow on their boots' were marching down Britain en route to France, to protect the country from invasion, was a compensatory counter-myth to the worst atrocity stories. Emerging in late August, it boosted morale when the Germans were believed to be near the Channel coast. This rumour spread widely without discrimination of age or class. Staying at Farningham in Kent on 9 September, Clare Howard was irritated that the newspapers were late. Like many others she had completely swallowed the story. 'We may get the official confirmation of the Russians,' she told Reggie excitedly. But he was 'sad to relate' that the story seemed definitely untrue, he replied six days later, after an evening with friends at the Cavendish Club. 'It is really extraordinary,' he declared, 'how circumstantial the evidence was . . . it seemed such a splendid move.'[78]

The peak of unemployment came in August with the first shock of war. The impact of the war on people's standard of living was less marked in rural areas than in manufacturing districts dependent on now disrupted overseas markets. Exceptionally, the textile business in Huddersfield and the Colne Valley enjoyed a boom with the unprecedented demand for khaki. In these autumn months there is striking testimony to how seriously people took voluntary economising. Violet Clutton commented on the encouragement it had given when the King had 'done away with all grand dinners at the Palace'. Setting an example by small sacrifices was common. The Reverend Andrew Clark noted how, in his village of Great Leighs in Essex, there was 'either butter or jam, not both' and 'no cake at tea at the Manor House'. Another Essex family 'agreed to do without sugar in their tea'.

Changes in the landscape were inescapable. Rudyard Kipling, from Burwash in Sussex, told Theodore Roosevelt in early December, 'I don't say all England is yet an armed camp because there are gaps where you can go for ten miles without seeing troops', but his local wanderings were teaching him that there were no longer roads 'where you can go twenty miles without running into them in blocks'. 'London is full of uniforms,' noted Lieutenant Basil Ryder in September, 'more officers and Belgian soldiers than Tommies . . . all the bridges and tube stations are guarded by two soldiers with fixed bayonets'.[79] There was constant tension in people's minds: on 22 December, woken by an aeroplane, Clare Howard sprang out of bed 'to inspect and be sure it wasn't the sound of a Zeppelin'.[80] Anti-Zeppelin searchlights started blazing across the London night sky, though it was not until September 1915 that Zeppelin raids on the capital began. The night that happened, Mary Wemyss was in the library with Yvo at her Cadogan Square home: 'the two housemaids rushed in gasping and shuddering with fright'.[81]

For many families it was separation that brought the war home. Departures broke people's hearts. With a million volunteers, few households were entirely unaffected. This made everyone think about relative sacrifices, for there was a general acceptance in the language of sacrifice that those who were most morally admirable were the soldiers. Theirs, whether or not they survived, was the blood tax against which everyone else had to justify their actions.[82] It was personal loss above all that the whole nation began to struggle to come to terms with. By 1918 no single family would be without some sorrow in their home.

Elsie Kipling realised in the autumn of 1914 that only one of the young men with whom she had danced at the beginning of the season that summer was not at war. When it was announced that one of these partners had been killed in action, she said with pardonable exaggeration that 'very soon she won't know any man who is alive'. Her father, painfully, found it was 'the uncertainty that kills'. 'The staple of conversation,' Rudyard Kipling wrote on 5 October, reflecting on his Sussex neighbourhood, 'when one meets is as to the where-abouts of such and such a one, son or husband or father of so and so'.[83]

Yet the overall impression left by a mass of comment is that, after some heady excitement in August, the months of September to December 1914 were the time when the British people settled into war. The rupture of the routine of Edwardian life had occurred with a finality that was palpable to all. There is clear testimony to a sense of a new era beginning, with the initiation of a pattern of living that was unknown and certainly different. What marked the change was the understanding that a new moral order had been born. Sir Alfred Dale, Vice-Chancellor of the University of Liverpool, remarked on 23 October that 'men and women who were cynical have become serious'. He detected a change of mood which, if it lasted, would signify 'the opening of a new chapter in the experience of the nation'.[84] By and large, it did last until the Armistice which, this book argues, is part of the explanation of why Britain and the Allies won the Great War. Arguments and disputes developed from 1915 about equality of sacrifice; but general disillusion only followed the war's end.

But when would it end? Predictably, this was an issue of great concern to most people, but the notion that the war would be over by Christmas was never widespread between August and October 1914. Hopes for a short war were the product of human nature. 'Wishful thinking in the face of adversity is one of the mechanisms by which people cope,' Hew Strachan has remarked.[85] But reality was setting in. People could infer from the immense mobilisation of relief and fund-raising to support those who went to war that this struggle would not be over quickly. They knew, once they felt able to face it, that Kitchener's prediction was probably right. Those who did expect that the war might be short, like the Reverend Andrew Clark, constantly readjusted their expectations in diary entries as the war progressed.[86]

This chapter has described how Britain went to war in 1914. The kingdom was virtually united in a cause one of honour as well as national expediency. In the course of this account four of the principal characters of the book – Reggie and Herbert Trench, Yvo Charteris and Julian Grenfell – have been introduced. The next chapter explores in greater depth and detail the patriotic idealism with which men went to fight. There is more about Reggie, Herbert, Yvo and Julian. But the chapter introduces nine more of the main characters whose fortunes we will be following on the Western Front.

CHAPTER 2

'Glad to Go'

Patriotic Idealism

Charles Carrington, the son of an Anglican clergyman, reflected in 1965 on how he had felt at seventeen years old about the Great War breaking out. He was then back in England, after time spent in New Zealand, preparing for a scholarship examination for Oxford or Cambridge.[1] Was he then, he asked, anything more than a 'juvenile delinquent, whose characteristics were a love for ganging-up with other boys, a craving to demonstrate his manliness and a delight in anti-social violence'? The mood was exhilarating 'because of the rare experience of finding inclination, actual necessity and the highest principles of conduct pointing the same way'. There was no one who wanted war; there was 'nothing that we could gain by war and much that we might lose'. A sense of adventure drove men to join up. How long this war would last was a matter of speculation: 'our major anxiety,' wrote Harold Macmillan later, 'was by hook or by crook not to miss it.'[2]

Thus the decision for war was a wholly moral one: 'there was no doubt what we ought to do,' Carrington wrote later, 'and the prospect of danger and discomfort gave an additional spur'. He thought himself lucky that his errant purpose 'was directed towards a task that was socially acceptable'. He had found himself, a mere teenager, 'joining in a spontaneous assertion of the general will'. Rupert Brooke, he remembered, had spoken nothing but the simple truth when he said that God had 'matched us with his hour and caught our youth and wakened us from sleeping'.[3]

A similar analysis was offered by a young officer in the Rifle Brigade, Malcolm White, writing home in 1916, the year of the Somme. He decided in his trench musings that 'the only thing which really produces idealism is, unfortunately, war and the thing called patriotism'. Then 'leisured young men', who have lived heedless of their country in peace, find it is 'absolutely their duty to die for it in war time and fling away their lives with heroism'. Even the poets, White noted, had not got much further than seeing war as the motive force that invariably activated idealism.[4] So we should start with the poets who wrote early in the war, like Rupert Brooke. Carrington and White both cited him. The war sonnets, Carrington remembered, 'so accurately expressed the mood of August 1914'.[5] Brooke 'seemed to welcome war as a release from materialism', declared White.

Rupert Brooke grew up at Rugby School where his father was a housemaster. He was good at games and a fine classicist, though, after he left in 1906, his real love became English literature. He studied this in a promising academic career at Cambridge. He was handsome and charismatic, moving in circles which included Bertrand Russell, Stanley Spencer, Eric Gill, Paul Nash and Virginia Woolf. The war startled Brooke, turning his mind away from his unresolved relationships with women and the emotional turmoil surrounding them. At ease with the highest in the land, he dined at Number 10 at the end of July 1914. He sat opposite Winston Churchill First Lord of the Admiralty, whom he had not previously met and who offered him a commission if it came to war.[6]

His writings in August 1914 document the emergence of the patriotism which, later expressed in verse, made Rupert Brooke so famous after his death. 'I know the heart of England,' he wrote to a friend from Warwickshire on 2 August, 'it has a hedgy, warm, bountiful dimpled air. Baby fields run up and down the hills and the roads wriggle with pleasure.' It was 'perpetually June', here the 'flowers smell of heaven', there were 'butterflies all the year round', and 'a full moon every night'. Motoring that day through William Shakespeare's Arden, he realised how deeply he felt about the English landscape.[7]

Later that month, Brooke wrote the disguised autobiographical piece he published in the *New Statesman* entitled 'An Unusual Young Man'. It described the ambivalent feelings he was having about Germany, a country he had previously enjoyed visiting. He contemplated with a 'tightening of his heart' a possible raid on the English coast, the notion of warfare on English soil. Understanding the holiness with which he perceived 'the actual earth of England', the full flood of his emotions engulfed him. This was the 'triumphant helplessness of a lover: grey uneven little fields and small, ancient hedges rushed before him . . . sedate houses of red brick, proudly unassuming, a countryside of rambling hills and friendly copses'. He felt, he wrote, 'extraordinarily happy', thinking 'often and heavily of Germany' and 'of England all the time'.

It was in this mood that Brooke grasped at the chance of the commission in the Royal Naval Division that Winston Churchill had promised him. He lunched with Churchill at the Admiralty in late September 1914.[8] Brooke's experience at the siege of Antwerp the next month, when he saw the flight of the Belgian populace before the German advance, confirmed his patriotic convictions. In December he wrote his five war sonnets, submitting them to the magazine *New Numbers* on 13 January, before leaving for Gallipoli. Dean Inge read the sonnet 'If I should die . . .' in his Easter Sunday sermon at St Paul's on 4 April 1915, seeing it as an example of 'pure and elevated patriotism'. Few listening that day already knew the poem. But Brooke was told of the sermon on the island of Skyros, where he was already sickening, on the 18th.[9] He is thought to have contracted the septicaemia, from which he died at sea sailing for Gallipoli on 23 April, from a mosquito bite.

Edward Marsh, his close friend, published an obituary in *The Times*. This stressed the inspiration which 'the incomparable war sonnets' left behind for 'many thousands of young men moving resolutely and blithely towards this, the hardest, the cruellest and the least-rewarded of all the wars that men have fought'.[10] Patrick Shaw Stewart recognised the significance of Brooke's death. His friend had 'the gentlest manner you ever saw', he wrote to Ettie Desborough: 'he will be a great legend now and have great fame'.[11] The chivalric image leapt to mind even though Rupert Brooke had not actually died in battle. In a memorial address at Rugby, Sir Ian Hamilton, commander of the Allied forces sent to land at Gallipoli, spoke in heroic terms of this man whom the world still hardly knew: 'I went into his tent, where he was lying stretched out on the desert sand, looking extraordinarily handsome, a very knightly presence.'[12]

'If I should die . . .', the poem called 'The Soldier', proved the best-known sonnet published in English in the whole of the twentieth century. It was as eloquent as anything Brooke ever produced, flawless in tone, a magical piece of verse making. 'A pulse in the eternal mind, no less/ Gives somewhere back the thoughts by England given.' The plangent harping on the word England, with all its historic and patriotic overtones, gave this poem overwhelming authority. Through it the message of sacrifice, which was becoming the keynote of a national mood, was firmly established in the common mind. Brooke's anthology *1914 and Other Poems* was published posthumously in May 1915; it went through fifteen impressions before October 1916 and was read in thousands of homes.[13] Reggie Trench's sister Margot bought a copy in July 1915; his wife Clare absorbed another copy circulating in her family home.[14] Brooke's war sonnets, Adrian Caesar has argued, created 'a cultural myth in which the poet came to symbolise both a golden age of pre-war Edwardian England and the tragedy of willingly martyred youth'. With the revulsion at the horrors of the Great War in the 1960s and 1970s, his work became both politically and poetically unfashionable. Now, Caesar suggests, we may begin to see him as representative of his time, 'articulating the manifest complexities of Edwardian masculinity'.[15]

Julian Grenfell's famous poem 'Into Battle' was quite different but equally important as a patriot's declaration. He recorded writing it in his diary on 29 April 1915, noting a time of 'wonderful sunny lazy days' back in billets after four days in the front line. Composing the poem gave him a task, on a day when he was, as usual, 'longing to be up and doing something'. He sent it to his mother, saying 'I rather like it', encouraging her to get it published. Ettie took this as permission to circulate her son's work. She sent it to the RSPB, who immediately reproduced it as a greetings card on nice cream paper, sending it out to members 'by special permission'. The RSPB illustrated the poem with a picture of a swooping kestrel which, in Julian's argument, 'hovering by day' bade the soldier be 'swift and keen as they/ as keen of sound, as swift of sight'.[16]

'Into Battle' is luminous and serene. It is about Julian's love of his life and his almost mystical connection with nature. Its message is about surrender to duty and destiny, *dulce et decorum est pro patria mori*, the glory of dying for one's country. At this moment Julian spoke for the minds of thousands. It was only in the terrible disillusion of the 1920s that, memorably recalled by Wilfred Owen, *Dulce et decorum est* became the 'old Lie'.[17] The fighting man, Julian argued, was at one with nature, with the 'bursting trees' and 'glowing earth'. The little owls and blackbird, as well as the kestrel, were beside him. There were also of course the 'dreary, doubtful, waiting hours'. But then came the 'burning moment', when 'all things else are out of mind/And only joy of battle takes/ Him by the throat, and makes him blind'. If death was the fighting man's destiny that day it would 'fold him in soft wings'. The glory would be won

Julian had joined the Royal Dragoons in 1910. His mother Ettie Desborough, the aristocratic hostess who presided with such grace at Taplow Court, was dominating and possessive. Her style of motherhood imposed an almost impossible burden on him. By 1910 he was desperate to get away and see the world. His solace, first in India, came from reading, writing poetry, hunting and his greyhounds. In July 1914, he announced that he would give up his military career and stand for parliament. War then suddenly intervened. 'Aren't you mad with excitement?' he asked Ettie, kicking his heels that August in South Africa.

Julian's letters home were full of the longings of a young man who had played with the idea of war too long and was now eager for action. 'It is hateful being away in a corner,' he told his father, 'I suppose the whole thing will be over in a very short time.' He was desperate to 'get somewhere in time for something!' He was sure it 'must be wonderful in England now'. His whole upbringing felt like a prelude to this moment: 'it reinforces one's belief in the Old Flag and the Mother Country and the Heavy Brigade and the Thin Red Line and all the Imperial idea'. All this was now 'a real enough thing'. From

South Africa Julian poured out his frustration to his sister Casie: 'just think of being here when the biggest thing in the world is going on'.

Julian harried his mother. 'Is Billa-boy going to fight?' was a crucial question. His brother Billy was commissioned as a second lieutenant in the Rifle Brigade on 14 September. Julian sailed at last on the *Dunluce Castle* on 25 August and docked at Southampton on 19 September 1914. Ettie travelled by train to meet him on the Wiltshire downs. He then joined the family for a brief weekend at Taplow. 'Awful ship for horses, with steep ramps and low ceilings,' he wrote, describing the embarkation for France on 6 October; 'however they rose to the occasion and went in like lambs'. The adventure he had lived for had at last begun.[18]

Ettie described her parting from Julian to her daughter Casie: 'I feel so strongly that courage is his due, one could not be anything but brave for him'. She wrote of things 'impossible to bear . . . and yet we do bear them'. She knew Casie shared 'the anguish of this and yet the uplift'. Patriotic endeavour, never questioned or doubted, bound the Grenfell family together with hoops of steel during that traumatic autumn.[19]

Only one other of our seventeen soldiers was in the regular army before the war. He was Jack Sweeney, son of a confectioner who had an unhappy and deprived childhood, losing his mother at ten years old (plate 7). He joined the 2nd Battalion of the Lincolnshire Regiment at the age of eighteen in 1907. The archive in the Imperial War Museum contains the pass issued by the recruiting staff officer in London for his journey on the Great Eastern Railway to Lincoln. It also includes a printed pamphlet history of the regiment detailing its battle honours from the reign of James II until the Boer War, which Jack noted with his initials was 'given to me at the depot on enlistment'. The next years were the happiest in his life until then although the discipline and training were rigorous. He was given a furlough for six weeks in 1911. The regiment served in Gibraltar in 1912 and 1913, before being sent to Bermuda early in 1914.

Jack waved goodbye to the sunny West Indies in the unthinking obedience with which Tommies invariably left distant lands. His first letter to his father from the Western Front, on 20 November 1914, was resolutely cheerful. The rain in the trenches had 'made us look like mudlarks'. Shells 'came very near our trenches but never hurt anybody and the boys was laughing every time one bursted'. But it was already a 'pitiful sight to see some of the towns here all in ruins'.[20]

The War Office hastened to reinforce the British Expeditionary Force. Old soldiers did not hesitate to return to arms. The call of duty in his blood was too much for Rowland Feilding: he could not sit around (plate 15). His pedigree was illustrious and colourful: one famous ancestor had been a prominent Royalist in the Civil War. Born in 1871, Rowland studied civil engineering at Manchester before qualifying as an associate of the Royal School of Mines. In Rhodesia during the Matabele rebellion, he joined Gifford's Horse, a force to protect white settlers. He had pursued his mining career, travelling in turn to every continent in the world. On his return home in 1898 he served for a time with the Lancashire Fusiliers before joining the City of London Yeomanry. Rowland married Edith Stapleton-Bretherton in 1903. At the outbreak of war in 1914, they had three daughters, Joan, Anita and Peggy. Despite being forty-three years old, Rowland yearned for action, so he lobbied a cousin in the Guards for a transfer from the Yeomanry.[21]

Robert Hermon was still at Oxford when the Boer War broke out, but abandoned his studies to answer the appeal to 'defend the Empire' and joined the Queen's Own Hussars (plate 16). He saw active service in South Africa until 1905, and his first daughter was born there. Settled at Cowfold in Sussex with four children by 1911, he could not bear to leave them behind when the regiment was due to go to India. So Robert left the regular army and joined King Edward's Horse, a Special Reserve cavalry regiment made up by and large of men from the old Dominions. He was promoted to Major and given command of the Oxford and Cambridge Squadron.

On his annual territorial army training at Canterbury, Robert wrote to his wife Ethel philosophically four days before war was declared: 'it seems as if it will be some time before you see me home again'. His CO had agreed with the General inspecting the squadron that six months' training was necessary, before final mobilisation, to bring the King Edward's Horse to the standard of a regular cavalry unit. Meanwhile, rooted as he was in the glories of Britain's naval past, Robert hoped 'the fleet will give 'em Hades before long'. This would 'put our tails up'. He had two personal preoccupations. The first was whether his manservant and groom would go with him to the Front: 'I don't know what I am going to do for servants but I think both Buxton and Harry are quite keen to follow master,' Robert told his wife on 4 August. The second was his mount. He opted to take with him from the Cowfold stables his own horse and his wife's: 'it strikes me that if it comes to fighting I should like to be as well mounted as I could be.'[22]

There was a rapid exchange of letters between Gordon Buxton, Robert's manservant who was a general factotum at Cowfold, and his wife Marie on 4 and 6 August. The squadron was about to leave Canterbury to mobilise at Alexandra Park. Writing on the 6th, Buxton told Marie the matter seemed to be settled:

I was very glad that you were all for my being a soldier. The Captain would like me to stop with him very much but he wondered how you would like the idea. If he does take me I think I have to sign on for four years but he would get me out as soon as the war is over of course . . . I told the Captain what you said and he was very pleased . . . It seems heartless to think of leaving you but I must confess I would love to go . . . If anything happened to me and I never came home alive you wouldn't think I went because I didn't care what became of you would you my love.[23]

Gordon Buxton's qualms are quite understandable. His dilemma was that of thousands of couples up and down the country.

Robert's doubts about Buxton coming with him were greater than his own doubts about going. He was wondering if he should send him home 'to take care of you', he told Ethel on 6 August. 'I should be more comfortable if I thought you had someone you could rely upon,' he reflected. But Robert Hermon's double chivalry at that moment, pulled in two directions, was quickly torn to pieces. For he found himself preoccupied by the business of mobilising and needing every ounce of Buxton's help. Some of his horses, unused to being picketed in the open, stampeded at Alexandra Park; one broke its neck and several were badly injured.[24]

Commissioning was a hectic, disorganised and unstructured process. Sometimes it followed a man's sudden decision to enlist. When the war broke out, Wilbert Spencer was only seventeen and had not expected to leave Dulwich College until the following year (plate 25). But, on his way home to Highgate from school soon after 4 August, he took it into his head to join up. His arrival home that day was engraven in his six-year-old sister Helen's memory. Many years later she told her daughter Nicola about it: 'he came excitedly into the house, throwing his hat in the air and rejoicing in the fact that the army had accepted him'. Helen's emotions that day stayed with her because they were traumatic, but she was too young to understand what it really meant for her family to be caught up in international conflict. Wilbert's mother was German by birth. Nicola relates the story of her reaction to his arrival home: 'my mother remembered thinking how displeased her mother was and not really understanding why she marched off crossly and shut herself in her room'. For Wilbert's parents, his impetuous decision was completely unexpected. They were horrified. Letting their youngest boy go off to war so young was bad enough; for him to go off to fight against her German relatives made his mother feel even worse.[25]

Somehow Wilbert's father, moving fast, managed to obtain an immediate place for his son on a three-month crash course at the Royal Military College,

Sandhurst. 'Life here is very healthy and extraordinarily interesting,' Wilbert told him on 14 August 1914. He sent a kiss to his baby sister. 'My word you do have to drill smartly here,' he continued, finding the parades 'six times smarter than the O.T.C.' at Dulwich. The raw recruit was struggling to find his feet. He was unbelievably young to have been thrown into this war. Wilbert requested his dressing gown from home.[26] In fact Wilbert was at Sandhurst for just two months, since he was commissioned and joined the 3rd Battalion of the Wiltshire Regiment in October. While training with his new regiment, he managed to find the time to buy a small ring for his sister Helen's seventh birthday. Coming at the bottom end of a large family they seem to have been particularly close.[27]

There is no record of Wilbert writing to his mother during this training period but he probably did get home once or twice from Sandhurst. When he wrote to her from Le Havre on 1 December, he apologised that she had no warning about his leaving the country except a telegram. He knew it 'took her by surprise'. But they were given only four hours' notice and no leave was allowed before sailing. He sought to reassure his mother by saying he had a new waistcoat and socks from the stores. It would 'be jolly if we are all home for Christmas', he told her.[28]

Lance Spicer, aged twenty-one, was the son of a Liberal MP. He gravitated to the lobby of the House of Commons on 5 August 1914, where he glimpsed Sir Edward Grey, the Foreign Secretary, announcing that Britain was at war. Lance's obvious first step was to register as an applicant for a commission with his OTC in Cambridge. He heard nothing so considered joining a 'Public Schools Battalion' of the Middlesex Regiment, where he expected to find men he would know from his days at Rugby. When, in the middle of August, he was accosted in Jermyn Street and found a woman sticking a pin with a white feather in his lapel he wondered if he was being dilatory (plate 13).

Meeting a Cabinet minister who was a family friend, Lance confessed the incident. He said he was considering enlisting since getting a commission was taking so long. But Lance was exactly the kind of man Kitchener was seeking as officer material. Within a few days, with some lobbying, Lance found himself reporting to the Oxford OTC. After a fortnight there, he received a commission in the King's Own Yorkshire Light Infantry, with which he served for the duration of the war.[29]

Graham Greenwell joined a public school camp on Salisbury Plain in September 1914, confident that he would soon be commissioned (plate 11). It was a 'temporary business', he explained to his mother, assuring her he was 'having great fun and enjoying it all immensely'. 'I am learning a lot of my officer's job,' he wrote. He was delighted that, learning to give commands, he was 'sandwiched between two of Asquith's sons'. As both were 'sadly deficient in the elements of drill I had to pull them through'. When he heard that his home regiment, the Oxfordshire and Buckinghamshire Light Infantry, required officers, Graham pulled some strings for a commission. Eager for action, he waited for news of going to 'India or Aldershot or Havre'. Relegation to the reserve battalion and delay going abroad, he noted, 'would be rotten'.[30]

Billie Nevill was the odd one out here since Dover College was the kind of small public school that did not win many commissions. But, planning to be a schoolmaster, he had completed his first year at Jesus College, Cambridge when war broke out (plate 14). It was easy to obtain a temporary commission in the newly formed 8th Battalion of the East Surrey Regiment, because he lived at Twickenham and his Cambridge OTC supported his application. He was fortunate, like Wilbert Spencer, to be one of the few of Kitchener's men to obtain a place on a month's course at the Royal Military College at Sandhurst. He was gazetted a second lieutenant on 27 November, the day before this course began.[31]

The timing could not have been worse for Yvo Charteris, whose idyllic childhood roaming the woods of the family estate on the Cotswold Edge was hardly over (plate 24). As the youngest he began everything early. He was hunting at nine, shooting pheasant and woodcock at ten, blooded when he shot his first stag at thirteen. At Eton he had gone bird nesting on the Thames Valley fields. But before he was eighteen, war turned the Eton dream sour. 'Back again with Alma Mater, Ugh,' Yvo wrote to his sister Mary in October 1914. 'I shall be very bored here, most of the best people have gone to the war . . . the O.T.C. no longer provides the opportunities for buffoonery it used to, we're very efficient now, we route march every Thursday afternoon.' 'We are very military here now . . . I feel a veteran, people are getting commissions every day,' he explained to his mother.

Yvo was truly overwhelmed by the nation's response to war. He wrestled with his family to establish his own patriotic commitment. When his second brother Guy was gazetted in September to the Shropshire Yeomanry Yvo thought he looked 'very well in khaki'. 'I bought a dormouse this morning called Portia,' he continued in the letter home reporting Guy's departure. Portia was a companion, he explained, to his field mouse Horace. Hugo, Earl of Wemyss, Yvo's father, made a rousing speech in the Stanway barn rallying recruits from the estate. Some thought he went too far by threatening dismissal of any servants who did not enlist.[32] But Mary Wemyss's honeyed words to the tenants put things right. A dozen able-bodied Stanway men marched off to enlist.

Yvo's sister Cynthia, married to the Prime Minister's second son Herbert Asquith, told him about her visit to France in October on a Red Cross mission.[33] She went within three miles of the firing line, where they 'heard, saw and smelt' the battle. The trip was 'the most wonderful experience . . . crowded with every possible beauty and horror'. Tommies had 'swarmed round our motor and cheered us', Cynthia said, as they distributed cigarettes. This involvement of young aristocratic women in war overseas was previously unheard of in Yvo's family. No wonder that in October he found it 'too disgusting' being back at Eton, which now seemed 'horribly irrelevant'.

But Mary Wemyss was devastated by news of family members killed early in battle and had felt stressed on seeing off two of her three boys to war. She was loath to let Yvo go too. But by late November he had made up his mind. His Oxford matriculation, achieved the next month, seemed to him an almost pointless ritual. Suddenly he insisted he wanted to apply for a commission over Christmas and leave school as soon as it came through. Throwing aside his uncle's proposal of a Sandhurst course on account of his youth, he set his mind on the King's Royal Rifle Corps. By March he was in training with the regiment at Sheerness. He told his sister Mary of his emotions on leaving Eton. 'I have left behind me for the last time that great nursery of England's manhood – picture my feelings . . . yesterday as I leant out of my window at night and heard the flooded river plashing over the playing fields I almost wept – but now I am glad to go.'[34]

A famous school behind one, the drive, confidence and ambition to lead as well as serve, and the right connections were what mattered in obtaining a commission in Kitchener's Army. In many cases, though, enlistment was the only option for men caught up by the patriotic fervour of the moment.

Herbert Trench had to emulate two elder brothers Arthur and Reggie. Arthur, eight years his senior, had been serving as a regular officer in the Royal Engineers in India for more than a year when the war broke out. Reggie, we have seen, was a leading figure in the Inns of Court Officers Training Corps. Herbert was the baby in a family with a long tradition of public service, ill at ease with a mother who found him clingy and difficult. He had never quite recovered from losing his father just after his eighth birthday. The family's hard times led his mother to choose Dover College, close to her home at Folkestone, for his schooling. Intellectual and deeply sensitive by nature, Herbert felt deflated by this, since his brothers had been to Charterhouse, a more prestigious boarding school. In 1910 Herbert did an engineering apprenticeship with the South Eastern and Chatham Railway. He followed this in 1913 with a probationary position in the General Manager's office of the London & North Western Railway.

In early August 1914, Herbert confessed to his mother Isabel that he was broke but did not say that he also owed his landlady eight weeks of rent.

Reluctantly, Isabel agreed to lend him £15 when he planned a motorcycle trip to help the French army.[35] He had inveigled his uncle into writing reassuringly to her about the escapade: 'it is very unlikely that we should be in or near the firing line – and the show can hardly last more than four months, or six at the outside'. Herbert's brief motorcycle dash on his Twenty Triumph into northern France expressed his need to live up to his brothers. Immaturity was concealed by bravado. He had a record of road accidents and was under the influence of his older companion, Eddy Burney, who was a budding journalist wanting to place copy about the war.[36]

Both Herbert's sisters had their doubts about his soldiering ambitions. Margot thought the trip was simply to seek excitement: 'he's only too delighted to get away from his ordinary work and rag about and be important ... I daresay he does care a little about fighting for England but not much'. She disapproved of their mother giving him £15 for his moment of glory. Cesca was more charitable and, closer to Herbert, also more anxious. 'He will be a despatch-rider for the French army, he hopes, speeding from place to place on his motorbike,' she noted in her diary. 'His experience of accidents will come in useful,' she added wryly, 'may they come safely out of it.'[37]

Herbert's own account to his sister Cesca just before leaving on 11 August was euphoric. He called the expedition the 'great adventure'. They would cross to Boulogne and make contact with the military: 'it ought to be the best fun on earth ... I have been waiting for this for about four years and I am not going to miss it now if possible.' But the trip was a fiasco. There was nothing to say about what they did, he told his sister, apart from admiring Amiens Cathedral and seeing lots of troops.[38] But hanging about, as we have seen with Lance Spicer, could be embarrassing in the feverish atmosphere of August 1914. Herbert enlisted a week after getting home.

Reggie Trench told Clare Howard how it came about. Visiting the HQ of the Honourable Artillery Company, he 'was asked for references so I got the Secretary of the Cavendish Club to write and in a rash moment wrote a line myself'. Herbert was one of the last twenty taken on that day, becoming number 1688, Number 3 Company, in the service battalion. The regiment was famed for its long and honourable tradition so young men like him were besieging its HQ, Armoury House. It appealed to Herbert to recover his standing by joining a regiment, founded in 1537, that represented the glory of the Tudor and early Stuart army.[39] He felt even better when the medical officer passed him as a fit twenty-two-year-old.[40]

Herbert spent just three weeks in camp before sailing for St Nazaire on 18 September. Reggie was astonished to hear that they had left 'at 3.0 am having been serving out rifles all night and without any meal'. He discovered that many of the men were 'utterly untrained'.[41] So far as Herbert was concerned though, he was proving himself as a fighting man. The war was still a personal adventure. He took the Triumph motorcycle with him, hoping it would carry his heavy equipment. In childish excitement, he told his mother about how he had offered its big headlamp to light up the loading of the transport wagon with kitbags and stores (plates 28, 29).[42]

Kitchener quickly realised the War Office needed help with the recruitment drive. Local authorities and leading citizens all over England were finding halls for bigger recruiting offices and collecting clerks to register volunteers. They sometimes housed and fed the men till they could be sent off to training centres. The formation of the Pals battalions in the great northern cities was the core of this surge of civilian effort. Britain was after all still a very local society. The Pals battalions there were bound together by close local links and motivated by a shared desire to protect urban and regional homelands.[43]

The Sheffield Pals initiative was typical, in reflecting Edwardian civic pride. It was the brainchild of two students at the recently founded university who approached the college authorities. When the plan was announced in the *Sheffield Telegraph* on 4 September, the emphasis was on professionals, businessmen and their office staff: 1,200 men in all were sought. Many early recruits were students and lecturers at the university or men working in the city. One of them, Reg Glenn, a survivor who lived until 1994, recalled with pride serving with 'the finest men in Sheffield'. Men came in from the districts around as the net was quickly widened. Reg made friends with a miner, Will Streets from Derbyshire. The tough regime of his work underground had given Will stamina. Three of his brothers joined up but Will was the only one in the family who went off to Sheffield to do so, taking digs in the city during his training.[44]

Will Streets, born in 1885, was the eldest in a family where all the boys went down the mine. His father had moved from Lincolnshire to Derbyshire in search of work, finding it at Whitwell Colliery which was opened by the Shireoaks Colliery Company in the 1890s. Number 16 Portland Street, Whitwell, a small terraced house, became the family home and remained so for fifty-six years. The Streets family was the very epitome of the respectable working class, attending the Wesleyan Methodist chapel close by their home. Will took Sunday school classes, leading the smaller children on nature rambles in the north Derbyshire countryside. The girls sang in the choir and Will's sister Clara played the organ. He was a voracious reader, and his talent as an artist shows in pen and ink sketches of the neighbourhood done at nine years old. He was writing poetry at twelve, evoking the skylark that climbed the morning sky 'to catch the songs that angels sing /and reproduce them on the wing'.

At sixteen Will began work at the colliery. He wrote about his sense of duty to a friend in 1916: 'I had dreams, I had ambitions, because I strove even in boyhood after learning, after expression'. Most of Will's wages went to his mother, but he spent what he called his 'saving pittance' on books, bought, as he told a fan of his poetry in a letter written during the war, 'with my own blood as it were'. In this letter he spoke of his fourteen years 'in the deep eternal shadows of the mine, working with men with hearts like diamonds, sweating, toiling, fighting death daily'. Will read books on ethics and philosophy but poetry was always his chief love. He sat up reading into the midnight hours. By 1914 he was steeped in the poems of Shakespeare and Milton, Shelley and Keats, Browning and Tennyson. He enrolled on educational correspondence courses. He wrote essays and submitted his own verse to a poetry magazine.

By 1914, when he joined the Sheffield Pals, his local life must have seemed changeless to Will. He had reached the age of twenty-nine. A few weeks after he began his training the first local wounded came home. Will told his mother how some 'looked worn out' and were oblivious 'to the cheers of women and children lined up along the route'. Imagining what they had lived through so recently he was inspired to follow their example: 'the fire-swept trenches amid the shriek and havoc of shrapnel last week and tonight in the fine city of Sheffield tended by patient, tender women.'

Writing home in October, Will was in no doubt about his locality's response to the threat posed by Germany. 'The pale faces are becoming flushed and hardened,' he noted, 'the bent bodies are becoming straight.' 'The fire of freedom and patriotism burns strongly within the British soldier's breast,' Will told his mother, 'even though he may seem to hold it and some other things lightly in the songs that he sings.' It was because it was so sacred that he hid this fire, 'as youth hides the sacred discovery of his first love'.[45]

Cyril Newman's school reports show that he had a creditable career at Bedford Modern School, which he attended as a day boy from 1902 to 1911 (plate 10). He was keen on sports and body building. As a hobby he studied the Crimea battle plans and was interested in the military history of the Peninsular War, the Franco-German war of the 1870s and the Boer War. His vigorous patriotism was founded on his notion of Britain's destiny and his strong Christian commitment. Not quite teetotal, Cyril treated himself to the odd glass of sherry, but cigarettes in the Newman household were on offer to guests only.

Cyril was an upright idealistic young man, passionate about the imperial tradition. When he was offered leave by the Board of Trade, enlistment became inescapable. He felt his path of duty was clear on 2 September when he joined the huge queue in Oxford Street to enlist in the Queen Victoria's Rifles. His friend Reg Noakes, who later married Cyril's sister Nellie, joined him. Till then he had thought, as he walked to his office each day, that the war might end by Christmas.[46] During October 1914, Cyril was in training daily in Hyde Park with the Queen Victoria's Rifles. He was one of the advance party which left London on 19 November to begin training in earnest. The night before, his girlfriend Winnie Blackburn sewed on buttons for him and helped him pack his kitbag. She asked shyly if she might write to him occasionally. Next day he left home in a hurry, sending a brief note to his Sunday school class. In his first letter to her, he thanked Winnie for her gift of *Daily Light on the Daily Path*, a devotional textbook. He was sleeping with it under his pillow.[47]

At the core of Great War patriotism was young men's sense of adventure, but older men found themselves caught up by this too. Maurice Murray was aged forty-seven when, as rector of a small Kentish parish, he started badgering his bishop to be sent to France to serve others. At Christmas 1917, having come through Passchendaele, he was with the 12th and 13th Sussex Battalions enjoying their sing-song which expressed their longing for home. Their tune 'Oh who will o'er the downs with me', he wrote in his diary, 'lays hold of me for some reason'. 'It always,' he reflected, 'to me suggests mystery and passionate longing and adventure.'[48]

But there was no one in those first months who articulated this dedication to the adventure of war quite like Julian Grenfell. Forty-five letters home between October 1914 and the next May, written in sustained ecstasy, explain his heedlessness of the danger of being killed. He had found his identity and sense of purpose, an identity which made nonsense of the social world in which he had been brought up by his mother. 'I adore war,' he wrote, 'it is like a big picnic without the objectlessness of a picnic. I have never been so well and so happy.'

'Isn't it luck for me to have been born so as to be just the right age and just in the right place to enjoy it most?' Julian asked his mother. The release war brought him was enormous. He was allowed to be dirty. 'I have not washed for a week or had my boots off for a fortnight,' he boasted on 3 November. He loved the outdoor life, the company of men, horses and dogs. The intensity of his involvement showed in his inability to realise that his men, whom he praised to the skies, were not usually as desperate as he was, after the briefest rest, to get back into the action.

War was about killing, and this was no problem for Julian. Killing provided the total confidence, even the insouciance, of the poem 'Into Battle'. He could project childish rage and violence, what he called his 'barbaric disposition', onto the enemy; relaxing with his own men there was mostly just laughter. Yet the account he wrote home of the sniping feat, using stalking skills learnt on Scottish moors, which won him renown and the DSO, was cold-blooded. 'I crawled to the parapet of their trench,' he wrote, 'it was very exciting . . . then the German put his head up again . . . I saw his teeth glisten against my foresight and I pulled the trigger very steady. He just gave a grunt and crumpled up. The others got up and whispered to each other.' In his game book Julian recorded having shot 105 partridges on his mother's estate during his short leave in October 1914. He made two entries after his sniping expeditions on the Western Front: 'November 16th: 1 Pomeranian' and 'November 17th: 2 Pomeranians'. There were probably few soldiers who saw the struggle with Germany in such blank terms as this.[49]

Great War patriotism in part was the logical outcome of an ideology of manliness developed in the late Victorian and Edwardian public schools. This manliness encompassed a raft of attributes, including loyalty, honour, duty and chivalry, besides physical courage, strength and endurance. Rupert Brooke and Julian Grenfell, born in 1887 and 1888 respectively, educated at Rugby and Eton, were members of a whole generation brought up to this exacting code. But Kitchener was able to recruit a huge volunteer army in 1914 because their single standard of manliness had, by then and in its essence, through some kind of osmosis, pervaded British adult male society. Public schoolboys were merely its leading proponents.

The public school values were steadily absorbed by aspiring upper-working- and lower-middle-class youngsters as boys' magazines appeared by the dozen between 1880 and 1900. The *Boy's Own Paper*, with an estimated readership of 250,000 in 1884, together with magazines like *Chums*, founded in 1892, spread the word. This literature for young men revered athletics. Rowing, cricket and football were seen as the most manly sports. Grammar school boys aped and absorbed public school customs and lore. Their organisation followed the public school model. Malcolm Muggeridge, at a state secondary school peopled by cockneys during the Great War, recalled how even its 'organisation was vaguely derived from that of the public schools', with prefects, colours and other trappings reminiscent of *Tom Brown's Schooldays*. His school, like so many others, had a Latin motto: *Ludum Ludite*, 'Play the Game'.[50]

Over 40 per cent of male adolescents belonged to some kind of youth organisation by 1914.[51] Public schools had their missions in the East End of London. The Boys' Brigade, for example, founded in Glasgow in 1883, sought to direct the aspirations of boys towards Christian manliness. The most famous of these youth movements was the Boy Scouts, founded by General Sir Robert

Baden-Powell, the hero of Mafeking, in 1908.[52] Urban boys were taken into the countryside to learn moral purity and practical Scoutcraft. They were trained to be worthy servants of the Empire. 'Be Prepared' was more than a vague command. 'Be prepared to die for your country,' declared *Scouting for Boys*, 'so that when the moment arrives you may charge home with confidence, not caring whether you are going to be killed or not.' This manual contained sections on Honour, Courtesy, Loyalty, Fair Play, Obedience and Discipline and Humility. The formula was triumphantly successful. Gentlemanly scout-masters and groups of working-class Scouts talked and laughed together round endless camp fires. Within two years of the foundation of the Boy Scouts, there were 100,000 members.[53]

Boys' adventure literature also did much to create this code of manliness. G.A. Henty, publishing two or three books a year from the 1880s to 1902, sold around 25 million copies by 1914. He sent his public school boys, thinly disguised in period dress, on adventures into every period of British history from *Beric the Briton* to *With Kitchener in the Sudan*.[54] But his readership was very much wider than boys who went to public schools.

There is no more striking shrine to Great War patriotism than Clifton College, Sir Henry Newbolt's alma mater, founded in 1862.[55] The figure of a knight in armour dominates the court between the cricket field and the formidable range of Victorian Gothic buildings. This memorialises the Boer War, when 300 were sent to fight and 44 were killed. The school chapel's Great War memorial windows have portraits of King Arthur and Sir Galahad, yet the faces that look out from under the helmets are unmistakably those of contemporary public school boys.

Newbolt imbibed the values of John Percival, Clifton's first headmaster, recognising the combination of devout Christianity and chivalric idealism which underlay his classical model of education imported from Rugby. 'It was a Roman rule,' Newbolt wrote, 'presented to us by a man of fine character and magnificent presence, demanding of us the virtues of leadership, courage and independence; the sacrifice of selfish interests to the ideal of fellowship and the future of the race.' Percival boasted that 'few members of the school would not have bartered away all chance of intellectual distinction for a place in the cricket eleven or football fifteen'. The report of the Royal Commission on the public schools in 1864 argued that, far from being merely places of amusement, cricket and football fields helped form 'some of the most valuable social qualities and manly virtues'.[56]

The culture of school songs and sporting doggerel reached its peak in the late Victorian and Edwardian periods, fusing the world of school with adult lives spent serving the Empire. That service could mean engagement in war, as it did in the Crimea and South Africa. There was an obsession with building character through physical exercise. The messages of male brotherhood, of loyalty, masculinity, chauvinism and decency, underlay the rhetoric of the patriotism of 1914. There were simple linear relationships in this ideology between youth and manhood, between physical effort, physical courage and moral worth, between sport and war.[57]

Newbolt made his name as a poet with 'Vitaï Lampada', riveting the reader by its famous opening line 'There's a breathless hush in the Close tonight.' It told the story of a cricketer who grew up to fight in Africa and, in the panic of battle, was stirred to heroic action by his memories of schooldays: 'his Captain's hand on his shoulder smote – "Play up! play up! and play the game!"' Newbolt felt encouraged to write and publish more school poems. In 'Clifton Chapel' another schoolboy hero was advised by his father to take inspiration for his life from his worship in the chapel during his youth: 'You too may speak with noble ghosts/ Of manhood and the vows of war/ You made before the Lord of Hosts'. In a single verse of this poem, Newbolt summarised the basic notion of patriotic manliness which inspired the British war effort. The crucial connections were made here between the soldier's mind, his body and the emotions he felt about his country:

> To set the cause above renown,
> To love the game beyond the prize,
> To honour, while you strike him down,
> The foe that comes with fearless eyes;
> To count the life of battle good,
> And dear the land that gave you birth,
> And dearer yet the brotherhood
> That binds the brave of all the earth.

This delineation of a manliness ready for martial action was so familiar by August 1914 that it was a simple matter to drive forward the national cause. On the first day of the war, The Times published Newbolt's 'The Vigil'. The poem evokes a nation prepared to arm to 'defend the Right': 'joyful hear the rolling drums/ joyful hear the trumpets call'. All his poems were suddenly in hot demand. Reggie Trench had been enthusing about them to Clare since early in their courtship. In July 1912, he confessed how they made him, a mere city clerk, 'feel rather a slacker'.[58] When he sent her a nice leather-bound edition of them in September 1914, she responded with a comment on how they exactly fitted 'one's present mood and the general atmosphere'. In 1917 Newbolt published his Book of the Happy Warrior, telling the story of English chivalry, with a chapter on Agincourt which he titled 'France versus Gentlemen of England'.[59]

From 1912 to 1914 Reggie fed Clare with the adventure literature, mainly Rudyard Kipling's tales, that he loved to read. The Sussex tales evoked the Weald landscape they both knew well, endowing it with a history that went back to Roman times. Giving her *Rewards and Fairies* for her birthday, he drew her attention to 'If', initially published there. He found it 'jolly inspiring'. No one, of course, got to 'be a man' by achieving all the counsels of perfection set out with such panache by Kipling. But it was the sheer impossibility of the scale of Kipling's agenda of performance that inspired Reggie.[60] 'You will like the stories of the Roman centurion on the Great Wall,' he noted, sending *Puck of Pook's Hill*.[61] He was referring to the centurion Parnesius, whose dogged defence of Hadrian's Wall against the 'Winged Hats' for two months and seventeen days brought respite for the Romans in the desperate last days of the Empire.

Charles Carrington declared, in the Preface to his biography of Rudyard Kipling, that his qualifications for writing it were 'shared with thousands of my contemporaries'. He, like Reggie Trench, had grown up with *Just So Stories, Stalky & Co.* and *Puck of Pook's Hill*. He argued that no pieces were 'more effective in moulding the thought of a generation' than Kipling's chapters on the defence of Hadrian's Wall. The centurion's task, he suggested, became a 'panegyric of duty and service' by junior officers. Remembering his days on the Western Front in old age, Carrington argued that the Roman centurion 'strengthened the nerve of many a young soldier in the dark days of 1915'.[62] In an article on the teaching of patriotism in 1915, Baden-Powell came up with a breezy manliness which cast ancient Romans in a different light. 'Don't be disgraced like the young Romans,' he warned, 'who lost the Empire by being wishy-washy slackers without any go . . . your forefathers worked hard, fought hard and died hard to make the Empire for you.' 'Don't let them look down from heaven,' he declared, 'and see you loafing about with your hands in your pockets, doing nothing to keep it up.'[63]

At the Front, duty became a family issue among officers. Robert Hermon was dissatisfied with his nephew Dick in 1916 when, passing his eighteenth birthday, he chose to stay on at school rather than showing the pluck to take a commission. 'Dick has no idea above a ferret,' he told his wife, 'though there's man's work to be done.' He hoped his boy Bob, if there was a war on, at that age would 'see his duty a bit plainer'.[64]

Harry Sackville in the Royal Field Artillery, killed in February 1918, pictured himself back in his study when he wrote from the Front in 1917 to his former pupils at Buxton College about the one thing 'which keeps life sweet and clean'. 'It's a Christian thing and it's a British thing . . . it's the story of the Crusaders, of the Reformation, of the downfall of the power of Spain, of our colonisation, of the destruction of Napoleon's might'. The thing was this, he insisted: 'playing the game for the game's sake'. They all knew what that meant: 'high honesty of purpose and the word duty'.

To illustrate his point, Sackville told them about how he once interrupted classroom pandemonium at Buxton when the fifth form raided the fourth form. 'Desks were not to be used for splinter-proof dug-outs,' he announced. Having caned those dragged into the fray in the fourth, he told the fifth he would be glad to cane those who felt they 'ought to turn up' in his study at five o'clock. Seven arrived. Then the 'guiltier party', as he saw it, were beaten. This was the stiff upper lip, the honesty of owning up and due submission which earned the privilege later of leading others. 'I'm very proud of you chaps,' he said before they left.[65]

The chivalric tradition was the essence of British manhood learnt from endless fictional adventures imbibed in youth.[66] Yvo Charteris, one of the youngest and most innocent of our subjects, read avidly the stories of battles long ago. C.W. Beaumont, a bookseller friend with whom he corresponded regularly, recorded his love of picturing himself 'taking part in the old French wars, the days of knighthood and chivalry when lance met lance and sword met sword'.[67]

Charles Carrington learnt from *The Brushwood Boy* Kipling's lesson that 'a hard conventional exterior might conceal a strange and sensitive inner life'. This was Reggie Trench's favourite Kipling story. It was a destiny tale about a boy's fulfilment in love and service to the nation. George Cottar, its hero, was moulded by subaltern training in India, but this concealed the man he was inside. The plot developed round his meetings at the brushwood pile with the girl who became the love of his life. In his dreams they rode together the Thirty-Mile Ride. Cottar was modest, gallant, diligent and dedicated to his romantic quest. 'I envy the knights of old time who could go off and perform deeds of "derring-do" for their loves,' Reggie wrote to Clare Howard during their engagement.[68]

Charlie May, a company commander, kept a diary at the Front in 1915 and 1916, in which he recorded his passionate longings for the company of his wife Maud, for whom he had gone to war. He was twenty-six. Taking a ride on his horse Lizzie, he enjoyed the French countryside, the 'larches, birches, wood-pigeons and magpies'. But, as it was for so many men once off duty, he could only, he wrote, think of Maud and his baby Pauline: 'the green rides of Epping came back to me in a flash. You in that black-spotted muslin dress looking cool and lovely so that I asked nothing more than to walk along and gaze at you dumbly, like any simple country lout gazes at his maid.' Another day he recalled a picnic in Darley Dale, 'knee-deep luscious grass . . . the Derwent gurgling along'. 'You knitted or made the kettle boil.'

Young men found themselves when they went to war. At the same time they discovered the depth of their love for their sweethearts. On 30 December 1915, Charlie recorded his thrill at the love Maud had poured out to him in her two most recent letters. He was, he wrote, 'utterly undeserving of such a deep affection as yours', the evidence of her 'goodness, bravery and perfect womanliness'. 'May our sweet babe,' he concluded this entry, 'grow into such another woman as her mother.' This diary, the single one cited often in the present book, has an intimacy that it was perhaps possible for a man to express only when he sat down to write about and concentrate on his inner thoughts.[69] Letters to be sent home at once, as we shall see, were bound to be dominated by accounts of the moment and the immediate challenges of trench life.

Cyril Newman was something of an exception. He told Winnie Blackburn in one of his letters that 'woman has always been nobler than man'. She should keep her life 'shining clear like a beacon light' to help him rise to his ideal. Three years after she had sewed on his buttons he recalled her gift of the book *Daily Light*. He was then 'her knight departing for the wars, to battle for her, and the gift was the symbol of a pinning of a plume on the casquet, the sign of her love and trust'. He would travel through numerous dangers. 'Wholeheartedly,' he told her after three years at the Front, she had 'placed her trust in my honour, to be a true man . . . so that if spared I might return unstained, worthy of the reverence of her pure womanhood'. 'And on this anniversary day,' Cyril declared on 17 November 1917, 'I renew my vows to you, I kneel before you and promise to be true.' Few perhaps stated their commitment to war as a crusade for a loved one quite so directly as this.[70]

Personal allegiances were usually a strong element in patriotic feeling. Significantly, one army song went 'Good-bye, Nellie/ I am going across the main . . . I'm going to do my duty/For the girl I love'. Sung with great sentiment the composition went to the heart of why men risked their lives in battle.[71] In several letters John Rapoport of the Rifle Brigade poured out his love to the girl he was engaged to marry. On 6 May 1918, back from leave, he had just received fourteen letters, five of them from her. 'Darling you were splendid when you saw me off at Waterloo,' he wrote, 'you just typified the women of England by your attitude, everything for us men and you have your dark times to yourselves so as not to depress us.' John asked her to pray hard for him: 'one is so apt to get slack . . . I do so want to remain keen and good, but it's awfully hard.' If she prayed 'for her boy, I feel somehow that God will listen to her prayers an awful lot'. He was killed ten days later.[72]

If men fought for loved ones – sweethearts, wives, sons and daughters – they also fought, indefatigably, for the land they sought to preserve against the German invader. Siegfried Sassoon, cycling through the Kent countryside on the last Friday in July 1914, saw it as threatened by the international crisis. 'The Weald had been the world of my youngness,' he reflected, 'and while I gazed across it now I felt prepared to do what I could to defend it.'[73]

For some, persons and places were so intimately connected that they could not disentangle the different elements in their patriotic endeavour. Reggie Trench felt the same about the Weald as Sassoon, for this was where he had wooed Clare. When he drove down to visit her Red Cross nursing camp at Rolvenden in July 1914, he returned to his Chelsea flat overwhelmed. 'My darling,' he wrote, 'it would be topping' for them to spend more time in that countryside. His journey had 'brought back so many memories of you and the beautiful part of the world that I can hardly think of anything else'. In the darkest days of 1917, Reggie declared that Clare was 'that ideal companion and friend that one used to dream of'. Her daily letters had 'always been the greatest comfort and help to me'. Now second in command of his battalion, he was still in his heart simply her Brushwood Boy.[74]

For most soldiers their England was a very local and particular place, bounded by streets they knew or the cottages of a rural village. Robert Hermon could appreciate his wife's mention of a holiday on the Helford river in Cornwall, which made him 'long for such another summer as we had last year'. But he was also likely to picture his wife and children in a French landscape similar to his own meadows and woods at Cowfold in Sussex. The Chugs, as he called his children, 'could have some fine rides round here as there is quite a bit of park to this chateau,' he noted in January 1916.[75]

People he cared for and places that mattered back home merged in the fighting soldier's mind. Conversely, French villages where men were billeted for some while created new attachments. Billie Nevill, liking the village of Tambour, even suggested taking his family 'all over this ground' after the war: 'we'll follow it all from my letters'.[76] Julian Grenfell told his mother that it was the high Chiltern country from Taplow across to Aylesbury which he really loved, finding it 'much prettier than the real hunting country in the Aylesbury Vale'.[77] Home was somewhere different for every one of those who fought, yet home also became generalised. The connection between their native land and the political values at the heart of the British Empire was much in men's minds. Christian Carver expressed this well, in a letter to a brother still at school with whom he shared his deepest thoughts. 'I always feel that I am fighting for England,' he wrote, 'English fields, lanes, trees, English atmospheres and good days in England – all that is synonymous with liberty.'[78]

Personal sacrifice, this book argues, was always at the heart of British patriotism. The soldier who may have put this best was not a Clifton or Eton boy but
the miner and poet Will Streets. 'Why should one sorrow if one goes out in the
morning instead of the evening?' he asked his mother before leaving for the
Front. He insisted that any Englishman 'ought to count it a privilege to die for
his country'. Women should not be sad when men died who had taken up arms
'for the reign of love and chivalry'. 'Rather be eager,' he implored her, 'to pin the
tokens on the breasts of the knights who are going out to fight a holy crusade.'
'As Kipling so truly put it,' he reminded her, 'who dies if England lives?'[79]

Something of the same attitude is evident in Robert Hermon's action in
posting a letter to his wife for her to open when he had gone abroad. It contained
a poem by Sheila Braine called 'Farewell'. If he died she should put grief aside
and accept his sacrifice as a soldier of England: 'I shall sleep well 'neath alien
soil, dear heart, sleep well – and dream of you'. Edith was to keep this poem by
her while he served in the trenches and in battle. The parents of a subaltern
who was killed in 1917 noted, reading over his letters home, that the words
'honour' and 'sacrifice' occurred more frequently than any others.[80]

Yet we should be careful to see the nuances in motivation for joining up
between the top and bottom of society. The patriotism of the working man was
more mundane and less high flown than that in gentry circles. The words 'duty'
and 'obligation' were the keynote here. In letters to local newspapers working
men made it clear that besides financial inducement, when work was sometimes hard to find, propaganda drove them forward. Unlike the upper class,
they could not see themselves as the initiators of a national enterprise. 'I never
had any doubts as to my duty to fight in this Great War for all that I held in my
life most dear,' wrote one man. 'A mortar shell blew our lance-corporal to
pieces. I got some of his brains on my arms and in my tea,' reported another.
'Ah, it's a bad thing is war and I don't want to go back but then, it's duty you see,'
wrote another. A third told a relative, after a bayonet attack which had given
him a 'night of hell', 'I know it is hard for you but when duty calls, one
must obey.'[81]

Last letters only to be opened in case of death were often written by officers.
They illuminate what men wished themselves to be remembered as dying for.
Eight such letters selected here show clear hearts about duty and the prospect
of death in battle. Four of these soldiers were killed in 1916, two in 1917 and
two in 1918. Edward Tennant, first, wrote to his mother just before he was
killed at the age of nineteen. 'Tomorrow we go over the top,' he explained. 'I am
full of hope and trust and pray that I may be worthy of my fighting ancestors.'
'The one I know best,' he reminded her, 'is Sir Henry Wyndham whose bust is
in the hall at 44 Belgrave Square.' Edward stressed his pride in being a member

of the Grenadier Guards and spoke of his communion before battle on a French hillside. He had steeled his heart: 'your love for me and my love for you,' he wrote in farewell, 'have made my life one of the happiest there has ever been.'

Eric Townshend's letter thanked his parents for enabling him to crowd into twenty years 'enough pleasures, sensations and experiences for an ordinary lifetime'. He wrote movingly and powerfully about how he saw his life on the canvas of history. 'But for this war,' he was convinced,

> I and all the others would have passed into oblivion like the countless myriads before us . . . but we shall live for ever in the results of our efforts. We shall live as those who by their sacrifice won the Great War. Our spirits and our memories shall endure in the proud position Britain shall hold in the future. The measure of life is not its span but the use made of it.

Eric's consolation lay in the reflection: 'I did not make much use of my life before the war but I think I have done so now.' His parents should 'be of good courage that at the end you may give a good account'.

Ernest Pollack gave a letter written to his parents to the chaplain of the Gloucestershire Regiment on the eve of the first day of the Somme. He had 'little to leave except my love and gratitude'. It was the thought of them and of his brothers that inspired him at that moment. Death had 'no terrors for me in itself' though, fearing pain through wounding, he was 'taking morphia in with me to battle'. 'Our cause is a good one and I believe I am doing right in fighting,' he declared. Claude Templer was a prisoner of war who escaped from Germany in 1917 and returned to the line. 'I used to think the glory of going back to the beautiful adventure was worth any price,' he wrote that April. 'I resolve to be a worthy warrior. To fight to the finish, to love to the finish, to sacrifice everything but never honour.'

John Engall was another who wrote home to his parents on the eve of the Somme. He described his communion with dozens of others who were going over the next day: 'I placed my soul and body in God's keeping and I am going into battle with His name on my lips, full of confidence and trusting implicitly in him.' 'Should it be God's holy will,' John insisted, 'I could not wish for a finer death . . . I ask that you should look upon it as an honour that you have given a son for the sake of King and Country.'

One of the main objectives of writers of letters of this kind was to plead with parents and siblings not to grieve too much and to accept their sacrifice as willingly given. John Llewellyn Jones addressed his letter to his 'dearest Dad, Ethel and Gwen', thanking God 'for giving me the best father in the world and two very dear sisters'. 'One has to face the prospect of being knocked out,' he wrote philosophically, 'as many other and probably better fellows than I have been.' War was cruel but its sacrifices were 'all in the game'. How better to make one's exit than 'fighting for the country that has sheltered and nurtured one all through life?'

Eric Lubbock set out his faith in this world as a nursery where we are trained 'to make us fit for another and better life'. 'So Mummy,' he entreated, 'if you lose me try not to let it be too great a blow to you, try and conquer your own sorrow and to live cheerfully.' 'Help Mum and look after her,' Eric wrote to his brother, hoping his life would be one 'of peace and happiness'. Arthur Heath wanted his mother to treat associations with him such as his love of the South Downs as a source of future joy, not somewhere remembered as a fact of the past 'but rather be transfused by you' so that remembering him would 'give a new quality of happiness to your holidays there'.[82]

One of the remarkable aspects of the letters is the capacity shown by these soldiers not simply to accept their ultimate sacrifice but to affirm it in such positive terms. They breathe the atmosphere and mores of Victorian and Edwardian Britain. They say things and put things in ways that we cannot conceive of today. These letters thus proclaim the immeasurable depth and intensity of the Great War's patriotic ideals and remind us how far off they now are.

CHAPTER 3

'Ready to Go'

Training

Six months of intensive training were planned at the outset for Kitchener's Army. The sheer military ignorance of the majority of recruits and junior officers was the government's main problem. While an officer coming from an Officers' Training Corps had benefited from some preliminary training, most of those who enlisted as private soldiers knew nothing about saluting, standing to attention, forming a straight line on parade or wheeling from line into a column of fours for route marching. The scheme envisaged graduation from weeks of drill in platoons and companies to training at battalion strength, with elaborate field days, entrenching schemes, rifle and bayonet practice. There were numerous difficulties in implementing this blueprint, not least the lack of sufficient experienced regular officers and NCOs to do so. In the last months of 1914, thousands of recruits and newly commissioned officers were struggling to come to terms with a new environment and a strange way of life. This was the biggest challenge ever confronted by masses of the British civilian population suddenly turned into soldiers.[1]

Our only soldier who went abroad with less than six months of training was Wilbert Spencer. Two of the officers who began training in 1914, Graham Greenwell and Billie Nevill, were at the Front after around six months. So was Cyril Newman. Will Streets trained for fifteen months before sailing from England, landing at Marseilles, after a short stay in Egypt, in March 1916.[2]

Letters home before they left England illuminate how thousands of soldiers came to terms with the new demands imposed upon them. Everyone had to adapt, on putting aside civilian life. An officer had consciously to adopt a military persona. His bearing and body language had quickly to indicate his confidence and ability to command. Tommies, by contrast, traditionally were considered trained when they had been taught to obey orders. The objective in the regular army had been to suppress all individuality, making men pliant and subservient. The new Tommies of 1914 certainly did get used to irrational demands and the constant bawling of intimidating NCOs.[3] Volunteers were not, however, by and large passive victims of the war. They retained their civilian identity, masking it with temporary patriotic engagement. No one knew how long the Great War would last. Thus the volunteers, whether officers or men, never deliberately or fully assimilated the values of the regular army.[4]

Reggie Trench, rapidly growing his neatly trimmed moustache, accomplished the adoption of his military identity with aplomb as he began drilling his men in Lincoln's Inn Fields. In September, Clare started driving across to Richmond Park to watch the Inns of Court Corps in training. 'I loved seeing you . . . I hope you enjoyed our "attack", Reggie wrote, having spotted her. Clare enjoyed his 'piece of drilling before you all marched off . . . your voice made a splendid noise and it was pitched on a nice deep note'.[5] Graham Greenwell was pushed into drilling his men for half an hour by the Adjutant on his arrival with the Oxford and Buckinghamshire Light Infantry in Essex. He was thankful for his practice at the public schools camp on Salisbury Plain. He told his mother: 'I got on remarkably well . . . the men all heard my orders and obeyed them pretty smartly for recruits'. He was self-conscious, feeling 'rather a nuisance to the sergeants who can't curse their men quite so freely in my presence'. Yet Graham knew his assurance on the parade ground was the first test of a young officer's mettle.[6]

There was little grumbling in the letters about the privations of military life. No one moaned at excessively hard and exacting orders. Extraordinary good-will on both sides in fact prevailed at the start of the war. Most wanted to equip themselves as quickly as possible for active service. The hierarchical structure within which men learnt their professionalism was taken for granted.

Yet an account by Cyril Newman of guard duty at his Crowborough barracks in February 1915 illustrates the punitive measures that were quickly applied when recruits did not stick to the straight and narrow. He was deputed with two other riflemen under a corporal to guard the divisional detention hut. Effectively, as he saw it, this was a prison. Sixteen men who had 'disobeyed orders, gone on leave without permission etc.' were incarcerated, not allowed to converse or smoke, deprived of reading matter and even of pencils. They were on fatigues for eight hours a day. 'One could not help being sorry for them,' Cyril confessed: 'the first time they had drill it made our blood boil – it was so hard and the Sergeant seemed such a brute.'[7]

The first months of soldiering, a test of the resolution and stamina of all ranks, were largely about fitness. Mothers heard from boys being driven hard. 'They are working us like the devil and a lot of chaps are cracking up,' wrote

Private A.K. Aston in the 8th Norfolk Regiment in September 1914: 'just listen to this for a day's work especially to put chaps to who are soft and untrained.' He detailed a fourteen-hour day of parades with reveille at 3.30 a.m., which included a three-mile march to the sea and back for a bathe.[8] In October 1914, Graham Greenwell told his mother about his 'first long march – 18 miles – from 9 o'clock till 2.30 … then paying the men's billets all afternoon till 6 o'clock, going into cottage after cottage till I was tired out'. He was not daunted, assuring his mother that life was splendid: 'I feel as hard as a rock.' It boosted his morale to be told that some of the messages picked up from Germany at the Chelmsford Marconi station where he did a spell of duty were being forwarded to London to aid strategic thinking in the BEF.[9]

Cyril Newman had been keen on keeping very fit since his schooldays. It quickly became a matter of pride to cope with the demands that training with Queen Victoria's Rifles imposed. In a long letter on 3 February 1915 he described the previous two days. One day he marched three miles in his draft of 250 men to the trenches they were digging, worked till 2.30 in a fast drizzling rain and 'got wet through to the skin'. Afterwards he walked over to Crowborough to the hot baths. 'I have not been affected by the wet and am wonderfully well and strong,' he insisted. After a twenty-mile route march the next day, he declared he was not a bit tired and 'enjoyed it very much'. At the battalion sports in March Cyril was chagrined to come only third in the mile and to fall in the obstacle race six yards from the winning post, giving him another third place. But for his size, he mused, this performance was 'not so bad'.[10]

The Sheffield Pals began their drilling at Bramall Lane football ground in blue suits and their workaday caps. A new purpose-built camp was being created on the city's outskirts near the Derbyshire moors. Had she kept that list of 'things I must have for my life as a soldier'? Will Streets asked his mother on 29 November. The family clubbed together to send him a generous cheque. A week later he reported a full kitbag, including a new cardigan jacket he considered a bargain at 7s. 11d. It was a severe winter when they moved in at Redmires, now equipped with rifles. 'The hail cut our faces in welcome,' wrote Will. He described some night operations: 'the scheme is one of outposts. Happily we are supports and are to sleep in a fir wood. It will not be so bad as sleeping out on the bleak moor, though while the majority are resting, we corporals and a few unfortunate privates may be sent out on reconnoitring patrols.'

In May 1915 the Sheffield Pals began training with other units in the 94th Brigade, including the Barnsley Pals and the Accrington Pals. 'What a good send off from Sheffield the other night,' Will wrote home after thousands had thronged the streets. Their new base was in Cannock Chase. He enjoyed the

Staffordshire moorland at Penkridge Camp, explaining that, with 'two minutes walk, we are knee-deep in heather with a vast view of hills and a lovely valley'. The pace was increasing. On a fifteen-mile route march in heavy rain, Will noted, 'all the fellows grumbled awfully, then a peculiar trait of the British Tommy asserted itself. We began to take it philosophically and humorously started to sing ... we sang jests at the weather and the army in general.' 'Tramping along with your thighs wet and feeling miserable and testy' was hardly their natural element.[11]

Billie Nevill's demanding timetable at Sandhurst began with physical training at 6.55 a.m. and included rifle firing, musketry and lectures on subjects ranging from sanitation to military topography and organisation. His stalwart sense of humour is evident in an account of arriving back late from weekend leave to find he was orderly officer next day: 'I spent three halfpence worth of matches learning up my duties and shivering with cold and fear of the morrow.' He enjoyed his Christmas at home with his three brothers and three sisters before joining the regiment.

Billie's training between January and July 1915 was then divided into initial weeks of drilling and field exercises at Purfleet, battalion and brigade training at Colchester and the final divisional preparation at Codford. 'I hope to be second-in-command of A company before we go out,' he wrote early on: 'the C.O. I know is very bucked with me.' Lack of equipment remained a problem for the East Surreys during these months. A hundred rifles had to serve for a battalion of around 1,100 men; there were no entrenching tools or haversacks; and very little khaki uniform had arrived. Nevertheless, when a full moon allowed a Zeppelin to drop more than four bombs and forty incendiaries on the main road his battalion was marching along, Billie took this first contact with the enemy excessively personally. 'It's rather a rag,' he wrote, 'as the Boches are trying to bomb us but they don't get the dates quite right.'

There was more variety to the training once Billie was on Salisbury Plain. 'We are going to see our artillery fire soon,' he reported, 'we are to stand and watch just between the guns and the target. Rather a rag, eh?' Billie urged his family to visit: 'I'll give you lunch in my hut and we'll go to the divisional horse show in the afternoon.' As departure approached he sought to reassure his mother. 'It's like hanging about at the end of your last term at school ... don't worry about me please, Mother, I feel as happy as I ever have in my life ... I shall be alright, really there's no danger.'[12]

Peter McGregor was an unlikely soldier, yet he shared the Scots' abiding commitment to soldiering when the cause was right (plate 23). Born in 1871, he belonged to a middle-class Edinburgh family. His father was a professional painter exhibiting at the Royal Scottish Academy. Peter married one of his students, Janet Davidson (plate 22), whom he invited to a piano recital in 1902 that he was giving with his violinist sister Helen. He became deeply affectionate to his 'dear darling sweet' Jen and every inch the family man, pursuing his career as a professional piano teacher in Edwardian Edinburgh, where he was organist and choirmaster at St Andrew's church. Peter was proud of his clan ancestry and had trained with a group of local volunteers before he decided to enlist in April 1915 in the Argyll and Sutherland Highlanders.

Peter's decision was deeply pondered. The war was at a stage when 'every man would be needed'. He explained it in a letter to Jen: 'I am quite ready . . . oh I would be sorry to leave you – fancy never coming back – only a memory – however I am ready to go'. He was sure he would 'give a good account of myself in the field of battle'. But he realised that if he revealed his true age he would be denied overseas service, which was the last thing he wanted. 'Don't for good-ness sake give my age to anyone,' he told Jen, 'my age in this battalion is thirty-six, born 1879.'

'I am doing my best to live the life of the men around me . . . I can swear and laugh at the most awful coarse jokes,' Peter told her after a week in training in June 1915. He reported in shocked dismay that two pals had taken tea 'in a house kept by two widows' who 'turned out to be – guess what!' Another told him about how 'they had a girl in a field – two of them – think of it!' 'You are the only person I care about,' he declared. Peter's transformation from organist and choirmaster into a Tommy in 1915 surprised himself as much as others. Back on the Edinburgh streets on leave in July, his new seriousness was noticed, 'never lounging or playing at his new business, but taking it in earnest like a soldier born'.

Inside, Peter reflected to Jen in an early letter, he was still 'the quiet Pete, who liked more than anything to be quiet, lazy perhaps – to love his wife and play Debussy – try and paint – draw and read – and dream the days away'. But he was becoming quite a hardened Tommy eight months after enlisting. He reflected, 'I am beginning to live now – life has a different view to me – my eyes are, I am sure, wider open than they have ever been.'

Peter McGregor was full of vigour training down in Devon, writing of how he loved 'marches in the semi-twilight, through narrow lanes and dusty high-ways'. 'I am as brown and weatherbeaten as ever I have been,' he declared, 'and feel very fit.' The scale of the operations he was part of when he moved to Aldershot impressed him. His troop paused for twenty minutes 'to watch rows and rows of soldiers and Army Service Corps wagons and artillery passing us: they loomed out of the mist with men swearing and tugging at mules' heads – engines drawing huge wagons laden with food'.[13]

Alec Reader, the eldest in a family of five children, was born on 8 December 1897, so when war broke out in August 1914 he was still five months from his seventeenth birthday, the minimum age for recruitment. His father, Fred Reader, worked as manager of the Clapham Hill Posting Company and his home, 4 North Side on Wandsworth Common, reflected the family's modest middle-class status. It was a detached villa and he had several servants. Alec was born out of wedlock; when he married Alec's mother, Fred falsified his son's birth certificate; he was not above seducing the servant he employed as a housekeeper at 4 North Side. Fred was a short-tempered, hard-drinking womaniser. Alec went to Emmanuel School in Wandsworth where according to his headmaster he was 'a splendid boy' who 'gave promise of a bright future'. He seems to have been rather quiet and shy but his good singing voice earned him praise as a soloist at St Peter's, Eaton Square. When he left school he began work as a clerk at the Telephones Department of the Post Office just across Wandsworth Common from his home.

It has been suggested that Alec may have enlisted to escape his overbearing father but his letters to him from the Front indicate they remained on good terms, as he also was with his brothers and sisters. To enlist in the Civil Service Rifles, Alec walked up to Somerset House one day that extraordinary August. He was tall and, though under age, was accepted without question when, crossing the open square, he went down to the drill hall facing the Thames embankment on the lower level. He was nodded through the medical and became Private 3623 of the 15th Battalion in the Civil Service Rifles, on a shilling a day. For a fortnight, Alec came in each day to the Somerset House square to learn the rudiments of marching and squad drill. Then the new recruits lived under canvas in Richmond Park. That winter Alec was billeted with the Dubois family in Gerard Road, Barnes. This was how the war began for many young Tommies: away from home, an uncertain future, home at weekends. Alec found initial practice on the rifle ranges at Rainham in Essex in November 1915 hard going. 'I felt quite lost without my mittens yesterday and messed up my firing,' he wrote home.[14]

His parents arranged a family photograph when he was home for a short period of leave in January 1916, just before his battalion joined a crowd of other units at Hazeley Down camp near Winchester (plate 6). Tall and patriotic, he stands behind his parents, brothers and sisters. His father, stocky with arms folded, fixes the camera with a confident look. His mother Rose, in her mid-thirties, looks careworn. Arthur, Lilian, Minnie and Constance all responded seriously to this formal moment in their Sunday best. He was 'nearly dropping', he told his brother, when they 'finally stopped' after they had marched in full kit nearly four miles from Winchester to the camp on Hazeley Down. Yet his spirits in these early letters were always good.[15]

Settling in was a matter of establishing whole sets of new social relationships. Officers, privileged to have a personal servant, reported home on how the Tommies who were deputed to serve them shaped up. Billie Nevill, in his first letter when he joined the East Surreys at Purfleet, described his servant as 'a fairly decent lad' who had 'sweated in with my valise' on his arrival. It was two months before Graham Greenwell told his mother 'I have at last secured a servant who suits me . . . he knows the ropes thoroughly'.

The cohesion of public school backgrounds often produced a cheerful and noisy camaraderie in the officers' mess. Graham Greenwell described the nervous but rowdy atmosphere when a raid on the Essex coast was rumoured in November 1914: 'all the pack ponies were loaded with ammunition . . . we had champagne for dinner to celebrate our departure . . . we then had a fight with soda-water bottles in which I got soaked . . . we kicked up a hideous din.'[16]

Some were more pensive. Charlie May was a freelance journalist with a penchant for short-story writing.[17] He kept a reflective diary we have seen, finding it an effort to settle to the life at Larkhill on Salisbury Plain in November 1915, having been appointed a company commander in the Manchester Regiment. He feared he would 'go red . . . and generally look a perfect ass' proposing the King's health as senior officer in the mess. He pined for his wife and his three-year-old daughter Pauline. Charlie found his colleagues' ragtime singing 'in loud and raucous tones' in the officers' club depressing, he confided to his diary. He could not bring himself to post his wife an unhappy letter he had written: 'I'm such a pippy miserable blighter that it would be a sin to convey it to you and just when you will want bracing up.' What spurred Charlie on was his sense of a marvellous keenness in his battalion. They were 'topping fellows and I do hope we can bring the most of them back with us'. They were wild about the company's effort to win the battalion soccer final. The mess, moreover, was generally 'great fun' with its endless joking and singing. Maybe, he thought, his battalion had it in them to 'carry the Regiment's name another rung up the ladder of fame'.[18]

Yvo Charteris hated his training at Sheerness. For a boy used to charming his way through society drawing rooms, the dreary Isle of Sheppey was the back of beyond. Transfer to the Grenadier Guards at Chelsea Barracks in June 1915 came as a huge relief. His mother arranged a bedsitter in the family's London house in Cadogan Square. She promised to 'try and get as many interesting people to dinner' as she could. Yvo was very pleased. Dropping in with his family 'to luncheon or dinner most days' and entertaining his friends in his bedsitter, he could remain for a while remote from the real war. But his attitude had not gone down well with his commanding officer at Sheerness, who considered him 'not a keen soldier'. 'I'm sorry to hear that,' Mary Wemyss wrote to him. Was it said 'in pique' at his request for a transfer to the Guards? In her heart she felt she knew the score: 'I know you are not really a keen soldier but I thought you could have appeared so.'

The Grenadiers, perilously, let young men go to the Front at eighteen. Yvo would not be nineteen till October. His mother understood the sense of his previous commandant's view that 'the country was much better for young men than London'. She also knew how he pined for his social life, wanted him 'to be more trained than you are now' before going to the Front and believed Yvo was too young to go to war. Yet she could not check his patriotic impetuosity. He greeted her on 4 September holding a paper in his hand and, in a voice tense with suppressed excitement, said 'I've got my warning'. She wrote in her diary that night of the 'strange and unexpected shock' she felt at the 'expected blow'.[19]

The Stanway Archive contains a poignant letter to Yvo from his mother at this time. 'It's a horrible wrench and terrible when it comes so real and near but there is no doubt that it's right though disagreeable and I am proud that you are going,' she wrote. Her youngest boy had suffered various bouts of ill health, always tossed off by him but serious enough to tug at a mother's heart. 'I don't suppose you know how I love you – and how fervently I shall pray for your safety and welfare – and your strength of nerve and body,' she promised. There are thousands of such stories of maternal sacrifice hidden in the narrative of the Great War.[20]

Partings were often traumatic. On the last day of Yvo's hectic preparation 'his kit-bag was stuffed tremendously full . . . we filled the mess tin with coffee sugar and tea'. His brother Guy joined his mother to see him off from Charing Cross on 11 September 1915. She noted how serene he was: 'Yvo looked lovely, his young fair face and beautiful figure, broad shoulders, slender waist and elastic tread'. With officers crowding the window as the train moved out, he leapt high in the air to catch a last glimpse of his mother. This allowed her a sight of 'his beloved face'.[21]

'Another thing Mother, just between ourselves, that I want to thank you for,' Billie Nevill wrote on 1 August 1915, 'is for being so jolly or rather brave when you said goodbye because I know you thought it was dangerous out here, but it's not really of course, especially where we are likely to be when we do go "up"'. Some though avoided any possibility of a scene. 'I do hope you did not think me too selfish in not letting you see me off,' wrote Ernest Smith from Le Havre in December 1914 (plate 19). The eldest son of a professional family in Muswell Hill, he had joined the Artists Rifles, a volunteer corps dedicated to 'fashioning

2. Ernest's room at training school, Blendecques, June 1915.

young men as rapidly as possible' as officers of other regiments. All its drafts underwent an initial tour of service in the ranks, providing a training which acclimatised them to the actual conditions of war before they were offered a commission.[22]

Wilbert Spencer, as we have seen, also missed out on parting from his mother. The war had not finally sunk in for him when he wrote home from Le Havre in December before going up to the lines. He did not actually believe he would be away from home for long; the story he heard going round at Christmas 1914 was that the war would not last much longer than another month.[23] Wilbert had fifty-two men under his command for route marches every day, he had told his father from Weymouth. Yet, despite his youth, Wilbert evidently made friends very easily. 'All the officers are very nice' was his first impression. 'I have grown very fond of them and I think they of me' was his judgement after a fortnight. 'This is all very sudden but it is a great chance if I meet with luck', he wrote somewhat nervously when he was suddenly ordered to conduct a party of Sherwood Foresters to France. 'Keep cheerful', he insisted, 'and don't let mother and Elsa get at all in the dumps.'[24]

Alec Reader's homesickness increased once he was put on a draft for the Front. His training was stepped up in early 1916. He pressed his father to get down to Hazeley Down to visit him on his motorbike. Trench digging, bomb throwing and bayonet practice were leaving him 'ready for the end of each day'. He had heard from a pal at the Front that the battalion was 'having a rough time'. He had kept pleading for twenty-four hours' leave, he related on 24 February, but now they were at Southampton. He sent the family a letter card showing twelve views of the town, promising to write every Monday once in France 'whether I have anything to say or not'.[25]

Peter McGregor was candid with his wife about his homesickness. 'Tell Margaret,' he wrote in June 1915, 'I saw a wee girl when out on the route march – and my eyes filled with tears thinking I wouldn't see my dear darling family for such a long time.' In November, he was writing 'my poor old heart feels very sore and terribly anxious about you'. Then suddenly there was leave and he was 'wild with joy' at getting back to Edinburgh. In June 1916 he was briefly home again, finding that his children Margaret and Bob had matured remarkably in his year of absence: 'I was quite struck with their grown-upness.'

This shy Scotsman once offered, when visiting his brother-in-law in hospital, to lift up his kilt to a passing crowd of girls who were discussing with some English Tommies whether he wore anything underneath it. But he thought better of it and 'escaped out of doors'. Yet his standing was such that, at the battalion's Christmas dinner in 1915, the chairman asked him to propose the Colonel's toast. 'The chaps said it was fine,' he told Jen. 'I got tremendous shouts at various points and at the end they yelled themselves hoarse . . . I was very much surprised at even being asked.'[26]

The emotional content of letters written by men preparing for war varied enormously. Will Streets, the eldest of twelve, was more deeply reflective than most. By the time he was training at Penkridge three of his brothers had volunteered and were in training or already in France. How could his parents possibly hope for all four to return? He admired the stoicism shown by his mother in her trial. 'I know,' he told her, 'that you will not be wanting at the supreme hour of your trial but will learn to turn your sorrow into a proud consciousness that the blood of your sons was true to England's finer breed.' What made the soldier's lot hard was 'the fact that those at home are agonising'. If she could accept the possibility of losing him, 'believe me I could go to face death as calmly as I rise to face the morning's existence'.

Will returned to the subject in October 1915, when he had received a letter from his father which made him feel that 'he at least has not yet faced the possibility that this war may bring'. He believed his parents had accomplished the struggle to bring up twelve children on a meagre miner's wage 'in a rare and supreme manner'. It was cruel that they now faced losing one or more of them 'just as benefits come'. Their boys had volunteered with the 'blood of freemen coursing through their veins', although they hated war 'as we hate our bitterest enemy'. 'It is your grief that cuts me to the quick and makes it hard for me to die.' Will knew it was 'woman who suffers in the bitterest extreme'. He had taught himself, he declared, to 'hide grief and give a Spartan front'.[27]

'Please, please don't worry about me . . . the only thing I'm worrying about is the crossing,' wrote Billie Nevill to his mother as embarkation approached.[28] Yet all knew there was a finality about this stage of going to war. Excitement mixed with nerves about what overseas service would actually bring produced a heady crop of emotions as men reached the English coast. Thousands of troops crossing the Channel by night experienced this strain between 1914 and 1918. Yet most of the comment in letters was about the physical impact of the journey.

Julian Grenfell, predictably, was at his most elated when telling his mother of his night-time departure from Ludgershall camp and early morning embarkation on 6 October 1914 at Southampton: 'it seems too good to be off at last. Everyone is perfectly bird about it.' Julian travelled with two squadrons of the Life Guards and two of his own Royal Dragoons. The elation lasted. Five days after landing he reiterated his conviction that war was 'the best fun one ever dreamed of . . . the uncertainty of it is so good, like a picnic when you don't know where you are going to'.[29]

Others were more sober. 'I slept or tried to on deck and partly in an open lifeboat,' Ernest Smith explained to his mother from Le Havre on 31 December, 'no blankets – very cold'. He had not been seasick. 'We were escorted by a destroyer with all lights out, the effect in the moonlight was rather impressive,' he related.[30] Wilbert Spencer describing his crossing to his father said how interesting it was 'to watch the escort and signals and then to watch the French escort recognising and taking over'. He had paced the deck full of the adventure but thinking it would be 'jolly if we are all home by Xmas'.[31]

The regular officers out of retirement, Robert Hermon and Rowland Feilding, were matter-of-fact about their crossings in April 1915. Escorted by two destroyers on a moonlit night with a glassy calm, Robert reached Le Havre uneventfully. He posted a card to Ethel which read 'landed alright, Robert'. Rowland described to his wife Edith how the regimental band had played his draft of 250 men and twelve officers of the Coldstream Guards through Windsor to the station, the men singing 'lustily'. The rough crossing from Southampton to Le Havre took nine hours. He confessed that his pack 'felt as if it was filled with lead' on the five-mile march to a camp at Harfleur.[32]

Cyril Newman described his seven hours on the Channel water to Winnie on 10 May 1915. 'The speed at which we went,' he explained, 'made the crossing choppy'. Nearly everyone, including himself, was sick at least once. He reiterated his Christian faith as in almost all his letters: 'we know that God knows what is best for his children and I am not afraid'.[33] Graham Greenwell was luckier on 11 May. 'Everything is, so far, splendid,' he told his mother; 'I had a most easy voyage over and slept on a very comfortable bunk'. He and two friends had 'a gorgeous lunch' at the Hotel Continental before taking a taxi to the huge rest camp outside Le Havre.[34]

Billie Nevill hit a stormy night crossing from Folkestone to Boulogne on 27 August 1915. Adopting the spirit of the censor's instructions and jovial as ever, he headed his first missive from France as written from 'I wonder, Try to guess, Hard to say'. Despite his earlier qualms, he tossed aside the general seasickness, declaring 'I did very well really and felt quite fit all the time'. He found it 'quite interesting watching our little destroyer escort sneaking along like a beetle – not a glow-worm'. Billie was exceptional in having someone from his family to welcome him to France, since his Aunt Annie was matron at the base hospital at Boulogne. He was 'in great form and so delighted to be out, dear old boy', she wrote after they dined together at the Hôtel Duvaux. 'We split a bottle of Veuve Cliquot,' ran his account of their meeting, 'it was awfully jolly seeing her'.[35]

Alec Reader told his family on 12 March 1916 that only three men on his boat had not been sick. He had been living mainly on bully beef and dog biscuits since landing at Le Havre but the food was not as bad as he had expected. His main worry was how the censors, officers and others would treat his letters. He wrote 'what I think I am allowed to' but needed feedback on what had been passed. This suddenly mattered a great deal as the importance he would now attach to writing sank in. His second report on landing was the 'longest letter I have written in my life'. 'I am still like Johnny Walker going strong' was a summary intended as much to reassure himself as those at home.[36]

Edwin Vaughan was a second lieutenant in the Royal Warwickshire Regiment. He kept a notebook diary which he appears to have written up from memory after the war. But his account of the journey to the Front at nineteen years old in 1917 seems wholly authentic. What is interesting is that it documents the same intense patriotic excitement, more than two years into the war, that Julian Grenfell recorded so vividly in 1914. Edwin noted moments of aching in his heart at leaving his family, yet, as his train steamed slowly out of Waterloo, 'the excitement of the venture into the dreamed of but unrealised land of war eclipsed the sorrow of parting'. A rough crossing did not bother him. Avoiding the hold, which he found uninhabitable, he stood alone in the bows watching the scene: 'I could see the tail light of our leading destroyer, darting from side to side, forging ahead and then waiting, and as it became light the whole escort became visible.' Edwin found that the destroyers 'lent a wonderful sense of power and security'. He went to breakfast 'soaked to the skin and feeling very fit'.[37]

How long it took men to reach the Front once they had crossed the Channel varied considerably. The huge Le Havre rest camp was a continuous hive of activity as adjutants struggled to get their battalions into trains and across France. Lance Spicer and Yvo Charteris were plunged into action within days, since they both arrived just before the Battle of Loos began on 25 September 1915. Lance left a letter home begun on 16 September unfinished till the 20th, pleading then that 'we have been worked fearfully hard here and are still feeling a bit weary but quite cheery still'. He expected very shortly to be 'right in it'. He promised field postcards, the soldier's standard reassurance tactic to those back home, when he could manage them.[38] Reggie Trench by contrast really got to know the company he was commanding during a whole month of marching and billeting them since, when he landed in early 1917, the Germans had recently retired to the Hindenburg Line.[39]

The journey to the Front was often pretty miserable for the Tommies but not as uncomfortable for officers. Graham Greenwell explained that his men were 'packed in fifty at a time' whereas 'we had one carriage between four officers'. When the train halted at Amiens on 22 May 1915, he was going out to breakfast. The men 'simply camp outside the train' and 'mayn't leave the place all day'. As the train inched along, they were 'shrieked at by the French peasants for souvenirs' and were answered by 'a constant hail of bully beef tins and iron rations'.[40] By June 1916, when the Argyll and Sutherland Highlanders crossed rural France in cattle trucks, Peter McGregor noted the lack of interest in them: 'folks went about their work sedately, didn't even make a wave as we passed'. The soldiers' discomfort must have been obvious. They were 'just lying all over the place – so mixed up that I am sure no one could separate us'. He remained cheerful. 'I laugh at myself often,' he told Jen, 'the quiet wee man living the warlike life'.[41]

The sound and the stories of battle and trench life, then the sight of those already living this life, prepared men for their own initiation. For days or weeks after leaving their training at home, coming under fire for the first time was continually a matter of nervous anticipation for new soldiers. Mature and hardened regulars, remembering past campaigns, naturally wrote their first letters home in a very different tone from young volunteers. They felt able to be analytical, descriptive, even matter-of-fact.

Rowland Feilding reached his battalion's billets by train and then in a car lent by a staff officer five days after landing. A company returning from the trenches met him on his way in. The men's clothes and boots were stained with clay and dust. The stretcher-bearers brought up the rear. 'I thought their faces wore a strained and tired look,' Rowland told Edith. This 'first contact with the war brought home to me its reality more than anything had done before'. He related that gunfire was audible 'almost continuously'. But he also spoke of fruit trees in blossom, the primroses, cowslips, and the French children who played 'apparently unconscious of the proximity of danger'.[42]

Just landed, Robert Hermon told Ethel about distant gunfire which 'fairly shakes the windows of this old pub'. Unperturbed by it, he was thrilled to find that Buxton, brought from home as his servant, was a 'top-hole cook'. They were only missing 'some cakes and a box of cigars'. Robert soon moved to a farm near Béthune close to the Front. On 30 April 1915, he was sent to reconnoitre the lanes up to the trenches with the squadron sergeant-major. Leaving their horses, they walked to a vantage point where they heard the snipers sniping 'but no bullets were coming our way'. The French were farming the land within 800 yards of the trenches 'just as though nothing at all was going on'. There were women and children in cottages along the roadside though fields around were pitted with shell holes.[43]

Young men experienced a strange unreality on French soil but not yet in sight of battle themselves. Reggie Trench learnt something of their emotions while censoring letters as he marched his men across the Somme battlefield in

1917. He was amused by one Tommy, he told Clare, who said the noise of the guns was 'deafening' when they were still quite ten miles from the line. If one heard the guns at all then they were 'only a dull boom in the distance'.[44] Cyril Newman had slept on the floor as his train rumbled inland from Boulogne. The reality came closer for him at the end of a short march, after fourteen miles in a bus with its windows boarded. He found men back from the line in the huts his company were given to live in. 'The stories told of trench life are not pleasant,' he confessed to Winnie.[45]

By 1915 the BEF had given a great deal of thought to the design and dimensions of its trench systems. There were usually three lines of trenches with a front line or firing line, depending on the ground, between 200 and 500 yards from the enemy. Networks of communication trenches were often complex, with names and signposts reminiscent of home like Regent Street and the Strand.[46] The constant rotation between firing and support lines, reserve and billets involved a huge amount of work for brigade staff officers. Adjutants were always busy. But the work was essential to morale. Tommies always knew their time in the firing line was short enough for them to see relief in sight. Regular rotation, which prevented men being in the posts of most danger for more than a few days at a time, secured high morale throughout the war.

Charles Carrington calculated from his diary that during 1916 he was under fire in the front line or close support trenches for 101 days. He spent 120 days in reserve and 73 days in rest well behind the lines.[47] Examples from a miscellany of battalions in January of four different years show that rotation was highly effective. The longest continuous period in the firing line for the 1st Battalion of the South Wales Borderers was two days in January 1915, 1916 and 1918. For the Oxfordshire and Buckinghamshire Light Infantry it was two days in 1915, one in 1916, two in 1917 and 1918. The 1st Battalion of the Black Watch was in the firing line for up to four days in 1915, up to three days in 1916 and up to two days in 1918. But the pressure increased considerably in 1917 and 1918. These figures may not be fully representative, and in some regiments much more prolonged stints became common towards the end of the war.[48]

Some, like Graham Greenwell arriving at Ploegsteert Wood in May 1915, were lucky to find themselves in a very quiet part of the line with time to acclimatise. He was in very good spirits in letters to his mother. The weather was 'divine', he found the bully beef 'excellent'. He considered his actual introduction to the front line 'the most interesting day of my life'. Riding up to the trenches with the Transport Officer, Graham told him, 'I could scarcely believe we were so near the war.' 'I am supremely happy,' he concluded.[49]

Yvo Charteris was very near the war indeed when he wrote to his three sisters on 21 September 1915. But unless they read carefully to detect the hints of nervousness behind his quiet courage these may have gone unnoticed. 'I was delighted to get your letters,' he began. He broke off to attend a dinner party being held by his fellow subalterns immersed in the mess tradition of high spirits. They were 'playing hunt-the-slipper on the floor and throwing Perrier water at one another'. He had 'just come away with a pigeon's egg on my forehead'. All day, Yvo reported, these pranks aside, he had 'heard the rumbling of guns like distant breakers reminding me of what awaits us'. 'The plans of this Division,' Yvo was convinced, 'are rather thrilling if everything goes right.' But he wished he had had 'a little more practical training'. He was looking forward eagerly to hearing 'a shot fired in anger', he declared with bravado.[50]

Ernest Smith had a very gentle introduction to the war. He told his company commander in January 1915 of his doubts about taking a commission and asked for parental advice. 'As far as fighting is concerned,' he told his mother six weeks after landing, 'I have been no nearer than when we saw some heavy artillery in action a mile or two from our domicile.' It must have comforted her to hear that the artillery gunners very rarely saw their target, 'the result of their shots being signalled by phone or aeroplane'. Ernest became concerned that his draft was getting a reputation for inactivity. He soon realised how well he was living, compared to the men in the trenches. He resented the monotony of life on the edge of the war. So predictably, like his pals, he yielded to the pressure to go forward for a commission. After cadet school he joined the Buffs as a second lieutenant in August 1915.[51]

Alec Reader, one of the youngest in his company at just eighteen, struggled to be a man as he learnt to be a soldier. He was just a boy when he sat down to write home. Yet, he insisted, his mother underestimated his 'capabilities when you say I can't smoke a pipe'. 'Why there is nothing I am unable to do now even work,' he remonstrated. There was plenty of that: 'work all day and every day', he noted on 25 March 1916: 'when I am not working I start thinking of home, which is the worst thing to do out here, I am glad I have my mind occupied.' Fifty men had fallen out, Alec related, after a ten-mile march carrying heavy packs. The meaning of army discipline was sinking in. The nearer they were to the line the more particular NCOs became about cleanliness, he explained at Fresnicourt. You were severely punished for appearing on parade now with a speck of mud on you. He pleaded for old magazines, chocolate and decent coffee.[52]

Billie Nevill's ebullience was not jolted during his fortnight's journey to the front line. He had committed himself heart and soul to the war. He was determined to persuade his family this was an extraordinary adventure which they would share through his almost daily bulletins. 'I am glad you all like my letters at home,' he told his sister Amy on 10 August 1915. Quickly he abandoned keeping a diary. Billie at once realised that it was his big sisters, especially the responsible twenty-eight-year-old Elsie, who could best put the Nevill family war story together, by carefully numbering and archiving each letter he sent home. He expected them to keep his girlfriend Muff Schooling up to date as well by sending on his letters.

Billie's insouciance, fearlessness and sheer excitement about going to war dominate his long, neatly written pages. 'That mysterious place, The Front' was about twenty miles away, he recounted from billets in Bertangles. Everything was 'toppingly managed'. With some 'top-hole looking eggs for our tea' and 'bacon about you really might be staying at the Ritz'. An old piano enabled him to 'oblige with my world renowned rendering' of 'Chopsticks'. They were expecting their box from Fortnum & Mason 'of dear old Piccadilly' too. It was less comfortable, he admitted, for the men in barns and sheds with no disinfectant at present and flies which 'send you fairly crazy'. He was beginning to understand how leadership was as much as anything about creating domesticity.

Yet not only was Billie happy but he honestly believed the men were too. 'Judging by the letters I have to censor every day,' he told the family, they 'thoroughly enjoy it all'. There was a kind of collective will to ensure that those at home did not worry. Billie was at the forefront of this campaign. His men, Billie was confident, were a match for the Germans, 'although of course I've not seen a Hun yet nor am I likely to, I'm afraid, for a long time'. His Tommies were not 'crawling in terror' of a sniper: 'we're as good or better than all their snipers and if one shows he gets "it" – hit'. The East Surreys spent 1 August, after church parade, on a picnic, taking lunch in the travelling kitchens to a river nearby to bathe, 'combining exercise and pleasure with cleanliness'. Billie's letters were exuberant. His mood was dauntless.[53]

Going to war took hold of many men just as they were on the threshold of adult life. It was at least a temporary career, and perhaps more than this. With energy and commitment at full flood, ambition was predictable. It was natural to think about promotion, within the officer class or from service as a private to NCO status. Their manhood was engaged. They yearned for the respect and credit of colleagues that promotion would mark.

After being dropped from the draft as under nineteen, Graham Greenwell sought to reintegrate himself into his peer group when he reached the Front. 'I am now at last among all my friends,' he informed his mother on 24 May 1915. He was shown round trenches being manned by his regiment. Expecting straight lines, he found himself moving along trenches which zigzagged endlessly: 'I kept meeting all my friends round different corners.' His captain, J.J. Conybeare, introduced him to others 'in a little dug-out . . . cakes galore and jam – very pleasant'. Conny at once made him Mess President, Graham explained, which involved responsibility for orders from Harrods each week. Overall it had been 'a most ripping day'. He was glad, censoring a letter, to find himself mentioned by one of his men as apparently 'mighty pleased to be out here'.[54]

By the time the day came for his company to take over a sector of the front line on 22 August 1915, Billie Nevill was becoming repetitive in telling his family how he loved it all. But the new note was his ambition to lead effectively. His company commander, whom he normally understudied, happened to be away. 'I simply love having to run the company in his absence: as long as you don't let people come and hustle you you're alright.' If you did try to deal with eight things at once, he was realising, 'you may as well go home'.

Leadership really bit Billie in the next weeks when his captaincy came through. He decided to take a gamble on how long the war would last. If he could get four years of seniority as a regular soldier by taking a permanent commission he would then make the army his career for life. If it ended sooner he would go back to his plans to be a schoolmaster. This was carefully considered. By November 1915 Billie had achieved one of the permanent commissions the War Office was offering to temporary officers.[55]

Until early in 1916 Reggie Trench was one of Lieutenant-Colonel Errington's closest and most reliable junior officers in the Inns of Court OTC (plates 2, 3). He built his military career on this dedicated service. The success of Errington in turning this unit into one of the foremost instruments of officer training in the war was remarkable. Its establishment was increased from two to four, then eight and then twelve companies by August 1915. By 1918 around 12,000 men had received commissions after passing through Errington's scheme of training. From the day war broke out Reggie felt he was in the right place at the right time. His ambition quickly became palpable. He was gazetted as a captain on 15 November 1914. Desperate to get to the Front, he volunteered for Gallipoli in early 1915, but Errington held him back through his influence at the War Office. Reggie's letters to Clare document a young patriot's zeal in training men to lead.

Reggie was intent on rooting the slackers and incompetent out of the Corps. 'I got rid of two men today,' he told Clare on 4 September 1914, 'but there are one or two others that are a nuisance.' Later that week he had a busy day taking over the Adjutant's role in his absence. Drills in Richmond Park were now the main routine. The move to Berkhamsted put the training programme of the

Inns of Court OTC on a much surer footing. Promoted to Captain, Reggie revelled in the command of C Company, with his closest friend Charlie Pollock as his second in command. When he was given twenty-one new recruits on 23 September he prided himself on getting to know their names quickly. 'Awful rabble!' he boasted to Clare, 'but we are putting them through it and in a week they won't know themselves.'[56]

Errington believed that, given the *esprit de corps* he created with his keen public school and university recruits, in two months he could turn out 'a useful officer, well grounded and able to instruct in drill, musketry and map reading'. The conditions at Berkhamsted were ideal for a scheme which placed a premium on fieldwork. The undulating country of Ashridge Park and the southern Chilterns was so varied that, working there for more than two years, Reggie never repeated the same battalion exercise. Fieldwork, cultivating an eye for the ground, inculcated the duties of leadership. Errington often gave Reggie important tasks. On an exercise when he was put 'in command of the enemy' on 29 October 1914, he borrowed a motorbike to get 'all the way down our successive positions'. On a night exercise, he was sent with his company to finish off trenches being dug on the common and await the battalion's charge. The commanding officer was 'quite bucked' with him, he reported.

Reggie quickly understood that corps identity was a crucial issue, so he used the formal writing paper with its fine embossed dark green badge. He joked to Clare about a photo of the sixteen corps officers 'taken for an Xmas card: appalling thought – I'll give you one'. But this concealed his pride in Corps fellowship. In November 1914, Errington chose Reggie to lick a new company of 200 raw recruits into shape. He had new memorandum sheets with ruled lines printed from 'The Officer Commanding H Company'. There was a touch of both pride and ambition in his grabbing one to use for a quick note to Clare.

This was when Reggie adopted the high standards of practical soldiering which he later clung to at the Front.[57] After a 'battle royal' with the Adjutant, who had billeted the men two to a bed, he ensured each man in H Company had a bed to himself. He enlisted Clare's support in planning a display of spring bulbs outside his orderly room: 250 yellow crocuses made up the H COMPANY emblem with thirty bulbs per letter.[58] Reggie kept his eye on his orderly's planting and care of the bulbs since company identity, besides corps identity, was now at stake. He bought a kitchen table for the orderly room: 'it will do excellently for our house when the war is over', he told Clare. Night operations were a baptism of fire for the volunteers: most of H Company, he discovered, 'did not know how to load their rifles, none had ever dug trenches in the day much less at night'. But again Errington was bucked with him.

Reggie had become an exacting officer, tough in his judgements. He had 'got one little blighter discharged', he revealed to Clare, 'as not likely to become an efficient officer'. Examining some of them as the course drew to an end he found that most 'wanted to stay and learn more'. In August 1914, men had seen delay in getting to the Front as suggesting irresolution. As the war moved into a second phase, young men coming forward for active service were calmer and more thoughtful about preparing themselves for service overseas. 'It is rather satisfactory really,' Reggie concluded. He kept a letter he received from A.J. Willmer, one of his H Company men who went on to Sandhurst. 'All this is probably quite bad form and contrary to all rules of military etiquette,' Willmer wrote, 'but I do want you to know how much I feel I owe you.' He and Charlie Pollock had been a great team doing 'a depressing and utterly thankless job'. It had been strenuous but a 'good life' at Berkhamsted. He was 'rather sore at having to come away'.[59]

Going to war was a prolonged process that profoundly disrupted men's civilian lives and expectations. Variations in the details are endless, yet the pattern was essentially the same for all: training, mobilisation, the Channel crossing, the journey to the front line. All the time there was news, rumour, hearsay of what battle held in store. It percolated worryingly into the soldier's mind. Men thought about the courage and endurance which would be demanded of them, the test of their manhood that lay ahead. Letters to and from home remained the bulwark of their emotional lives. These need fuller assessment. Then will come the question: when they faced a baptism of fire would they flinch from danger? An account of their actual service on the Western Front has to start with their fears and how they mastered them.

PART II

AT THE FRONT

CHAPTER 4

'Write as Often as You Can'

Letters and Parcels

Collections of letters take us into the private worlds of loved ones and the most intimate concerns of family life. Our soldiers were always in close touch with home. Letters used in this book express the sheer comfort to be obtained by writing to a member of the family. Thousands watched for the post in eager anticipation of a buff or green envelope with familiar handwriting. We have to read between the lines, perceiving the understanding and sensitivity with which the soldier's words would be greeted when the envelope was opened. Replying was a recognition of the massive encouragement that the bursting mailbags brought to the Front. 'Write as often as you can. I long for letters now,' Peter McGregor told his wife.[1]

Three of our soldiers rejoiced in well-settled marriages. Their broods of young children pored over paternal missives. Another large group were young men that were the oldest offspring of sizeable families, with siblings who looked up to them, admiring their courage in going to war. A few were not yet married but had sweethearts whose dedicated support, in the form of numerous letters and parcels, sustained their endurance. This was very much a family war. Men's emotions were always more than half left behind them in Britain. Crumpled pages filled soldiers' pockets until, bulging out, they had to be replaced by new missives of love and care from across the Channel.

Rowland and Edith Feilding trusted each other completely. 'I continue writing to you of all the dangers of the war,' he confirmed in May 1917, 'remembering that you once said that if I hid anything you would know it and only imagine worse things than were really happening.' His 261 letters home are powerful testimony to the war as it was lived by a senior commander in the field. 'Snowball', with his shock of white hair, was a familiar and much-respected figure at the Front from 1915 to 1918.

The Feildings had three daughters. Fifteen times he wrote to his eldest Joan, who was ten at the outbreak of the war. She acted as a channel of communication with her sisters. She packed up candles to send him soon after he left for France. He sent her a German soldier's shoulder strap, booty he seized at the Hohenzollern Redoubt. When Edith told him about Joan's efforts at Auntie Agnes's bazaar, making £5 in all, he was proud of her. More solemnly, when his men were suffering in the freezing cold of the 1916 winter, he told his eldest girl to 'remember what they are going through for you and pray for them'. The others were much in his mind too: 'I use Anita's soap box every day,' Rowland wrote gratefully, 'and I carry Peggy's chocolate in my haversack to eat when I get hungry in the trenches.' 'I am sending each of you a poppy to put in your prayer books,' he wrote in June 1915.

By 1917 Rowland had a fourth daughter. He thanked Joan in February for her latest letter: 'I send four German postcards choose the one you like best and give the others to Anita, Peggy and Pru'. He thought he could guess which she would choose. He had found the postcards on a dead German. In October, he was back on the Somme, reporting 'miles of devastation' to Edith. 'I rode through one of the flattened villages near here', he told Joan. The church was 'a mound of stones and dirt' but, beside it, he found a great crucifix standing undamaged. 'One sees that so often in France nowadays', he explained.[2]

'My pockets are so full of letters that I have to burn them,' wrote Peter McGregor. 'I've had a letter almost every day from you since I came here,' he noted wonderingly on 2 July 1916. Margaret, ten years old, and Bob, who was nine that year, were every day in his thoughts. He lived for and fought for them. He treasured all Jen's news of the family's doings. Grannie McGregor, too generous, needed to limit her parcels. 'I wonder if it would hurt Grannie's feelings,' he asked, 'if you told her not to send so many oatcakes. I am in one place for so short a time and to carry extra weight is just a bit too much for me.' Peter was always full of gratitude. The sheer ardency of his love for Jen shines out of his letters. 'I seem to love you deeper and better than I have ever done,' he declared shortly before embarkation.[3]

Robert Hermon's letters to his wife Ethel were equally touching. He usually began 'Darling Mine' or 'my dear old Lassie'. Before his leave in October 1916, he wrote 280 letters to her in reply to 303 she had sent him. He was easily disappointed when she missed a day, as on 23 May 1915, which brought 'four from the Chugs which I liked very much'. His children were Mary, Bob, Meg and Betty (plate 17). His eldest boy and girl both wrote to him very frequently, amusing him by their spontaneous but chaotic spelling. Mairky sent him bullseyes; Meg cake and candles. When the children enclosed hairs from the dogs in an envelope, he kept them with his photos of them in his pocketbook.

It was almost unbearable when Ethel sent accounts of time on the beach at a rented holiday home near Worthing: 'I would give anything to see the Chugs and you,' he wrote, but he was 'glad to hear my little Meggie is so brave in the sea'. He sent Bob a bayonet, rather a gruesome memento, he confessed, which he suggested should be 'firmly nailed to the nursery wall'. Away from home Robert remained very much the paterfamilias. There was a controlling aspect to his correspondence. Betty shook the camera, spoiling some photos of the family. 'Teach her to put it on a chair,' resting it if possible, he advised. He was horrified by Lloyd George's suggestion that women should work in the munitions factories. This was for spinsters and widows: 'your first duty to your country is the efficient upbringing of your children to be useful members of society,' he told Ethel. But he consoled her when she had to see Bob off to boarding school for the first time on her own. After six months, Robert found himself 'rather homesick' and 'just longing to be out of this wretched business'. 'I hope all the doggies are well,' he wrote plaintively. Accustomed to the life of a country squire, it had not been easy to come out of retirement.

The children were never far from his mind. 'Would to God this damned war was over and we were together to pursue the even tenor of our ways with the little Chugs once more', he declared in early 1916. A few weeks later, he sent Meg 'a small birthday present of some French buttons worn by a soldier who gave his life for his country at Souchez'. When Ethel reported to him the children's enjoyment of a birthday party in the village, he reflected that they were 'lucky to have so little knowledge of what is going on. . . . I look forward to the time when I can bring them out here and show them what war means', he reflected, showing them the landscape around Loos. 'They would never forget it', he believed, peering uncertainly into the future of his world, 'and perhaps later on when questions of conscription ... cropped up it might be very useful for them to have seen it.' Meanwhile he was 'simply starving' for a sight of them. 'I think old Mairky's little pencil effort simply sweet and old Bet's 'pres' too', he told Ethel.[4]

Reggie Trench's double correspondence is unique among these collections, containing 245 letters to his wife and 35 to his mother. The contrast in the tone of these letters is striking. To his mother Isabel he was factual and unemotional, like the little boy he had been when reporting from boarding school, but regaling her now with the domestic activities of his military life. Indeed he wrote once 'I can tell you we are very like boys at school here and look forward to the mail with eagerness every day.' He knew the power of her love and her need to support him. 'A fortnightly parcel would be very welcome,' he soon prompted, 'chocolate, coffee, butterscotch, toffee ... tinned fish, fruits and meats, potted meat, sardines, anything that will make a change in our diet'.[5]

To Clare he was above all a lover. He treated her incessant letters as texts, in replies which often took her news and queries point by point, creating an intimate conversation. He tried to write every day, explaining the reason when he was occasionally unable to.[6] Their married life since early 1915, long delayed, had been blissfully happy; their daughter Delle was a precious bond (plate 30). Reggie's physical longing for Clare was somewhat alleviated by the scarf she sent him after he had been away three months. 'It is quite priceless,' he insisted, 'I sleep in it every night and wind it round my head. The feel of it makes me dream of you, my love. I know it so well over your dear shoulders around your sweet neck.'

The scarf created Clare's presence in bed with him. It was 'particularly comforting', he confided in a moment of candour about his vulnerability, because he had 'an empty tooth' needing filling. Soon after returning from leave in 1917, Reggie stressed just how crucial Clare's letters were to his morale. 'I can truly say that my whole day is made bright when I get a letter from you,' he wrote, 'it always feels as if I have had a talk with your sweet self when I have read your letter.' In October Clare sent him her silhouette, the new form of photographic profile just in fashion in England. He was ecstatic: 'it is a remarkable likeness – it stands opposite me now – standing on my pistol, leaning against my flask.'

On his leave Reggie and Clare organised the purchase of identical rings to be worn on corresponding fingers as symbols of their troth. Their little girl was always present in their letters. Clare plied Reggie with photos and word pictures of her activities. 'I think they are quite perfect,' he declared, thanking her for a 'ripping' consignment. He had mounted his favourites, he reported, calling them 'The house that Mummie built', 'Dare I knock it down?' and 'Oh so careful', which showed Delle walking in her bonnet and coat, her 'eyes on the ground quite intent on her feet'. He sent suggestions, for example a rocking horse, for Christmas presents. He wanted her to have a donkey and cart; with 'promotion to a pony perhaps when peace comes'. His was a caring, besotted fatherhood of the mind and imagination.[7]

Clare's parcels, carefully thought out, were a constant joy. An early one included porridge, shoes, cigarettes, soap and cocoa tablets. What about boxed kippers to provide variety at brekker on a fortnightly basis? Reggie suggested. Clare began supplying Reggie with alcohol, ranging from claret to curaçao and liqueur brandy, besides consignments of high-quality wines from her father's cellar. He was delighted to find that all this travelled well.[8]

There can have been few more energetic correspondents with a whole circle of relatives and friends than Cyril Newman. In the front line during April 1917, he counted his unanswered letters, finding 56 to which he owed replies. He

3. Letter from Reggie Trench to his mother with poppy attached, 16 April 1917.

asked his fiancée Winnie to explain to his six Sunday school boys and others at church the need to understand the impossibility of his writing as regularly as they did. He had sent off 66 postcards to friends the previous Christmas. But Winnie had to come first. When for a short time officers sought to limit letters to three a week, saving them time on censorship, he was quick with plans to evade this by enclosures in letters to his mother. His very emotional stability and strength depended upon contact with Winnie. His letter to her, almost without fail when time allowed, was the highlight of his day. He usually found something from her in the mail. When there was a gap caused by the vagaries of the post he pined: 'four days without a letter from you seems so long a time'.

Chalking up fifteen months away in April 1917, Cyril yearned 'if only I might see you again even for a few minutes, to hear your voice, to feel the touch of your hand'. This was another passionate love affair, recorded in 544 intimate letters between them which were later edited by Cyril. The difference between Cyril and Winnie and Reggie and Clare was that theirs was unconsummated desire. Everything that mattered lay in a wholly uncertain future. In Cyril's case, the entire war was an ordeal by fire. Over and over again, in one form of words or another, he described this crusade: 'sweetest and best of women, Queen of my heart, accept the gratitude of my heart and the dedication of my life for all you have been and are to me'.

They had a running battle about the parcels Winnie sent. 'How the other signallers enjoyed those oatcakes . . . will you thank your mother for the excellent cake and pudding,' he wrote in the winter of 1916. But she was not to send another parcel 'until I say so'. Cyril counted the costs of her normal correspondence, noting that each week she spent on him 'at least one shilling and sixpence for papers and stamps'. Parcels on top of this 'cost a lot of money and self-denial'.[9]

When Jack Sweeney went to France in 1914 he signed a will leaving all his belongings to his father. Not long at the Front, out of the blue, he received a parcel from Ivy Williams in Walthamstow. We know how she learnt his name. Jack's sister had a little boy in Ivy's Sunday school class, who had piped up when she asked if any of them had fathers in France 'My Dad ain't, Miss, but my Uncle Jack is'. Jack Sweeney's archive is one of the outstanding collections in the Imperial War Museum, rivalling that of Cyril Newman in its size and emotive power. There are five volumes of letters, 878 pages in all, addressed to Miss Ivy Williams at 7 Maude Terrace in Walthamstow (plate 7).[10] Like Cyril's, this is the record of a wartime love affair which ended in marriage and domestic happiness. Ivy must have told him a great deal in her letters about her household, her mum and dad and her siblings Olive, Florence, Frank and Charles. Jack constantly refers to them all. He felt that, by some miracle, a new family that cared about him had come into his life across the English Channel.

Jack fell in love with Ivy from a distance, well before he saw her face or even her photograph. She recalled in old age the day she came home from work in May 1916 and found him in their living room: 'he was much quieter than I expected, gentle and with a lovely face . . . for him I think it was love at first sight. For me the real love came later.' But their correspondence became increasingly intimate once they knew each other face to face. It meant a great deal to Jack that he was able to obtain a good supply of the green envelopes which Tommies used to escape the prying eyes of their officers. Fifty-seven of these green-envelope letters reached Ivy between December 1916 and the end of 1917. The standard declaration read 'I certify on my honour that the contents of this envelope refer to nothing but private and family matters.' Their love affair not only survived the war but also dissolved a class barrier, for Ivy's father was managing clerk in a firm of solicitors. She had been to technical college and worked as a solicitor's secretary. Their terraced home was a world apart from Jack's father's tenement flat. 'Please remember that I am not a city clerk,' Jack wrote in one of his early letters, deeply conscious of his humble origins and lack of education.

Julian Grenfell found solace at the Front in the loyalty of a hunting companion he met on leave called Flossie Garth. He carried her photograph when he went into action. His passion for her was undoubtedly primarily sexual but was at the same time, as letters to her in 1915 show, shot through with a mixture of bravado and macho dominance. He was both alarmed and fascinated by her reputation as 'fast'. She needed 'someone strong and capable with a strict sense of duty and morality' to look after her, Julian insisted. It was obvious whom he had in mind. She needed 'a good talking-to'; he would have to 'get leave to come and administer it to you'. He plied her with requests for more riding photos, best of all with her buttocks 'flying off the saddle' as she jumped another brook.[11]

Every soldier needed a girl in his life who he knew adored him and believed in his chivalric quest. Men found romantic release in writing to the woman of their dreams. Yet many of our young soldiers were simply too young, too caught unawares by the war, to have acquired a regular girlfriend. A devoted mother was the next-best thing.

This was Graham Greenwell's saving grace during a tough period when the Oxfordshire and Buckinghamshire Light Infantry held the Ovillers trenches eight weeks into the Battle of the Somme. Refusing to admit he was depressed or downhearted, Graham nevertheless stated that a letter, arriving 'with the rations even up here, cheers me up tremendously'. Two days later he received his mother's 'dear anxious letter' about a small wound he had mentioned, not in itself very serious. A parcel came too, 'containing – oh! sacred Joy! a Fuller's cake and some haversack chocolate which dropped like manna from Heaven in our midst'. On an evening when his headquarters was strewn with 'five casualties together with a few shellshock cases', the cake reposed incongruously as 'a veritable Snow Queen' among 'the variegated litter' of the dugout. In an earlier discussion of the items his mother might order in her Harrods parcels, he had remarked 'I need not tell you what I want because you always know best and anticipate me'.[12]

The contrast between Graham's relaxed and confident relationship with his mother and Herbert Trench's anxious one with his mother Isabel is striking. Only two of Herbert's surviving twenty letters home were to his mother. Both were written in the first flush of adventure and bravado while twice crossing the Channel. He was the only officer aboard in July 1915. This allowed him to feel important. Placing guards at each end of the ship to watch for submarines, he made himself comfortable: 'I grub with the captain and sleep in the saloon.'[13]

Many of our letter writers knew their stories would be devoured by a wide circle of family and friends. Billie Nevill's 203 letters home consistently show a cheery jauntiness. 'Bill in Stillets' he headed one after the previous one had begun 'Still in Billets', adding 'please laugh'. This was schoolboy humour but then, like many going to war, Billie had just recently been a schoolboy. The inventiveness of the greetings which started his letters displayed his delight in family cohesion: 'dear family and people all', 'cheer up family', 'everyone', 'anyone', 'cheer ho all', 'beloveds' and 'all and sundry whom it may concern' were among his favourite formulations. Elsie, seventeen years older than him, was the closest to Billie of his three big sisters. When his Dover College friend Donald Campbell was sent home badly wounded, Billie quickly asked his mother and Elsie to visit him in hospital. Donald was thrilled, as Billie told the family: 'I gather he likes you all very much.' Thus soldiers drew men they cared about into newly created networks of friendship and support.

Mrs Nevill, more than ten years a widow by 1914, was the centre of Billie's emotional world. Her numerous parcels were meticulously packed. Besides these the family arranged regular Fortnum & Mason consignments which went down very well with Billie's colleagues. 'May I take this opportunity,' Billie told her once, 'of saying how splendid you are in sending out <u>exactly</u> what I ask for and not something you <u>thought</u> would perhaps do.' Mothers were the crucial trusted link between young men and their families. Among 5,000 letters written by unmarried men to their families now held by the Imperial War Museum almost half were addressed to a mother.[14]

Lance Spicer wrote man-to-man letters to his father which sometimes discussed the progress of the war. He was more intimate as well as reassuring, ready to show his softer side, to his mother. His tummy ache was quite recovered, he reported in November 1915, thanking her for her enquiry. He held too much food and 'too little actual walking exercise responsible'. This letter gave her a cheerful account of the state of his trenches. 'The army makes us experts in strange things,' he reflected. 'I have become quite a drainage expert.'

Suffering the blow of losing all his kit in the chaos of Loos, Lance confessed how essential letters were to sustaining his confidence: 'I must say I have never appreciated letters more in all my life than I do out here and I know everybody says the same.' He was thrilled with the new Gillette razor his sister Marion had packed up. This was 'so beautiful that I hardly dared shave with it this morning'. But he did so, greatly boosting himself by the smooth face it revealed. The results of his shave, Lance was emphatic, restored his self-esteem. The razor brought a real sense of how he was cared for.[15]

Loos was also Yvo Charteris's baptism of fire. He tried hard to write to everyone back at Stanway. Mama, Papa and his sisters all had news from him in September and early October 1915. He was always cheerful, enjoying the spectacle of war with childlike innocence, as his regiment marched towards the ruined town. 'The march was very thrilling,' Yvo declared, as 'the guns grew louder and the flashes more distinct'. He congratulated Mama on 'a very skilfully chosen parcel of food-stuffs', which included much-appreciated partridges. But, so incredibly young, he was inevitably needy. 'Please send me some pencils soon,' he asked Mary. 'Write to me again,' he implored his youngest sister 'darling Bibs'.[16]

Ernest Smith's first letters show him setting up an effective personal support system. 'I am going to give you a list of things which I should very much like at your convenience,' he told his mother. This included carbolic soap 'or something powerful', matches, handkerchiefs, shirts and envelopes. Sisters Gracie and Sybil were making mufflers which he was sure would turn out 'the warmest things that ever happened'. Calling his brother 'my dear old man', Ernest gave him an account of a Royal Engineers officer listening to German voices as he tunnelled close to them, which might have been taken from an adventure story. He thanked Aminda for her cakes and tobacco. His three sisters were soon plying him with butterscotch. 'Thank you so much for your funny little letter and the lovely parcels!' he wrote to Gracie in September 1915.[17]

That kind of regular and dependable family support did not come quickly enough for seventeen-year-old Wilbert Spencer. During December 1914, it sank in that his fantasy of the war being over for Christmas was just that. He had received one parcel and no letters for weeks, he told his mother on

26 December. He longed for cigarettes. 'Please give Baby something from me,' he pleaded, clinging to his big brother status. With too much expected of him so young, Wilbert needed a touch of regression. 'MUCH LOVE AND HEAPS OF HUGS FROM BOOBA' he wrote to baby Helen in capital letters. But parcels did soon pick up. He could not carry anything more, Wilbert explained in January. Chocolate, cigarettes and acid drops, immediate dope, were the best things to send. There was comfort in sending home photos. He felt the one in his waders, intended to comfort his mother, was quite good of him. Wilbert noted receiving his fifteenth parcel in February 1915.[18]

Older boys at the Front sought to be protective and encouraging to younger brothers. Billie wrote affectionately to Tom still at Dover College. 'Go in for everything,' he urged with regard to sports, 'don't be shy of entering for things and don't overtrain to start with.' Tom collected butterflies so Billie sent him specimens from France. Will Streets urged on his brother Ben who was taking singing lessons and planned a public performance: 'you have to put your soul into music to succeed. Study hard, lad, and when I return I hope to hear you sing.'[19] Alec Reader promised his brother Arthur, three years younger, 'you will end up by doing great things'. There was inevitably some bravado in his account. His pal had 'stopped a bit with his leg' and was 'now in England'. But things would get back to normal before his birthday came round in September, Alec assured Arthur. Then they would have a spree just like old times.[20]

Alec Reader struggling to cope, still only eighteen when he reached the Front, never really pretended he was happy. But he did have massive and persistent family support. Grandparents and aunts are frequently mentioned in his letters as well as his brother and sisters. So he managed to show a certain grim sense of humour. Writing once, after endless days of digging, he declared he would one day answer the question 'What did you do in the Great War, Daddy?' with the response 'Dug up half France, Sonny'.[21]

'It is wonderful how people think of one,' Ernest Smith marvelled soon after landing. 'I have received letters from all kinds of people.' The unexpected letters from acquaintances back home meant as much as those of familiar family correspondents. Cyril Newman commented to Winnie on hearing from Mr Stewart, an assistant cashier at the Official Receiver's Department, his workplace in London. He had got up at 4 a.m. to see Cyril off when he was returning from his leave on a cheerless morning, 'a side-whiskered man, you may remember him'. This lowly office colleague, Cyril reported, wrote of them all being 'tried in the fire'. The letter confirmed his conviction that 'we out here and dear ones at home' stood shoulder to shoulder in the patriotic struggle.[22] The immeasurable courage and persistence that mountains of letters brought British soldiers is summarised in such examples.

Men leaving behind a male, however young, found comfort by projecting on to him their absent household role. 'Tell Bob to write one of his stories to me,' Peter McGregor wrote to Jen, 'tell him I don't forget him – he is looking after you and Margaret – I asked him to do all this – poor wee chap.' Husband, protector, caring spouse – Peter mentally loaded everything on little Bob's shoulders. His schoolboy son bore his mantle of family and public duty. 'Tell Bob to have a good term,' he wrote, 'not to be shy – soldiers always seem to be enjoying themselves and laughing – Bob wouldn't have to be shy here.' Bob would surely one day live up to him at war too.[23]

Men at war quite evidently remained engrossed in the lives of their families and friends.[24] They did not for one moment neglect their duty and love towards wives standing in for them. When in Zeppelin raids on London with bombs falling nearby, Edith Feilding explained how she kept the children entertained with games in the cellar, Rowland was full of praise. 'I admire the way in which you have never woken the children till, in your opinion, the danger has become imminent . . . you are becoming a veteran now and I have every faith in your leadership.'[25] Ethel should realise that danger from Zeppelins was negligible in rural Cowfold, though, Robert Hermon advised his wife. Anyway it was 'infra dig' to 'go diving about in the cellar when so many in the village haven't got a cellar'.

Robert was more sympathetic to Ethel's sorrowful tale of seeing Bobbo off to boarding school. 'I was so very sorry for you old dear and that I wasn't there to help you through . . . I was so glad that the old boy was so brave.' Little Mairky had gone in the car to comfort her brother. The whole story, he confessed, his emotions suddenly collapsing, 'brings home so close and makes one long so for another glimpse of you all'. In his next letter, fully recovered, he was back to planning Bobbo's entry to Eton in 1920.[26]

Sons at the Front naturally thought too about their own fathers, who although beyond service age were still the family breadwinners. 'How is Dad,' asked Will Streets, 'working hard for nothing as usual down the pit?' He thanked two of his brothers for their letters and apologised for not writing to them and his father separately due to lack of time.[27] In October 1915, Ernest Smith thanked his father for a copy of his latest pamphlet about his system of muscular training for pianists, a somewhat risky business venture. He was glad 'the summer has been well tidied over' and hoped for 'yet better business' that winter.[28]

There was always solace in the mental escape that caring about a sweet-heart's day-to-day life could bring. Reggie Trench regularly pondered Clare's stresses in her work in the Orpington VAD hospital. He was rooting for her promotion, knowing her dedication, so the news that she had been passed over for a senior post was disappointing. 'It is very annoying Pet,' he wrote, 'after all the trouble you have taken and all the time you have spent there.' But some months later he was thrilled by the account of her cross-dressing role in the hospital's music hall for her wounded patients: 'I would love to see your acting … I wonder which pair of breeches of mine you have got hold of?'[29] Cyril Newman's letters endlessly commented on Winnie's daily activities. He liked to know exactly where she was going to be every day. Thus, on 17 June 1917, he insisted 'I do hope and pray that you will have a good holiday at Haslemere'. He wanted her to let him know about it later on but to take a rest first, 'even from letter-writing'.[30]

The soldier's life was a long-endured act of defence of family and friends. Men at the Front worried ceaselessly how best to reassure those at home. Aware of the terrible tales of battle and casualties in the British press, they knew how much contact meant. This is why collections of letters are full of the faded field postcards which – with their option of crossing out all items except 'I am quite well' – could bring some balm when the postman called. Everyone seems to have sent them.

Reggie Trench's letters to his mother brimmed with reassurance about his living conditions. Typically, he enumerated his comforts in a letter on 16 April 1917: his fleece-lined trench coat which could be scraped with a knife when the mud became too thick, a visit from an officer who brought a bottle of port which they drank from enamel mugs, a 'good comfortable dug-out quite dry and warm', a hot bath 'in half a German beer barrel'. Some of the colour remains on the purple pansy he chose to attach to a letter to Isabel Trench a few weeks later, a mute symbol for almost a century of his defiance of mud and dirt. In June, after a chatty account of trench life he added a PS to his valediction as her 'loving son'. 'I am extraordinarily fit.' Isabel, writing over his pencil words as she did with all his letters, has added her own words of gratitude for this missive: 'my precious son'.

There was nothing Reggie liked more than providing a colourful account of his domestic environment, if possible with lighter touches, as well as references to roofs of elephant iron and earth benches. 'A blue and white little cloth' he had found in Amiens, with flowers on the table in empty fruit jars was one such vignette. Even when he landed on a previous battleground scarred by shell holes and deep in mud, Reggie made something positive of his quarters, describing 'a little hut covered with sandbags' and a trench railway past his door as 'an excellent billet'.

Reggie was equally solicitous to Clare. Once in the early days he let himself get depressed after being kept awake by messages and cold. But, by confessing

NOTHING is to be written on this side except the date and signature of the sender. Sentences not required may be erased. If anything else is added the post card will be destroyed.

I am quite well.

I have been admitted into hospital
{ *sick* } *and am going on well.*
{ *wounded* } *and hope to be discharged soon.*

I am being sent down to the base.

I have received your { *letter dated* _____ _____ __
{ *telegram ,,* _____ _____ __
{ *parcel ,,* _____

Letter follows at first opportunity.

I have received no letter from you
{ *lately* _____
{ *for a long time.*

Signature only) *Ree Trench*

Date ___ 4 / 5 / 17 _____

[Postage must be prepaid on any letter or post card addressed to the sender of this card.]

W₃. W3597/283. 2924L 6000m. 9/16. C. & Co. Grange Mills, S.W.

4. Field postcard, Reggie Trench to Clare Trench, 4 April 1917.

it to her, he was able to stress how this was a break with his usual strong morale. Responsibility for 250 men prevented one 'thinking too much of oneself. We are really happy,' he summarised, 'we grumble at the discomforts and we all share alike in every officers' mess and don't do at all badly'.[31]

Cyril Newman warned Winnie whenever he saw on the horizon a difficult period for writing. 'Only become anxious after a lapse of three weeks,' he emphasised. During battle it was only the most determined soldiers from the ranks who found ways of getting a friendly officer to see a letter was posted. 'You know that during the Somme period no letters were officially possible for a fortnight yet I managed to get one or two through to you,' Cyril boasted to Winnie later. His carefully edited correspondence reveals the detail of this. He managed a brief note confirming he was safe and well on 4 July and a fuller 'green envelope', brimming with intimacy and affection, the same evening. The battle for Combles between 13 and 26 September was a period of 'indescribable horror', but Cyril managed to persuade Major O'Shea to send three letters with the ration transport returning back behind the lines. Many soldiers were less dogged about maintaining such scrupulous contact.[32]

Soldiers constantly worried over how much to come clean about and what to conceal. At times it was difficult to avoid entirely the rigours of military life. Graham Greenwell confessed he was struggling against bitter cold in the 1916 winter. The hard frost, he tried to insist, was 'rather fun' but woe betide them when the thaw came. He was clinging to the prospect of four days behind the lines, 'motor drives' to local towns and 'some dinner parties'. 'So you see I am fairly cheerful,' he concluded, then, checking himself against looking pathetic, he wrote 'I mean very cheerful'.[33]

The Nevill family, much as they loved Billie, knew the kind of reckless character he was so he was not disconcerted when his protestations about his safety were blown apart in September 1915. Some of the wounded East Surreys in hospital near home talked to a nurse about his bravado. This got back to the family. 'Of course it is all rot about my being too venturesome,' he insisted. He simply had to do his leadership duty: he would not tell anyone to look over the parapet 'without doing so myself and, if necessary . . . talking to them a minute or two till they get confidence'. This care of his men he saw as 'nothing at all'. 'My invariable rule,' Billie wrote later, 'is unless you are directly helping to kill a German don't run the tiniest chance of getting killed by a German.'

In October 1915, the biggest German mine on the Western Front so far exploded close to Billie. Through his swift action and that of his fellow officers, the casualties were 'pretty light' but he had never 'been in such a tight corner before'. Pleased with his performance, Billie could not resist telling the whole story, giving it weight by comparing the tongue of flame to 'that big clump of trees in the bottom of Marble Hill Park' near their home. Significantly, though, he began this long letter by confessing how he had pondered whether to reveal what happened at all. He was doing so 'as you've been so good about not getting nervous about me'.[34]

Providing honest matter-of-fact accounts of performance yet making light of the worst aspects of trench warfare, soldiers were walking a tightrope. Emotions slipped out; hints of the strain they were under marked the most thoughtfully constructed letters. For there was sometimes a desperate wish and need to tell.[35] Ernest Smith had done a pretty good job for four months in the line preventing his family from being alarmed. Then his colleague Ford went on leave and visited them in Muswell Hill. In a sense this was a relief, because he saw that he needed to moderate his descriptions of trench life in view of what he found the Smiths could take. 'No doubt Ford gave you graphic details of the working parties we had to take up to the front line at the time he left us,' he told his mother. 'I was quite glad' to get that over, he confessed. That was enough from him on the subject.[36]

Alec Reader, we have seen, constructed elaborate plans for reassurance. But once in the line his offer to write every week looked more problematic. It would be 'as near Mondays as I can', he declared, completing a very long letter from Le Havre. He did his best to stick to this, reproving his mother when she fussed about whether he was coping. Nevertheless, Alec's disintegration during his first months in the trenches is vividly apparent in his letters. He progressively abandoned his determination to protect his family from the full truth about his state of mind. By 4 May 1916 demoralisation had got the better of him. 'I have undergone the various emotions caused by war, have seen most things that happen in war and don't think much of it.' He had 'seen men killed and wounded and have had to carry a mortally wounded man to the dressing station on a stretcher . . . the poor chap was dying fast and knew it. It was awful . . . war is a rotten game.' But a few days later he was racked with guilt about this letter. It followed a particularly horrible spell in the front line, he insisted: 'don't take any notice as we all have our rotten moments'.

With his mother's anxiety at fever pitch later that month and press reports of his Division's being almost wiped out, it must have cheered her to hear that Alec had spent four days in hospital after a minor wound and was then in rest camp. At the end of June he reported he had still not fired a shot. When he was told he could leave service because he was still under age there was no chance to consult his family. 'The temptation to get out of this ghastly business,' he confessed, 'is far greater than you can possibly conceive, but of course there's only one decent thing for me to do, that is to stay here, but oh! it's going to be very hard.' He reiterated this decision, using the usual euphemism, to 'stick it out here until I get knocked out' a week later.

Manfully, Alec decided that his survival depended on the war being quickly over. So he began to offer a new kind of reassurance. The war could not last 'longer than August', he declared on 8 July 1915; he was 'absolutely sure', he insisted on the 22nd, peace would come by Christmas, 'so make a lot of puddings'. Two possibilities of escape held back his creeping fatalism: that his dad, now in service, would arrange a transfer or he would get a 'blighty one' a minor wound that sent him home. His mother still talked 'all that bosh about bravery'. But, 'horribly fed up with this game', he admitted he was now 'only too pleased' for his father to rescue him since he could not rescue himself. Caught in a trap between his mother's feverish concern and his sense of duty, he was unable to resolve this. As his fatalism took hold, the censor's pencil began to run through many of the passages he wrote home.[37]

In Jack Sweeney's first letters to Ivy Williams there was much less inhibition than normal since this was a new relationship and he was testing the ground. His very first letter, sent to 'my dear friends' in July 1915, painted a lurid picture of Ypres as 'a heap of ruins with dead civilians and soldiers everywhere'. He used hearsay to illustrate his case that Tommies dreaded going there: 'anywhere except there is the cry'. 'You will think me a lively feller telling you this but I do like to speak my mind.' Yet, anxious about Ivy's reaction, his next letter was apologetic about his honesty: 'I was wild with myself afterwards because I wrote such horrible stuff.' Jack gradually came to see that trust depended upon some guarding of his tongue. But his fourteen-page account of battle the following April spared the girlfriend he had still not met very little indeed. 'I am sure this war will send us all mad,' he summarised: 'people at home cannot realise what the lads out here go through.'

Jack battled through the Somme having declared his love for Ivy after his leave in May 1916. He was one of 435 men out of 1,150 in the Lincolns who survived, he told her in his account of the Big Push. Jack now regularly let his emotions show, confident in the intimacy which gave him daily strength. It was the censor who checked him, erasing his saying he feared he would be killed in the next assault on 10 September, but doing so rather ineffectually. 'Keep smiling, enjoy your holidays,' he wrote in the same letter, veering between personal fatalism and cheery encouragement to those back home.

It was November before Jack, still reliving it, began revealing to Ivy his personal story of the Somme. Fearing bad dreams if he let himself recount the experience of Mametz Wood, Jack decided 'it is too horrible to mention'. But on 6 November he felt an overwhelming need to confide a crisis he had survived nearly two months earlier: 'I was wet to the skin, no overcoat . . . I had about three inches of clay clinging to my clothes and it was cold . . . do you know what I did – I sat down in the mud and cried. I do not think I have cried like I did that night since I was a child.' Then, soon after this, Jack let himself go and had a good moan on paper, which Ivy found it hard to take. He replied, 'but I really was fed up at the time. I am so sorry that you get downhearted.'[38]

Older men might be but were not necessarily more open than younger ones. Rowland Feilding, we have seen, had a close understanding with his wife Edith.[39] Peter McGregor was also middle-aged but had been flung into war, whereas Rowland had years in the army behind him. Peter was entirely candid and uninhibited with his wife Jen because, feeling in desperate straits, he often needed to be. Moving up to the Front in June 1916, he had to purge himself of the sights he passed through by getting them on to paper. A ruined town 'made me shiver – wooden crosses on the roadside and in places in the town marking the heroes' death – what devastation – a day of judgement more like'. He found it helped him to recount the gradual mastery of his fear. 'Dodging rum jars, bombs, has become quite an art with me,' he told Jen, 'I can look back on the experience with amusement now but at the moment the agony of fear is awful.'[40]

Yet it was the young men who undoubtedly found writing home about violence and disturbing events the most painful, since they had not had time to acquire an adult armour against life's traumas. Wilbert Spencer's letter to his mother about his first dose of shelling is instructive. One of his men was killed and four were wounded. A slip of the pencil dropped a clue to his confused feelings. 'One of the worst parts of the war,' he wrote, 'is the sights one has to endure.' No wonder he was traumatised when writing this letter: he was recalling his care of the man who died: 'the fellow who was killed lived his last minutes with his head on my knee'. He was thankful, he related, that men in this case were 'usually unconscious and can suffer little pain'.[41]

One of the most difficult letters Ernest Smith had to write to his mother followed a three-day battle fought by the Buffs soon after he joined the regiment. On 13 August 1915 he was recovering from 'a bit of a nerve shaking', hunger and thirst. He explained that, at the time, 'the sense of having to see after others and set an example prevents one from thinking much'. This was why he had difficulty in recalling much about the first hours of the show, when the Buffs consolidated a position won by another regiment, repairing trenches, burying the dead and helping the wounded. 'The taking over of that line,' he concluded, 'seemed an unreal sort of dream to me.' 'I am not going into details,' he announced.

Ernest could not stand the introspection involved in writing a detailed narrative of the battle, but what he did write powerfully conveyed his feelings.

It also allowed his mother to understand what the experience meant for him three days later. It seemed, in Ernest's words, 'as though there was an infinity of time and space separating us from anything beautiful or desirable and the weird effect was increased by the half light and mist, which prevented us from seeing very far or even distinguishing the Bosch lines'.[42]

What is remarkable about this letter is the delicacy of Ernest's balancing act. While emphasising the bravery of fellow officers and the spirit of his men he downplayed his own role. He sought to check his mother's alarm, by insisting 'you must not run away with the idea our losses were exceptionally heavy'. When he wrote again on 21 August, Ernest had read of her gratitude at his having written at such length. The account on the 13th, he assured her, had helped him come to terms with the battle on his second full day of rest: 'I was longing to tell someone all about it'. He did so in a way that effectively managed her emotional state as well as securing his own emotional stability.[43]

The assignment set the 2/5th Sherwood Foresters on 4 April 1917 was to take the hilltop village of Le Verguier on the Hindenburg Line, in broad daylight, using a flanking movement to attack where the Germans appeared weakest. Reggie Trench led the third of three companies which swept down a long hillside in the early morning, meeting sustained and accurate machine-gun fire. Only 150 men reached the comparative safety of some dead ground in a hollow before the village. Reggie became the senior officer left in the action. He halted his men, too weak to move into the planned attack and unable to retreat. They were saved by a snowstorm, which turned during the morning into a blizzard, depriving the German gunners of the chance to set their sights. Under this cover the survivors got back and the stretcher-bearers laboured long and hard to bring in the dead and wounded. When the count was made the casualty figure, in a battalion whose fighting strength had stood at around 600, was 104, including 20 men killed.

So what of all this could Reggie relate to his wife and mother? Clearly he found it hard to write about his first battle. His letter next day opened with a full account of his makeshift company headquarters where, he asserted, all was 'snug and cosy', with a wooden and felt roof that kept out the worst of the snow and 'a big fire going all night'. Coming to the failed attack, he confessed 'I'm sorry to say that Captain Adams was killed'. Then he wrote and crossed some words out. Next he spoke about how Milner, his subaltern, had been wounded, 'a nice cushy one in the leg – he was awfully bucked!' 'One of my men was wounded for the fourth time,' he continued.

There was nothing in this letter about how they had stood that morning at the burial, conducted by the much respected Padre Judd, of most of the twenty men who had been killed. It was a lovely sunny day on 5 April. Reggie's clothes, soaked during the battle were drying out. But the last sentence of his report, in its sheer emotional force, set the rest of the letter he wrote aside. 'I am thankful to say,' he stated, 'my nerves under fire are perfect – this is very comforting as one's responsibilities are very great.'

Clare read enough to realise the seriousness of the battle Reggie had been in. She at once pressed for more information. Two of her letters reached him in the same post on the 8th. Three days had given him a little more perspective. So after some chat about how nice it would be if she sent some dry kippers, since all her parcels had arrived in perfect condition, he responded to her clamouring. 'Yes my love, I have been under fire and pretty heavy too – in that attack the other day their barrage caught us before we had started and they had a lot of machine guns too which did much damage. I lost some of my best men but thanks to a snowstorm was saved excessive damage.'

This time Reggie sought to reassure Clare that the battle had been an effective test of battalion morale. He was encouraged by his men's spirit: 'the men were splendid – laughing all the time at their escapes and following their officers perfectly.' Writing to his mother on 13 April, he felt strong enough to come clean about what had happened at Le Verguier. 'We attacked a village – my company was forming the third line but there was only one line left after a little time and I was in that with those that were left. Poor old Adams, our company commander, was killed, such a good chap . . . I came through without a scratch and best of all – it was my first "action". I found that my nerves were all right. My company did very well.' The Sherwoods had won praise. 'The GOC sent a most complimentary message to the "gallant fifth battalion",' he told her.

Clare went on worrying. She was struggling to come to terms with what she had long expected: that her husband was now regularly in acute personal danger. A bundle of five letters received by Reggie on the 18th, written between the 7th and the 13th, dwelt on the battle and how little she knew of it. She was now fully aware it had been a 'bad day'. He agreed, admitting 'we had more casualties than I liked'. But it was only after another packet of her letters, on 25 April, that Reggie responded to her insistent pleading for information about his own escape from injury.

Three weeks after the battle, fourteen letters from him later, he at last told Clare how close that shave had been. He had been 'a couple of yards from Adams when he was wounded – he died shortly after I believe though I had advanced and did not know till later'. She finally dragged the crucial information she wanted out of her husband. He had avoided telling too much, seeking to protect her, hoping she would not imagine how close he had come to death. But in the end his honour impelled him to tell the truth.[44]

Letters brought endless comfort, support and encouragement. In return soldiers offered involvement in the lives of those at home. But the attachment to home went deeper. Soldiers needed to confide their feelings about their homes. Thus nostalgia is a dominant emotion expressed in many of these letters. Men found the more stressful their situation became the greater their need for their homes as a heaven. Nostalgia distracted soldiers from the tedium of trench routine. At times it offered escape from anxieties that threatened to become intolerable. Emotional survival could be purchased by drawing upon the power of distant love.

When Robert and Ethel Hermon's wedding anniversary came round in January 1916, distracted by one of his best sergeants being killed that day, he forgot to think of her or write. 'I'm awfully angry I forgot,' he confessed. Keeping marital romance alive was hard work. Ethel had been teasing Robert about the early days of their love affair that month. He picked up her challenge to name what happened on a certain summer's day long before. He managed to guess she meant the day he proposed and was not instantly accepted. In a letter full of exclamation marks, he then teased her about a 'day when you nearly chucked away a damned good bargain'.

Revealing how his hopes of leave were shattered that December, Robert asked Ethel to teach the children a prayer they knew which spoke of God watching over 'the sentry on watch this night, that he may be alert'. In an elaborate imaginative exercise, he sought to draw Bobbo and his sisters into his leadership at the Front. 'I would love to think that the kids were saying it or had said it when I go round the front lines at midnight'. The special appeal of this prayer for him was that he saw 'so much of the sentry and know what he has to go through, with no protection against the weather bar what he can put on his body'.[45]

There was comfort in recalling family routines with happy memories; for example 'Waste not want not'. Alec Reader reminded his mother about her reprimanding words across the kitchen table. Did she remember 'the way I used to spread the butter and jam?' Escaping into memory when he wrote to his father after his 'pretty rotten time' in May 1916, having just survived a 'most unpleasant' sally over the top, Alec's mind went back to their rides together on his motorbike in the English lanes. He was looking forward to their 'spin on the Enfield' on his return.[46]

'As I came into the trenches last night,' Rowland Feilding related to Edith on 11 June 1915, 'the mud was just like very thick soup'. Whereas it impeded the work of his men, it lightened his mood to think of Anita and Peggy's childhood play. This, he joked, was 'good mud wasted – how they would have loved it'. Peter McGregor's mind conjured up 'the long stretches of sand' at Burntisland, the Scottish resort where the family always took summer holidays. They were back there without him in August 1916. 'How lovely it was,' he mused, 'I am sure you will be having a good time – how the kiddies will enjoy the sea and shore – how I long to be with you.'[47]

The reflective Charlie May, we have seen, liked to find time on his own when he could set aside the pressures of his company command in the 22nd Battalion of the Manchester Regiment. A 'stroll out' on Lizzie, his charger brought from England, written up afterwards in his diary, did much to restore his equanimity. He could lose himself in the landscape, daydreaming of his wife Maud and Pauline their baby girl. 'I longed that you could have been with me,' he recorded after a ride towards Canaples. Christmas made Charlie homesick, as he remembered the glorious family times of previous years: 'how the lamps will gleam, the fire leap and the laughter ring'. He sat up with fellow officers, drank to absent friends 'and thought pretty hard'. But at the New Year in 1916 he could not bring himself to join this throng. He needed time alone to immerse himself in 'such sweet, sad memories'. Just after midnight a shooting star he saw cross the heavens seemed 'a good omen for our future New Years'. His diary was a haven for Charlie May just as letter writing was for others. As the Somme offensive drew near, he drew strength, he noted, from Maud's regular and 'ripping' letters. In quiet moments he let his mind wander to her word pictures of their daughter. 'Peace, comfort, all that is sweet clean' overwhelmed him when he allowed these thoughts of her full rein.[48]

Reggie Trench permitted himself a burst of nostalgia after Le Verguier. Clare's wonderful letters, he suddenly exclaimed, 'never tell me anything about your very own self and I long to hear that you still walk with short skirts and a smiling face about the place in all weathers'. He had been thinking in their rest period 'of our many happy days spent together' during their peripatetic wartime life in England and Ireland. There was 'the jolly time last Easter at Broadstairs ... that topping holiday in Brighton ... Folkestone that was good fun too though it was only two nights ... Clan Rye that was topping and above all Potter's End ... that inn in Kent? What was it called? We had some fizz I am glad to remember ... finally Thurston Lodge which was perfect'. One vision of his wife encapsulated this whole catalogue of wartime living from place to place. He dwelt on it in writing about Potter's End, the village where they took a house near Berkhamsted: 'you looked so topping in our room looking onto the apple blossom'.

Some of their letters related past pleasures to anticipated excitement. 'I got your letter ... yes my love I should love to camp with you again in Devon, somewhere near a river or even the sea,' wrote Reggie. Their camping holiday near Totnes in 1913 came flooding back. As a married couple it would be different and better next time. Though 'the privileges of a lover were not inconsiderable were they Pet', he avowed, recalling chaste but passionate love-making by the River Dart. 'I shall never forget those happy days', he told her. One of his billets, he related in another letter, was in a farm with an orchard, 'quite like our joy camp at Totnes'. Did she remember that night they had slept out, 'together in one blanket', until, to his sorrow, Clare thought it proper to retire about midnight to her tent?

Sex was always present in Reggie's passionate longings, as in his dreams of Clare, at the Front. After finding 'the waking reality very dull' once more on 19 September 1917, he urged her to stop worrying in letters about how it would be for them when he came home. 'I think even if you were very sleepy darling,' he insisted, 'I could manage to ring the bell all right . . . it does not require much effort after this long absence . . . it would be like having our honeymoon again.' How he longed for the end of the war, epitomised by a contented family life. He longed for a son and was sad that, four months after his leave, no 'little Chennie' was arriving. He reflected that 'perhaps we will have better luck' when he next came home.[49] Friends had called him Chennie at school.

Clare needed to plan for and set hopes upon their future too. In January 1918 she sent Reggie the Harrods details of a dream house she thought they might possibly afford. But perhaps 'a farm and fields' were 'too expensive a luxury'? Reluctantly, he agreed. Nostalgia became even more necessary to help Reggie through that dark winter, when peace seemed as far off as ever and they were still apart on their third wedding anniversary. Her letters were 'so delightful', such a solace, especially the one written on 28 January. He had timed one full of memories of the day to reach her: 'how clearly I remember it all . . . my anxiety about arriving on time . . . how sweet you looked in your wedding dress and "going away" dress . . . those two dear nights when I had you to myself at last'.[50]

But writing could also be a deliberate act of dissociation, a kind of going home, during present stress at the Front. Reggie chose to relieve 'a period of suspense that is not pleasant', when he had sent a platoon out trench digging, by writing Clare a long letter about the drama of an aeroplane being shot down that day. He paused to see to the rum ration and, sure enough, he declared, returning to his pencil, the men returned 'within five minutes of the time I estimated'.[51]

But correspondence had a special privacy and intensity for the soldier which parents, when they were on the receiving end, did not always fully grasp. Wilbert Spencer was very unhappy when his father sent one of his letters to the *Daily Mail*, chiding him that he found it 'a bit thick' to be publicised behind his back. When he subsequently sent photos of himself to his mother, including one in waders to assuage her concern about the mud, he insisted sharply that they must not reach the press.[52] Writing letters, it is evident, fulfilled many functions. Those at home wanted news, as did soldiers far from home. Just keeping in touch mattered a great deal. But, at the deepest level of men's emotional survival, there was nothing more crucial than the opportunity letters provided to leave aside the harrowing present. The happiness of the recent past or hopes for fulfilment in a new world yet to come could give men great solace.

CHAPTER 5

'Sticking it Out'

Fear and Shell Shock

In traditional patriotic thinking war was a test of manhood and character. But the Great War taught lessons which struck at the very heart of Victorian and Edwardian manliness. Neither attendance at a public school nor training in an Officer Training Corps prepared men for the emotional reality of the Western Front. The adventure literature and patriotic verse had swept fear aside. G.A. Henty, Rudyard Kipling and Sir Henry Newbolt did not write about danger in terms which alerted boys to how they would cope when faced with battle. These writers assumed that men schooled in heroic virtues would be able to wave away their vulnerability. Emotional repression together with sheer willpower would be enough to see them through. Service on the Western Front involved a sharp and accelerated exercise in growing up.[1]

Predictably, by 1918 huge numbers of soldiers had collapsed with shell shock, a condition diagnosed for the first time in 1915. In 1939, 120,000 men were still receiving pensions for psychiatric disability caused in the Great War. Everyone had moments of fear at the Front.[2] But at the same time men desperately wanted to hide their fear and prevent their families at home from worrying.[3] Remarkably, our letter writers, though chary about being in real danger, almost all provided some kind of account of their first experience of being under fire. They needed solace, and they also believed their families expected to hear about it.

Soldiers at the Front were hardly ever entirely out of danger. One walking in the woods near Poperinge, well behind the lines, in 1915 was killed by a single stray shell which took his head off. When Will Streets found himself, for the first time since he reached the Front, away from the sound of guns in June 1916, he told his mother about the 'blessed relief' this gave them all.[4] 'It is lovely to laze on the grass without fear of shells,' wrote Cyril Newman behind the line at St Amand during the Somme battle. There was renewed sweetness in living when one could see and hear 'the green grass, the singing of birds, even the hum and buzz of insects'.[5]

Men mostly narrated their anxieties, times of dread or moments of terror without analysing them. Those who did write reflectively about fear did so within a straitjacket of mental assumptions. Will Streets, so perceptive generally about the strains of war, was elliptical about his feelings after a largely uneventful spell in the trenches in May 1916: 'of course there are great moments of excitement, of intense animal fear, when the spirit dominates and all that is best in man stands out . . . we gave them tit-for-tat and blazed away. It gives you greater confidence and spirit when you meet them with a bold front.'[6]

The padre Donald Hankey wrote pieces in 1915 about the experience of trench warfare which were published in *The Spectator*. They gained such celebrity that they were published as a book, *A Student in Arms*, in 1917. One of his essays, 'The Fear of Death in War', dealt with the irrational fears men felt when their nerves were tried for hours on end by 'sitting in a trench under heavy fire from shells'. Hankey described this graphically: 'you see them slowly wobble down to earth, there to explode with a terrific detonation that sets every nerve in your body a-jangling. You can do nothing. You cannot retaliate in any way. You simply have to sit tight and hope for the best.' Groping for adequate words, he wrote of 'an infinitely intensified dislike of suspense and uncertainty, sudden noise and shock'. He called this 'nameless dread'. It was a wholly physical sensation in his account which could be mastered only by sheer willpower.[7]

Writing in 1915, Hankey was innocent of psychic explanation of fear in battle. There was not yet any understanding of war trauma. The term 'shell shock' had only just been invented. The psychological analysis, under Freudian influence, of fear as memory, which later proliferated in literature, drama and memoirs, lay well ahead. All anxiety and trauma simply had to be put out of the mind or obliterated by strenuous activity.[8] Charles Wilson, who became Lord Moran and was Winston Churchill's doctor, much later became an authority in this field.[9] He published his observations on the stress of war in *The Anatomy of Courage* in 1945. His career as a medical officer on the field of battle long before, in 1914–18, was a striking example of integrity and thoughtful investigation. It was not without reason that he dedicated his book 'To my father who was without fear by his son who is less fortunate'.

Wilson's classic account is both a personal war story and an acute analysis of the psychological effects of war. He knew what difficulties he had borne in containing his own fears. His diary account of the first time he was shelled merely hints at his own terror. When a shell fell on his dugout on 20 December 1914 and the fumes gradually cleared, 'there was a hole in the wall of the cellar where the shell had come in . . . I foolishly expected another shell to come in at the same spot, and wanted to move out of the line of this hole, and had a feeling the Boche could see this hole and was watching it for any sign of life.' It took him time to realise he had work to do, with men injured all round him. Three were lying dead. As he worked he 'could not help feeling cheerful now that it was over'. But the diary account gave more space to his and his men's emotional responses to the incident than to his work of seeing to the wounded. One day in 1915 Wilson found himself shaking like a leaf under bombardment. He contained this fear and soon after noticed a sergeant alongside him 'shivering like a reed in the wind'.

His observations of men under stress were a constant theme in Charles Wilson's diary of his time in Bernafay and Trones woods during the Somme. When followed by Germans into a trench, he saw some of his men run 'like frightened cattle that push and jostle and are harried into the fields through the open gate by barking dogs'. He saw faces 'which sleep might not have visited for a week'. He watched men 'who had sat for days under heavy shelling without leaving their trenches, the supreme cold-blooded test of this war'. It was only later that he understood the toll this had taken: 'even when the war had begun to fade out of men's minds I used to hear all at once without warning the sound of a shell coming. Perhaps it was only the wind in the trees to remind me that war had exacted its tribute.'[10]

Wilson later developed a highly influential notion of courage which, he argued, was expendable. 'Courage,' he wrote,

> is will-power, whereof no man has an unlimited stock; and when in war it is used up, he is finished. A man's courage is his capital and he is always spending. The call on the bank may be only the daily drain of the front line . . . his will is perhaps almost destroyed by intensive shelling, by heavy bombing or by a bloody battle, or it is gradually used up by monotony, by exposure . . . by physical exhaustion.

A chapter on 'Moods' in his book exemplified the extent to which he came to adopt Freudian languages of the self. Churchill refused to write a preface to *The Anatomy of Courage* because it contained too much 'damned psychological nonsense'.[11]

Nothing induced fear like being shelled. This was the primary preoccupation of the new soldier. At the Western Front soldiers quickly learnt how explosive and jagged shell casings, the dreaded shrapnel, tore at men's bodies. Almost three-quarters of the wounds in 1914–18 were caused by shells. They usually went septic because foreign matter entered the body with the splinters. Close bursts of shellfire produced many predictable reactions in frightened men crouching in their trenches: blackouts, numbness, trembling eyelids, shaking hands. Men often had to struggle hard to control their nerves.[12]

The real barrage, a continuous stream of fire, could send soldiers half mad. In his later memoir Wynn Griffith recalled a youngster's extreme reaction under such a barrage. Following 'a thunderous crash in our ears, a young boy began to cry for his mother in a thin boyish voice "Mam, Mam . . ."' He had not been hit, yet he screamed in terror for his mother 'with a wail that seemed older than the world'. After some muttering in the platoon, 'we shook him and cursed him and even threatened to kill him . . . the shaking brought him back'.[13]

Predictably, accounts by men from all ranks of their first experience of being shelled have a stark immediacy. 'It was an awful time,' wrote Private Horace Bruckshaw in his diary at Vimy Ridge on 3 June 1916. For almost an hour, 'instead of our superiors leading us out of it they kept us in the centre of it all sheltering as best we could under the ruined walls, all of us expecting every minute to be buried under bricks and mortar at the least'. He saw one man killed and others injured jumping down from 'the wagon just behind us'.[14] Lance Corporal Roland Mountford wrote to his mother after his first sentry duty on 7 November 1915. He came down from the firing step, he explained, and crouched in the trench when shells began to fall thickly about him. He confessed to being 'in a terrible funk'. Moreover, judging by the faces of others, he believed he was 'not unique in that'. 'The row shakes you to pieces,' he added.[15]

A week after arriving at the Front, dreaming of the glories of the cavalry charge, Julian Grenfell was explaining to his parents there was simply 'no job for cavalry', so the Dragoons had become infantry in the trenches. In November 1914 the full reality of their job came home to him. 'We've been doing all shelled work lately and it's horrible,' he told his mother, Lady Ettie, in a week when the German barrage was normally seven hours: 'you just lie there, hunched up . . . the noise is appalling and one's head is rocking with it by the end of the day'. After a single day in the front line, Julian accepted, 'one's nerves are absolutely beaten down'.

Julian yearned for escape, being the kind of man he was, and for action. He pleaded to be allowed to have a go at the bothersome German snipers. Hence his famous stalking raids on 16 and 17 November which won him the DSO. He was as frightened as the next man inactive under shellfire but these stalking expeditions, bagging 'three Pomeranians', restored his composure. Is this not the hero you wanted? his account home effectively asked. Julian was happy killing the enemy. It was being under attack that confused him.[16]

Cyril Newman sent a letter about his 'baptism of fire' on 24 May 1915, asking for it to be read to his Sunday school class. This was a consciously constructed exercise in studied bravery for the benefit of youngsters back home. His 'heart was kept in peace', he narrated, because he constantly repeated 'The Eternal God is my refuge'. He had survived a long night out trench digging in no-man's-land 'with bullets whizzing round and over us all the three hours'. There was a chlorine gas attack on the way home at dawn which left him coughing and choking. His fear was no more than hinted at in the mild comment 'I did not like the experience at all'. His interpretation, dramatising the experience for his boys at home, stressed a demonic presence: 'the Devil was doing with nature as he liked'.

Writing nearly three years later, Cyril had acquired a reflective stance on how he had taught himself to endure front-line shelling. In March 1918, he told Winnie how the 'ear-splitting and sickening crash' as a shell burst forced to the surface of his mind 'reserves of stern endurance and a hardness of heart so that for the time being one becomes Spartan'. By this time, Cyril could give a factual account of his own practice of playing the man: 'keeping under all sensitive, tender-hearted feelings that, if indulged in, might render one a coward'. It was after each such trial, he admitted, that he craved 'for a woman's love'.[17]

When Graham Greenwell suffered an hour's bombardment with the Oxfordshire and Buckinghamshire Light Infantry in Ploegsteert Wood on 6 June 1915 he described it as 'the nearest approach to a battle' since his regiment had come out. Machine-gun bullets whistled outside the door of the dugout: 'it seemed as if they must come in though, of course, they couldn't'. Simultaneously the whole wood was being shelled. 'I found it difficult to smoke my pipe with my usual insouciance,' Graham admitted, 'although I was in comparative safety the whole time.'

There were several periods later in 1915 when Graham was worn down by prolonged shelling. Fear for him, as for many, was a cumulative problem over long hours expecting a direct hit. He had a 'ghastly time' on front-line duty in October 1915. A letter afterwards contained an especially clear account of why soldiers saw being shelled as a process of 'wind-up'. The row made by a shell, a 'low whistle', was incredible, he explained. Graham reached the state when 'every puff of the wind startles me and I feel as nervous as a cat'. What finished him was 'sitting still throughout a solid day listening the whole time to shells and wondering if the next one will be on the dug-out or not'. At the end of a 'hateful' day on 31 December, one detects the tension behind Graham's conscientious scribbling of 'my usual line' home. He had been back from the trenches for a full hour, yet he was sure shells were 'still whistling in my ears as they had whistled all day, accompanied by deafening explosions'. They still 'seemed to be all round me'. Graham was wholly 'wound up' and hours must have passed after writing this letter before he recovered his composure.[18]

Graham Greenwell was far more candid than Billie Nevill. But this was a difference of temperament and personality as much as one of policy on what to tell. Billie had schooled himself to retain the conviction that war was all a game. He managed to maintain his bravado in the front line. Mentioning his first time under fire out trench digging at night on 12 August 1915 almost casually, he turned at once to an excited account of watching star shells and fireballs, 'awfully pretty, very like an ordinary regatta display'. Boasting a few days later of sitting out 'in some long grass in "No Man's land"', he confessed he 'got about four shots round my tail' when he bolted back, 'but the poor souls are too slow'.[19]

Captain Jimmy Wilson, a Sherwood Forester, explained his feelings when first under fire to his mother in March 1916: 'I was horribly afraid – sick with fear – not of being hit, but of seeing other people torn in the way that high explosive tears. It is simply hellish. But thank God I didn't show any funk. That's all a man dare ask, I think.' The next month he wrote to his aunt describing his trench: 'piled earth with groundsel and great dandelions and chickweed and pimpernels running riot over it'. There was 'corrugated iron, a smell of boots and stagnant water . . . and over everything the larks and a blessed bee or two'. Twenty or so shells had come over that morning. His word picture was powerful: 'you hear a sound rather like a circular saw cutting through thin wood and moving towards you at the same time with terrific speed – straight for your middle it seems until you get used to it'. Then 'a terrific burst . . . and sometimes a torn man to be put out of sight or hurried down to the dressing station'.

Painting the same scene in another letter to a teacher in May, Jimmy wrote that the thunder of a shell landing could be just 'an interesting phenomenon' to newcomers. To men hardened as he was 'it is a terrible and fiendish thing'. 'Mangled bodies are obscene', he came to feel; 'war is an obscenity'. Why had schoolboys been taught the romance of war? Jimmy asked. Why had they all grown up soaked in the poetry of war? Their reading masked the personal horror of war. The stories showed 'nothing of the sick fear that is tearing at the hearts of brave boys who ought to be laughing at home'. In this letter, Jimmy Wilson reflected, 'it isn't death we fear so much as the long-drawn expectation of it – the sight of other fine fellows ripped horribly out of existence'.[20] An important element in the soldier's nameless dread was the tension between the distress of others around him and his own trauma.[21]

Alec Reader was fortunate in encountering a 'fairly quiet part of the line' for his first days of service. He was very miserable after his second tour, confessing 'I was so nervy I buried my head in the mud and I was not the only one either'. But he put a good face on it to his brother Arthur when asked if he had won a VC yet. Sensible men like him stayed in the bottom of the trench, he replied, 'when things get a bit hot'. Yet there was a touch of bravado in his claim 'we all have to do dangerous work. I had to carry boxes of live bombs up to the firing line with shrapnel shrapping all round.' That was on 8 April 1916. By the 28th, relating a frightening incident to his mother, he was beginning to go to pieces. He had been in a party carrying rations up to the line 'when shells started bursting about five minutes walk in front of us'. Alec saw no chance of surviving the barrage: 'it needed all my willpower to keep walking. I felt like dumping my load and running.' Mercifully, the shelling stopped when they were 300 yards from the trench.[22]

Peter McGregor was another soldier who first faced shellfire in the early summer of 1916. It occurred as the Argylls marched the last thirteen miles to the line. 'By Jove to say I had no fear would be a lie,' he wrote to Jen. 'I was full of fear.' He related hearing the whistle of each shell then the 'sharp nasty crack' of the explosion. He was on his tummy 'in double quick time'. Two days later, he tried to write home 'sitting on the fire step with shells flying overhead', but he found himself looking at a blank page for a long time. It was too hard to find the words for his pencil against the noise. Back in reserve on 21 June, Peter confessed that his first tour of duty had turned him upside down: 'no man can experience such things and come out the same'. He struggled to master his nerves. Waking from a night's sleep to a 'most terrible roar', he thought himself back in the trenches but 'it was only a chap banging on a tin tray to wake us for breakfast'.[23] The Reverend Maurice Murray made reference to that personal struggle to keep a tight rein, writing to his elder brother during Passchendaele: 'everyone must funk in a sense . . . the only thing is not to show it as it is infectious and bad for morale'.[24]

Some deliberately made light of the strain of being shelled. Quizzed by his wife about coping with gunfire, Reggie Trench confessed that the guns did not worry him at all but the largest German shells were 'rather trying'. His account was vivid: 'they come along with a noise like an express train, getting louder every second and ending with a scream and loud bang!' A pillar of earth was usually thrown up, but, to be consoling, he insisted that the 'effect was very local'.[25] Others by contrast found shellfire almost too difficult to relate. They felt the need to unburden themselves by writing, yet the act of writing and the recalling this required were unsettling.

Wilbert Spencer, much younger than Reggie, described his first involvement in heavy fighting. His letter to his mother displays crossings-out and incoherence. In the first dose of shelling he had seen one of his men killed and four injured. 'This is the most awful part of war,' he wrote, hinting at the depth of pain he was feeling.[26] Frightening experiences were easier to convey to relatives slightly less close than mothers or wives. During his first days in the front line in heavy rain, Wilbert Spencer gave himself a minor injury through sheer panic, he told his Aunt Vie. Surprised by an enemy rocket on a wiring party 'in my hurry I jumped down on top of a bayonet which ran about three quarters of an inch into my arm . . . not serious but quite painful.'[27]

Everyone felt safer in a dugout than in the open trenches, yet a dugout could become a tomb. 'We thank God for our dug-outs,' wrote Graham Greenwell after a bombardment that had lasted an hour at Hébuterne. But he confessed to feeling the same undercurrent of 'anxiety as to the strength of the lusty beams and boards above us' as the sailor felt about the stoutness of his ship.[28] Billie Nevill at last admitted having been 'a bit jumpy' throughout the next day when a shell had landed on his dugout. It exploded, he explained, 'just the other side of three foot of earth and timber from our heads'. Inspecting the damage in daylight, he found one row of timber and only an inch or two of earth left protecting them.[29]

Recalling a miraculous escape, Edwin Vaughan remembered seeing where shrapnel had gone through his valise 'and would have gone through me had I been in bed'. The notion of German destruction of their domestic refuges terrified soldiers. The dugout was a treasured haven. Vaughan carried in his mind, when he wrote up his diary after the war, the biscuit tin, tobacco tin and whisky bottles which were smashed to pieces in that attack.[30] Eric Marchant described in a letter a direct hit that buried the knives, spoons, plates and food of some of his fellow officers, besides 'killing one or two men'.[31] All this paraphernalia of daily living symbolised security and a minimal kind of safety.

Those who suffered burial alive, however briefly, were bound to experience trauma. Jack Sweeney had just finished serving his officers dinner on 24 February 1916 when the dugout with its corrugated iron roof caved in under shellfire. 'My God,' he told Ivy, 'I thought my last moment had come.' He could not answer shouts from the officers because he and another man were buried. It was pitch black. 'How long I was buried I do not know . . . at last a party of men came and dug me out, also the other man who I expected to see dead.'[32] Coping with a shell that buried men by landing close by was a particular test of resolve. Charlie May and his subaltern Lieutenant Bowby experienced this together in March 1916. A trench mortar threw them to the ground leaving them smothered and badly shaken. 'I trust the men did not see that my grin was feigned only and that really I was in the deuce of a funk,' he noted in his diary. Back in his dugout, he found himself shaking. Bowby had 'brassed it out quite successfully but I knew it had given him a turn'.[33]

Wiring after dark in no-man's-land, making men vulnerable to machine-gun and sniper fire, was particularly nerve-racking. Will Streets spared his mother the story of his first wiring party in the front line. He told his brother Ben about it with the warning 'I do not want you to speak of this at home.' Few men, he said, had experienced this degree of danger so quickly. He had found it valuable to get it over and was proud of his self-mastery. He believed he had earned the respect 'of one or two senior NCOs' who before had been loath to give it: 'I kept my nerves and fear in hand and kept the lead unto the end, even in retiring.'[34]

When veterans wrote about the war they sometimes recalled and dwelt upon fear. How they had overcome it was integral to their stories of survival. Patrick Campbell went to war at the age of nineteen in April 1917. 'We were setting out together, knights in shining armour, on the Great Adventure,' he wrote in a memoir in old age. 'I had no thought of fear in my head in spite of the unknown that lay ahead.' It was when the train stopped and he first heard the guns on the horizon that he knew fear. 'My heart had failed,' he recalled, 'my courage had turned to water.'

The next weeks were difficult for him, a green public school boy. But Captain Cecil, ten years his senior, looked after him 'like an elder brother, warning me how to take care of myself.' One memory remained especially vivid. It was of a dinner out, 'the glittering lights of the restaurant, laughter and noise, pretty Belgian waitress'. He had just been under fire. Patrick knew that night that he had won his spurs. Captain Cecil told the others at dinner 'that I never turned a hair, but was as cool as a cucumber.'[35]

In November 1914 Dr Charles Myers, a laboratory psychologist from Cambridge, studied cases of mental breakdown in a hospital at Le Touquet.[36] He began developing the notion that their nervous collapse was related to shells bursting near them at close range. In March 1915, Myers returned to France, having been appointed consultant neurologist to the War Office. He toured the hospitals along the Channel coast selecting, as he had been directed, cases of 'nervous shock or neurasthenia' for transfer to England. Myers was up against the military frame of mind, rapidly finding himself expected to advise courts martial. The Higher Command saw the intervention of psychologists like him as simply making the task of winning the war more difficult. Shell shock was not regarded as a valid defence for cowardice or desertion in the field.

Myers's initial energy was replaced by frustration and anger as he began to understand the human tragedy which lay behind the emergence of the phenomenon of shell shock. The Royal Army Medical Corps was cautious and conservative. Its labels were clear cut: men were either sick, well, wounded or mad. Unwillingness or incapacity to fight made a man a coward. The issue of mental disorder was shrouded in attitudes to honour, self-control and comradeship. Mental illness was equated at the Front with weakness, to be treated by disciplinary methods.

There was more sympathy for sufferers from war neurosis at home. Not that there were any suitable facilities for those who broke down except mental hospitals until four private hospitals were opened in 1915 for short-term rest cures for officers. The medical profession in Britain very gradually came to terms with the real nature of shell shock. In a discussion at the Royal Society of Medicine in January 1916, it was accepted that this covered a series of nervous disorders ranging from concussion to sheer funk. A man's loss of control of his nerves was the single feature these disorders had in common. It began to be noticed that war neurosis took different forms in officers and men. Whereas physical symptoms, such as paralysis, blindness, deafness and mutism, appeared primarily among the men, neurasthenic symptoms such as nightmares, insomnia, depression or disorientation were more common among officers.[37] As he developed the theory of shell shock, the psychiatrist W.H.R. Rivers began to see clearly how the differences in education and socialisation of officers and men accounted for this variation in symptoms. The public school officer behaved in ways which showed mental effort to repress traumatic memories. The rank-and-file soldier, less able to control his raw instinct for survival, was closer to a child.[38]

The medical debate, with its scientific qualifications, was taken up by public opinion and the media in an oversimplified way. During 1915 and 1916 'shell shock' entered the national consciousness. The very vagueness of the term made it a useful, neutral, physical label for a psychological condition that could be accommodated within an ideology of patriotism focused on courage and heroism. The complex reality of the war neurosis being investigated by doctors, meanwhile, passed over the heads of the public. People were thankful to find there was a term they could use for emotional stress and breakdown in combat.[39]

Shell shock once diagnosed was always seen as an illness by the medical profession and those who made reference to it on the Home Front. Even in the worst conditions only a minority of men broke down psychologically. Shell shock was also viewed as largely curable, though it was accepted that, as with other illnesses, there could be relapse. Its victims no doubt often felt guilty. But British psychologists during the Great War never associated shell shock with dereliction of duty.[40]

Herbert Trench, our only letter writer to suffer shell shock, broke down early in the war while the national confusion about what exactly the condition was persisted. His story, told in a series of increasingly desperate letters from the Front, is illuminating. It illustrates the process of breakdown in a young man whose bravado had been unwavering. He found it possible to be needy and plaintive to his two sisters Margot and Cesca, though he could not let the mask of bravado slip with others in the family. Above all, his mother had to be placated: in his first postcard on 26 September he asked Cesca to 'impress on Mother how absolutely safe I am and shall be'. Yet the first family member to receive hints of how he was feeling was, significantly, another young woman of his own generation. Amy Howard was just a little older than Herbert. On a postcard which Clare saw, also dated 26 September, he related that, though not yet near the firing line, he had talked 'with a Black Watch man, who said amongst other things, that it was more like hell than anything else.'[41]

Herbert was soon loading Cesca with demands. He started with reading matter, especially poetry; quinine for his cold, zinc ointment, cigarettes and baccy. The first hint of real stress came with the specific request for Marich cigarettes on 14 October when he was near the front line in Belgium. He was asking for these since 'they are mostly opium'. On 29 October he reminded Margot of the address in the City of London where they could be obtained. It must have been a day or two earlier that Herbert was first under fire. 'Just come in,' he wrote in an undated incoherent note, 'we lay low in soaking rain in the trenches and betted on which of the six the next one would fall on – shell, I mean.' He requested Oxo cubes and meat 'tabloids', adding, 'I hear there is a chocolate famine in England – if this is so peppermint creams are the next best thing.'[42]

When he wrote to Margot on the 29th, Herbert summarised his condition after two spells in the front line and 'some pretty strenuous marching'. He was 'fairly fit except for the deuce of a cold and general rottenness'. His eight pages expressed gratitude for chocolate and baccy which was 'absolutely topping' and for copies of the *Irish Times* and *Punch*. He 'hoped to goodness' his brother Arthur remained out of it all, posted to Shimla in India. This first full account of front-line duty managed to be poetic as well as graphic. Herbert spoke of the last two miles of the five-mile night march there through the 'land of snipers' and the frozen or slushy fields which were 'damnable to march on'. 'As soon as it is light you look around and see the German trenches, perhaps eighty or perhaps a hundred yards off.' At eighty yards, Herbert reckoned, you were 'safe against shelling and shrapnel' which would go overhead while at a hundred, he believed, 'you are more or less safe against a raid'. 'Anyhow,' he continued, 'you stick there, shoot, eat and sleep and swear at the older men as the case may be till you're relieved . . . then you march back, feeling nearly dead and see the rosy fingered dawn over the purple hills and realise that for that alone, life is worth living.' 'Personally,' he declared with masterly understatement, 'I do not mind how soon this is over.'

Herbert Trench was coping but he was becoming worn down by insomnia. 'I want some sulphonal,' he told Margot on 29 October, instructing her that Burroughs & Wellcome's was 'the most convenient', in five gram tablets. Or if that was difficult she should send five gram Veronal. He seems to have known a good deal about barbiturates then available for insomnia. 'One can't do this sort of thing without sleeping,' he insisted.[43] A few days later he still had the sense of humour to write a postcard to Reggie signed Herbert St Omer, which was a cunning dodge to pass the censor and reveal his whereabouts.[44]

Herbert's next letter to Margot, on 15 November, made no mention of the insomnia but hinted, in a narrative account of a trench-digging fatigue, how working under shellfire was affecting his nerves. The day before he had paraded at 6.30 after cold bacon and bread, setting out along roads 'comparable to an Irish bog and no exaggeration with a sixty pound pack'. They started digging, 'half hour after shells drop over mostly "coalboxes" and a little shrapnel – lie low and go on digging'. More shrapnel meant an hour's wait 'lying in a soaking ditch till one's frozen' on the march home. There was no food on return, just 'cleaning a rifle thick with clay'. The last straw was 'except for charity of others no baccy'. Nor was there a parcel for him in the mail 'just in'. This more desperate letter ended with a plea, given four underlinings, for chocolate, baccy and matches. He also asked, via Margot, for cash in five-franc notes from his mother Isabel.[45]

Writing a postcard to his young cousin Sheelah Trench and to his brother Reggie at Berkhamsted a few days later Herbert managed to compose himself. The bravado was back. 'We're having a great time out here – a night attack a short time ago and trench digging under intermittent artillery fire – best time I've ever had,' he told Sheelah. Her father was so impressed he forwarded this to his sister Isabel, Herbert's mother, commenting 'these young people seem to write in a marvellous cheery strain'. Experience of shellfire was 'quite entertaining', Herbert assured Reggie, and their night attack had 'a sort of "Brocks benefit" Crystal Palace touch'. He was sure the war could not last another year. German casualty figures were reported as enormous. They were said, he had heard, to be entrenching Waterloo for a last stand. The downfall 'of another Emperor' there, repeating 1815, would be 'curious'.[46]

By late November press reports of the Honourable Artillery Company in action were alarming his mother and sisters living in Dublin. Isabel sent a friend in London to the War Office to ask if Herbert had been wounded. On 28 November Cesca recorded sending off 'another pound of spare lumps of chocolate . . . and one and a half pounds gingerbread, soap and matches'.[47]

When he began his next letter to Cesca on 14 December Herbert was low. He was just back from three days in the front line: 'water and mud up to one's knees practically all the time – try and realise it'. Nor had the sulphonal arrived. 'I've got nerves,' Herbert now confessed. The silver lining was new letters from both sisters assuring him they would not stop writing: 'the mail is the one thing one lives for out here'.

This letter was continued on the 20th after a spell of better weather in the trenches and a spate of parcels from the family. Herbert had received the sulphonal, marble sugar and Vaseline for his gun. He was suddenly hugely grateful for everything but it was apparent that he was warding off collapse by forced optimism. The battalion had been reduced in less than three months, he reported, from 800-odd to about 450 fighting men. The Allied cavalry would soon see it through, he asserted, keeping the Germans running 'until the final debacle on the line across Waterloo'. 'It is <u>very nearly</u> over now,' he dreamed.[48]

About ten days after he sent this letter Herbert's incipient shell shock turned to complete collapse. Mercifully for him, this took the form of a physical collapse. He simply fell out on the march back from three days and nights in the front line. He was not at once missed, since he fell into a ditch and lay there unconscious for some hours, till an ambulance travelling the road picked him up. He spent one day at the military hospital on the coast at Wimereux. The casualty form recorded his transfer to England on 2 January with the diagnosis 'insomnia as nervous debility'.[49] Briefly in hospital in Leicester, Herbert discharged himself on the 5th, contacting Reggie. It was he who informed the family in Dublin that Herbert was home. There was panic in the household while it was assumed that he was injured, but a wire soon came from Herbert himself with the message 'nervous breakdown only trouble, home Sunday'. Ten days of cosseting and an Irish doctor's attentions cleared up the bronchitis contracted from his hours in a French ditch and restored his mental stability.[50]

On 28 January Herbert attended Reggie's wedding to Clare Howard at Orpington (plate 9). His twenty-eight days' leave had almost expired. He took advice from his uncle Jack Mackie, whose Berkshire home had become effectively his base in England since his mother's return to live in Dublin the previous summer. His uncle, a magistrate, agreed to sponsor him for a temporary commission in the mechanical transport section of the Army Service Corps. He applied on 2 February, attaching a testimonial of his three-year apprenticeship from the chief engineer of the South Eastern and Chatham Railway. On 18 February his employers until August 1914, the London & North Western Railway, confirmed his satisfactory performance. Herbert claimed experience in driving cars and a steam engine and riding motorcycles. He had owned, he stated, three motorcycles and two cars. The last motorcycle, the Triumph, was the one abandoned smashed in a French ditch in November 1914.[51]

Herbert, mad on motors, believed he could serve the country best by managing an army transport depot (plate 5). He hoped this would be well behind the lines. After satisfactory interviews, a shell-shock victim who had made a rapid recovery, he was formally recommended for a commission on 28 February 1915. His territorial service expired and he took up his second military career a month later. There was initial training for his work with the Army Service Corps (ASC) at Aldershot from April to June. On 16 July 1915, full of enthusiasm for his new job, Herbert wrote to his mother on board ship. From Boulogne, he explained, he would go to brigade headquarters at Armentières to take up his new duties.[52]

The Somme brought home to the military authorities in 1916 the magnitude of the threat mental collapse posed to the war effort through severe wastage of manpower. It was at last accepted in the BEF in the autumn of 1916 that shell shock was a genuine disorder with psychological not physical origins. An important policy shift was implemented. This was proposed by Charles Myers and Gordon Holmes, respectively now consulting psychologist and consulting neurologist to the BEF.[53] Four receiving centres on the Western Front were set up for diagnosis and initial treatment. Holmes did crucial work on the various states of shell shock, its association with states of exhaustion and the intensity of battle and the rarity of its symptoms in soldiers seriously wounded. Policy on who should be evacuated was refined. During Passchendaele the epidemic of shell shock was arrested. The acute management strategy practised there was temporary respite from battle, along with sleep, food and some comfort, followed by return to active duty. Only 10 per cent of shell-shock patients were now being returned to England. There remained the issue of relapse. Holmes claimed that 10 per cent of casualties relapsed once and 3 per cent twice or more.[54]

Some regimental medical officers quickly showed a pragmatic understanding of shell shock. Captain Chevasse, in the Liverpool Scottish Regiment, had a sixth sense for noticing men about to collapse. He began having vulnerable men removed from the front line to rest in fatigue companies behind the lines early in 1915. But he could pick out the shirker. Hearing that a Gordon Highlander had shot himself in the leg he poured iodine into it. 'The shrieks of the poor man,' we are told, 'were awful.'[55] Resort to self-infliction of wounds was common enough among men feeling close to the edge. There was the favourite old trick of shooting one's finger off when cleaning one's rifle.[56] Thomas Marks, in a memoir in old age, recalled seeing men 'stand on the fire-step and hold both arms above the parapet in the hope of getting hit'. He believed there had been those who 'got to England with as cushy wounds as they could have desired'.[57]

Max Plowman was seen by his biographer as 'a generous and enthusiastic but often tormented spirit'. He commented on variations in the attitude of medical officers to shell shock in *A Subaltern on the Somme*, a generally careful and unsensational memoir published in 1927, based on letters and diaries.[58] Recounting his experience as a young officer at High Wood in August 1916, he found one of his men, a survivor of Gallipoli where he had suffered a fever, 'lying on the ground breathing heavily and apparently unconscious'. The Medical Officer (MO) pushing him with his foot, declared it was 'just wind up, the bloody young coward ... don't waste my time with these damned scrim-shankers'. Plowman and his sergeant kept their eye on the youngster, giving him 'all the easiest jobs'. Predictably, he had a similar attack after a long march: 'the battalion now having changed doctors, I send for the new M.O. who orders the boy to hospital'.[59]

Some doctors suffered a degree of shell shock themselves and were subsequently much more sympathetic to others. James Dunn, MO with the Royal Welch Fusiliers, had seen training and discipline as the invariable answer for men he thought were skulking or 'trench-shy'. But, finding himself sheltering in a shell hole at Passchendaele, he realised with dismay that his own nerve was failing. The emotional strain of surviving, for more than two years, fresh intakes of all ranks who were subsequently killed or wounded had told on him in the end.[60]

During 1915, 1916 and 1917 references to shell shock became common in letters and diaries. There was complete moral neutrality and considerable sympathy for the victim in these accounts. Twice in the autumn of 1915, Graham Greenwell told his mother about incidents when 'the Huns put a shell plum into the trench'. The first time, a sergeant was buried by earth, had to be dug out and had 'gone a bit off his head'. On the second occasion, the bombardment was prolonged. Graham himself felt 'most frightfully shaken and pretty rotten but after about half an hour it passed off'. This time 'a bomber broke down' seeing men around him killed and wounded. 'Bucked to death' with his lads later at Ovillers on the Somme, Graham admitted that one of them had to be removed from the line to the depths of his headquarters dugout when he 'suddenly went groggy with shell shock'. 'He can't keep his hands still,' he narrated sadly, 'and waggles them the whole time.'[61]

In May 1915 Rifleman Reginald Prew described how he and his chum George were acting as 'bomb carriers' running the gauntlet in the line at Festubert. He noticed someone lying on the ground who 'every time a gun went off would jump about one foot in the air'. He checked and found it was George, 'suffering from shell shock, his nerve had evidently failed him running across the open'. Writing home in April 1916, Alec Reader mentioned the 'rotten experience' of one of his draft, about twenty-five years old, who 'lost his nerve and laid in the mud groaning and crying the whole time'.

Innes Meo was a second lieutenant who recorded his own gradual break-down in a series of tiny diaries on the Somme. 'I shall probably get the sack as my nerves are no good,' he wrote on 24 September. He saw the doctor the next day, survived a 'terrible bombardment' and by the 30th was in the casualty clearing station. 'Officer in next bed with awful shell shock, also airman with broken nerves,' he wrote, 'God what sights.' At Messines, Lieutenant A.G. May noted two soldiers going 'completely goofy' during an attack. One of them cradled 'a tin hat as though it were a child' and was seen smiling and laughing in the midst of falling shells.[62]

Bert Fereday, who reached the Front aged eighteen in May 1918, confessed to his minister in Wimbledon in August that the horrors of seeing men killed around him, bandaging wounded pals and getting them to safety after a push had left him with incipient shell shock. It was difficult to compose a letter home since 'I have had such a horrible shaking and have not quite got over it'. 'If only everyone knew of the horrors of this war it wouldn't last another five minutes,' he insisted, 'but until its over we have got to stick it'. Yet he could not conceive facing another day like the one he had just had 'with the same fortitude or steady nerve'. Had he not been killed the next day he was a predictable shell-shock victim.[63]

Everyone's understanding of the problem of nerves and of the universal vulnerability to shell shock increased as the war went on. In a long, reflective letter to his brother Phillip after the Battle of Loos, Sir Oliver Lyle explained how he himself had lost his nerve for three days and found himself, during sleepless nights, getting up to check everything each time a shot was fired. 'Luckily we were relieved soon after and I recovered,' he explained, 'but at one time I thought I was going to break down.' Previously he had scoffed when apparently fit men told him about the problem 'but I now know that one seems quite fit but feels perfectly bloody'.[64]

Officers learnt to watch themselves, their fellows in the mess and their men in the trenches for signs of cracking up. Geoffrey Donaldson reported two officers sent back from the line with nerves in July 1916 'as it was essential that they should not be near the men while the sort of ague which is the visible and outward sign of the disease was upon them'. The Tommies' nerves, he argued, depended so much on the strength of mind of those leading them.[65] 'Poor old Gordon has had a breakdown after all his experiences of July 1st,' reported

Lance Spicer from the Somme. He himself was still fit, he said at the start of his letter but he ended it admitting he was 'not quite up to the mark' so was being sent to hospital for 'a rest cure'. Writing a fortnight later from an 'Officers Rest Station' twelve miles behind the line, he described his symptoms, suspiciously like incipient breakdown, as 'sundry aches, headaches, neuralgia etc'. He enjoyed the quiet and a charming garden to lie about in, declaring 'all that is wrong is that I am a bit run down and tired'. He recovered and was soon back on duty.[66]

Robert Hermon had 'the whole show to run' when the Northumberland Fusiliers assisted the Canadians in the attack on High Wood on the Somme, because his second in command collapsed the first evening with a nervous breakdown: 'I had to put him to bed where he was till morning. Poor bloke he wasn't very fit and he was one of two who came through the 1st July and it wasn't to be wondered at'. Robert believed the strain the Somme was imposing on the BEF should be told directly in England. 'I saw a man of mine with genuine shellshock,' he related to Ethel, 'he was deaf and dumb and though 500 yards away and held by two men he was shaking so you could see his arms going continually.'[67]

Survivors' worst memories after the war were often of times when they came very close to breakdown. Charles Carrington was one who sought to deal with such memories with ruthless candour. Twice, in *A Subaltern's War* in 1929 and in *Soldier from the Wars Returning* in 1965, he engaged in harrowing self-analysis in relation to the assault which he led with a company of the Royal Warwickshires at Passchendaele in 1917. On his worst day he came close to total and humiliating breakdown. He was under constant shelling in a circular pit five feet in diameter with two other subalterns, one of whom had to steady him when a shell burst close enough to shower them with clods of earth and splinters. But he recovered his nerve. In retrospect, writing forty years later, he described himself as having led his company as a kind of zombie. He was able to observe of himself that he 'was a quite good company commander and kept up appearances except when, rarely, the live man took charge in a state of high panic'. Yet courage was born from somewhere. Carrington won an MC that day and was promoted Captain.[68]

It is likely that Herbert Trench confided something of his experience of falling into that French ditch to his older brother. Reggie must have supported his efforts to get back to France. Herbert undoubtedly did well in the ASC with the 21st Siege Battery at first, earning promotion to Lieutenant in March 1916. In a progress report to Cesca in September 1915 he was confident and optimistic: 'my company is certainly one of the best out here . . . we've just dug a well, built a rifle range, got our own canteen and I'm now laying a cement floor'. The only grouse was that he had not managed to get a car of his own yet. But he would have one by Christmas 'if I have to steal it'.

Herbert had won credit the previous week handling the movement of some large guns from England into their positions. His colleagues let the guns get ditched when taking an inadvisable short cut. Herbert went to the rescue. 'General Currie and the gunners were awfully pleased,' he told Cesca.[69] He sent her a sketch of Ypres, done he said, from his 'bathroom', with one of his lorries, 'not a beetle' he assured her, moving towards the Cloth Hall.[70] He had fought back after his experience in December 1914 and could console himself that he was contributing to the war effort in his responsible transport role.

On leave in early 1916 Herbert enjoyed family visits in London. He was given responsibility on his return for managing a base for the motor transport company of the 15th Corps heavy artillery outside Ypres. For his hut, he built a brick open fireplace with help from his sergeant. Cesca sent him crocus bulbs, which he planted outside. Uncle Benny had promised him a gramophone and 'some decent records', he announced on 20 February. There was a hint of future trouble in the comment that the Huns had been dropping some shells uncomfortably close to him, just across the road from his hut by the lorry park. Beyond that, he ended cheerfully, 'there's nothing doing'.[71]

In his next letter to Margot in July Herbert described his compound and sent her a plan of it: the park for thirty-three lorries, the canteen, men's huts, the stores, ammunition dump, his hut and private bathroom. There was 'feverish activity – ammunition stunts for various people'. Rats were bothering him. More seriously, he was finding it essential to play the gramophone to drown the sound of gunfire. There was a strafe going on and he had Tchaikovsky's 1812 Overture at full volume as he wrote.[72]

It is not clear what exactly caused Herbert's relapse. But in September 1916 he was invalided home. His service papers include notes on a medical examination on 6 September. Herbert confessed that one of his motorcycle accidents had caused a head injury shortly before the war. He also said there had been marriages of first cousins in his family for some generations. He described his nervous breakdown in 1914. The doctor, noting reports of his having recently become 'very eccentric and nervy with insomnia', suggested that 'rest and a change of climate' might be sufficient for a second recovery. Herbert was treated briefly in a London mental hospital, escaping when he was allowed to the magazines and companionship of the Cavendish Club.

Herbert obtained permission to visit his family in Ireland.[73] In October he heard that the War Office's Medical Board had decided he was 'permanently unfit for general service overseas or at home'. He pleaded that he had been promised two months' sick leave and was confident he would be fit sooner than

5. Herbert Trench sketch 'Ypres Oct. 1915 From my bathroom!'

that. But, his appeal unavailing, the *London Gazette* announced on 12 October that Herbert Trench had relinquished his commission 'through ill health'. He was devastated. Herbert was just one of many such casualties. Yet his recovery on this second occasion was much as he himself predicted. By January 1917, he had obtained work in the Ministry of Munitions in Chiswick and he held down office work of this kind for the duration of the war. 'Herbert seems to have a job he likes, I hope he sticks to it,' Reggie commented from the Front in May 1917. Early the next year his indigent state led him to raid Reggie's wardrobe for decent clothes for the office. He could have neither his blue suit, nor his grey one, nor 'that green tweed one', Reggie told Clare firmly, but he could take 'that black coat and any collars and shirts that he wants'.[74]

It was five months after Herbert Trench left the Western Front that Reggie arrived there with the Sherwood Foresters. He had learnt about shell shock by observing his brother's two truncated episodes of service. When one of his fellow officers soon showed persistent nervous symptoms, his summary to Clare in September 1917 indicates how shell shock for him was simply another kind of illness: Captain Smith was 'ill again, nerves I'm afraid'. Reggie returned to the subject when writing to his mother in February 1918. His colleague Stebbing, the only other one of twenty-nine officers with the battalion for a full year, was going home for six months as 'war-worn'. Stebbing seemed all right to him but his well-earned break was a reminder, Reggie reflected, of 'how some fellows' nerves go'. He had been speaking the day before near the front line with a subaltern who 'suddenly started crying'. He was 'a great big healthy chap', who had seen much fighting: 'apparently his nerves have gone suddenly and I think only temporarily so I bundled him out of the trenches and gave him leave to go to Amiens for a day – he'll be alright in a week or two but at present it would be madness to expect him to do his duty'.[75]

The recognition of shell shock as a serious but often curable medical condition did not involve the repudiation of conventional standards of manliness. As they recovered from shell shock men like Herbert Trench did not lose their patriotic commitment or sense of duty. At one level, shell shock became a political metaphor which was much spoken of yet never received an objective or final definition. At another it was a very real disability that removed men temporarily or permanently from the Front, causing lasting damage to huge numbers of soldiers.[76]

Once shell shock had become an accepted fact the treatment of men's emotional distress in modern warfare would never be the same again. There was no way that the simple heroic Victorian and Edwardian ideology of manliness could survive intact. It had been established that fear was a basic, a constitutional, perhaps a universal reaction to war. Even the bravest might succumb. Any man's bank account of courage might run out. If, as shown here, fear was often discussed by men writing home in 1914–18, it became an obsessive theme in memoirs and the retrospective accounts of the Great War during the 1920s and 1930s.

One of the reasons for the immense and immediate success of R.C Sherriff's play *Journey's End* was that his argument was about the emotional costs of dutiful service. Here, in the breakdown through drink of an officer commanding his small dugout, was a hero with a troubled male identity. No Edwardian audience could possibly have tolerated such a stage hero. Yet this was an identity that by 1929 audiences found instantly recognisable. The hallmark of Stanhope's courage in Sherriff's play, instead of an unbending traditional stoicism, was emotional suffering. 'Sticking it out', he declared, was 'the only thing a decent man can do'.[77] This was how far the world had travelled during the Great War and after it.

CHAPTER 6

'A Certain Sense of Safety with Him'
Leadership

His men must surely love him in view of all he did for them, Reggie Trench's besotted mother insisted when he had been four months in the trenches. 'No, you are quite wrong,' he replied, 'the men do <u>not love</u> or even like me but I think they will follow me.' 'Very few men and I'm not one of them can keep good discipline and popularity.' Reggie explained, 'I think I have the first but I know I have not got the second.' A couple of weeks earlier, Reggie had told Clare of an incident which exemplified the respect in which the men held him. He had fixed up a 'very good shelter . . . large and airy with a shelf of earth to lie upon' as his company headquarters. Some of the men were improving this makeshift home while he took a nap. Waking briefly he heard the man in charge say 'come on lads: we must make the bloody skipper comfortable; he deserves it.'[1]

Officers, NCOs and men on the Western Front were caught up in a web of relationships permeated by trust and dependence. Ernest Smith made each man 'tell me his name which I compared with the rolls' when he took command of his company in the Buffs. 'I can see it will be some time before I know them all,' he reflected.[2] Hierarchy was taken as read. This was the governing principle of management in the British Expeditionary Force from the brigade down to the platoon. But trust humanised day-to-day life. It was 'wonderful the things some of our lads think of', commented Reggie, telling of a wounded man in great pain who had asked him to see that his fellow officer got a revolver he had lent him: 'this chap had an arm and a leg broken and some damage to his head and yet could think of that.'[3]

Captain Edwin Venning found it comforting that his affection for his men was reciprocated. 'Oh, I am so pleased,' he wrote in May 1915, 'my Quarter-Master Sergeant (QMS) was asked to go for promotion yesterday . . . but he heard it meant leaving me for another company and refused to take it.' His servant had refused a similar opportunity 'because he would not be able to look after me'. 'I think I know the ways and peculiarities of every man of mine,' he reflected: 'it surprises them and they like it and work well for it'.[4] Charlie May's emotions were similar when he found his QMS reluctant to leave, declaring 'I was a leader of men and he would never feel the same under any other captain'. He wrestled with an innate modesty in the privacy of his diary, writing 'please God I may always justify half such faith. It's marvellous. I cannot understand it . . . I am such an ordinary sort of clout-head'.[5]

There was pride in trusting relationships across the BEF's hierarchy and much genuine warmth between many rank and file and their officers. Cyril Newman thought the world of Major O'Shea, 'a jolly good sort, kindhearted and generous and straight'. Setting aside his censorship role, he let Cyril seal his letters home before initialling them. Cyril was an incessant letter writer and obviously trustworthy. Just as well, he noted, in May 1918 when he had written fifty-one letters in the last fortnight. His officers, 'very decent not to complain', did a lot of initialling that month.[6] Lieutenant W.E. Charles wrote home in March 1916, 'I can't express my admiration and love (I really mean it) for Tommy Atkins. The way he treats everything is wonderful, the names he gives things is extraordinary, you hear him talking of rubber-headed shells because you can't hear them until they burst'. Charles was deeply affected by his task of censoring letters, which gave him insight into the minds of those he commanded: 'I feel like crying when censoring letters which begin "Dear Wife and Kiddies" or " Darling Mother". It may seem superfluous but every word is really meant'.[7]

Many officers confessed to learning a great deal from reading men's letters. Ernest Smith found the job of censorship 'both amusing and sometimes a little touching'. It made him 'the more anxious to approach them as separate individuals whenever possible'.[8] Captain Parkin described the letters he censored after the Battle of Cambrai as 'offering a peep into the soul of those who had acted so bravely for three days of battle'.[9] It is easy to dismiss officer attitudes as patronising, which they were not meant to be. Second Lieutenant H.A. Munro copied typical opening lines into his diary. The most common he reckoned, and one that Yvo Charteris also commented upon, was 'just a line to say I am still in the pink'. Munro was struck by directness of expression such as 'Dear Mother, I am getting on alright, but life out here is a pure bugger!' Among the 'wonderful conventions' Yvo noted was telling a sweetheart not to forget there was 'someone somewhere in France'. Latent snobbery was always there but seldom became explicit. Seeing his men as 'all good fellows and very keen', Graham Greenwell could not resist slipping in a mention of his repugnance at how they 'perspire freely!'[10]

At the same time, letters written by the rank and file were often a source of encouragement when officers spotted remarks about themselves. Wilbert

Spencer, seeking to reassure his father about how he was doing, said 'I try to cheer them up.' 'I think they like me,' he added, 'anyhow it appeared so in one of their letters which I had to censor.' Graham Greenwell was pleased to find his men saying he seemed 'mighty pleased' to be with them. When he was mourning the loss of his colleague Ernest Dashwood, who was killed by a rifle grenade in Ploegsteert Wood, he also found it 'very touching' that letters home from his men reflected his grief at this loss.[11]

Young officers were often more than ready to respect age and experience among NCOs. Yvo Charteris, just landed near Wimereux in September 1915, hastened to tell his sisters about his 'charming platoon-sergeant Sergeant Stagg'. 'Few people can have seen much more of this war,' he remarked. Since the previous August he had been 'through the retreat, Ypres, Givenchy, Festubert, Neuve-Chapelle'. 'I shall greatly rely on him,' Yvo felt certain. Stagg himself later wrote of his pleasure at 'how much Mr Charteris thought of me' and the interest he had taken 'in giving him the benefit of my experience'.[12] Ernest Smith, in a similar manner, developed a close friendship in his first weeks in the Buffs with Sergeant Mould, who was much older than him, and he confided in Mould about his family. 'My platoon sergeant is a splendid fellow and takes great care of me,' he told his mother; 'the difficulty is to persuade him to sleep at all.' His mother sent Mould cigarettes. He 'asked me very especially to thank you', wrote Ernest. 'I think he was greatly impressed.'[13]

If hierarchy was the framework and social divisions always underpinned it, officers quickly learnt that it was empathy which secured their leadership role. Francis Snell, trained by the Inns of Court OTC at Berkhamsted, told his wife how he totally cast aside lessons on 'the proper deportment of an officer before his men' that he had learnt there. At the Front it was men's courage, cheerfulness and humanity that drove him to break these rules. 'One may stand in relation to these men as a father or an elder brother,' he explained to her, but 'quite as often the boot is on the other foot, even as officers and men'. Any bluff would be detected: 'they know what you are worth and if you are fit to lead them they will follow you. But even if not, and you are honest and sympathetic and do your best – your level best – they'll lead you.'[14]

Selfishness or weakness among officers was invariably found out. One captain in the Liverpool Scottish regiment was remembered for his 'ridiculous habit of going about in the trenches in an almost crouching position'. This 'drew ribald remarks when observed by some of the old sweats'. It was easier for public school men to escape derision they may have sometimes deserved where a clearly defined social class barrier was present between officers and other ranks. But the Liverpool Rifles and Scottish were both newly raised regiments. Local men from middle-class urban districts who knew each other from business and social life had enlisted together in these Pals battalions. In this case many in the ranks had the credentials to lead and could perfectly well have been effective officers. This meant those who were commissioned and set in authority had to display high standards of leadership to meet their scrutiny.[15]

Leadership was built upon paternalism and deference, but it was integrity that counted in the stresses of everyday existence. Yet although officers were tested to the hilt, this testing seldom occurred during leadership in battle, an exceptional event. The conduct of raiding, wiring or digging parties more regularly put officers on their mettle. But it was the weary marches to and from the front line for periods of trench duty that gave structure to Western Front service. Junior officers for the most part were domestic managers of an army in the field. Their performance at this task is explored in detail in the next chapter, on their care of their men.

R.C. Sherriff's account of his recruitment from a grammar school background to the officer class was written in 1928. It reflected the specific perspective of his own eventual commission, once the war had winnowed the early mass of public school entrants to the officer class. His father had scrimped and saved to send him to Kingston Grammar School, and Sherriff then found work as an insurance clerk.[16] When *Journey's End* proved a hit on the London stage he realised that some thought he gave too much attention to the public schools, either glorifying them or discrediting them. He had written, though, with no axe to grind and had hardly ever met anyone from a public school until he joined the army. If he had cut public school boys out of *Journey's End*, he declared, 'there wouldn't have been a play at all'. He never pretended that all officers came from public schools but his memories were coloured by having worked with many who had.

In a classic statement of how leadership was exercised in the Great War, Sherriff argued that junior officers 'played the vital part in keeping the men good-humoured and obedient in the face of their interminable ill treatment and well-nigh insufferable ordeals'. As he grew older, he saw British society change. So, in 1968, it was with conscious nostalgia that Sherriff wrote of a time when class distinctions were recognised by everyone 'and accepted without resentment so long as they were not abused'. The deference of the Western Front was under intense scrutiny by the 1960s: the humble workman had been 'content to obey a foreman who had risen from his own class so long as the boss was socially a cut above the foreman'. By the same token, Sherriff explained, privates obeyed non-commissioned sergeants and the sergeant majors. Tommies saw in officers that mysterious 'something more' which they could not define in words but which, he believed, originated in the public school ethos.

Yet close personal relationships, developed through working together, always cut across the officer–ranks divide. Cyril Newman often spoke in his letters to Winnie of the Medical Officer in the Queen Victoria's Rifles, Captain Clarke, who befriended him. During the Somme, he explained, it was only with difficulty 'through the kindness of officers especially the M.O. that I am able to get a letter to you'. In reserve a year later, Clarke invited Cyril to use his hut 'for writing and reading', to 'just come in and sit down', whether he was there or not. 'We have had several talks on religious and other matters', Cyril related. Clarke once said 'I admire you Newman', confiding personal matters such as his devotion to his mother. Clarke was proud of her descent from Sir Thomes Picton, who fought with Wellington in the Peninsular War.[17]

Junior officers, R.C. Sherriff stressed, 'led from personal example, from their reserves of patience and good humour and endurance'. Winning men's respect involved much more than sharing their physical privations. The key was 'an understanding of their spiritual loneliness'. These boys, often just eighteen, he remembered, 'were only happy, perhaps, when they were on sentry duty alone, with the moon and stars for their companions'. He recalled how he would chat when visiting them. 'If you could break through their shyness, they would sometimes talk to you of their homes and you could lead them on to tell you of their work and small achievements, their hopes and ambitions if, one day, they returned.' These conversations stuck in his memory: 'you might be able to help them see a glimmer of light at the end of the dark tunnel that enclosed them'.

Enlistment meant surrender of individuality, giving oneself up to the army machine. The Tommy expected dedicated leadership in return, 'an officer who thought for him' as Sherriff put it; 'better still an officer who thought with him'. Private Horace Bruckshaw's cautious approval in his diary of 'several new young officers' who joined his battalion in July 1916 is instructive: 'they seem rather nice chaps if they are not spoilt'. Revealing how he came to find himself on a wiring party though very tired and shaky during the Somme, Jack Sweeney explained that Mr Kirk had asked for volunteers. He was asked by name and agreed, since 'he was a gentleman any of us would follow anywhere, the bravest and best officer in the regiment'.[18] It was fortunate, Sherriff concluded his analysis, that the great majority of officers with whom he worked did prove worthy of the trust placed in them.[19]

Superior living conditions was the outstanding privilege enjoyed by officers. This above all, with its degree of protection from shelling, was what the men coveted. Officers were usually relatively warm and dry. 'The worst billet is better than the best bivouac,' as Robert Hermon put it.[20] 'The great advantage about this village is that you have bags and bags of fuel,' related Billie Nevill in November 1915. Men of the East Surreys were systematically demolishing a 'pretty little village' for the officers' benefit. 'You live in one house and send your servant next door to fetch the bathroom ceiling in for your early morning fire,' he declared insouciantly.[21] Officers could take for granted some kind of shelves and boxes to store personal possessions. Reggie Trench described 'many flowers in empty jam jars' around him in the company headquarters dugout. Such trappings of domesticity mattered.[22] It was wholly different for the Tommies. They conveyed the exigencies of their more makeshift domesticity with patient humour. Their dugout had a board over it, Cyril Newman wrote from Carnoy, which read 'Sanatorium. Fresh Air treatment. Plain food (if any). Plenty of hard work provided.'[23]

Camaraderie and better living conditions made life, even in the trenches and immeasurably so in billets, not just bearable but often enjoyable for officers. Letters show how privileged they were in the pleasures of good food and drink. His promotion to Major and second in command of his battalion in July 1917 enabled Reggie Trench to expand his role in the social life of his officers' mess. He saw mess etiquette as a deeply serious matter, taking it upon himself to give the subalterns a lecture on the subject 'as they are a little casual at present'. He arranged for wine to be sent over from the cellar laid down in Kent by his wife's father. 'I think I shall broach that case,' he told her when General Romer was coming to dine. The dinner was 'conspicuously successful', with 'fizz' provided by the new commanding officer, Lieutenant Colonel H.R. Gadd, as well as his wine. The evening ended riotously: 'we had blindfold boxing which was very amusing'. Reggie's colleague Captain Stebbing 'went quite mad, knocked two holes in the wooden wall of the mess hut, charged the table where the General was sitting, knocked a candle over on to the Brigadier's best jacket and a whisky and soda that went up his sleeve!'[24]

In June 1915 Graham Greenwell and his friend Conny dined in their village billet with the battalion transport officer and quartermaster. 'The woman cooked us a most recherche meal,' he told his mother; 'tonight I am giving a return dinner in my chateau and have spent fabulous sums on fresh fruit, cauliflowers at one franc each etc.' Another dinner party that summer was 'a great success and the cheese straws beautifully hot'. The Oxfordshire and Buckinghamshire Light Infantry had enlisted a cook from Oxford's Magdalen College. Graham quickly recruited him for his mess. At one of these social evenings 'the jam omelette and the mushrooms on toast contended for the chief honour'. When they celebrated the award of three Military Crosses in the battalion, oysters and Moët et Chandon 1906 appeared on a seven-course menu.

Menu

Hors D'oeuvres Russes .
Crème Zéro.
Saumon Mayonnaise .
Boeuf Rôti
Pommes de Terre .
Choux Natures.

Pouding Victoria.
Savours.

Café. Liquers. Cigares.

2/5 Batt The Sherwood. Foresters. Aug 18/17.

6. 2/5th Sherwood Foresters dinner menu, 18 August 1917.

Yet, proud of his own record while mess president, Graham was dismayed at the fall in standards when he retired. They were feeding 'like Gadarene swine on ration beef and tinned fruit without alteration', he wrote in June 1916. Things improved again the next month when, training up a new company 'from the wrecks of the old' after the first day of the Somme, Graham found a subaltern with fluent French willing to be mess president. He admired the way this man secured 'wines, pigeons, salads and fruits with the greatest ease'.[25]

Lance Spicer related the pleasures of trench life candidly. In December 1915, he wrote at length about a local teashop, previously a 'high-class patisserie', now for the use of officers only, in the battalion's rest area. The room was comfortable and had a good piano. Someone could usually be found to play. In September 1917, Lance was living a busy office life as acting Adjutant. But he usually managed to put his papers aside by 7.15, he explained, changing for a convivial hour and a half or so in the mess before dealing with evening correspondence until bedtime. That month he initiated a regimental guest night, 'hiring a complete dinner service from Amiens' and arranging for his divisional band and battalion bugles to entertain those who attended.[26]

Château de la Haie. 18.10.17.
.: MENU.

Oysters
Soup
Fish
Plaice
Ducks
Peas
Potatoes

Joint of Beef

Omelette

Anchovy Toast

Cheese
Biscuits
Coffee

7. 178th Brigade dinner menu, Château de la Haie, 18 October 1917.

In his early days at the Front, Billie Nevill sent his family colourful accounts of how well the officers lived. There was a good deal of toing and froing between the messes of the four East Surrey companies. 'I had breakfast with D company this morning,' he wrote on 10 August 1915, 'it was quite a rag.' They started with tinned peaches, 'then sardines and finally eggs and marmalade, all on the same plate of course.' He had an eye as he wrote on 'our mess waiter-cook-manager (a charming Tommy called Potter) mauling two fowls' for dinner that evening. Things were tougher when winter came. But there were still some treats for Billie. 'We're in an old chateau place,' he reported in December, 'and while we were feeding tonight the old Madam produced some ripping little glasses and two bottles of wine dated 1878.' In a break from the trenches at Flixecourt during February 1916, Billie and his fellow captains enjoyed 'a ripping champagne dinner at the Godbert restaurant' in Amiens. He sent home a schoolboyish sketch of the bus that transported them there, with nine grinning faces on the upper and lower decks.[27]

There was much support from senior officers for their juniors. Graham Greenwell received encouragement from the new Colonel of the battalion when he took command of his company in June 1916. He was told he was very

8. 'We all went into Amiens on Saturday'. Drawing by Billie Nevill, sent to his family, 17 February 1916.

young for the role: 'thank God the responsibility doesn't worry me and seems to give me a new interest in life,' he told his mother. Reggie Trench's first letters made references to how much he was learning from Colonel St Hill, commanding the 2/5th Sherwood Foresters. 'I <u>am</u> glad he is back again,' he wrote when St Hill returned from leave in May 1917. But the officer who taught him most was Brigadier T.W. Stansfield. He was 'a priceless man', Reggie declared, 'and knows a great deal – in fact more about practical soldiering than any man I have met'.

Reggie respected Lieutenant Colonel Gadd, who replaced St Hill, killed by a sniper, in July 1917. He was 'a very clever chap' with 'a great deal of practical experience so that we know we shan't be let down', he told his wife. But Reggie found him reserved. 'The CO never speaks about his people,' he replied when Clare pressed him about their relationship. There were nuances of deference between senior and junior officers. Conscious of what was now expected of him as second in command, Reggie was anxious when General Romer caught one man falling out on a battalion march. Yet 'he seemed quite bucked' with its general performance. 'The band were playing a tune on the pipes at the time – this I think braced him a bit.'[28]

Officers, as we have seen, could let off steam by descending into buffoonery after a convivial meal, but mess hospitality also oiled the wheels of the hierarchical command structure. Young and aspiring officers saw it as the quid pro quo for the encouragement and approval they won from those above them. Charlie May noted in his diary how he dined with his CO in the Manchesters when his company took over the line. He had his cook 'put on a regular beano for him: soup, fish, a joint, coffee, dessert'.[29]

Tensions emerged only when junior officers felt called to account unreasonably or there were fears of snooping. Graham Greenwell was livid when the General got back to the safe entrenchment of his office after a visit to his forward trenches where he had discovered men asleep with their boots off. The General sent a stinker via his Brigade Major. Graham decided to excuse his men by explaining he had ordered them to remove their boots 'for medical reasons'. His CO laughed about his being rebuked, suggesting he should 'have invented a better yarn than that'.[30] Reggie was once in the midst of a letter to his mother when a sentry reported 'a General on the horizon'. 'I must go and meet him as one never knows what these fellows will do if not carefully watched,' he told her. He took the precaution of having a sentry track him with field glasses, expecting an imminent visit to his lines.[31]

Several junior officers expressed their feelings about 'brass hats' who did not live up to the privileges of their rank: 'I cannot help feeling an officer makes a fatal mistake in not endeavouring to win respect and affection of those who

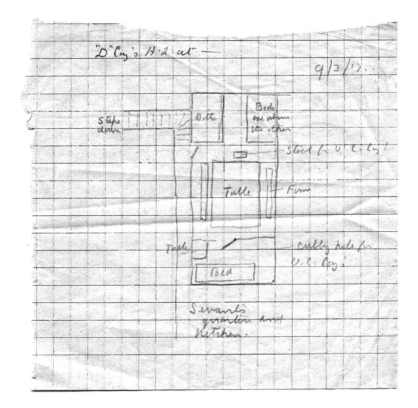

9. Reggie Trench's sketch of D Company headquarters, 9 March 1917.

serve under him – we are so ready to make a hero of him,' wrote Charlie May. As he learnt the rigours of the front line he became bitter about some of his senior officers. It was 'easy to order men here, there and everywhere whilst you sit in an easy chair in a warm chateau.'[32] 'I never once saw any of the Brigade or Divisional Staff come up to the trenches,' declared Gerald Burgoyne after five months in the trenches in Belgium. He was scathing about their ignorance of this 'terra incognita'.[33] After Loos, Lance Spicer told his mother 'the Divisional and Brigade Staffs were absolute washouts.'[34] Discussing the system of collection of names for mention in Sir John French's despatches in September 1915, Graham Greenwell groused about what a farce it was. 'All the Staff have their names sent in,' he realised, 'as does everyone who is miles away from the trenches.' In fact, he reckoned, 'the further back you get from the trenches the more promotion and plums you get!'[35]

Relationships between officers and their batmen epitomised the paternalistic tradition. This was a cap-doffing society, imbued with reverence for its rural and country house lifestyle. Every regimental officer had the right to a batman, essentially a manservant, with a wider remit than any single figure in the country house hierarchy: the batman was valet, butler and cook. In the first role he was forever organising clothes and polishing buttons, in the second he was on the staff of the mess, in the third his credit rose and fell with the quality of the meals he scratched together for officers.[36]

The documentation enables us to examine in some detail the special relationships between three of our officers and their batmen. In two cases the batmen came home when their masters were killed. Close friendship between an officer and his batman could arise in various ways. In the most straightforward case, Robert Hermon took his manservant with him from his home at Cowfold (plate 18). It never really occurred to him to do anything else. While the squadron was still in training the following April, Robert reported that he had discovered new skills in his previous valet: 'we are really doing top-hole at present', he wrote to Ethel.[37] For the next two years Robert and Buckin, as he called him, became very close. In billets at Noeux-les-Mines after a strenuous time at Loos, Robert reported it as 'a capital place to be in as Buxton calls me every morning at 6.30 and brings me a cup of tea and bread and butter and the previous day's *Daily Mail* which I read till 7 a.m.'[38]

It is hard to exaggerate the strength a personal friendship like this brought to men in war or its contribution to the morale of the British leadership. In April 1917, Ethel was reading each day in the papers about preparations for the Battle of Arras about to be launched. The intensity of her mental involvement with her husband across the Channel comes across in her letter of 12 April. 'Laddie my own', she wrote, 'it must be awful never getting a moment's peace from the noise of the guns.' Then she explained that the children had rigged up a tent to protect their goats from a snowstorm but it had just collapsed. 'I went and had a bit of a talk with Mrs Buckin today', Ethel confessed: 'she tells me you tried to persuade Buckin not to go up with you the last time you went up into the line but that he said "rats" or its equivalent in language more in accordance with discipline!' Mrs Buckin 'altogether was very nice and rather splendid about it'. 'She's been awfully good in that sort of way all through', reflected Ethel Hermon, remembering their numerous chats about how the war was going. Here, in microcosm, is the courage with which thousands of women coped back home while their men were in great danger.[39]

Neither Captain Charlie May nor Private Arthur Bunting was a career soldier. They met during the training period of the newly formed Manchester Pals Regiment in late 1914 and 1915. There was a certain social distance between them: Charlie was a freelance journalist and Arthur a coach builder and sprayer. But it was not enough to hinder two volunteers who hit it off from socialising together in those tense days of a war only just begun. Neither was imbued with or shackled by the traditions of the service, which precluded officers and men from that kind of social life together. First at Morecambe and Manchester then at Larkhill, Charlie and Arthur spent much time together in local pubs. Once, when they were tottering home somewhat the worse for drink along the canal near Old Trafford, Charlie lost his footing and slithered into the water. Realising he was missing, Arthur ran back, jumped in and hauled his drinking partner from the water. What could have been more natural than for Charlie and Arthur to cement their friendship and preserve their camaraderie before the regiment embarked at Folkestone in 1915 by Arthur becoming Charlie's batman? (plate 21)[40]

Albert Lane became Reggie Trench's batman when the Sherwood Foresters were in Ireland in 1916. By the time they crossed to France in early 1917, they knew each other very well indeed and had established a deep mutual loyalty. It was a great joy to Reggie that he had introduced Lane to Clare when they were on the Curragh, so he was free to write often about him in his letters knowing she trusted him as he did. Returning to battalion headquarters at 3.30 in the night after settling his company into forward positions in April 1917, Reggie was expecting to be out again for 'stand to' at 4 a.m. 'Now all I can remember,' he told Clare, 'is some conversation I had with the C.O. and eventually his calling my servant and Lane coming in and putting me to bed.' He later reflected on 'what luxury we live in' with 'my servant to put out my shaving tackle – water, towel etc, my groom to have my pony ready . . . our cook to provide us with meals.'[41] Reggie assumed that Lane would be one of the household at home. Corresponding about Clare's house hunting for the period when he expected to be back for a course at Aldershot in March 1918, he took it as read that Lane would live with him, Clare and Delle.[42]

The best testimony to how close Reggie and Albert became comes in a letter Lane wrote to Clare in the 1950s. This tells of how they once crawled under occupied German trenches and found large earthenware jars there, which Lane was then sent to collect with help from others. Ever resourceful, Reggie had realised that his men could use these jars 'to wash and wash up with'. Lane's reflection on this and other such expeditions is illuminating: 'I was always quite happy and felt a certain sense of safety while I was with him'. Writing more than thirty years later, Lane was wistful about what he lost on Reggie's death. 'We used to have such homely heart to heart talks in the evening while he was changing for dinner,' he recalled. 'Things would have been rather different for us all,' he told Clare, 'because he always promised I would go with him to Barracks.'[43]

The job was no soft option. 'I know the captain can't stand the sight of apricots,' says Mason the batman in *Journey's End*, fretting that when his canteen could not supply pineapple chunks he had to serve apricots instead. But it did carry certain appealing advantages. There was extra pay besides access to warmth, shelter, better food and exemption from many drills and parades. Servants lived in the officers' world, though on its lowest rung. They ran the gauntlet of taunts about their cushy number. The work could be seen as unremitting drudgery, yet for many who sought it the prize was honour and pride in serving an officer respected for his leadership and courage.[44] Their present cook, Ernest Smith told his mother in December 1915, 'shows – for a Tommy – the most remarkable ingenuity', when serving up 'what he was to call "devilled" chicken' for breakfast.[45]

Servants were not invariably happy with their lot. Alfred Hale wrote a long and bitter memoir about his life as a batman, 'the lowest and most despised being in the Royal Flying Corps', in 1917–18. George Coppard seems never to have learnt to be at ease with his officers in the Royal West Surrey Regiment. He was glad to go back to the ranks, noting in his memoir that, despite the job's good points, 'somehow I felt less than a complete soldier'. It was certainly easy to blame the batman when things got rough. Graham Greenwell, frustrated by five days without a proper wash in the trenches at Hébuterne, complained to his mother about the relentless shelling, 'which has prevented me having a shave this afternoon as my servant can't get near me or doesn't want to'.[46]

Timorous Jack Sweeney was glad to be taken on as a batman by his captain, whom he had come to respect while working with him on a machine gun at Neuve Chapelle. 'He is a gentleman, not one of those who are always bullying their men,' he wrote home, 'and he gets a lot more work done by treating men as men.' Jack's problem was that his obvious personal vulnerability left him open to ragging when he did the mess cooking. His Captain, he recorded, once knocked his hand when putting pepper in the soup, then at dinner 'he had the cheek to say there was too much pepper in the soup'. Other officers in the mess hid his utensils: 'they enjoy it very much if I happen to burn myself'. Yet, after a spell in the line, Jack was glad when he returned to his job in the mess in December 1915. If it was difficult cooking the kind of dinner expected of him 'working on an old pail with coke', it was 'better than sentry duty'.[47] He was sad when he had to report in August 1916 that 'my Captain the one who was such a gentleman' had been 'killed on July 1st in the Big Push'.

Evidence of deep affection and loyalty between officers and their servants abounds. Billie Nevill wrote about his orderly, Miller: 'I should love you to see him ... he's simply ripping. He's as tough as "bully" and as strong as ration cheese, man of few words, very quick and intelligent withal and possessed of that dog-like fidelity and cheery countenance which characterises the personnel of C Company.' Billie asked his mother to send Miller a decent parcel. He suggested 'lots and lots of cigarettes, cake, a pair of khaki mittens, a little chocolate and some Bull's eyes.' 'It came as a surprise to me and I cannot express my thanks enough,' Miller wrote in gratitude. He had been with Billie 'on several occasions within easy reach of the German trenches and as a man for pluck and courage he cannot be beaten'. Billie was equally fond of his batman Marker but ready to tear him off a strip for letting him down. 'I strafed Marker tonight till he moaned with remorse,' he wrote in April 1916, 'because the silly blighter had handed in all my blankets when we moved, because he thought they weren't mine!!'[48]

When he sent home 'one or two things which I gathered at the Somme', Lance Spicer included in the parcel a 'Hun helmet' which his servant Stancliffe had found. He assumed the Spicer family would be able to pass this on to his family. Stancliffe served him very well for nearly another two years. Then, on 25 April 1918, he was finishing a wash and shave outside his dugout 'when a shell pitched about five yards off him and he stopped most of it'. Lance, nearby, did not expect him to live more than a few minutes, but he got him to the casualty clearing station since he proved 'extraordinarily plucky'. Stancliffe died within a few days. 'He was a very nice little fellow (though uncommonly stupid at times) and I shall miss him very much,' Lance told his mother. He kept a photograph of Stancliffe and when he published his letters home in 1979 he included it in the book. Harold Copperwheat became Lance Spicer's new batman. Lance had known him since early in the war. He was a survivor of the first day of the Somme when, as he recalled on writing to Lance long after, in 1975, he went over the top at 7.30 a.m.[49]

After the war, Robert Hermon's wife Ethel wrote to the authorities explaining that his valet and batman Buxton had been in her employment before it began and offering him work 'as a motor driver immediately on his return to civilian life'. He brought up a family of seven of his own children at Cowfold, living there till after Ethel's death in 1930. This was simply a fulfilment of Robert Hermon's plans. In August 1916 he was turning his mind to how he could reward Buckin adequately for his devoted service. 'I would like you to have the cottage thoroughly whitewashed and repapered,' he told Ethel in a letter. In his mind their friendship had become a lifelong commitment.[50]

A batman, it was generally accepted, was supposed to stay by his officer's side in battle. Rowland Feilding had a batman who was always thirsting to 'pop over the sandbags' and insistent, if he ever had to do so, that 'he would like to be by my side'. 'This I think,' Feilding added, 'is not mere talk.' The special bond between an officer and his attendant servant was at its most powerful in battle or in talking about battle.[51]

Collections of letters home written by men from the ranks have a common pattern. The war was seen as a blurred succession of periods of activity and comparative inactivity. Their experience of it was essentially passive. Work was 'all day and every day'.[52] Life was a story of parades, inspections, marches, fatigues, digging or wiring parties and spells of sentry duty. Thus Horace Bruckshaw's diary was an account of repetitive and often irksome duties.[53] But the routines officers organised in support trenches or behind the lines were crucial to the overall war effort. Cyril Newman reflected on how the burden of duties in reserve could make one glad to be back in the front line. There were always rations and water to be carried up and digging had to be done. Officers spent much time on necessary management of routine tasks. Guarding lines of communication, cleaning rifles and billets, Newman noted, could feel irksome to 'soldiers who had come to fight for their country and their dear ones'. There was something heroic, he felt, about facing the enemy even if many soldiers went for months without seeing a German.[54]

Active leadership meant marching the men, taking charge of a wiring party, managing trench duty or going into battle. At such times for officers the war became dramatic, personal and heartfelt. 'The sense of having to see after others and set an example,' concluded Ernest Smith after his initiation into battle, 'prevents one from thinking much' about the shellfire.[55] Officers were usually positive about their leadership in the field. There was exhilaration in Charlie May's diary entries on a march in December 1915. After a long day's sixteen-mile trek on the 4th, he noted with satisfaction getting 'the men tucked in good clean straw'. On the 6th, A Company in the 22nd Manchesters was still going strong: 'they bucked up to pass the other companies swinging along at a great rate and singing'. Only he 'knew how done the poor devils were'.[56] When Graham Greenwell marched his men on a six-hour journey under a broiling sun, he was mounted. On foot beside them twice for an hour at a time to set an example, he found the march 'quite hot and unpleasant.' But it delighted him that only four men fell out, 'all absolutely exhausted and whacked, three of whom had only returned the night before from hospital with trench fever and enteric.'[57]

Reggie Trench was responsible for the march south to the Avion sector of the Front by the 2/5th Sherwood Foresters on 10 October 1917, since Colonel Gadd was on leave. His operation orders were meticulous. No man would be allowed to fall out 'without permission in writing from an officer' or to 'enter an ambulance without a written order by a Medical Officer'. He detailed one of the subalterns to lead the billeting party ahead of the battalion on bicycles or horses; another subaltern would lead a 'slow party', of those whom company commanders judged 'unable to march at the same rate as the battalion', in the rear.[58] Unfortunately the mayor of the first village where billets were needed had just died, so Reggie had to engage in much haggling to settle around

800 tired men after a long day. After a third day on the march he was able to speak with satisfaction: 'I am glad to say that not one man fell out'. They were into a 'fourth day of trekking and the men are a bit tired' but the remaining journey was shorter. His pride was at stake since, as he told Clare, he always had to report the numbers of men who fell out on the march to Brigade headquarters.[59]

'This morning I went up to the front trench with my Platoon in the grey and misty dawn,' wrote Graham Greenwell to his mother on 16 October 1915, 'so again I find myself in charge of two or three hundred yards of the British front.' His report could have been repeated by junior officers thousands of times over during the years from 1914 to 1918. The mist was still down at eleven o'clock as Graham scribbled at Hébuterne. The deathly quiet was often broken by the crack of a sniper who he knew was in the grass outside his wire. 'I have started one or two of my men on to answer him to keep him amused,' he explained.[60]

Reggie Trench gave his mother an almost lyrical description of his earlier sentry duty there as a company commander in November 1917 when Flesquières was for a few days in all the British papers during the Battle of Cambrai. 'Many times at dawn,' he told her, had he watched the ground in front of that hilltop village: 'first one could see our barbed wire – then our "posts" crawling back to our line – then the Boche trench – then the roofs of Ribecourt and finally on the hill with a belt of trees on one side of it Flesquieres growing clearer every minute'. At 'stand to' there was the relief of another night seen through, and satisfaction with his role as a cog in that extraordinary military effort of defending 150 miles of the Western Front. 'I knew my duty was at an end – so to my dug-out – a cup of tea made ready by Lane – some rum in it – a signaller to take down my reports.'[61]

The march back to billets after a spell in the front line demanded special care and attention from officers. They were often weary enough themselves. Charlie May's diary account on 29 February 1916 celebrated the standards he sought: 'the officers went in and out carrying a rifle for this man, giving a cigarette to another, helping a lame duck up onto his poor swollen feet again – cracking feeble jokes with them all'. He made a special note on 8 March when 'coming out men sang to their step for the first time in weeks'.[62]

Work out in no-man's-land was always testing, especially for a green young officer like Wilbert Spencer, less than a month at the Front. He told his Aunt Vie about an upsetting incident when no one came to harm. He was in charge of seven engineers working at night over the parapet about 400 yards in front of his trench. Hearing a party of the enemy approaching who might have caught them, he ordered his men to get ready to fire. A 'nervous fellow let off his rifle by mistake,' which warned them off. Without him, Wilbert reflected, 'we might have surprised them and captured them all'. As it was, they simply got back safely.[63]

Erecting the crucial barbed-wire entanglements in front of the trenches to hinder attacks was a much disliked duty which had to be done at night. Billie Nevill supervised an eventful wiring party on 27 October 1915, spending four hours in no-man's-land with a sergeant and eight men. There was a full moon and they were quickly spotted and peppered by an enemy machine gun, which caught one of the men in the legs. This gave Billie the immediate task of getting him back: 'we tore his clothes to shreds pulling him in through some low trip wire and he was soon nice and comfy on a stretcher on his way to Blighty'. Predictably, after this Billie had 'some bother getting some of the men out to work again' and it took over three hours to finish the job. Billie was then put in charge of all wiring for the battalion. He made his terms for this leadership task with the CO. He was given a young lieutenant whom he knew to be 'cool as an icicle' to help him, and four parties of men, with three days allotted to specific training. 'Each party is one corporal and eight men so I've plenty to amuse myself with in billets,' Billie reported happily. 'I can change the men about and relieve them.'[64]

Several of our collections of officers' letters contain reflections on actually leading men in battle. Lance Spicer's first long letter home followed the Battle of Loos in September 1915. His nerves under fire proved good, he implied, because he was so busy. What 'exactly happened' after the attack at 11 a.m. 'I don't know . . . all I know is that I spent my day collecting small bodies of men, putting them into trenches, getting them out again, generally because we were shelled out of them . . . the total thing was rather chaotic'. At Loos, Lance learnt about leading without support or direction from seniors. Moreover, 'it was our first experience of "shot and shell" and therefore memorable', he wrote later in old age. What was most harrowing in this schooling in battle, which undoubtedly stood him in good stead when it came to the Somme, 'was the sight of dead and dying, lying in large numbers on the open battlefield'.[65]

Lance Spicer was in a group of twenty-four officers who toasted their battalion, the 9th King's Own Yorkshire Light Infantry, on the eve of the Somme. Twelve of those who led the regiment's attack on the German lines near Sausage Redoubt north of Fricourt were killed, three soon died of wounds, eight more were wounded. It was Lance, one of the group of officers chosen to remain 'ready to go up after the first attack had begun', who ended the day leading the battalion. He walked up to the battlefield that afternoon with Lieutenant Basil Hart, two other junior officers who had remained in reserve, and their batmen, reporting at Brigade Headquarters at 7.30 p.m. Twelve hours previously the long-planned assault had been launched. 'I was to endeavour to reorganise the battalion,' he related.

'Is that you? Thank God, thank God,' called his colleague Gordon who had kept up the morale of survivors on the deeply scarred battlefield. Lance managed to establish a battalion headquarters. Working closely with a signalling officer in touch with Brigade Headquarters, he consolidated ground that had been taken during the night of 1 July, through the 2nd and until he was relieved on the afternoon of the 3rd. Over forty-eight hours 'full of hard work and anxiety', he attested, 'the men worked in a way of which I had never thought them capable'. They never lost their spirits. Lance was just twenty-three when fate thrust this exacting responsibility on him.[66]

Lance spent the months from September 1917 to April 1918 back in England following a serious wound to his arm in the attack on Gueudecourt on the Somme. When he returned to the Front his career went from strength to strength. 'The officers are nearly all from the same districts as the men and they all talk a good broad Yorkshire accent,' he wrote, joining a Territorial battalion of his old regiment. He soon became its adjutant. He distinguished himself at Passchendaele, winning a Military Cross. The citation spoke of his constant successful reconnaissances 'regardless of personal safety' and of how he 'encouraged the men by his example under heavy fire'. Effective both in the field and in staff jobs, Lance was torn between them. He returned from leave to work at 64th Brigade Headquarters in November 1917, becoming Brigade Major the next April. But he found he did not enjoy this role with its endless 'silly little jobs'.

Lance was in action twice in the last months of the war. On the first occasion, he assembled assaulting companies for an attack under very heavy shellfire. He then made a reconnaissance of his battalion's position under heavy machine-gun fire, sending in 'most valuable information'. He was awarded a bar to the MC for this action in July 1918. In October he was given a DSO for his gallantry at Miraumont. He carried out an immediate reorganisation of the Brigade when his brigadier was wounded. Later, when the force was entirely surrounded, he crawled out and brought back a report which provided the intelligence necessary for the relief of the Brigade. Fired by his performance on the Somme, Lance Spicer had acquired the drive and sustained courage that enabled further distinguished leadership in battle.[67]

Robert Hermon was ordered to lead a party consisting of a subaltern and six men on a mission to clear Loos of guns, ammunition and stores, with the town on 28 September 1915 still partly under German control. Describing this work under heavy shellfire in a long letter to Ethel, he wrote, 'I don't mind admitting I was terrified.' Robert knew that above all Ethel would want to know how his nerves had stood it. Did he 'feel shaky'? Two full days of work under continuous shellfire had certainly made him 'feel very frightened about myself as I didn't at all relish the idea of my nerve not standing the strain'. It was working with others near collapse that was hardest. The first 'beastly' day in Loos Robert had to meet a man to show him where the guns were:

> he was in such a state of nerves that I had to send him back, he had certainly had a bad day there and there was every excuse, then I had another fellow with me who was too awful too and he kept on explaining to me all the time that it wasn't that he was really a funk, but that it was his nerves. I must say that at the end of the time I was feeling pretty much the same.

Yet in September 1916, promoted to Lieutenant Colonel, Robert was in command of the 27th Battalion of the Northumberland Fusiliers, which was in the front-line trenches at Contalmaison on the Somme. 'For concentrated hell,' he told Ethel when he found a moment to write properly, 'the attacks on High Wood absolutely take the biscuit'. Responding to her request for news of 'what my feelings have been', he reported he had never been calmer 'or had a better grip of things' after his second in command had collapsed. Robert's adjutant was amazed at his performance at High Wood. He was after all a cavalry officer without training in running infantry actions in the trenches. Friends were joking about his deserving a DSO.

Robert was glad to be able to tell Ethel 'that I wasn't so frightened that I couldn't carry on'. When she worried about his safety he explained that his direction of the Contalmaison action from behind was very much a matter of policy: 'during a show of this sort I don't go right up there as I have to sort of hold the strings behind, as one must be in touch with one's companies and the Brigade too'. If a CO goes 'messing about up in front on occasions like that he is quite out of touch with his command and the result is chaos,' Robert assured her.[68]

Rowland Feilding was invalided home with a badly infected knee in November 1915, returning fit for service the next April. Keen to 'be in the swim', he was frustrated that his seniors held him back from the front line by giving him charge of the Coldstream Guards' entrenching battalion. He felt Edith would agree that 'if I inspire any confidence in the men it is certainly right that I should be with them'. But, reputed to be 'too chancy', Rowland accepted his role and watched the first day of the Somme. He found it 'inspiring and magnificent' and summed up the start of the battle as 'a wonderful day'.

Rowland was transferred to the command of the 6th Battalion of the Connaught Rangers on 7 September 1916. The Somme campaign was then in

TELEPHONE, 3. COWFOLD.
STATION, WEST GRINSTEAD.

BROOK HILL HOUSE,
COWFOLD,
SUSSEX.

most cases one side sits on one side & the others
on the other & hurls bombs at one another.

The chief advantage is that eventually if
you can consolidate your side alright it
gives you a high
point between the
lines from
which you
can get good

observation of the other blokes line. An ordinary
crater runs to anything from 60 to 100 feet across
the top with banks up to 15 feet high.

There is no crank handle in an aeroplane so you
see the starter has to stand outside & pull the
propeller round & having to have the throttle fairly
wide open for starting she is very apt to run
over you if you are alone or else go off across the
field alone! When the engine starts you have got
to have some one holding the beast's tail or else

10. Robert Hermon describes creating a bomb crater 'from which can get good observation
of the other bloke's line' in letter to his wife Ethel, 4 May 1916.

its ninth week. Consolidating territory recently gained after huge losses in the Delville Wood area, his first task was far from easy. He hardly knew his officers and did not know his rank and file at all. 'I shall require all your prayers,' he wrote to his wife after a briefing with General George Pereira. After parading his 250 Irishmen, all, 'kneeling down in the ranks', received General Absolution before the battalion moved into the district won since 1 July at Bernafay Wood. Rowland's account of his capture of the village of Ginchy, in three long letters written on the successive days from 8 to 10 September, was cool, assured and matter-of-fact. He found the men 'in no condition for battle of this strenuous order'. But his sober report shows the strength of character Rowland had acquired as a seasoned Great War campaigner. His casualties over three days amounted to 92, nine of the sixteen officers and 83 of the 250 other ranks with which he had started.

Junior officers held Rowland in high esteem for his courage in the field. One of his company commanders wrote that he 'could always be trusted to be in the middle of the worst trouble the battalion was suffering, and could be trusted to see that the most ridiculous orders of High Command were inter-preted in a sensible way . . . he was to all appearance completely fearless, either of German shells or General Officers'. Two matter-of-fact accounts of his actions confirm Rowland's remarkable self-command. Neither in the account he wrote of the taking of Messines Ridge in June 1917 nor in his description of the German bombardment on March 1918, which decimated his battalion, was there a trace of fear for himself. Friends were surprised at seeing him, he wrote jokingly after the March retirement, since 'for the fourth time during my mili-tary career I had been reported killed'.[69]

The little-known bid by the 2/5th Sherwood Foresters to dislodge the Germans from Le Verguier on 4 April 1917 went down in the battalion annals as a day of drama and courage. This was their blooding and, as we have seen, Reggie Trench's first battle. Some of his men had enlisted in August 1914, had trained through 1915 and into 1916 at Swanwick, Dunstable and Watford, then served on the Curragh in Ireland. They were eager at last to prove their mettle. The village occupied the high point of a prominent ridge in front of the country chosen by the Germans to create the Hindenburg Line. In early 1917, the German High Command had moved back strategically from the Somme to hold this more easily defensible frontier.[70]

Reggie took command of those who survived the first phase of the attack down the slope in front of the village. From their hollow, the battalion history records, Reggie and the others 'could see dozens of inert forms being gradually covered by snow'. Away back lay Adams, killed in the advance. Some 100 yards short of immunity was Lieutenant Rossiter, badly wounded by a bullet through his lung. His batman, a nineteen-year-old Yorkshire lad Private Brown, went and covered him with his waterproof sheet, remaining by his side. Gentle snow now turned to a blinding storm, reducing visibility to 100 yards and spiking the enemy's guns. To Reggie's relief, in a little while Colonel St Hill came striding down the slope through the snow. It was some time after nine o'clock that he handed over.

Reggie's emotions following his first battle were powerful. He spent part of the next night searching for the bodies of some of his men that had not yet been recovered, finding only one. There was pride in the men's morale, which he had consciously been seeking to build for months. 'The men were splendid, laughed all the time at their escapes and following their officers perfectly,' he wrote. Reggie recognised how much he was learning about the men he led: 'I have lost some fine men but we have all been tried now and I have found out the men I can rely on at any time.' Collective leadership spirit by the battalion's officers was illustrated by the return of Rossiter, tended insistently till he was safely in by his loyal servant. Rossiter was 'a jolly good fellow and he was so cheery as he was carried in – he just told me where he had got them – one through each arm and one or maybe two in the lungs – and then began to talk of trivial matters such as the snow etc.'[71]

With St Hill on leave, Reggie was given a prominent role in the next attack, planned for the 2/5th on 3 May, on two farms held by the Germans as outposts of the Hindenburg Line. He was overawed when attending his first council of war at Brigade Headquarters, where he heard the scheme in full from two generals and two staff officers. With 350 men under his command, his objective was Malakoff Farm. He wrote to both Clare and Isabel before the night operation. It was anxious work, he explained to his mother, as he would be issuing orders by telephone to men in forward positions supported by signallers. It was hard, Reggie felt, leading from behind like this. 'Please God there is no hitch,' he told Clare. 'I feel quite confident myself but one never knows what may arise.'

Daylight made it clear that the position achieved overnight was precarious. But it was his subaltern William Alliban's forward platoon, not his, that was left most vulnerable to enemy forces. 'You will be glad to hear,' Reggie told Clare, 'that my half battalion captured their objective ... everything seemed to be going well next day, a deserter came and gave himself up and said there were 50 more who wished to do the same.' 'I was never in any danger practically speaking and the attack so far as I was responsible was quite successful,' he assured his mother. Then came the expected counter-attack at dusk, 'around 750 men against my 160', in Reggie's calculation. He kept his head in managing the Foresters' inevitable withdrawal, but he was devastated to lose his right-hand man Alliban in this action. The battalion history, published in 1920, concluded that in both the Le Verguier and Malakoff Farm shows 'it was given an impossible task to perform'.[72]

These short accounts of leadership in full-scale battles show, in the context of long runs of correspondence, how infrequent battle was. Over fourteen months Reggie Trench was only in battle twice. Robert Hermon, arriving in May 1915, was in action at Loos in September and then on the Somme the following September. Lance Spicer and Rowland Feilding both served from the spring of 1915 through to the Armistice, yet neither was in battle more than half a dozen times. Leadership on the Western Front was not largely about front-line action. It had its daily grind at every level, the battalion, company and platoon levels most particularly, whether in the front line or in reserve. It was about authority in enforcing day-to-day chores. It was sustained by friendship between officers and their men as well as by discipline. Leadership, officers knew, was best demonstrated by caring for the men, the very essence of what Reggie Trench called the 'practical soldiering' which service on the Western Front required of them.

1. Reggie Trench had been a keen member of the Inns of Court Officers Training Corps since 1911, soon after leaving Oxford. He was at the annual camp at Ludgershall on 3 August 1914, when a declaration of war loomed. He became a leading figure in the Corps from then on until March 1916, when he joined the Sherwood Foresters to go to France. 'Recruiting apace' he wrote to his fiancée on 4 August, having returned to the London Headquarters of the Corps in Lincoln's Inn.

2, 3. Lieutenant Colonel Errington, writing about the work of the Corps at Berkhamsted, stressed that his aim was leadership 'on a solid foundation of drill and discipline, with practice in command and full emphasis on the moral qualities needed in those who have to lead men in the field'. In entrenchment practice, men learnt about digging and revetment. One in ten men was selected in interviews of 130,000 candidates for the Corps. Around 12,000 of these received commissions: more than 2,000 of them men were killed and another 5,000 were injured by 1918.

4. Bramall Lane Football Ground, Sheffield. 'I have just finished my first day as a soldier', Will Streets wrote to his mother on 16 September 1914, 'but I am not so tired as I thought I should have been'. Recruitment for the City's Pals battalion had been launched on 4 September. The intention was to enlist 1,200 volunteers.

5. Second Lieutenant Herbert Trench was in command of a lorry park outside Ypres in 1916. He is shown here, holding his pipe in the midst of his twenty-eight men of the Army Service Corps 363 company. One of his lorries is in the background.

6. Private Alec Reader, a mere boy in man's uniform, stands behind his parents and siblings in this family photograph, taken five months after he enlisted in August 1914. Flanking him, besides his parents, are his brother Arthur and his sisters Lilian, eleven, Constance, two, and Minnie, seven.

7. In July 1915, Private Jack Sweeney, a regular soldier, received a letter with a parcel out of the blue from the Williams family in Walthamstow. This parcel was to change his life. He wrote nearly 878 pages of letters to Ivy Williams from the Western Front. They married in March 1918.

8. Will Streets is one of the most dynamic and compelling characters in this book. A Derbyshire miner, the oldest in a family of twelve, he had worked down the pit in his village for twelve years by 1914. He loved poetry and wrote a great deal himself on the Western Front.

9. The wedding of Reggie Trench to Clare Howard took place at Bark Hart, at Orpington in Kent, on 28 January 1915. The family group includes Clare's brothers Hal, Stanley and Walter Howard, her sisters Amy and Ida, Reggie's mother Isabel, his sister Margot and his brother Herbert Trench.

10. Lance Corporal Cyril Newman, a civil servant, created a meticulously organised archive telling his story of service on the Western Front. He sent this photograph of trench duty with a pal (right) to his girlfriend Winnie Blackburn during the war. They married after the war.

11. 'I look back on the years 1914–1918 as among the happiest I have ever spent', wrote Captain Graham Greenwell. He was introducing an edition, published in 1935, of letters he wrote home to his mother.

12. 'It seems too good to be off at last', Julian Grenfell told his mother embarking at Southampton for France in October 1914. He had joined the Royal Dragoons in 1910. His poem 'Into Battle', written on 29 April 1915, was luminous and serene.

13. Captain Lance Spicer noted on this photograph that it was taken on 'my first day in uniform'. Publishing his memoirs in 1979, he recalled seeing the Royal Navy to 'action stations' in the English Channel on 4 August 1914: 'it was a thrilling if somewhat frightening sight'. When soon after in Jermyn Street, he 'felt a pin being stuck into the lapel of my jacket', he was being accosted by 'a little woman with a tray holding white feathers', who told him he should be 'out in France fighting for your country'. Lance was quickly commissioned: he served in the King's Own Yorkshire Light Infantry for the whole war and had 'kept in close touch with it ever since'.

14. Captain Billie Nevill had bought the footballs dribbled across no man's land by his battalion on 1 July 1916 at home before the first day of the Battle of the Somme. A subaltern friend recalled how, just before 7.30 a.m., he strolled up in his usual calm way and 'we shared a last joke before going over'.

15. Lieutenant Colonel Rowland Feilding published his letters home. He explained that they were written 'while the events described were fresh in mind – often actually on the battlefield or in the trenches'. He had added dates and place names from his diary. 'That is their claim to interest', he declared, 'coupled with the extraordinary luck which permitted an individual to survive so long in the front line'.

16. Lieutenant Colonel Robert Hermon wrote almost 600 letters home to his wife between 1915 and 1917. When his granddaughter, Anne Nason, untied the bundles of them, following her mother's death in 1991, they had lain untouched for more than seventy years. Editing them, she added dates from original postmarks on the envelopes and locations from war diaries.

17. Lieutenant Colonel Hermon with his children, left to right Mary, Bob, Meg and Betty, and two of the family dogs at Brook Hill, Cowfold, during his leave in 1915. He fondly called his children the 'Chugs'.

18. Lance Corporal Gordon Buxton was Lieutenant Colonel Hermon's batman from 1914 to 1917. He had previously worked for him as a general factotum. After the war he returned to Cowfold, working for Ethel Hermon till her death in 1930, then for her daughter Mary until after 1945. His daughter Jessica Hawes helped the author with material for this book.

19. Captain Ernest Smith was commissioned in the Buffs, following training in France with the Artists Rifles, in early August 1915. He summarised trench life to his mother: 'one is strung up to take almost anything' but he was helped to concentrate by 'the sense of having to see after others and set an example'.

20. Captain Charlie May asked his adjutant to care for his wife Maud and daughter Pauline if he was killed on the eve of the Battle of the Somme. 'I do not want to die, not that I mind for myself. If it be that I am to go I am ready', he wrote in his diary.

21. Private Arthur Bunting (seen here) and Captain Charlie May made friends during training in England. Arthur became his batman in France. It was he who sent Charlie's diary, a moving account providing insight into his patriotic mind, home to Maud when he was killed.

22. Janet McGregor's last letters to her husband in France are poignant. Their son Bob, she told him on 13 September 1916, was 'getting to be a fine bold laddie'. 'I wonder what you are doing poor old darling', she continued, 'I am always thinking about you'. He was killed that day.

23. Without a white lie, Private Peter McGregor would never have reached the trenches. He took eight years off his real age when he enlisted in 1915. His letters show the ardency of his love for his 'darling sweet Jen', and his children Bob and Margaret. Bob was over sixty when he opened the old suitcase where he knew the letters were kept. He copied the letters out, word for word, in sixteen exercise books. 'I was deeply moved', he recorded, 'it was like a voice coming to me'.

24. Yvo Charteris was not quite seventeen when this studio photograph was taken in 1913. He was still at Eton when war broke out. He insisted on leaving school early to take a commission and train for the Western Front. His mother wrote 'he was so young when he first led his platoon that the older men used to chaff him on his extremely youthful appearance.' They even 'chipped him by singing "and a little child shall lead us."' Yvo, she said, flushed and 'flung back some retort'.

25. Wilbert Spencer left school early at seventeen years old. After a three month crash course at Sandhurst in August 1914, he was commissioned as a Second Lieutenant in the Wiltshire Regiment. 'It is wonderful how one gets to know and love one's men in a very short time,' he told his father on 6 December, while in training at Weymouth.

26, 27. Delville Wood and the ruined village of Wytschaete, 8 June 1917. Lieutenant Colonel Rowland Feilding chose photographs showing places devastated by the war that he remembered well when he edited his letters to his wife for publication, eleven years after the Armistice, in 1929.

28, 29. The postcard sent by Private Herbert Trench on 26 September 1914 to his sister Cesca carried the standard reminder it should not include any details of the writer's location or movements of troops. His tone, just arrived in France, was optimistic: 'everything is perfect here . . . it is very unlikely we shall ever get to the Front. The army will probably be in Germany by the end of the year'.

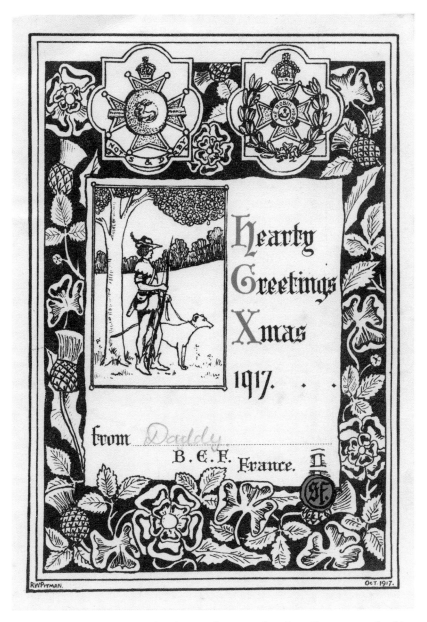

30. Major Reggie Trench sent this Sherwood Foresters battalion Christmas card to his daughter Delle, aged two, at Christmas 1917.

31. The Earl and Countess of Wemyss took the original grave cross, made in October 1915 for their son Yvo, home to Stanway, when this marble headstone to Yvo Charteris was set up in the war cemetery at Sailly-Labourse. They chose the following words to commemorate their son: 'They carry back bright to the coiner the mintage of man'. Yvo's sister Cynthia had used the same words, writing to Lady Ettie Desborough about the death of her son Julian Grenfell in May 1915. She may have begun to think of the words as a general message of consolation, after her own youngest brother joined the toll of the fallen later that year. The Earl and Countess may have been influenced by their daughter Cynthia's conviction in choosing these particular words after the war.

CHAPTER 7

'Such a Helpless Lot of Babes'

Care for the Men

Trench life was a fight against the elements. In summer there was heat and dust, in winter cold and mud; cold was the greatest enemy. 'The cold crept under our clothes, our fingers and joints ached with it,' wrote one soldier in his diary, 'it seemed to congeal our blood and kill the very marrow of the bones.' Mud enveloped men in the front line; lice were everywhere, infesting men's clothes. With surplus food and corpses all over the place, rats multiplied with amazing fertility.[1] On their return to billets, washing and cleaning their clothes were men's priorities, yet obtaining clean and hot water to do this was itself often a struggle. 'I am getting the men bathed in water of a sort by degrees,' reported Reggie Trench after the attempt to capture Le Verguier.[2]

Management of housekeeping activities was not an optional extra on the Western Front. Attention to them was the very core of the junior leadership role. Many young officers relished the responsibility this gave them. Joining the Buffs, Ernest Smith told his mother in June 1915 how he felt that it was 'rather nice to think that a platoon commander's job is a much more human one than that of a higher command, as one is held personally responsible for the comforts and good spirits of the men and [must] try to make them respect one as a man as well as a soldier.'[3] Reggie Trench emphasised the range of his domestic activities in May 1917. His day had been about 'anything and everything in fact except fighting the Boche': 'I have been either fussing round the latrines or arranging to build houses or improve billets or building a kitchen or supervising sump pits or grease boxes or setting men on to ablution benches or baths or arranging distribution of rations and diet sheets for the next day and general office work.'[4]

The obsession of the staff of the regular army with what seemed like trivialities was rooted in fear that temporary officers, as most of those studied here were, might neglect their paternalistic duties. So thorough was military bureaucracy that there was no chance of their doing so. 'This concern, this anxiety and interest, minute and unceasing,' Wynn Griffith recalled in his memoir *Up to Mametz*, published in 1931, amounted to the notion that 'every man above the rank of private is his brother's keeper'.[5] The survival activities of finding or constructing shelter for the men and providing food were permanently at the front of the minds of officers. Keeping them healthy and fit was seen as important in maintaining morale and unit bonding. Entertaining them with occasional treats mattered as well. The 1915 handbook *Duties for All Ranks* set out in detail the officer's overall responsibility to care for his men's 'comfort and well-being'.[6]

Officers' accounts of their own living conditions, as we saw earlier, were positive and cheerful. They assumed their men's quarters would always be primitive by comparison. Nevertheless, they did seek to ensure that billets were as decent as possible. Ernest Smith was arranging everything himself for his platoon, as he explained, when the first battalion of the Buffs were in scattered farms in the winter of 1915. Whereas he enjoyed a soft bed and sheets in a farmhouse, the men were 'in a barn adjoining with plenty of dry straw'. 'I have been making up to Madame at my place,' he recounted; 'she lets the men sit in the kitchen during certain stated hours and gives them coffee and beer.'[7]

Settling his men from the East Surreys into billets prior to going up to the line in 1915, Billie Nevill was concerned about keeping their quarters healthy. His problem was 'no disinfectant and no drains and a lot of men . . . after each meal there are heaps and heaps of bully beef tins, biscuit crumbs and perhaps fat off bacon, eggshells etc and everything has to be burned or buried'. He had never seen so many flies before. 'They send you fairly crazy,' he confessed, explaining how he had spent a 'morning trying to devise every possible improvement'.[8]

Beginning his winter march across to the Front, Reggie Trench was very concerned about getting his men well billeted. He had them break up ration boxes for firewood and had strips of wood tied to each man's pack. Since D Company was at the rear in the marching order on 28 February 1917, it was almost ten at night when 'I got all the men in'. But he was pleased to see them bedding down in the barns with good straw. Checking in the morning, he found that 'out of fourteen billets eight had got hot tea last night'. 'I have just been round with the medical officer viewing our latrines – he pronounced them good,' Reggie informed Clare. Two days later, now ten miles from the front line, he was offered some huts with rabbit-wire beds for his men, a marked improvement.[9]

Wilbert Spencer found it wonderful how men 'keep up and keep cheery', and told his mother how, just back from his first spell in the trenches, 'the Tommy stands or sits down in a cramped position nearly all the time. He gets no shelter from the rain for three days.'[10] Men, however, did often complain about these cramped conditions. K.H. Young in the London Regiment described his dugout on the Somme in July 1916 as 'a hellish place three foot high with five men crowded at the bottom and quite six on each of the stairs'. The following month he was in a 'very poor dugout, four men all sleeping on stairs as the bottom is too foul for human habitation'.[11]

They had moved forward to about 3,000 yards from the German trenches, Cyril Newman explained in May 1915: 'I and my friend Wally have secured an airy and roomy hole ... we improved it by digging recesses in the sides for shelves to hold our candle, food etc.' 'Had a comfy little dug-out just big enough for one, with a little shelf and cupboard recess,' he reported another time, 'not long enough to lie down at full length.'[12] In rest at Laventie in January 1917, his billet was a garage attached to a house: 'we have straw mattresses as well as our two blankets so are "in clover"'. But a few weeks later he was back in the front line and it was freezing hard. 'I have my feet in a couple of sandbags, my leather jacket wrapped round my knees, my overcoat done up and gloves on as I write,' he related.

Cyril was resourceful in taking initiatives, under the benign eye of officers, when the chance to improve his lot arose. In September 1917, a letter home included a lyrical description of 'Sunnyside', the name he and his pal Reg Nakes gave to their scratch accommodation in reserve. 'We scrounged some sheets of tin from an R.E. dump for the roof and built up walls from debris ... we formed a window span and doorway, made a chimney and found part of a cooking stove.' Their china, set out on their do-it-yourself shelf, included 'a cut-glass decanter rescued from rubbish inside a blown up house'.[13]

The wartime government was convinced of the inextricable connection between food and morale. Food was 'a matter of paramount importance', insisted the 1915 *Manual of Military Cooking*. The duty of managing the catering 'should be attended to by the officers themselves'.[14] British soldiers hardly ever went without, enjoying a balanced and healthy diet. Their only complaint was its monotony. Undoubtedly it was a better diet than many were accustomed to at home.[15]

In the trenches the men were fed either with tinned cold rations for them to cook or with hot food prepared behind the lines in horse-drawn wheeled cookers. 'The cooker remained at the transport lines,' Stuart Dolden explained in his memoir *Cannon Fodder*, published in 1980, and 'two cooks stayed with it and daily cooked meat, bacon and vegetables, which were sent up to the trenches nightly with the rations'. The prototype Tommy's Cooker was constantly being updated. It was a small tin holding a chunk of fuel or a pot of meths on which a mess tin with water or food was heated.[16] Reggie Trench enthused about schemes for new models of the cooker in the autumn of 1917. A mixture of fat, paraffin and petrol as fuel in an old bully beef tin was one version. 'We mix three parts dripping and one part paraffin,' he wrote explaining another version, 'in an empty cigarette tin . . . cut some holes in the tin very near the top to make a draught and put a mess tin on top.' He used a piece of sandbag to act as wick: 'they work very well and will boil two pints of water and fry bacon for half a dozen men'. 'I am arranging to make at least 200,' he declared, convinced he had found the most reliable answer.[17]

Tinned bully beef with vegetables, the standard subsistence food, was called Maconochie's. The name came from the Aberdeen manufacturer of the most common brand. It was notorious for its monotony and its unreliability.[18] Julian Grenfell enthused about it: 'delicious when you heat it up,' he said, so thrilled was he to have reached the Front. But typical complaints were that there was too much liquid and that the origins of the lumpy pieces of meat were highly dubious. The trench newspaper the *Wipers Times* sought to allay derision, carrying spoof advertisements with testimonials from delighted customers: 'please forward to me the residential address of Mr Maconochie as when next on leave I wish to call and pay my compliments'.[19]

Resourceful officers understood the need to get their cooks to serve up something different and more interesting behind the lines. 'I have been experimenting on the company in the food line recently,' Reggie Trench told his mother in May 1917. 'I find they appreciated very much a "spinach" made of nettles.' He would like to have offered the men another dish tasting like young asparagus that his mess enjoyed, young hops boiled with margarine, but 'we have not enough at hand to make dishes for the company of this'. In his next letter Reggie boasted about the nutritious and wholesome food he was providing from 'the rations issued to us made up with a little care and forethought'. 'My men's diet sheet today,' he related, 'was Brekker, bacon, bread, tea – Dinner, roast and boiled spinach – jam pudding – Tea, dripping bread, tea – Supper, Bran bread, tea and lime juice.' Not a bad day's feed is it?' he commented.[20]

Reggie was fanatical about feeding his men better and more efficiently than any other company in the Sherwoods, or anywhere if possible. He put the highest priority on the standards of his cooks. 'Captain Trench was dead nuts on field kitchens,' noted the battalion history, 'everything had to be IT or someone was for it.' He was jubilant in June 1917 when he won the competition for the best field kitchen in the battalion: 'and so we ought to as we have better diet sheets and cleaner cooks than anyone'. The prize was three suits of linen for the cooks, which 'looked very smart and saved the uniform a lot'.[21] W.G. Hall, writing the story of the regiment, noted Reggie's obsessive pride in his kitchens: 'woe to the senior cook whose brass work was not brightly polished or whose dixies showed the slightest trace of grease'. He had bowls of disinfectant to hand, and instructed the cooks to use them before touching food. In a famous story a visiting staff officer noticed these. 'What's that, eyewash I suppose?' 'No sir that's to dip our hands in,' replied a nervous cook.[22]

It was his promotion to Major that gave Reggie his head in catering management. 'It could not have been in better hands,' wrote the historian of the 2/5th Sherwoods, since 'he was to be found at all times visiting the lines, the cookhouse, helping to invent fresh dishes out of old material.'[23] 'I now have to supervise the messing of the whole battalion and find it very interesting,' he told his mother, 'and having had to run a company I know a good deal about it.' He said how pleased he was to have secured 'a motor lorry to bring us fresh vegetables for the men'. Obtaining these, supplying the men with a diet adequate in vitamins, was a massive problem at the Front.[24] Fresh cabbages were unknown, because they rotted on the long journey from Channel ports whether by 'train, lorry or horse transport'. When he managed to buy 185 cabbages at 35 centimes each he simply had to relate this to Clare.[25] Sausages, Reggie decided, would be 'a pleasant variety for the men'. He could buy the skins at the canteen but he needed an attachment for his mincing machine to force the meat down the tube. Could his mother visit some good ironmongers in Dublin to obtain what he wanted?

For Reggie, practical soldiering was solving problems like this. Isabel Trench could not find the sausage attachment but the moment for it passed. 'I have procured bigger skins which I intend,' he declared, 'to fill with meat, minced herbs, fat, bread and biscuit crumbs etc: then boil and serve in slices.' 'I think it should be rather good and very portable,' Reggie mused; 'if the men like them I shall arrange for some to be made for sending up' when they were in the front line.[26] A few months later, he attended a school of cookery for officers with catering responsibilities, where he saw 'a very cunning arrangement for cooking rissoles'. This was 'simply a piece of tin about twelve inches square with holes pierced in it and a wire handle': on this the rissoles were 'lowered into boiling fat'. He was having 'one made up for each company'.[27]

Canteens were a huge boost to the Tommy's morale. Divisional ones were the most highly organised but battalions often had their own canteens, with officers putting up some capital and providing the administration. Civilian organisations like the YMCA and the Church Army also helped to keep soldiers behind the lines occupied and under control. The Church Army established more than 800 canteens and recreation rooms on the Western Front and in Italy. The

YMCA had ten in the Ypres salient alone in the later years of the war. Among other services the YMCA distributed free magazines to the troops and offered libraries in its recreation huts. Major General Powell spoke for the whole Ulster Division in 1915 when he congratulated the YMCA organiser in Belfast on the Association's achievement in 'cheering men up during the monotony of their lives in camp'.[28]

Charlie May organised a canteen in an old butcher's shop near Corbie in March 1916, finding he could obtain beer locally. The men, he reflected, would be 'braced as blazes with their chance of buying a pint'.[29] The Second Royal Welch Fusiliers were very proud of their battalion canteen. When Captain J.C. Dunn, the Medical Officer, started it in March 1916, it was quickly in 'steady business'. Slices of cake and cups of tea or coffee were very popular, at a penny. Tobacco, biscuits, sausages and chocolate were bought from the makers 'and sold at shop prices'. Meat and fish pastes, sardines, writing paper and note-books, soap and candles, tooth powder, button and boot polishes and laces all sold well. Dunn related that NCO colleagues were amazed at his determination never to raise prices, even when there was good excuse to do so. Dunn sought to plough back every penny into canteen funds.[30]

Marking time with his squadron of the King Edward's Horse in March 1916, Robert Hermon was thrilled by the immediate response to the field canteen he opened as an offshoot of the main BEF canteens. 'One gets one's things from them and sets up on one's own,' he explained, 'trade is very brisk . . . it is really wonderful how the men appreciate it.' But there were items he needed from home too. Ethel was drummed into action despatching parcels. Besides the solid alcohol refills for the model of Tommy's Cooker he used, he needed aspirin, quinine, EnoFruit Salts and Beecham's Pills. He wanted her to tell him the prices item by item 'so I can see their cost and make a small profit'.[31]

Lance Spicer started a dry canteen for the King's Own Yorkshire Light Infantry. 'I happened to talk to an Army Service Corps sergeant who was already running a canteen,' he explained to his father. There had been discussion in his mess about the exorbitant prices men were being charged for a packet of Woodbines, that crucial narcotic: 'Tommy Atkins will get what he wants by paying a little more for it, but the small French shopkeepers will not be able to increase their supply and consequently the French people have to go without.' He was putting 'a fair amount of time' into the canteen, Lance confessed in April 1916; it was a 'thorough success', he declared the next month. Five hundred francs in profit had already been distributed 'to provide extra messing for the men'. Lance was talked into a plan for a wet canteen too but difficulties in obtaining a regular supply of beer, and then the Somme, swept that idea aside.[32]

Reggie Trench began a battalion canteen for drinks, selling 617 litres of beer in the first weeks. Encouraged by this, he was delighted in September 1917 to find a couple of men in the 2/5th Sherwood Foresters, grocers by trade, to run a dry canteen. He had them send in the mess carts to buy supplies in local towns, supplementing their efforts by a weekly order for cigarettes from the base canteen at Le Havre. 'Yesterday I took in 490 francs,' he told Clare jubilantly. He was amazed at the scope and variety of sundries he had to keep 'to satisfy all tastes'. He listed 'cigarettes, chocolate, biscuits, tinned fruit, candles, pencils, notebooks, boot laces, soap, mirrors, shaving brushes, tooth brushes, boot brushes'.[33]

'Winter has come on to us suddenly,' Reggie reported on 7 October 1917. He 'had to purchase a couple of trees yesterday for the kitchens', since there was no coal to be had. The canteen was proving very popular with machine-gunners and sappers billeted in his village. He was forced to send the mess cart twelve miles into St Omer for supplies 'as we are very rapidly cleared out here'. Moves disrupted canteen arrangements. But Reggie was quick to establish a canteen when the 2/5th Sherwoods settled into new trenches in preparation for the assault on Cambrai at the end of October. By early 1918 his canteen was a highly successful permanent feature of his sector of the Front. It was 'creating quite a furore', he told Clare, catering for two battalions and sundry signallers, tunnellers, machine-gunners and sappers.

Reggie listed the range of goods he stocked by this time: 'chiefly whisky, eggs, plaice, kippers, cauliflowers, cabbages, sprouts (officers only all of these), chocolate, biscuits, cigarettes, cigars, tobacco, pipes, salmon, lobster etc.' He had taken to returning profits to the men in the form of small comforts that he distributed as he did his rounds. 'Today each man in the front line,' Isabel Trench learnt from his letter of 14 February 1918, 'got either an apple or a piece of chocolate or a packet of cigarettes.' He had also collected enough newspapers to hand round 'two to every seven men in the front line'. He understood the importance of some kind of reading matter to help bored men 'get through the day when not on sentry'.[34]

Officers sometimes put their own cash into treats for their men. After the rigours of the march across from Le Havre, Reggie deputed the padre, Alan Judd, to obtain a pound's worth of cigarettes at his own expense 'for my company as they have worked so well'. He explained to Clare his ingenious scheme for subsidising cigarette purchase in bulk. He used his English bank account to buy 1,000 or 1,500 cigarettes: 'if the men cannot pay me I note it down and they will get pennies sent from home in parcels to recoup me, also I told them I would take one penny stamps in limited numbers'. He would be sending some of these home, he warned.[35]

Officers often made a special effort to treat the men at Christmas. In the Royal Welch Fusiliers, a well-organised regular unit, officers subscribed to the Comforts Committee which provided a slap-up Christmas dinner in 1916. There was roast meat with potatoes, carrots, turnips and onions, followed by plum pudding. One of the most popular young officers acted as Father Christmas. The sergeants had 'whisky, port and cigars'. After tea there was 'a sing-song in each company hut' with beer for the men: 'after dinner we all fore-gathered and had a jolly'.[36] Reggie planned a kipper per man as a Christmas treat for the 2/5th Sherwoods the following year. Clare ordered 700 in November for despatch to France in good time. To repay her he drew upon some funds held by the regiment's Notts & Derbys Support Committee collected in England.[37]

Grace and favour mobilised at home enabled officers from prosperous families to gratify their men. Letters home early in the war are full of this. Preparing for battle at Loos in September 1915, Lance Spicer told his mother his men were existing on very little but bread and hard biscuits, which they 'do not like at all'. He wanted his father to knock off his £5 a month allowance so he would feel less guilty about asking her for things for them. A large cake 'would be very popular' and cigarettes also, which they were always asking for in the letters he had to censor.[38]

Flattering Ettie Desborough as the best of all 'War Mothers', Julian Grenfell's demands for himself and his men during the autumn and winter of 1914 were unceasing. His squadron of 150 Royal Dragoons probably did much better than most soldiers in the line. 'It is too angelic of the servants to send things for my men,' he wrote on 13 November, returning thanks to the Taplow household. Ettie also arranged collections of money among her Panshanger tenants and had the people of Maidenhead make clothes to be sent out. Julian thanked one of those who organised the generous Panshanger contribution, which would 'surely keep my troop well supplied with much appreciated comforts for a long time to come'. He later sought more cigarettes 'out of the Panshanger money'. 'The great thing,' he emphasised, 'is that they shall have a fairly continuous supply . . . if ever the Taplow people want to send anything more, the thing to send is cigarettes.' Underclothes – vest and pants – were another priority. He requested three dozen pairs there and then.[39]

But as time went on and officers from the social elite were replaced by men promoted from the ranks, this largesse mostly dried up. One subaltern, concerned that his men needed socks, asked his seven sisters to knit them. Each sock arrived with five Woodbines tucked inside.[40] Many in his regiment were 'very poor and from the poorer parts of London', Edward Chapman told his mother in January 1917. 'I want to do all I can for them,' he declared, asking her to go on collecting and sending comforts.[41]

Since the formation of the Royal Army Medical Corps in 1898 health had been central to command and planning. Hygiene and sanitation were crucial issues. Junior officers understood the importance of getting the men bathed regularly and checking that latrines were efficient and well attended. Many hardly mentioned all this routine in letters home except to comment upon something unusual. Ernest Smith's man Piggott, who 'smelt so that there was not a man in the platoon who would consent to sleep with him in the same tent', was a nightmare that lasted several weeks. Sergeant Mould's order that he 'wash every morning in billets' made no impact. The others 'give him no peace', Ernest reported. He felt like encouraging them to be rougher, 'as all gentler measures have failed'. If his section commander told off a couple of men 'to arrange a thrashing' and heave him into the castle moat, Ernest would wink at the discipline issue. Release came when the Medical Officer took the case on. To Ernest's amusement, Piggott was found a job in the Division's laundry.[42]

Lice were the bane of men's lives and they made bathing – which gave temporary immunity – a huge relief. 'I've hardly scratched since, it's ripping', declared Billie Nevill after a really hot shower. But the louse was only beaten if new clothes were issued, which seldom happened. Parties of fifty men were normally marched to the bath house, leaving their clothes outside to be soaked in creosol, their uniforms left wrapped with their identity discs. Billie took his men from his Ribemont billet down to Heilly for the hot baths there, after their first spell in and out of the trenches was over in September 1915. Nude young men en masse were noisy and vigorous. Almost everyone took pleasure in restoring their personal cleanliness. There were large boilers in the cellars of a big disused cheese factory. 'Each man', he explained, 'has a whole churning tub to himself, which is a huge thing'. Exceptionally, clean clothing was provided there afterwards, 'if you want it, quite free of course'.[43]

Reggie Trench was triumphant about rigging up a bath on the march in 1917, when he found his men were without proper washing arrangements. He managed to borrow a huge tarpaulin from the Army Service Corps and had water carried in petrol tins from his field kitchen nearby. 'We have put about 100 men through so far', he related. When the CO 'looked at my bath' it 'rather bucked him'; the town's mayor reckoned it was 'the only one in the whole corps area'. At his next billet, with the help of an efficient sergeant major, he 'got into trim a huge tank with two fires underneath heating water for baths, a fine ablution bench draining via a grease trap into an old shell hole'.

Writing from the front line later, Reggie fussed about sanitation, 'a great worry to me just at present'. His apprenticeship in caring for men in trench conditions was proving testing: 'it is usually difficult to get to all one's men in daylight and if the trenches are not kept clean one is bound to get sickness especially with hot weather as it is at present'. 'I have creosol solution scattered all about the place,' he assured his mother.[44] Reggie's most impressive domestic achievement was the invention of a virtually fly-proof latrine. The technical details took nearly a page of one of his letters. Wooden biscuit boxes were adapted with a leather hinge to form a lid and placed apart over a two-foot pit. The lid was held up when the latrine was in use by a pole along the back.[45]

Sport, we have seen, was at the root of patriotic fervour. Keeping fit at war was as much a necessity for officers as for men. 'I'm fed up with billets, you get so fat and lazy,' Billie Nevill complained after a month at the Front. He saw the issue of how to keep fit as 'an enormously difficult problem both in and out, particularly out, of the trenches'. Comparing his men's present state with their training period in Wiltshire, he was alarmed: 'we're all as well as anything, but we couldn't march now with packs half as far as we could at Codford.'[46]

Yet a common culture of rough physicality did sustain and enhance the performance of the British Expeditionary Force. Young men with high spirits had to let off steam. 'I've just been having a tremendous fight against Conny and Freddie Grisewood armed with long sticks and apples . . . much more fun than real war,' Graham Greenwell commented to his mother. Tommies enjoyed watching officer horseplay as much as scrapping among themselves: 'we had a grand apple fight in the orchard . . . the men were regaled with the sight of six officers all pelting each other'.[47]

'Being back in billets is really ripping fun,' decided Billie Nevill after a taste of the trenches. He gave his family an account of organised recreation in the East Surreys, in addition to football 'as often as we want it'. The Aquatic Sports had kept the battalion enthralled: 'the tub race provided the usual laughter and sore skins for the spectators and competitors respectively. No one got across the greasy pole at all. The sun went out during the water polo match.'[48] It was accepted that diversity of sporting activities reflected social divisions. Equestrian sports, hunting, shooting and fishing, were the preserve of the officer class. 'We have started hunting here,' announced Reggie Trench in the middle of the 1918 winter. 'We have three real hounds, two war dogs, two chien-de-chasse and a terrier,' he explained, 'we meet twice a week and have a field of about twenty officers.'[49]

Football was a great mental escape for the men from stress and horror.[50] 'Could you send me two footballs for the men, as soon as poss, out of the Panshanger money,' pleaded Julian Grenfell.[51] In August 1917 the Assistant Adjutant and Quartermaster General of 36th Division issued a directive about the coming winter months. Though there was uncertainty about how suitable the ground would be for football, they assumed that 'the game will be properly organised by officers and a liberal supply of footballs maintained'.[52]

Sport at the Front became much more than a cure for boredom during rest periods. With recognition of its value and popularity it increasingly became the norm that when units were in rest formal training would end at lunchtime. Afternoons were given over to sporting activities such as football. Just as at home, where sport offered an arena of some autonomy and creativity away from the rigid obedience of the workplace, so at the Front it provided escape and excitement, free from fear, besides affirmation of a community life. W.G. Hall, historian of the 2/5th Sherwood Foresters, noted the benefits of time in reserve in 1917 when a new draft arrived, bringing the battalion up to 992 all ranks. It was stronger than it had been since its days in England: 'five weeks of intensive outdoor training beneath an August sun, hard living and healthy games showed itself in the lean forms, bronzed faces and clear eyes of the men'.[53]

The Medical Officer was getting up a battalion team for a rugger match, Cyril Newman related. A keen sportsman since his schooldays, he hoped to be chosen again as scrum-half. Cyril graduated to an organising role for the London Regiment's games. In August 1917, when he was up for a commission, he was asked by the MO to collect a team against one the Adjutant was getting up so he went round the companies recruiting. He was pleased that in a 'rough and tumble sort of game', on soft ground, it was his team that won five: nil.[54]

Much of this sporting activity served to bond officers and men. Battalion sports involved men in healthy competitiveness. 'I feel most braced about it, the men will be bucked,' wrote Charlie May when his company carried off the prizes in April 1916. 'Good old B company they always rise to the occasion,' he declared.[55] 'We had the battalion races . . . a damned good show, officers from the whole division . . . thousands of men,' reported Reggie. 'Hammer (the new subaltern in the company) and I played in an inter-platoon football match,' Ernest Smith told his mother in December 1915, 'it was very rough and very muddy but we enjoyed it.'[56] When, 'feeling warlike', Julian Grenfell issued a challenge to anyone in the room at a boxing show, he had to face a 'very large private in the A.S.C.' In 'a terrific fight while it lasted', he closed Julian's eye right up in the first round; 'in the second I caught him a beauty and they had to carry him out to hospital'. Both were all right the next day.[57]

Junior officers understood the benefits for morale as well as fitness of a vigorous sporting calendar. 'We had a jolly day there with footer and cricket matches and after mess a rowdy rugger match,' ran one of Reggie Trench's accounts. In August 1917, pressure for cricket led him to search for flat ground, having found 'cocoa nut matting to put down for the actual pitch'. The officers took on the sergeants. Reggie also initiated a riding school during that summer break before Passchendaele. Nursing an old-fashioned pride in the army's cavalry tradition, he inculcated in green young subalterns 'the gentle art of sticking on a horse with toes in and back straight'.[58]

Ordering those not playing in the football match between A Company from the 2/5th and D Company of the 2/6th to parade for close order drill, Reggie reflected, 'I expect we will have a fair crowd of onlookers on our side.' Trench journals record matches in which the antics of officers 'afforded much amusement to the spectators'.[59] Never fond of the game himself, Reggie felt bound to turn out in a match between the Sherwood Forester battalions since he had just become second in command of the 2/5th. 'It was very exhausting,' he confessed to Clare. But he 'struggled through', coming down early in the game with 'a little sprain in my arm'. In the winter days that followed, there was enthusiastic interest in battalion boxing matches. Reggie, pleased with the competition he had set up, did the honours in the CO's absence. He felt the 20 francs each he gave the winners and the 10-franc prizes awarded the runners-up were well earned.[60]

When Rowland Feilding commanded the Connaught Rangers, a match was arranged with an Ulster battalion. It created a sporting contest 'cleanly fought between the two great opposing factions of Ireland'. He estimated the crowd of soldier spectators at over 2,000. This caused him some anxiety as the senior officer present, since he knew there was a hostile aeroplane overhead and a German battery nearby. But how could he stop a match in progress, played 'in a spirit of friendliness which, so far as I am aware, seems unattainable on Ireland's native soil'? Feilding sent his wife a vivid account of the battalion sports later in 1917, when 'Lance-Corporal Pierpoint played the clown', entertaining the crowd as a contortionist and 'a buffoon of a high order'. 'By Holy St Patrick, look at that,' Rowland heard a man call out, as they watched the way Pierpoint kept goal in the football match for the company championship.[61]

The Western Front was a supremely macho social world. The irony is that middle-class young men, cosseted in their youth, applied the models of their own homes there when they acted as domestic managers. They consistently mothered their men.[62] Occasionally someone commented upon this maternal aspect of caring. In 1980, for instance, R. B. Talbot Kelly published a memoir entitled *Subaltern's Odyssey*. He recalled his feelings walking round his gun-pits during heavy shelling one evening: 'I felt like a mother going round her children's bedrooms in a great thunderstorm, but in this case the thunderstorm was one of explosive and gas.' This mother, he reflected, was 'many years younger than any of her children'. 'Metaphorically,' as he described it, 'I tucked each detachment up in bed, told them they would be all right.'[63]

Ernest Smith's concern for his men at the Front was on his mind during a period of heavy rain in the line near Hooge. His long letter to his mother, written over three days in October 1915, provides insights into the perplexity of a youthful commander under stress. 'I am out a good deal', he related, 'as one does not feel comfortable sitting in one's dug-out small and insignificant though it is – when the men have practically none.' Working round the clock to repair parapets which kept collapsing under the rain, he worried his men could not 'stand it much longer without cracking up'. Ernest feared the wrath of senior officers falling on his men as much as the impact of German bombardment. Hence the 'horrible dreams' mentioned in this letter, 'about my entire platoon being convicted of something dreadful and being left out in the filthy rain all night with practically nothing on'. This dream was so powerful that Ernest returned to it three days later, hoping that night he would not dream again of 'finding all my men lying out in the pouring rain with only underclothing on'. Had he, Ernest seemed to be asking his own mother, been a good enough mother to his platoon?[64]

'They really are such a helpless lot of babes!' declared Lance Spicer, busy fitting his men up with winter clothing six weeks into campaigning. Reflecting that he was now having an easier time after being thrown into the Battle of Loos, he continued: 'one can never have a real holiday here because one always has the men to look after and they do take a lot of looking after'. Yet, as he wrestled with distribution of the men's waterproof cap covers, he reflected that with so much discomfort they certainly needed 'all the comforts they get'.[65]

This deep personal commitment to their men comes across through small incidents related by officers in letters home. Billie Nevill was abashed in a family letter describing the only injury sustained by his troop after their first front-line experience: 'we got home all safe and sound except one man who got a pick about three inches into his, well – he was bending over at the time shovelling'. Billie's first aid was proficient: he soused the man's buttock 'in iodine from his ampule' and put on his first field dressing. Reporting on him ten days later, it was obvious he had given this man careful attention, while keeping him in action. He was 'better but can't walk far, however, I've managed to smuggle him up somehow'.[66] Kindness could be simply a mark of basic humanity. Gerald Burgoyne noted in his diary sending a man suffering dreadfully from frostbite over to the dressing station in the middle of the night. 'Oh God, take me out of this,' the soldier had been moaning outside Gerald's dugout.[67]

Finding a youth in his company unable to sleep with toothache, Reggie Trench improvised. 'I got the lid of a tin, filled it with hot tea, told him it had laudanum in it and made him rub his finger dipped in this on the gum.' Reggie had him 'cured and asleep in half an hour'. 'Operation of faith and a little eyewash helps a lot with the lads,' he noted.[68] He needed supplies of castor oil, Reggie told Clare in another letter, having heard some complaints about constipation. 'It would be a blessing to have some,' he explained, 'as one does not see the M.O. in the trenches and it is a bore not being able to do anything for such men.'[69]

Conscientious junior officers knew about caring for men's feet. They always gave careful attention to the state of men's boots and tried to keep them supplied with dry socks. The subject crops up in Max Plowman's memoir of his war experience.[70] Recalling his billet at Bonnières on the Somme, he wrote about 'ugly feet at my parade for foot inspection this evening . . . these fellows seem to have a very elementary idea of how to look after their feet . . . I am keen on these parades and insist on regular washing'. If that surprised some of his men in the West Yorkshire Regiment, he concluded that nevertheless they were 'beginning to appreciate my administrations from the greasepot'.[71] Gerald Burgoyne noted he had men marching in boots with toes worn away and broken at the sides. He confessed in his diary he merely offered advice about the remedy: 'I must warn my men to grease their feet with any grease they can find but I know they won't do it, far too lazy'.[72]

Reggie Trench quickly became preoccupied in early 1917 by the destructive effects on his men's boots of the long march to the lines. All in perfect condition when they left Salisbury Plain, within a few weeks many were in 'an awful state', since 'the mud simply pulls the soles off'. 'Boots, boots, boots have been on my brain ever since we arrived at our last billet,' he wrote later, 'thank goodness I have forty pairs arriving tonight.' Learning from experience about the trials of long marches, on the autumn journey south to Cambrai later that year, whenever possible he reserved a big dugout 'as a drying room and rest station'. He explained to his mother: 'all socks that are wet are sent there, dried and issued again; also any men who are "trench-worn" are sent there and allowed to sleep for a day'.[73]

Care of men's hearts involved seeking to fill such leisure as they enjoyed with some fun, interest and laughter, besides healthy exercise. His new recreation room was a success, Reggie Trench reported in January 1918: 'we sell cups of tea and provide the men with papers and games – it's chock full at present!'[74] Billie Nevill was reputed to have written almost all of the East Surreys' trench gazette. He recalled that it was 'somewhat bawdy, full of local "jokes" and the men loved it'. His modest account of these jokes noted that 'everyone pretends they are very funny as they are all topical allusions'. There are over a hundred titles in Cambridge University Library's collection of trench journals.[75] The *Wipers Times*, written, edited and printed close to the Front, is the most famous. This literature, reflecting morale and helping sustain it, was well summed up by the military historian Richard Holmes as 'part-funny and part-serious, proud and self-deriding, cynical yet supremely confident, an echo of a generation brought up to endure'.[76]

'A corporal has just looked in to say that the men are having a concert at 7.0 and will we go?' wrote Ernest Smith to his mother. Later in the letter he described its success, with someone acquiring an old piano and a stage constructed in the open of boxes of ammunition. Another time, he commented on the mouth organ band started in his company of the Buffs 'which – as such – is quite good'. They were 'kicking up a din in the barn' as he wrote.[77] This was the music hall age and its traditions quickly permeated the Western Front. The 4th Division's Follies led the way in December 1914. The typical repertoires at divisional or battalion concert parties were songs and sketches, both ensembles and individual 'turns', often extempore and reflecting life at the Front. The concert troupes, which became almost universal in the divisions of the BEF on the Western Front from 1915 to 1918, were usually led by an officer. Performers were almost invariably other ranks.

Officers were sent up and the audience's pleasure was all the greater if the victims were present at concerts. Officer participation, indeed, sanctioned the release of tension which these occasions afforded. No one could stand on their dignity in the hubbub. Young men with a penchant for playing female leads in drag were much in demand. Many were very convincing, for these female impersonators took care over their fripperies, often having lingerie sent out. Their songs fed men with the stereotype of soft and romantic femininity, so glaringly missing from their lives. They loved it. Thus concerts did much to assuage men's 'Blighty hunger' and were of immeasurable value in raising morale. Edwardian music hall had treated poverty, drink and marital strife as subjects for humour. It was a bold but successful stroke to treat mud, lice, the army's discipline and even the war itself in a similar manner.[78]

Officers writing home often commented on the bonding they observed while attending such performances. Graham Greenwell enthused about driving over from his billet at Courcelles on the Somme to see the Follies. By early 1916 there was a full-size orchestra. 'It is quite the best and cheeriest performance one would wish to see anywhere,' he remarked, 'and is crowded every night with officers and men from every regiment for miles round.' His men from the Manchesters were 'as excited as schoolboys, yelling the choruses and whooping the band', noted Charlie May in his diary after a battalion concert that April.[79] J.C. Dunn, chronicling the leisure time of the Royal Welch Fusiliers, described Béthune in the spring and early summer of 1916 as 'the most cheerful town near enough the British Front to be accessible to front-line troops'. In the theatre there taken over by the BEF, the 33rd Divisional troupe of squabbling actors, who took as their title 'The Shrapnels', and other divisional troupes gave their performances to crowded audiences.[80]

Rowland Feilding noted the discovery of the brilliant Second Lieutenant Stanley Holloway when he organised his first battalion concert. Leslie Henson had signed him as a juvenile lead at the Gaiety in London just before the war. Commissioned in December 1915 and serving in the Easter Rising, he joined Rowland's battalion of the Connaught Rangers in July 1916. Rowland rated Stanley Holloway highly as a 'very clever professional', little imaging what a long and astonishing career in comedy lay ahead of him.[81] Shortly before the Armistice, Leslie Henson himself, already renowned as a prolific stage performer in the West End, did a tour entertaining the troops. He was an actor-manager, his biographer has written, who 'revelled in the chaos and spontaneity of composing an entertainment off the cuff'.[82] Rowland found his show, in which the men delighted, 'altogether splendid': 'it is a fine thing for them and goes far to keep them happy'. There were 'as usual', he told Edith, 'some good female impersonators'.[83]

On one sector of the Front there were twenty-five cinemas attracting at least 40,000 soldiers a week in April 1917. 'Charlie Chaplain was there, figuratively, and at his best,' reported Rowland, visiting the Ovillers divisional cinema in November. The soldiers loved him, welcoming his image on the screen 'with such shouts of approval that it might be the living Charlie'.[84] But many of the cinemas available at this time were not sufficiently robust to tour extensively and when they did so primitive equipment was prone to break down.[85] It was noted that the men running the Sherwood Foresters' cinema did their best, 'but sometimes the flickers would obstinately refuse to flick'. Yet one day in September 1917 Reggie Trench's battalion was lucky. Obtaining use of the divisional cinema 'we rigged it up in a big barn'. 'We got a full house,' he related, 'I took the two kids from the billet aged nine and ten – they had never seen one before and went nearly mad with delight. Altogether it was a great success.'[86]

The officer class included regimental chaplains, generally recruited from a public school and often a university background. Their motivation was strongly paternalistic but there has been much debate about their effectiveness. The tradition of church parades was well established in the regular army before the war. But beyond this the padre's brief was poorly defined, which did not help because of the deeply rooted social divide at home between Anglican clergy and less well off parishioners. Yet, because they had no effective military responsibility, padres could afford to show more familiarity with the men than could regimental officers. Many were brave soldiers and insisted, though technically non-combatant, on accompanying their men into battle.[87]

By August 1918 there were well over 3,000 chaplains in the BEF, around 1,941 of them Church of England, 803 from the Nonconformist churches and 643 Roman Catholics. One hundred and twenty-one chaplains won the Military Cross, 81 were mentioned in despatches, 26 won the DSO.[88] One of them was Harry Blackburne who, serving with a field ambulance in 1915, was awarded the Military Cross and was seven times mentioned in despatches. He became Assistant Chaplain General of the First Army, and published his story in 1932 from his letters and diaries. *The Times*, in an obituary in 1963, summarised Blackburne's Great War career: 'he organised soup kitchens, recreation rooms and cinemas, wrote endless letters to the relatives of the fallen, visited units and was the friend of all whether Generals or Privates'.[89]

Rowland Feilding and his wife Edith were strong Roman Catholics so his letters contain much about their faith. Early in his service, Rowland sent Edith a weed he found which a colleague told him was 'Flos Crucis', or the flower of the Cross. 'The legend,' he related, 'is that it grew beneath the Cross and the black spots are supposed to represent the stains of our Lord's blood.' Joining the Connaught Rangers as their CO during the Somme, Rowland was astonished by their faith. 'It is like living in a new world to be among these Irishmen,' he told Edith, 'they are intensely religious, loyal to their officers and they are an exceedingly satisfactory body of men to deal with.'

Rowland supported the chaplain to the regiment to the hilt. There was an issue in 1916 about where the Christmas Mass should be held. The place suggested allowed all but those manning the fire trench to attend. It was not more than 500 yards from the German line 'in a depression in the ground . . . concealed from the enemy'. Expecting perhaps a hundred, 'I consented', Rowland's account states, 'though, like most soldiers they will shirk fatigues if they get the chance, these men will not shirk what they consider to be their religious duties and about 300 turned up'.

Church parades held in 1917 by the Connaught Rangers were a nationalistic affair. 'I must say I felt very proud of the battalion,' Rowland told Edith: 'the men had all groomed themselves up like new pins'. He described 'an enormous green flag with a yellow Irish harp upon it' but no crown, which 'the men carry about with them on the march'. Yet, in the year after the Easter Rising, Rowland never doubted their 'loyalty and devotion'. Preparing for their role in the Battle of Cambrai, he noted that 'the whole battalion flocked to confession'. He saw this as a mark of 'the intense devotion of these Irish soldiers who have come to fight in France'. Rowland watched as for hours 'the priests were engaged, the men crowding up silently, passing one by one to the canvas confessionals in the far corners of the old ruin, which was dimly lighted by a candle or two for the occasion'.[90] When he joined the London Regiment in August 1918, Rowland was again 'fortunate in our padres'. The Church of England man was 'not so long from Eton and quite charming'. He admired Father Benedict Williamson, the Roman Catholic chaplain, known for his incurable optimism. Carrying the Host with him always, he was ready with it in need: 'the shell-holes serve him as chapels'.[91]

Roman Catholic chaplains gained exceptional credit from their performance in the front line, when necessary administering extreme unction. John Bickersteth was an Anglican chaplain who took up tending the wounded and dying in the same way, carrying a pyx containing the sacrament in one kind, bread marked with wine. Guy Chapman, in his 1933 memoir *A Passionate Prodigality*, contrasted the 'serenity and certainty' of a particular Catholic priest he remembered with 'our bluff Anglicans'. Yet in declaring that the Catholic Church contrived to send 'a man into action mentally and spiritually cleansed', while the 'Church of England could only offer you a cigarette', he fell into repeating a crass simplification.[92]

Anglican ministration nevertheless did vary in quality. This was a matter of concern to many officers who were genuine believers. 'I walked this morning to hear the poorest parson I have ever heard in my life,' Robert Hermon noted one day. He was glad he had not taken any of his men since they might have mobbed this padre.[93] Reggie Trench was dissatisfied with a new padre posted to the 2/5th Sherwoods, who was 'quite a good chap off parade but at a service he mouths every word in a most annoying manner'. In charge of D Company, he tried to hold church parades as regularly as he could, sometimes deputing the task to his subaltern William Alliban. Reggie formed a close bond with the battalion's padre Alan Judd. He noted how glad he was to have him back from leave in August 1917.[94] Years after the war, his colleague H.P. Greaves wrote to the *Evening Standard* about Judd, confessing that at first the men of the Sherwood Foresters 'treated him very lightly'. But he 'proved himself a great-hearted Christian' in France.[95]

The middle-aged Maurice Murray emerges from his diary as a modest, courageous and highly conscientious padre. Reading it after his death, his daughter Joan commented rather defensively 'I am sure he got closer to the Tommies than the diary suggests.' She remembered his reticence about his faith. The diary is a factual record of his service which, unassumingly, never asserts openly that he achieved closeness to those he served. 'I took the men some cigarettes and talked with them,' was his account of a first visit to the front line; 'they were all full of jokes.' Numbers seem small but we cannot estimate how Murray's pastoral care helped men along. Twenty-two men attended a morning service he held when the Royal Sussex was in reserve, ten staying for communion.

During the Battle of Passchendaele, Murray says nothing about its progress, instead recording services, with fifty men at a time 'according to order', the men sitting on fallen logs while he preached on 'Thankfulness'. He spent much of his time leading burial parties. Each time he found a body, he recorded, he dragged it with the corporal into the nearest shell hole, where his men made the grave. Systematically he recorded belongings, then packed them into a canvas bag, before saying the committal words of the Prayer Book burial service, with additional words about the soldier's bravery and eternal rest 'for the benefit of the corporal'.[96]

The diaries kept by Victor Tanner, a public school chaplain who also served at Passchendaele, record a very similar pattern of activities. Censoring his men's letters in the Worcestershire Regiment, he found one replying to his wife's enquiry about their padre: 'no, I don't know his name but he's a nice chap and gets about among the men as much as possible'. Victor conducted a pre-battle service in September 1917. A crowded congregation sang 'Jesu, lover of my soul', 'Through the night of doubt and sorrow', 'Through all the changing scenes of life' and 'Soldiers of Christ, arise'. Many stayed for communion. 'It was a wonderful time,' he wrote in his diary.

During the battle that followed, Victor was posted in a concrete pillbox which served as a first aid post. In a graphic account written to his mother afterwards, he described how he left it to encourage a group of Tommies in a nearby trench. 'About twenty men were huddled there for protection,' he explained, 'so I talked to them and tried to liven them up a bit . . . I also dished out cigarettes all round to try to take their minds off things a bit.' He had the soldiers close their eyes while he led them in prayer 'that God will protect the boys in the front line and that He will extend the protection to us'.[97]

For a militant Christian, like Cyril Newman whose faith was all consuming, denominationalism became a minor issue at the Front. What Cyril wanted was ministration and he took every opportunity to grasp it. Once, in rest, he and a friend walked to a village where they attended the Roman Catholic Mass with its full panoply of elaborate ceremonial. He told his fellow Baptist Winnie about the bowed heads as the 'Host' was carried in a procession of fifty men with lighted tapers: 'no one is supposed to look'. 'What a change,' he declared, to attend a Church of England service that evening. He reported 'a helpful address on "What is life" by the Reverend Girdlestone'.

When padres were not available, Cyril was quite ready to improvise, if he could find a small company willing to pray and worship with him. With seven others, he organised 'a little service in our dug-out', in November 1916: 'our altar consisted of an upturned ammunition box with two lighted candles one on each side of my bible with a Cross resting upon it'. Two of their men had been killed that morning so the group said a Prayer for the Faithful Departed. Cyril led prayers and read from the Psalms. The hymns included 'O God, our help in ages past', 'Rock of ages' and 'Fight the good fight'. They recited the Lord's Prayer together.

Cyril learnt from his conversations with friends that what most men wanted was an affable and undemanding padre. He found Captain Clarke's frankness with him about religion as well as other issues 'jolly decent'. Cyril respected his view that 'soldiers on active service are attracted by a "manly man" – by the heroic in religion – by consistency'. In September 1917, he quickly made friends with a new chaplain appointed to the Queen Victoria's Rifles, who had recently returned from missionary work in China. He found him quiet and rather shy, noting his 'gentlemanly manner and winning voice'. A few days later he related that this padre had joined a patrol 'in No-Mans-Land which is very wide here'. 'That's the sort of thing that appeals to the men,' Cyril told Winnie.[98] All in all it can be said that religion certainly helped those with some belief to keep up their spirits. Many soldiers were able to draw comfort from a padre's ministrations and many who did not have any real faith were glad of an occasional packet of cigarettes.[99]

So there is massive evidence that British officers did their utmost to care for their men. Mostly young and inexperienced themselves, their resourcefulness was impressive. They grew up by responding to responsibilities for others which were thrust upon them. Their care ranged from the routine and essential matters, such as food and shelter, to exceptional and irregular events like concerts and cinema shows. Mutinies in the French army in 1917 arose from anger at failure to meet the daily needs of soldiers. In response Marshal Pétain instituted periods of total rest, improved food provision and instructed officers to attend more carefully to the welfare of their men.[100] Life in the British Expeditionary Force was made tolerable and even at times enjoyable through the spirit with which junior officers tackled the issues of organising and managing its domestic environment. This made an incalculable contribution to maintaining good morale.

CHAPTER 8

'Drops of his Blood on my Hand'

Horror and Endurance

Two words sum up the tragedy of the Great War in popular memory: mud and horror. When men stood in the cold, the wet mud of the trenches promoted trench foot and frostbite. Moreover, mud carries associations of excrement and dead soldiers, of shrapnel and barbed wire, associations which throughout the twentieth century portrayed this war as utterly opposed to nature. Thinking about mud leads to thinking about the bodily struggle with it, how it could engulf men, choke them and drown them. It took time, when it was over, for men to find meaning in such a cataclysmic struggle, which thousands had endured so heroically for more than four years. In the 1920s and 1930s, as Dan Todman has argued, 'the war was perceived through the filter of the post-war years as an experience which had destroyed even those men who had survived it'. It was then that a version of the war still dominant today, the myth of mud, horror and futility, was created by a small group of established writers who had in many cases been junior officers in 1914–1918. They provided the scripts on the basis of which other veterans later composed their memoirs and told their stories to interviewers.[1]

This chapter begins by exploring how far men sent home horrific stories of their fighting lives. Why did some do so, while others seem largely to have kept particular incidents which troubled them to themselves? Horror could be seen, heard or actually endured. It could be related objectively and almost impassively or told relentlessly, out of anguish, exhaustion and anger. Senior officers had a very different experience from junior officers; even more so from the Tommies. Every tale of misery, dejection, dread, hideousness or panic has to be evaluated in the context of the soldier's age, seniority and length of service.

Rowland Feilding, in France almost continuously from April 1915 till the Armistice, spared his wife little of the ghastliness of war. He was particularly incensed by incidents of French civilian casualties. 'It makes my blood boil to see this useless and vindictive shelling of towns,' he wrote in July 1915, reporting how he had looked out of his hotel window in Béthune as children scattered when a shell fell in the square. They scuttled to their mothers and homes, 'but two little ones were killed'. When, more than three years later, he was advancing in the path of German retreat, he had to watch French country people returning to pick over their homes. Many 'wore sad faces as they searched the ruins with handkerchiefs to their eyes, picking out bits of broken crockery or any kind of rubbish and collecting, with the utmost care, old, ragged, shell-torn or half-burnt clothing'. Endless villages, towns and cities, he knew, had been treated to German destructive vengeance. 'Thank God, I say on this occasion, we British are not famed for being "thorough".'

Rowland's longest letter, in 1915, was his account of the Loos battlefield. There are hundreds of descriptions, either in letters or in recollections, of this battle.[2] His was as graphic and sorrowful as any. 'We have seen much of the ghastly side of war,' he told Edith, relating casualities of 300 from his battalion of the Coldstream Guards, 'including thirteen officers, seven of whom are dead.' Reconnoitring a section of the German line captured the previous day by his troops, he confessed, his first experience of this kind was 'an ugly sight'. He had to pick his way through wounded men lying thick on the ground: 'I felt a beast for not being able to help them but we had no stretchers.' When he wrote he thought of some of those wounded two or three days previously, 'who had been lying out ever since in the cold and rain, without food or water'. Yet he knew many had by then been collected in: 'this is the most horrible aspect of this horrible war'.

If Loos tested as seasoned a soldier as we know Rowland to have been, a man of forty-four with South African fighting behind him in his youth, the Somme did so even more severely. He was up at Mametz, where the British had won ground on 1 July, three days after. 'Scarcely a wall stands,' he wrote home, 'the ruins present an appalling and most gruesome picture of the havoc of war, seen fresh, which no pen or picture can describe. You must see it, and smell it, and hear the sounds, to understand.' Although he considered himself hardened to such sights, it nevertheless 'brought a sort of sickening feeling to me even now'. Seeing the wounded carried back in streams a few days later, Rowland commented: 'it looks more and more as if Hell cannot be much worse than what our infantry is going through at the present moment'. At such times, Rowland told the authentic story of Western Front horror. He was an observer and an able commander who seemed himself to live a charmed life.[3]

Robert Hermon's account of his action at Loos was less reflective than Rowland's. He was sent in twice with a specific task, rather than as a senior officer reviewing the battlefield. His order on 28 September was to clear Loos of war material – shells, rifles, bombs, etc. He headed a party consisting of a subaltern and six men. 'Of course,' he admitted in his narrative, 'my first twenty-four hours in Loos was beastly.' 'I simply hated the idea of going near the beastly place again,' he told Ethel. Thus he 'disliked it very much' when he was ordered to do so on 30 September. But, gritting his teeth to control his nerves, he found to his surprise that he never felt a qualm: '[I] was simply delighted when I found my fears to be groundless.' Robert kept his head with horror all around him because he 'had so much to do'.[4]

Predictably, it was on the Somme that Robert encountered the full hideousness of mechanised modern warfare. Yet, like Rowland, he did so as an observer only, commanding from a few hundred yards behind the front line. 'If you could have seen what I have seen,' he declared to Ethel on 12 September 1916, 'you would wonder how men could come through it without losing their reason . . . the attacks on High Wood, for concentrated Hell absolutely take the biscuit.' It was his runners, he felt, who that day set him and everyone an example, 'going through heavy shelling just as one would go for a walk in the rain and not making any fuss about it at all'. He was furious that the British press, with propagandist intent, played down the horror of the Somme: 'why shouldn't the folk at home know that the men do suffer, suffer beyond endurance . . . damn it, they'd think a bit more if they did.'[5]

The devastation of the Loos battlefield became engraved on the mind of the young officer Lance Spicer. When he edited his letters in later life, he recalled the 'not to be forgotten sight of dead and dying, lying in large numbers on the open field'. Yet his account at the time was evasive, written in denial of what he was too young fully to cope with. 'We really have been in action and pretty fierce fighting at that,' he began. He could not give 'a coherent idea if [he] tried' of the battle, 'because I really don't know what did happen'. This was a classic case of a young man's repression of horrific memory following his first experience of Western Front warfare.[6] What his account did provide was a description of successful efforts to rally his men. Lance, as we have seen, learnt tough self-management, distinguishing himself as a young, untried officer. Both mentally and in his letters home, he taught himself to edit out the horror.[7]

Some other young officers could not bring themselves to describe horror except in chance references to the suffering of others. 'Thank goodness I wasn't there,' Billie Nevill wrote, describing how he missed a massive shell at Tambour which burst 'like a torpedo'. One chap had caught a machine-gun bullet in his head 'the other day': 'I saw him just after. He'd no eyes, forehead or nose left.'[8] Graham Greenwell needed to comfort himself by telling his mother about some of the most harrowing times he experienced. He was hurled backwards into a dugout concussed when a shell fell close to him: 'I felt most frightfully shaken and pretty rotten but after about half an hour it passed off'. He described leading his men back to reserve trenches after thirty-six hours' duty at Ovillers on the Somme. He left his front-line trench 'all blown in and littered with filth and bodies'. He thought 'the awful stench much worse than the shelling'.[9]

Reggie Trench suffered a horrific personal experience which was too shocking to relate in full for several days. He almost died caught by a fire deep in the headquarters dugout of the 2/5th Sherwood Foresters during the Battle of Cambrai. So traumatised was he that he could only list for Clare the possessions he had just lost in the fire, relics littering his disordered mind. Reggie told his mother the full story first, two days afterwards, on 7 December 1917: 'the servants were making something hot for us, when one filled the kettle with paraffin in lieu of water. This was not discovered until the mixture was very hot when it burst into flames.' Then 'the place was a blazing furnace in a short time'. He could not yet bring himself to write of his near escape, focusing instead, as he had done to Clare, on his goods, not his life. His 'shaving and cleaning tackle', trench coat, sleeping bag, cigarette case containing Clare's and Delle's photos, were all lost.

The battalion history describes how the fire was noticed when columns of flame began 'pouring from the dug-out shaft'. 'Men were tugging for all they were worth at the arms and clothing of Major Trench whose body was being slowly wriggled through a hole.' Fearful onlookers, knowing four men at least were down there, saw Reggie emerge 'like a cork from a bottle'; a runner followed, almost overcome with smoke and fumes. Three others still down there could not be rescued and subsequently died. The story lingered in Reggie's letters. 'Nothing could be done to save them,' he explained sadly to his mother at Christmas; they tried to dig the men out but were stymied by the concrete of a closed shaft.[10]

Hardships were usually much more extreme for Tommies than for officers. Peter McGregor's escaped when a 'Rum Jar', the largest German shell known, left him without his rifle and his boots, 'knocked into the water and mud'. 'We are rats in a hole,' he wrote, 'hounded out with shot and shell.'[11] The green envelope scheme undoubtedly allowed more honest reporting of horror to reach England than would otherwise have done so. Charles Tames, a private in the Honourable Artillery Company, did not mince his words in a green envelope account of the Second Battle of Ypres. 'This is my private letter I therefore intend to tell you everything,' he explained: 'the chap next to me had the back of his head blown off and the fellow next but one on my left was shot through the right lung, seven of our transport horses were killed, three were blown to atoms.'[12]

Jack Sweeney used his green envelopes to tell tales of horror to make people's blood curdle back home. 'There is one of our officers hanging on the Germans' barbed wire,' he wrote on 16 May 1916, 'he must be riddled with bullets by now . . . he was leading a bombing party and got fixed in the wire.' His account of the first dead man he touched, a lifeless body under a sandbag, came when he was explaining about fetching bombs in Mametz Wood. 'Something seemed to tell me to look in his pockets . . . I found a few photos of himself and his wife and children.' Looking at letters he also found on the body, Jack realised the man had been Private Salway, whose address he recognised and whom he had known. He was glad that he plucked up courage to send back a letter from Salway's wife which reached the Front soon after, for she had replied, thanking him. Back from leave in the midst of Passchendaele, Jack hastened to send a dramatic account of the 'terrible sights', declaring 'the Somme was bad enough but this is a thousand times worse'. Maybe it was not right, he admitted, to worry his girlfriend Ivy with 'all these horrors but perhaps you don't mind as I am only telling you what the papers are forbidden to tell – the truth'.[13]

A letter from Captain Edwin Venning to his sister in 1915 was unusual in its candid reflections by a man in his early thirties who had just come through a terrifying week when he had 'had to lead two bayonet charges'. 'You can't really gather what that means and I can scarcely tell you,' he wrote. It was a time for him of 'queer goes and weird escapes'. In a duel with a German sniper, 'he sent one across that burst the sand-bag in front of my head; the bullet came clean through the bag but there was just enough sand to turn it a little sideways and the heat and whir of it all I felt.' What struck Venning in this 'mighty business', so full of horror stories, was 'the utter smallness of it all, the infinite smallness'. He was finding it difficult to get across to his sister what he meant 'but quite literally it all seems far smaller to me than prize-giving or sports day at school'. He confessed himself 'never more disappointed: where I looked for grandeur I find pettiness lost sight of almost since my schooldays'. He was killed himself three months after writing this letter.[14]

Men experienced death and mutilation on the Western Front as a kind of normality they had never known before and never would again. Death was everywhere, on old battlefields, in no-man's-land, as decomposed bodies appeared with new earthworks or were exhumed and then reinterred by shellfire. Lieutenant Brian Lawrence, in a letter home, described his traumatic encounter with it on the Somme. He found himself in a dugout that 'was beastly and smelt most terrible'. There was 'something extra as well, I don't know for certain what it was, but as half a stale Boche fell out of the wall during the night, I might guess'.[15] Many were shaken by their first experience of death in the front line: it presaged their own mortality with frightening immediacy. J.S. Handley, a sergeant in the Liverpool Territorials, recalled the death of his captain in a later memoir: 'I was stunned, shocked. I saw myself lying there.'

Private Ellison made a diary entry in March 1915 about the first deaths in his platoon: 'I wanted to be physically sick . . . but we quickly realized that would never do . . . I cleaned myself up a little and managed somehow to swallow some breakfast.'[16]

Yet letters home, one finds, contain far more material about the deaths of colleagues, their injuries and broken comradeship than about mud or the horrific physical aspects of trench service. Daily discomforts, whether of mud, lice or even falling shells, could be borne. Grief at the ever-present stalking figure of Death, who, often close by, regularly stared men in the face, occupied men's minds more intensively than anything else, testing their endurance to the utmost. So did frightening premonitions of wounding. Scanning newspaper casualty lists for people he knew became one of Reggie Trench's preoccupations. Sometimes he told Clare about friends and relatives who had been killed before she could tell him. Respect for all who made the ultimate sacrifice, known or unknown to him, was always present. 'Yesterday,' he wrote in February 1918, 'I found a body out in the open, which I am having buried with a cross on the grave: "to an unknown British soldier. R.I.P."'[17]

Cyril Newman's deep piety helped him keep the fallen in his mind as, month after month, he maintained his patriotic effort as a hard-pressed signaller. On the last day of June in 1917, he shared his emotions in a letter home about the first anniversary of the Somme: 'what memories are evoked – sad sad memories, yet to us who survived a sense of satisfaction at having stood the test. Nobility was there.' Back in reserve two days later, debate grew quite passionate over one breakfast about whether it had been appropriate to hold a memorial service for 1 July the previous year. Three of Cyril's fellow signallers 'did not agree with it. No good to recall memories of the fallen'. But surely, Cyril insisted, 'memory of noble self sacrifice is good'.

Cyril was conscientious about doing all he could to keep in touch with the relatives of men in his section, whose addresses he knew, when they were lost. In May 1917, he heard from the mother of a missing fellow signaller, Walter Crook. They had worked together for nearly a year. When his body was found and he had been buried, Cyril performed the 'sad duty' of passing on the news. He found solace in sending home crucial information about such burials of lost colleagues. He was sufficiently well informed to be able to give the mother of Sergeant Hickman, another comrade, a detailed account of where he was buried.

The 17 November 1917 brought especially searing grief to Cyril Newman. Dr Clarke, medical officer for the Queen Victoria's Rifles, had been a wonderful friend to him, going out of his way to encourage him by providing the use of his hut for Cyril's reading and writing. He and two other officers, whom Cyril knew well, were caught by a huge shell which landed on the bivvy where they were sheltering. Two of the three were killed and the other, 'who was my first platoon officer in September 1914', was wounded. Major O'Shea, another officer who was good to Cyril, promised to hand on Clarke's address so he could write to his mother. Meanwhile, Cyril found comfort in his wife's understanding of how good the doctor had been to him: 'it is pleasant to recall his kindness and gentlemanliness', he wrote. In the great scheme of things, 'happy and good memories' were what each of us could hope to live on. When he heard from the bereaved Mrs Clarke, it was a consolation to discover that her gratitude for his letter was so patently 'very deep and sincere'.[18]

Most correspondents held back from writing home too much about deaths and injuries, though their contact with both was ever present. In diaries, though, deaths could be recorded as a ritual of mourning. In some cases men made lists of those in their unit or mess who had died; in others they found it cathartic to make notes about men's personal identities as a means of remembering the dead. Wrestling with death often preoccupied men. One noticed all around him 'a sort of subdued preparedness', as men became 'more silent' in hazardous situations. Putting personal loss aside was a constant struggle. 'Had pheasant for dinner,' ran one diary entry after the loss of a friend, 'it was good but it stuck in my throat at times – but one must steel one's heart to this, many times it will happen.'

A small story of personal loss that Charles Wilson recorded in his diary on the Somme and later which was used in *Anatomy of Courage* tells us much by the very sparseness of its narrative. His men had just taken over the front line near Delville Wood 'when we lost a company commander. I went to tell Toby: Pat and he were inseparable. I found him making out a return for the Brigade . . . he did not look up but sat without a word making holes in a piece of blotting paper with his pen. Then he said "Thanks old thing" and went on writing.' Pondering his diary entries many years later, Wilson found there was 'only phlegm, a vast imperturbability in the face of death, which gave to a few soldiers sway over their fellows'.[19] Charlie May recorded the emotional impact of mass deaths. 'It was a pitiful sight, poor English soldiers battered to pieces,' he wrote in April 1916, seeing the stretchers go down the line. The comradeship he had known since Salisbury Plain was shattered during the 1916 campaign: 'there are so many new faces with us now and so many old ones missing that the battalion hardly seems the same – and one cannot let oneself go with the new like one loves to with the old boys.'[20]

But attitudes to casualties varied very much according to circumstances. Billie Nevill was scathing when one of his sergeants lost his life by foolishly 'looking over the parapet in day time at a dangerous place . . . you'd credit a sergeant with more sense'. He was philosophical when his girlfriend's brother was shot in the head and never regained consciousness on his second day in the front line. 'I'm so sorry for poor old Muff and the others,' he told the family, 'mais c'est la guerre as everyone says and it's very true'. Yet the loss of his subaltern Thorne, who was shot on a patrol a few yards from the German line in September 1915, was quite a different matter. Billie had worked closely with him and 'liked him awfully'. When Thorne's elder brother Cornelius heard about it, he and his servant Private Hine went straight out under fire, found the brother in an old shell hole and carried him in. Billie saw this as 'an awfully plucky thing to do'. Such a display of family loyalty flooded the young officers in the East Surreys' mess with emotion. When, shortly after, Cornelius received the Military Cross for his bravery, Billie, his feelings still raw, declared 'it's a small consolation, but I'm jolly glad; his people will be so pleased'.[21]

When they wrote, the loss of highly valued and respected men was often on soldiers' mind. On the Somme, Rowland Feilding reflected on his grief about Steuart, one of his captains in the Connaught Rangers. 'I had known him only two days, but had formed the highest opinion of his character . . . he was full of life and spirits and daring – the acme of the perfect soldier. But such men are rare: they often die young.' 'I keep hearing daily of the loss of friends,' Rowland wrote a few days later. Did Edith remember Pike Pease who had died in a recent battle when his previous regiment, the Coldstream Guards, sustained heavy losses – 'a typical specimen of the clean English boy, with a fine brain and a promising career before him, and he was only nineteen'? He soon grieved too for his acting second in command Parke, killed by 'a direct hit from a chance shell'. Parke's recent marriage and return from a short leave to see his wife 'makes it all the sadder'. He was 'a cheery fellow and I shall miss him very much'.

Back on the devastated Somme battlefield a year later, Rowland recalled a melancholy ride to Ginchy or the site of that village, where, as he related, he came across 'a little group of Guards' graves, including several of my old battalion . . . one away from Pease was Walters – a machine-gun officer of the Irish Guards – a splendid type of boy, whom I knew well'. One day in February 1917, Rowland lost six out of nine of his best officers from the Connaught Rangers in a raid. This toll included Ivan Garvey whom he characterised as 'the ideal Company Commander – the bravest, the cheeriest, the most loyal and perfect of men'. 'I fly to you when I am in trouble,' he told Edith, 'I am feeling very sick at heart tonight . . . My God! If the people at home could actually see with their eyes this massacring of the cream of our race, what a terrible shock it would be to them.'[22]

The chemistry between the subaltern William Alliban and his captain, Reggie Trench, ten years his senior, was immediate when they managed D

Company together in the 2/5th Sherwood Foresters during the early months of 1917. Reggie admired the nineteen-year-old, finding him 'a host in himself, always cheerful and quite fearless . . . he cannot stand so much as older men but he is full of heart'. William showed him photos of his mother, and in no time Reggie was seeking to draw her into the family network, through the notion that Clare could retail such news as she had of the Sherwoods to his mother at Tupton Hall, near Chesterfield. 'I think she must be a charming person, she would I know be very bucked if you wrote a line to her', Reggie told his wife.

When William did not come back from the Malakoff Farm show on 7 May 1917 Reggie was totally devastated. 'I do not know what I shall do without him – he was my best friend in the battalion, the best officer I have ever met and the nicest fellow'. A short letter breathes his desperate feelings: 'he was seen to fall with his hand to his head in the midst of the enemy shouting a final order . . . Jordan was cut off with Alliban and had to cut his way through the enemy to regain his men. It is awfully tragic. I cannot write more now'.

For Reggie, the worst aspect of losing William was that he knew nothing of his friend's fate. 'I cannot think that he was taken alive by the enemy though they might have found him unconscious', he told his mother Isabel. Almost all this letter was in praise of his fallen colleague. The pain he felt reflected the knowledge that William had led a difficult attack on an impossible target quite brilliantly and yet lost his life in doing so. This was promise cut off in the bud. And his own dependence on the young man was hard to cope with. 'He was my right hand in everything', wrote Reggie, 'and any good times we have had (and as a matter of fact most of the time hasn't been too bad) have always been made jollier by his cheeriness'. For weeks Reggie had taken inspiration, without realising what it did for him, from this light-hearted and always sparkling youngster. Suddenly deprived of him he fell into nostalgia: 'I have heard his voice at the rear of the company encouraging men and helping them along – have seen him carrying one or two rifles in addition to his own equipment and later have seen him when out of sight of the men lying exhausted with lack of sleep and general fatigue'. Reggie's verdict was impassioned: 'his spirit was indomitable'.[23]

Constantly thinking of William Alliban, Reggie clutched at straws. No news, he related, but 'a man turned up who had been out two nights'. 'I wish we could get news of him', he yearned after three more days. The quartermaster was going on leave. He would 'see the Allibans as he knows them'. Mrs Alliban would surely be comforted by 'news of the district where her son fell'. A fortnight later his grief was still overpowering and, in this sudden vulnerability, he needed his mother's arms. 'I have had such a pathetic letter from Mrs Alliban tonight but what can I do? I can't tell her any more than I've told her, that news is bad enough. I don't know what to do and his loss is very great to me. I have no one to discuss things with now; he was my best friend . . . if you have time, would you write to Mrs Alliban in sympathy as she is heart broken, you know what I thought of him . . . I think he will get some decoration and have put him forward most strongly.[24] During the next months, Reggie found solace in regular correspondence with William's mother. She replied with long letters. Soon Clare was corresponding with her as well, offering her emotional support. 'It is very good of you to write to her, poor soul,' Reggie noted in March 1918.[25]

Graham Greenwell made friends with a subaltern called Hermon who came from his part of Oxfordshire. 'We sat down and had a long chat,' he wrote on 26 May 1915 from Ploegsteert Wood; 'he asked very much after you all'. They visited the grave of another of their friends. Dashwood, 'such a splendid fellow', the heir to Kirtlington Park, one of Oxfordshire's finest estates, who had been killed by a rifle grenade in that wood a fortnight before. Graham had written to his mother, Lady Mary Dashwood. Then, two days later, Hermon was shot in the head and died instantly. 'I shall go and see him buried this afternoon if I can,' Graham's brief grieving message declared.

Some months passed for him without more personal losses but Graham mourned the death of his adjutant early in 1916: 'quite one of our best and most useful officers . . . I liked him awfully'. Yet these casualties paled beside the slaughter he witnessed among officers in the Oxfordshires on the Somme. Two more 'of my late brother-officers have died of wounds', Graham related after two months of the battle: 'I can't help feeling more and more like the survivor of some great disaster . . . we had nine officers in this company alone and of them only myself and two others are left.'[26]

Officers and their NCOs often bonded closely. When his sergeant Macaulay was killed, Robert Hermon called him 'our first real casualty'. His own wedding anniversary on 14 January 1916 slipped from his mind due to this grief: 'he was one of my best sergeants and was in charge of the snipers'. He knew Macaulay left a wife and little girl. Like Reggie following William Alliban's death, Robert unselfconsciously looked to his own wife for help. He explained his feelings about Macaulay's instant death from shrapnel: since his enlistment in 1914 he had always been in Robert's squadron, and his wife lived at Ascot. 'I wish you could go and see her,' Robert urged, 'perhaps she would come and stay with us, she has a nice little girl about Bet's age'. Ascot was not so far from the Hermons' home at Cowfold. When Mrs Macaulay replied to his letter, Robert sent it straight on to Ethel, agreeing with her comment that it was a 'wonderful letter' from a 'brave woman'.[27]

Bereavement of friends was often noted sensitively in diaries or letters. Charlie May was sad for him when his colleague Towney's younger brother, in another battalion of the Manchesters, was 'put out by a hand grenade whilst instructing a class' as its bombing officer. Charlie knew him as 'a keen young chap, rather delicate but a promising officer'. He was very concerned, he noted in his diary, at seeing how it had 'rather knocked the guts out of Towney'.[28] Observing a close relative's distress was something many found particularly hard. Rowland Feilding had to write to the parents of a 'good lad' who had become 'incurably careless'. His inseparable brother had been serving with him. They buried the lad in a grave behind Le Rutoire Farm: 'the poor brother sobbed on his knees by the grave side, while the guns flashed and boomed in the darkness'. Such sights made Rowland melancholy, blotting out the more romantic images he had cherished of martial life and bringing home to him 'the cruel side of war'.[29]

When a commanding officer was killed in an unexpectedly sudden and tragic way battalion mourning was deep and heartfelt. The death of the commanding officer of the 2/5th Sherwood Foresters, Lieutenant Colonel G.H. St Hill, in a quiet sector of the line on 7 July 1917 took everyone by surprise. The battalion history records the general disbelief. Notoriously fearless, he was caught by a sniper while pointing out features of the landscape on his usual round of the line in a shallow portion of the trench. In a short message that day to Clare, Reggie Trench noted 'he was a very tall man and would never stoop enough'. Reggie's confidence as a young officer had been built upon St Hill's experienced advice. Now he was in shock at losing 'the finest gentleman that ever trod the earth . . . he has done a great deal for me – and an enormous lot for this battalion. I tremble to think what may happen now'.

We can set the record of Reggie's personal feelings in this case against the battalion account that we have of unaffected mourning. St Hill had endeared himself to officers and Tommies alike by his 'large genial presence and homely commonsense, his love of humour and fair play'. Three weeks later, when Reggie rode over to the little cemetery at Neuville-Bourjonval to pay his respects, he found 'a nice oak cross erected'. Soon he was in correspondence with St Hill's widow in London. When she sent some lettering she wanted to be put on the cross he passed it on to Padre Judd, who took the matter in hand and produced a new cross which Reggie thought personally was 'too much ornamental'. Commemoration was experimental and disorganised, an outlet for immediate needs when establishing sites of mourning, during the war. Mrs St Hill was one of thousands struggling to create a language of commemoration of her own that somehow salved her loss.

'Do go and see her,' Reggie urged Clare. A close friendship between his wife and the widow of his commanding officer developed, and Mrs St Hill started sharing her strong spiritualist beliefs with Clare.[30] She also sent cakes, 'about two feet square', at intervals to Reggie for her husband's men at the Front. Gifts of 'a priceless cake, a large cheese and two bottles of cherry whisky' arrived in November 1917 and 'went pretty quickly I can tell you'. We cannot measure the depth of emotion Reggie felt for his lost leader through references such as these. But his comment, in November 1917, when he had passed near the spot where St Hill died, about seeing this as 'a place of tragic memories', is eloquent.[31]

Even an apparently matter-of-fact account of the loss of comrades could conceal raw emotions and depth of sorrow. Horace Bruckshaw related in his diary being sent in wagons to work up at the line at Aix-Noulette. The wagon behind him was shelled 'just as they jumped down, killing one man and wounding three. Fisher one of the wounded died soon after.' 'A party of our chaps went to bury the poor lads who were killed last night', his entry the next day ran. Peter McGregor wrote home vividly about Jock Burns, killed instantaneously by shrapnel just after they had been chatting together. 'One of the chaps came rushing out of the next bay – stretchers quick – "who is it", I called – "Jock Burns" – I could say nothing but "O Christ" – I never felt so miserable in my life – such a nice young boy. When the stretcher came with its burden, there lay poor Jock – I could say nothing – I had two drops of his blood on my hand for two days.'[32]

Concern about friends when they returned wounded to England was very common. 'I'm awfully sorry to lose him,' Billie Nevill commented when his old wiring sergeant, Sergeant Ruffles, had his thigh bone smashed in a crater but managed to crawl in to the line. 'He's doing well and probably home by now,' he noted cheerfully.[33] Ernest Smith was thrilled when his pal Ferguson, whom he had got to know during training in the Artists Rifles, joined as bomb officer in the same company. In their first action together, however, Ferguson, doing 'more than his duty', was hit in the cheek by a bomb while 'hurling them and holding the men together in the most wonderful way'. 'I rushed down and found him being bandaged and about to be got away.' Ernest was deputed to take over. He sent his mother details of his friend's home address in Cardiff so that she could send commiserations to his family. He soon had letters from Ferguson himself, his mother and his sister, taking heart from the news that the only damage Ferguson had suffered which might be permanent was complete deafness in one ear.[34]

Reggie Trench remained anxious about his colleague Rossiter, wounded at Le Verguier. Hearing he was invalided home and in the London Hospital, he urged Clare to visit him when she was in town: he was his friend Stebbing's subaltern, 'a most charming chap, old Inns of Court man'. Reggie was always thinking of how to involve his wife and at the same time help her to gain information about the Front: 'I think you would like him and he might give you some news.'[35] In early 1918, it happened that Corporal Redgate, the stretcher-bearer who had brought Rossiter in at Le Verguier, also went home on the casualty list. By then Clare was alert to showing compassion to any Sherwood Forester in convalescence. Reggie remembered Redgate as a 'very good cornet player' in Stebbing's company, as well as a stretcher-bearer on that traumatic day of his first battle. He knew how Stebbing was feeling his loss: 'I should be glad if you could manage to take him to a show – I am sure he would enjoy it. Can he walk though?' Social hierarchy was set aside, in Reggie's eyes, by regimental loyalty. But deference, of course, would remain as a corporal and the wife of his major at the Front sat together in the West End stalls.[36]

Men on the Western Front grieved often and deeply. For many, grief was one of the hardest parts of all in their precipitate growing-up. But, as grief for the fallen and concern for the wounded were shared, it enabled the making of new family links and encouraged new ways of widening wartime friendships. The bonding that came from shared loss, moreover, was a crucial way in which families at home and men at the Front understood and shared the nation's commitment to the patriotic struggle. More and more that initial and eager patriotic commitment, for soldiers at the Front, became a commitment to simple endurance.

CHAPTER 9

'I Merely Did my Duty'

Discipline and Morale

Morale is the impetus which drives a soldier to conquer fear and carry out his duty. Discipline is the external force which substantiates this. Morale can be defined as 'the common shorthand for military resilience and combat motivation'. It is

> the thinking of an army . . . the way it feels about the soil and the people from which it springs . . . the way it feels about their cause and their politics as compared with other causes and other politics . . . about food and shelter, duty and leisure, weapons and comradeship, discipline and disorder.

Morale was maintained by a combination of factors in the Great War with patriotism acting as its wellspring. Leadership, we have seen, gave it direction and force. Care for the men's well-being by junior officers, it is clear, secured its continuation. It depended, Alexander Watson has argued, on training men to 'act in ways totally at odds with most civilian experience . . . to endure severe discomfort, place themselves in mortal danger and even break the ultimate taboo of taking life'.[1]

In the regular army, morale was traditionally seen in terms of coercion. There were very few initiatives taken at the level of Higher Command during the Great War simply to foster morale.[2] Regimental and junior officers were left to use their own efforts to promote it within the context of the army's disciplinary and administrative system. The recollection of Charles Carrington in 1965 is instructive: 'a memory that disturbs me,' he wrote, 'is the hint or warning that came down from above, now and then, that morale needed a sharp jolt . . . it was expedient that some man who deserted his post under fire should die to encourage others'. Carrington recalled how discipline would then be 'screwed up a couple of turns'. This might involve both death sentences being confirmed and, at the battalion level, field punishment being 'lavishly imposed and harshly administered'.[3]

Much attention has been given to capital courts martial and death sentences. It was books like Julian Putkowsky and Julian Sykes's *Shot at Dawn*, published in 1998, which fuelled the recent campaigns for a parliamentary pardon for soldiers who were executed in the Great War. The brutality of these executions has captured the imagination of a wide reading public. The facts are as follows: 346 men had their death sentences confirmed. This was 11 per cent of the men who were sentenced to death by courts martial and 0.006 per cent of the British army as a whole.[4] The military historian Richard Holmes confessed that for him the issue of these capital sentences 'divides head from heart'. While his head applauded their logic they still broke his heart.

Higher Command put great emphasis on external aspects of discipline, such as saluting. A routine order in December 1914 stressed that there was to be no relaxation in saluting in the field except during active operations. There were often reminders from commanders at various levels about the importance of it. Hardened regulars and NCOs found it difficult to adjust to the influx of commissioned middle-class volunteers. These men resented the army's bullshit, feeling themselves landed in an alien world. Ernest Smith put this particularly clearly, commenting on how pleased he was, after six weeks in the Buffs, that his pal Ford, with whom he had trained in the Artists Rifles, had joined him. 'The other officers in the company are all too military for us and will talk of nothing else,' he told his mother. Men like Ernest sought to manage things differently, creating their own universe of moral authority at the level of junior command. Yet they were always wary of being called to account.[5]

The rules and punishments prescribed by the official army manuals, we now know, were applied flexibly. The type of unit largely determined its disciplinary record.[6] The commanding officer of a battalion was allowed to try soldiers for twenty-three military offences and to apply summary and minor punishments. These included the standard field punishments, detention, fines, deduction of pay, punishment drill and admonition. Company commanders could deal with minor offences by delegation. Thus there was considerable autonomy for commanding officers in how they managed their men and in how far they allowed others to deputise for them. Tradition and practice varied widely.

Flogging in the army had been retained until 1881 but then replaced by field punishments numbers 1 and 2. These were intended to fulfil the need for a campaign punishment that was exemplary.[7] In field punishment number 1, known as crucifixion, men were tied to fixed objects such as posts or wagon wheels for set periods of humiliation. Number 2 was effectively hard labour, for a period of up to twenty-one days, without the daily two hours of ritual public immobilisation.

Field punishment number 1 was administered on 60,210 occasions during the war. About one soldier in fifty served it at some time.[8] It was a severe physical and psychological ordeal. Field punishment acted as a constant reminder of the power that the army exercised over men's bodies, hearts and minds. Higher Command believed it was effective as a deterrent. There is some evidence to support this and some to the contrary.[9] But it is clear that it aroused powerful emotions among both officers and men. One NCO, A.W. Feen, described crucifixion as 'disgusting and humiliating', especially with French civilians looking on; another NCO, G. Buckeridge, said it made him 'sick with resentment' and that was likely to 'embitter a man for ever'.

In a diary entry on 4 July 1916, Private A. Surfleet wrote of seeing a man secured to the wheel: his 'head lolled forward to drive away the flies . . . I'd like to see the devils who devised it lashed up like that.'[10] 'One of my early memories,' wrote Lieutenant F.P. Roe in his 1981 memoir, 'was the sight of a garrison artilleryman on a very hot day handcuffed to the gun wheels of his battery's gun carriages . . . he was sweating profusely and covered with flies.' The experience, he confessed, had haunted him for a long time. Victor Archard saw a colleague given fourteen days' number 1 'for swearing about an officer in his absence and to his fellow gunners'. He was set 'against the railings of the main entrance to camp with his arms tied to the rails about a foot above his shoulders'.

The BEF sought to exploit the deterrent effect of tough visible penalties. Occasionally lack of officer supervision could produce sadistic and illegal versions of the punishment. Arthur Moss recorded in his diary seeing a man tied to a wheel which was turned round 'ever so long until the head is downwards'.[11] When a soldier who had witnessed the sufferings of nine men who had been awarded number 1 field punishment at the Calais base camp sent an account to Sylvia Pankhurst, she published it in an attempt to arouse opinion in England.[12]

Rowland Feilding, though, coping with an epidemic of crime and insubordination while commanding the Connaught Rangers in 1917, reflected that field punishment could fall 'so flat that the hardened offender cares nothing for it'. Some delinquents awarded it were still with him, providing 'a constant source of trouble and annoyance'. However, he understood the General's difficulties. Some of his men had received heavy sentences of imprisonment at his courts martial which the General had commuted to field punishment: 'a certain kind of scrimshanker, scenting danger ahead, is apt to commit some crime, hoping thereby to get imprisonment and so be removed from the firing line'.[13]

Research in the National Archives and its own archives has illuminated the wider disciplinary framework in the 6th Liverpool Rifles. A relaxed disciplinary regime was firmly entrenched there as part of its Territorial tradition. The casualty books of the Rifles, together with centralised courts-martial ledgers, reveal the extent of punishment. The only weakness of this record is the omission of offences dealt with by company commanders not considered sufficiently serious to warrant entries in the casualty books. Between February 1915 and March 1919, 176 soldiers were tried by the CO and courts-martial were invoked forty-two times among a population of 5,000 men serving abroad. Formal discipline thus affected a small minority in this battalion.[14]

Self-inflicted wounding was the most frequently occurring court-martial offence in the Liverpool Rifles. It seems to have been a significant threat generally to the operations of the BEF, with 3,478 soldiers tried for self-inflicted wounds before October 1918.[15] Nine men from the 6th Liverpool Rifles appeared for shooting themselves in the hand, neck or foot. The pattern of these prosecutions interestingly mirrored Charles Wilson's analysis of endurance in the trenches. In five cases, self-infliction occurred within a month of joining the battalion, suggesting the new soldier's debilitating fear of the unknown. In other cases, where fear was slowly corrosive of morale, men took on average eighteen months to resort to self-mutilation.[16]

Reggie Trench told his wife about the 'annoying' incident of one of his men shooting himself in the foot with his revolver, and explained how he saw self-infliction: 'any man who does this is put under close arrest immediately and is inevitably court-martialled. Unless there is very strong evidence that it was quite accidental he gets a pretty heavy punishment. You see a mere bullet wound in the foot is nothing (to some men) to the risk of sudden death.' Reggie was convinced he had men who 'would choose this method of getting out of service for a few weeks anyhow', if punitive deterrence was not enforced.[17]

Six men in the Liverpool Rifles were court martialled for sleeping on sentry duty at the front or in a support line. Their suspended sentences were six months' imprisonment or five years of penal servitude. This severity indicates the seriousness with which the authorities viewed the risks they had posed to the security of the units concerned. But junior officers found lenience and concealment tempting for an offence that carried the death penalty.[18] Ernest Smith related a case to his mother. 'I found a couple of men asleep last night,' he explained, 'when they should have been on the look-out and – weakly I suppose – brought them up for "inattention" only as I knew they had had hardly any sleep for a long time and could not bring myself to take the worst view of the case.'

Ernest expanded on the dilemma he had found himself in as a civilian in arms. If his action was known, he 'should be hauled over the coals pretty severely'. His dressing-down of his men was designed to impress them and obviate its happening again. 'I shall feel bound to go the whole hog the next time,' he comforted himself. When he had ordered one of his sergeants before the captain of his company for a minor offence, he confessed he found it a 'beastly job'. His mother, he believed, knew how soft he was: 'as you may imagine I would let anyone off on the smallest excuse'.[19]

Max Plowman once or twice tackled sleeping on duty in his own way, he noted in his 1929 memoir. A 'dud' sergeant fell asleep during a bombing party under cover of night. He should have had him before the CO but he let the man off because he knew another was shortly rejoining 'to take the worthless beggar's place'. He related the story of how he startled Old Bert, when going on his rounds of the front line. 'I load my revolver and fire it over the top, almost in the man's ear, shouting "Hands Up!" . . . there follows a short and vehement address . . . I don't think Bert will sleep on sentry again.'[20]

Between 1914 and 1918, 25,844 men were sentenced for absence without leave in the British Expeditionary Force. Whereas there were only three courts martial for absence and three for desertion in the Liverpool Rifles, this was apparently a more common offence in regular battalions. Between 1915 and 1918 there were fourteen courts martial for absence and fifteen for desertion in the 1st Gloucestershire Regiment.[21] Both offences can be seen as alternative manifestations of psychological collapse. Gunner Peter Fraser recorded in his diary that he had allowed a sergeant who had absconded from the Royal Field Artillery to sleep in his billet. He was 'very near a complete breakdown'.[22]

Desertion, which carried the death penalty, could be the casual act of a confused soldier. Max Plowman dramatised an authentic example when he had to act as 'prisoner's friend' in 1916. The court-martial, according to his memoir, took place in the town hall at Molliens-Vidames, temporarily converted into a music hall for the divisional entertainers, with Pierrot drapery still adorning the stage. The man, a miner in the habit of drunken bouts at home, had slipped away from the battalion, taken off his shoulder-straps and reached Paris, where he was arrested ten days later. Plowman, questioning him under oath, sought to show he had not deserted 'but, after getting drunk, had wandered off like a fool and then, putting off the day when he would have to face the music, had not troubled to seek out the battalion'. 'I knew he was a brave man,' Plowman declared, 'who had often volunteered for patrols in the trenches.' Later in this narrative, he noted that his 'deserter' was not to be shot. He was sentenced to two years' hard labour, which it was expected he would wipe out by meritorious conduct in the trenches.[23]

Charlie May reflected in his diary on the tension between exacting the letter of the disciplinary code and supporting his men. It was stupid, he felt, to use power over them as a bludgeon. When his servant lost control of himself and drank too much, leaving chaos in the kitchen and unwashed debris in his scullery, he could 'not find it in my heart to blame him'. But he smiled when Bunting fell into a pond, returning 'bedraggled and repentant'. When he spent a 'happy afternoon' out training his Tommies and they 'did everything wrong they possibly could and were most cheerful about it', he reflected 'I could have strafed them'. But he could not bring himself to do so. When he had a bad tummy and, investigating, found the cook's utensils were in a disgusting condition, he gave him another chance because the man was so sorry about it. But he swore he would impose seven days' pack drill on him for another 'spot of grease on pots and pans'.[24]

But, believing that officers' standards of conduct put them above the men, Charlie was shocked when his subaltern Bowby was arrested, together with his sergeant major, for drunkenness. Angry with his colleague, he feared trouble to the company and that 'the good name of the battalion will be lost'. Bowby himself, he wrote on 29 March 1916, was 'pitifully drawn': 'what his poor mother will do I shudder to think'. Four weeks later, he noted that Bowby, soured by the suspense of waiting for his court martial, had taken the outcome badly. His sentence of dismissal had been reduced to forfeiture of seniority and transfer out of the battalion. Charlie felt he could not 'trust him again as one who drinks'.[25]

It was predictable that unofficial punishment was often winked at. When he was cheeked by a man in his section, Corporal Charles Arnold knew he would get away with giving him a good hiding. 'The fellow thanked me afterwards,' he noted, 'because if I had put him in the guard room he would have got about three months imprisonment.' Captain Stanhope suggested, when a man was brought before him for being 'always late and always filthy', that the company should see he washed properly. Later, in the bath house, hearing yells he looked round to see the man being forcibly cleaned with a hard scrubbing brush and nearly boiling water. NCOs were sometimes prepared to use violence to bring their comrades under control. Sergeant Reeve gave three drunken Tommies what he called a 'quiet hint'. They 'looked lovely objects', he recorded in his diary, 'as they crawled out of the green pond'.[26]

Thus archival material does not support the view that military justice in the Great War was usually an oppressive and cruel system which paid no attention to the reasons for men's behaviour.[27] There was more flexibility than was at first apparent. Horace Bruckshaw recorded a minor incident in his diary. Disturbed by a rat scrambling across their heads in his billet, someone struck matches 'to see where it came from'. 'In comes an officer taking our names etc for having lights and creating a disturbance . . . we were reported this morning but after I had spoken out we were discharged.' 'They will shove a chap in the rattle for any mortal thing,' was the cynical comment of this hardened Tommy about some cases of harsher discipline he had heard about.[28]

Our officer letter writers did not much like sitting on courts martial. Graham Greenwell 'sympathised sincerely' with the defendant, when he spent an unprofitable morning in February 1917 judging 'some poor devil who had tried to keep warm by drinking a pal's rum ration as well as his own'.[29] Reggie disliked sitting on a General Court-Martial when a fellow officer was charged with being drunk: 'it was not much fun trying an officer – I am glad I did not know him'. But when a man was charged following an incident which led to a serious fire in his dugout, Reggie had no choice but to give evidence for the prosecution. Questioned about his character, he insisted he was 'certainly one of the cleanest, smartest, most hardworking men' he commanded. The Tommy, who, as we have seen, in a silly mistake had put paraffin not water on to boil, was acquitted. Reggie, believing his evidence was crucial, was delighted at this outcome, writing ruefully, 'I expect I have now spoilt him for all time'.[30]

Armies sought to socialise men into a martial culture of obedience and group loyalty. This has been the underlying theme of our examination of going to war. Recruitment was followed by the oath of allegiance to serve the King faithfully and pay superiors 'due respect and obedience'. Recruits had to promise to prove themselves brave and loyal soldiers. Individuality was eliminated by uniform clothing which identified rank and expressed hierarchy. Punishment marked certain behaviour as unacceptable. Men to a considerable extent were frightened into compliance. The degree of adaptability in enforcing the rules that we have discussed here simply stressed the power officers held over their men. Tommies always lived under close supervision. The Corps of Military Police expanded from 405 to 13,414 men during the war, though day by day it was officers and NCOs who ruled men's lives.[31]

Promotions, awards and medals were the positive incentives that encouraged both officers and men to go beyond the call of duty. Back from leave, Reggie Trench learnt on 27 July 1917 that he was to be appointed second in command of the battalion. 'This would mean my long deferred Majority and better pay,' he wrote to Clare triumphantly. The promotion was signified by a crown and another ring on his cuffs, he explained, 'in lieu of two rings and three stars'. 'My appointment is definite as far as the Brigade is concerned,' he wrote two days later, 'the Brigadier called me aside at church parade this a.m. and told me he wished it put forward.' He reminded her to watch the *Gazette*, regularly published in *The Times*, under 'Territorial Forces, Sherwood Foresters', for his name to appear.[32]

Promotion from company command to battalion second in command meant another kind of life. 'It is different in a way as one has not got one's own absolute authority,' Regggie reflected. He was sorry to lose contact with D Company, which he had commanded since disembarkation in February 1917. Yet the scope of the new job fully made up for this. He threw himself into manifold new responsibilities. One of these was making recommendations for medals to be awarded to his Tommies in the 1918 New Year's Honours. He took this confidential business very seriously, making six copies of his final selections himself to send to Higher Command, so that the orderly room clerk would learn nothing of them. Realising how much a medal meant to the men, he worried over this when the recommendations came round again in February 1918: 'it is very difficult to choose who to send in,' he reflected.[33]

Although he never spoke directly of his own motivation in his letters home, it seems clear that Lance Spicer was another officer whose distinguished career acquired some of its drive from public recognition. His work on the Somme brought promotion to Captain. His contribution at Passchendaele won him an MC. Reconnaissance of his battalion's position under heavy machine-gun fire brought the award of a bar to his MC in July 1918. Lance carried out an immediate reorganisation of the Brigade when his CO was wounded in October 1918, earning him the DSO just before the war ended.[34]

Promotion within non-commissioned ranks was purely meritocratic. Will Streets, the miner just out of the pit in Derbyshire, set his sights on rising through the NCO hierarchy. He did so steadily. His talents were quickly recognised in those first training days in Sheffield. Just before the battalion settled at Redmires he was awarded his first stripe. As orderly corporal he was in charge of the parade of men reporting sick, he explained on 4 December 1914, so could not get home that weekend. His promotion meant 'more discipline, more endurance and less time off'. Notes in his papers from this time indicate some of his responsibilities, including a list of his duties, about musketry practice and on the rations in bacon, bread, cheese and jam that he was required to order daily.

In May 1916, when the York and Lancaster Regiment was preparing for the Big Push, Will became a full sergeant. He reflected in a letter home on the change he had watched in himself since his training in England. His diffidence had gone: 'from the first in the trenches I felt a great confidence come over me'. 'You see I am in a position to show my worth now,' Will told his mother on 23 June: 'I never did fancy myself in the drill square, but leading men into action I am at home.'[35]

Cyril Newman, surprisingly given his efficiency and utter reliability, never became an NCO. This may be explained by the specialist role he took up in

May 1916 as a signaller in the London Regiment. He remained a signaller, becoming expert in the technical requirements of the job, until he was invalided home in August 1918. The chapter structure he created for the unpublished typescript he made of his letters, nevertheless, highlights two key moments in Cyril's military career. In 1917, he was recommended for a field commission; in 1918, his work during the German spring offensive earned him the Military Medal.

Letters to Winnie explain Cyril's emotions at these times. The offer of a commission came on the initiative of the commanding officer of the battalion in August 1917, who evidently recognised Cyril's exceptional standing and the respect in which he was held. Cyril, knowing field commissions were then highly unusual, felt it was 'a great honour'. He prayed earnestly about it, realising 'it would mean more responsibility, easier conditions but perhaps greater risks'. He decided to accept. Both the Adjutant and the Medical Officer, a particular friend, were 'quite sure I should do well'.

'Beloved one,' wrote Winnie, 'I shall love Lieutenant Newman but had you remained an ordinary Tommy to the end of the war I should have loved you just as much.' There turned out to be comfort in those words because in September Cyril had to tell Winnie that the War Office had, just at this moment, stopped all direct field commissions. They reckoned the cadet schools in England were cram full of men preparing to go to France. The news of the offer to Cyril meanwhile had spread rapidly at home. His Sunday school class and office were full of expectations. Embarrassed that Winnie had to let them down, he sent her the Adjutant's letter of explanation to make carbon copies for all concerned.

When Cyril won the Military Medal in April 1918 he sent the telegram from the Corps Commander about it back home at once. He was one of two men in the regiment so honoured, he explained. His medal was for 'mending telephone lines under shellfire and for gallantry in keeping up communications during the recent fighting'. Winnie related the rejoicing in Muswell Hill. When the telegram was read out in the Sunday school 'everyone clapped heartily' and 'twas as much as I could do to control myself'. When she got home, 'there I knew it,' exclaimed her sister Dorothy, 'I dreamt last night that he had done some great deed.' Dedication to duty needed recognition as much as did acts of bravery. Cyril would not have it said that he had been heroic. 'I merely did my duty,' he declared, 'under difficult and dangerous conditions.'[36]

Regimental loyalty was a potent source of morale. It was a sound move to equip new battalions with an instant pedigree by founding them within the existing regimental framework.[37] Dress distinctions and ceremonial parades imbued soldiers with a sense of belonging to unique and arcane communities with glorious traditions to uphold. Captain Yoxall, serving with the King's Royal Rifle Corps, told his mother, 'when you're a member of a great regiment like the Sixteenth you feel yourself in a sense immortal'. Shared historical memories, customs and a myth of descent all defined the culture of particular regiments. Rowland Feilding described a march at the head of the Connaught Rangers: 'each time the drums struck up and each time they stopped, a wild Irish yell went up'. They marched to 'Brian Boru', the ballad of the Irish chieftain who became King of all Ireland in 1002. There was a cry marking certain bars in this spirited tune which, Rowland believed, always brought 'either tears or laughter' to the eyes.[38]

At the battalion level, association with local communities was crucial in 1914 and 1915, sending men to war with a shared identity. Of Kitchener's service and reserve battalions, 215 were raised locally. Bristol, Liverpool, Manchester, Birmingham, Hull and Newcastle all contributed Pals battalions to the war effort. Such battalions necessarily became more heterogeneous during the war. Yet many of those from large conurbations did manage to preserve local identity by additional recruiting from their own counties.[39]

One of the tasks Reggie Trench tackled with gusto as second in command of the 2/5th Sherwood Foresters was reviving its regimental fife and drum band. 'These lads are supposed to set an example to all the battalion in smartness,' he explained to Clare. He was getting 'new paint for the eight tub drums, Notts and Derbys crests to paint in . . . new uniforms for the lads, button polish, boot polish . . . everything new'. The band became a serious preoccupation. Reggie's letter to Isabel Trench on 16 September 1917 was full of it. He had 'a very good corporal in charge – aged twenty with two good conduct stripes'. His drummers and buglers were 'quite good now despite the fact that only two can at present read music'. Would she feel able to present a tenor drum to the battalion? he asked.

'Our band progresses,' he reported to Clare in October. It was still largely in one piece since it had not gone into the line at Passchendaele. Reggie was thrilled with the handsome baton, 'wrapped round with white leather with a large silver knob with the battalion coat-of-arms on it', that he had obtained. Other battalions would be 'green with envy' when they saw this being carried by the band leader. Isabel's tenor drum arrived, making 'an awful lot of difference': 'they play retreat now finishing up with the regimental march and then "God save the King"'. Music from a well-drilled band on parade, it was understood, was the very essence of sustaining battalion morale.[40] 'I forgot to tell you,' Rowland Feilding informed Edith soon after taking command of the Connaught Rangers that we have 'a band of drums and fifes and Irish bagpipes'.[41]

Morale, Reggie believed, expressed the cohesion of battalion officers and men. The three group photographs he organised in October 1917 signified both hierarchy and *esprit de corps*: warrant officers and sergeants, with himself as commanding officer in the middle since Lieutenant Colonel Gadd was on leave; the band; and the twenty-one battalion officers as a group. In the back row of the officer group Lieutenant Woolley-Smith held the terrier bitch Betty, the battalion mascot, standing between Captain Judd, the padre, and the Medical Officer.[42]

In a thoughtful letter to his headmaster at Marlborough, written on the first anniversary of the outbreak of the war, Charles Sorley, still only twenty, reflected on the officers with whom he had 'rubbed shoulders unceasingly for the last nine months'. 'They are extraordinarily close, really, these friendships of circumstance,' he had found, 'distinguished as they remain from friendships of choice.' It was incorrigible circumstance that had 'kept us together, rubbed off our odd and awkward corners where we grated: developing in each a part of himself that might have remained always unsuspected, which could tread on common ground with another.'[43]

Charles Wilson had wise words about how anti-German propaganda by the generals fell on deaf ears. 'To cultivate the aggressive spirit men must be made to see red,' he noted, 'and the only way they could think of goading them to the required pitch of ferocity was to picture the enemy as infamous.' But the magnanimous Englishman did not respond, finding 'no help at all in blackening the enemy'.[44] The emotional gulf that existed from 1914 to 1918 between hatred of the Germans at home and the attitudes of men in the front line has been commented upon. Descriptions of killing in letters home rarely identify the enemy as a fellow human being. Depersonalistion was a predictable emotional defence.[45] But at the same time the padre Maurice Murray, back in Kent with a minor wound during Passchendaele, found his gardener horrified that 'we had tended almost as many Boche as our men in the aid posts'. The German 'is really not too bad and a great fighter,' Maurice believed, recalling the 'extreme pallor of German prisoners and their expressionless faces'.[46]

Yet there were others besides Julian Grenfell who gloried in killing and found huge joy in war.[47] Lieutenant Colonel Neil Fraser-Tytler complained to his father that 'only too many people . . . quite forget that the essence of war is to kill. They seem quite content to sit in their trench . . . and grumble at being shelled.' He kept a game book of 412 German casualties, which he claimed as his personal responsibility between February 1916 and September 1917.[48] John Fitzwilliams, captaining an artillery battery with cool efficiency, quickly learnt the ropes. 'I had a very pleasant little shoot,' he told his wife in one of his letters in March 1915, 'and quite enjoyed it though I would like to know what damage I'd done.' Technical mastery of his battery gave him considerable satisfaction. His letters home were a pleasant diversion 'between going out to let off a bit of hate to the Huns'. Invalided home in 1917, he was keen to get back to 'start repaying the Hun' in the hope of giving 'him a good trouncing'.[49]

Robert Hermon was a hardened campaigner. He was ready to agree with a friend who insisted the enemy was implacable: 'there was only one thing to do with a Hun and that was to kill him and then look for another and kill him too'.[50] But many found killing extraordinarily difficult unless it was sufficiently impersonal. Cyril Newman told of a Taube aeroplane it had been 'fun firing at' over his lines. He confessed he was glad that 'one seldom sees the result of one's firing: I do not want to *know* that I have killed a man'. But, he consoled himself, 'we have to do our best for our side'. The Roundheads in the Civil War had after all been 'indomitable fighters' for Christian truth.[51]

It was easier to be matter-of-fact about killing Germans as an aside in accounts of battle. They became impersonal, pawns in the game. 'Yes we captured Malakoff Farm right enough,' Reggie told Clare, pleased to find his own field of action reported in the British press, 'we had got the ground east of the farm in the morning and we killed several that were walking about there with their hands in their pockets.'[52]

'Live and let live' was actually much more crucial to sustaining morale than to sustaining the aggression involved in killing Germans. It has been suggested that combat motivation decreased during some periods of trench warfare.[53] That morning, Reggie related from the Cambrai sector on 24 October 1917, he had gone out at 'stand to' to the front line. 'Everything was very quiet – usually the quietest time is at about 7.0 a.m. when the Boche is having his brekker and a sleep after the night's work – our fellows ditto.'[54] The trenches were maintained on both sides by night work. But, day and night, soldiers had a sense of living with the enemy as an unseen but often active presence merely yards away.

'We have rather a sporting crowd of Huns opposite,' reported Billie Nevill late in 1915, 'as when we shell them they crawl out next night and put German flags in the shell holes!'[55] In October 1917, Rowland Feilding told of his young sniping officer's getting the signal of a 'miss' when he had found a target one morning. His intended victim was spotted 'raising and lowering a stick above the parapet'. Rowland knew of this being done with a shovel too. 'Our enemy evidently has some humour,' he remarked.[56]

It was the singing he heard that stuck in Wilfrid Ewart's memory from his first night sortie: the Austrian national anthem 'and every now and then there came too the sound of a mouth-organ, cheap and bizarre'.[57] The sounds of the war were always in the air on duty or off it, on patrol or on a digging or wiring party: one moment the crack of a rifle, the next the whistle of a bullet. Yet so often men could see nothing ahead of them but deserted countryside and mounds of earth. 'Except through my glasses I have never yet seen a Fritz,' reflected Charlie May in March 1916. He had been at the Front since the previous December.[58]

In long months of proximity without battle the temptation of fraternisation was often irresistible. This was spontaneous. Reinforcing morale, it gave junior officers and their NCOs some control over the conditions of their existence. In the lull after Loos, Lance Spicer saw nothing odd, on the 'eerie business' of patrol, about shouting across forty yards to start a conversation with the enemy. 'I don't think I have laughed as much for a long time,' he wrote, relating an hour spent talking to a German with a sweetheart in London who had lived in the Euston Road.[59] Technically this hour of conversation was a minor truce, an exchange of peace, not war. It was tacit, unofficial and illicit. Yet Lance wrote home about it triumphantly and quite unselfconsciously.[60]

Very unusually at Cambrin, the trenches were close, only twelve to fifteen yards apart. Rowland Feilding related communications by the Coldstream Guards across the intervening waste ground and mine craters. These were not, he understood well, intended to seek any kind of truce. Tommy Robartes, heir to the Cornish mansion of Lanhydrock, he explained, played a 'ruse de guerre' on 4 August 1915 to celebrate the declaration of war exactly a year before. Rousing the enemy with 'Die Wacht am Rhein' and 'Rule, Britannia' by the band, posted forward in a sap, he organised a huge bombardment, launched as the enemy swallowed the bait and clapped with shouts of 'encore'. The next few days there was desultory and vacuous chat across the lines with shouts of 'Kamarade', 'Tommy' or 'Fritz'. More to the point for Rowland, in a show of decency the Germans recovered the body of a corporal killed in no-man's-land, whose captain had crawled out and retrieved some of his belongings. They put up 'a notice saying that they had buried this man properly'. Such incidents, he believed, did much for the Coldstreams' morale.[61]

The tension between compassion and aggression was at the core of handling morale. For there was a fine line between hatred and mercy in the fraught conditions of trench warfare, as Francis Snell explained after hearing of the killing of a prisoner in cold blood. A German officer taken prisoner in a raid was being escorted back to the lines when a chance bullet hit one of the escorting party. They 'turned on him and killed him'. Snell's mess was divided by this 'rather rotten story'. 'More Bosche you kill the better,' said two colleagues. 'Deliberately, in their calm considered moments', Snell noted, by July 1916 'even lots of awfully nice chaps have simply put the Germans outside the range of all human sympathies.' He found it 'rather awful' to observe how war was hardening men's hearts.[62]

But our letter writers were generally sympathetic in their attitude to prisoners. Graham Greenwell visited a prisoners' camp on the Somme, concluding from what he saw that 'they are a rum crowd, but pretty human when they have got off their high horse and have had a bit of a rough time'.[63] Rowland Feilding could not but admire his countrymen's warmth towards Germans in captivity. Passing them in their cages on the Somme, he found prisoners laughing and smoking 'and eating bully beef supplied to them by our soft-hearted soldiers . . . I even saw one man go to the trouble of opening a tin of beef before handing it through the wires.'[64] Referring to an incident reported in the British press about four Germans discovered by the Buffs isolated in a dugout, Ernest Smith knew the story. 'They were very abject poor fellows,' he heard, 'but I am glad to say that our men treated them well.'[65]

The year 1914 was critical for the BEF when, facing demoralisation and disciplinary problems, the old regular army struggled to stabilise the line and resist German attempts to break through at Ypres. Self-inflicted wounds occurred more frequently that autumn and winter than at any other time during the war. It was in this still almost entirely professional army that desertion reached record levels. Surrender rates were also higher in 1914 than in any other year of the war. A degree of capitulation was a major but unmentionable reason for the virtual destruction of the regular army by the end of November 1914.[66]

Conditions on the Western Front worsened with the approach of the harsh 1914 winter. Morale in many units was at rock bottom.[67] This was when empathy began to develop between the opposing armies. The brekker ritual, Captain Liddell Hart wrote later, emerged when 'the homely smell of bacon gained its conquest over the war reek of chloride of lime and in so doing not only brought a tacit truce to the battle front but helped in preserving sanity'.[68] Men were basically forced to take account of each other's behaviour in order to stay alive. Thus rations were brought up to the respective trenches about the same time each evening. The impact of this on truce formation in quieter sectors of the Front was noted as early as November 1914.

One NCO spoke of ration parties becoming careless and laughing and talking on their way back to their companies. In the 2nd Scots Guards, where night raiding was common, 'almost a tacit understanding as to no firing' developed in the early mornings that winter. 'I saw eight or nine German shoulders and heads appear and then three of them crawled out . . . and began dragging in some of our fellows who were either dead or unconscious,' wrote

Sir Edward Hulse. 'I passed down the order that none of my men were to fire and this seems to have been done all down the line.'[69]

The famous truce of December 1914 was assisted by the onset, along the Front, of seasonal weather that turned the trees into Christmas ones, froze the mud and rimmed the barbed wire with snow. Suddenly savage fighting was replaced by fraternisation. In the sector held by the Scots Guards, Hulse noted in his battalion war diary, the truce was negotiated by a scout given a glass of whisky by a German patrol. This truce was observed with varying degrees of fraternisation almost everywhere in British no-man's-land. Second Lieutenant Chater told his mother of 'one of the most extraordinary sights today that anyone has ever seen'. He described the ground between the two trenches 'swarming with men and officers . . . shaking hands and wishing each other a Happy Christmas'. Some kicked footballs about in no-man's-land; some even chased hares.[70]

So crushing were the warnings from Higher Command that nothing like this truce recurred. Yet, in a much modified form, the Christmas truce continued in places throughout the war. Tradition and a shared European culture of friendly greeting on that one special day of the year is some explanation. But distrust and barely veiled hostility were a feature of truces in years after 1914. Waving to each other across no-man's-land felt harmless enough. But, watchful for foul play, men slipped Mills bombs into their pockets when sheer boredom induced them to engage in informal chats and exchanges of gifts in a mine crater. Neither in 1914 nor in later years was there relaxation of the will to win or of wariness towards a brave and respected enemy.[71]

Local truces to recover the wounded continued throughout the war and were accepted by junior officers despite official disapproval. Rowland Feilding described an incident during battle at Kemmel in February 1917 'as remarkable as any that this most unchivalrous of wars can have produced'. 'Our dead and wounded still lay out in No Man's Land,' he explained. His men responded when the Germans shouted 'send out your stretcher men' in English. He found them dressing wounded soldiers: 'one of my officers and a German were bending over a wounded man alongside the enemy wire'. 'The Germans, in considerable numbers, were lolling over and even sitting upon their parapet, watching the proceedings,' narrated Rowland; 'my own men were doing the same.' Taking charge, he told Private Collins to remove the bombs still bulging provocatively from his waistcoat. He 'rather sheepishly' did so. Once the British dead and wounded were recovered, Rowland ordered his men back below the parapet.

The war resumed. Rowland's management of this affair was statesmanlike. As commanding officer of the Connaught Rangers he had the sense, in the interest of morale, to collude in something he knew was 'highly irregular'. The battalion war diary for the month, interestingly, went astray. The episode is known only through his account of it in a letter to his wife Edith.[72]

The chronological story of morale on the Western Front is the key to understanding Britain's role in the eventual defeat of Germany. Kitchener's Army began to arrive in France in May 1915 when three divisions landed. Eighteen more were sent during 1915, leaving only five to arrive in the first half of 1916.[73] This made the summer of 1915 the real testing time for the New Army, the largest corporate body that had ever been created by the British state. Inevitably, senior commanders were handling enormous problems of man management and logistics. They were also seeking to come to terms with an entirely unfamiliar battlefield environment. This imposed its own logic on how the war could be fought. Weapons technology was developing very fast, yet communications technology was in its infancy. Officers at various levels were wrestling with the tactical and operational conundrums posed by trench warfare. Solutions, such as use of a brief but heavy artillery barrage to precede a limited infantry advance, were tried for the first time. But constraints on effective command and control in 1915 and in 1916 remained great.[74]

Our letter writers provide snapshots of the ups and downs of personal morale at this time. Graham Greenwell's vivid missives to his mother were often positive. One in August 1915 caught him in a reflective mood about how it would all end. Noting that 'most people seem to think that any peace would be satisfactory', he observed that 'as usual the great majority who are fighting don't know what they are fighting for'. But there were a few who realised by this time not to expect a final decision, but 'a salutary blood-letting to cool the overcharged European atmosphere of the last ten years'.[75]

Lance Spicer, thrown into the Battle of Loos within days of landing, remained convinced in his old age it was a 'fiasco'. But, spending the autumn of 1915 in an 'extremely quiet part of the line', he adopted a philosophical tone in his letters. 'I am inclined to think that we shall never have a real advance in this war unless we are a great deal more ruthless than we are at present,' he told his father, a Member of Parliament. He believed for instance that the logistics in battle of getting ammunition and fresh troops to the scene of the action, currently hampered by motor ambulances congesting the roads 'most fearfully', needed a fresh approach.[76]

'The day has been a hard one but the men are in fine spirit,' reported Rowland Feilding on the first day of Loos, when his Coldstream Guards still had some marching to do. A private, asked about the last few miles, had sworn 'if we can't do it on our feet we will do it on our hands and knees'. Rowland's view was that his men were 'looking forward to a scrap in the open, when they know, man for man, that they can beat the Germans'. The two-day battle did not turn out like that at all. Yet, Rowland told his wife a few days later, the army's experiences at Loos were 'wonderfully exciting' and 'the results have been to some extent satisfactory'.[77]

Major General Maxse, writing in November 1914, gave what may have been the soundest assessment of the strengths of Kitchener's Army compared with the regular army that it largely replaced. He was particularly impressed by the 'zest and fearlessness' of the junior officers. Kitchener's volunteers came predominantly from the skilled working class, with a high proportion of middle-class men. Maxse was in no doubt that the New Army units had recruited men 'of a higher standard than that of the average men we usually recruited in the old Army'.[78] We have seen how lengthy and thorough their training had been. On the Somme the New Army showed its mettle.

At the core of morale is the notion of duty, inculcated by a mixture of belief in the cause, willingness to endure and unit cohesion. It was sustained, as we have seen, by paternalistic leadership, by religion which brought solace to some, or by cigarettes. Patterns of leisure activity, from football matches to concert parties, which were familiar back home helped a great deal. Coercive discipline emerges as playing no more than a minor role in combat motivation, but in another sense, as self-discipline, it was crucially important. For it was through self-discipline that the relationships of mutual trust and respect between officers and men, which we explored in Chapter 6, bore fruit.[79] The British Expeditionary Force was on an immense learning curve as it came to grips with trench and attritional warfare between 1914 and 1918. Rowland Feilding's remark on his arrival back from leave in August 1916 – 'I left them boys and returned to find them men' – could well be applied to the war on the Western Front as a whole.

CHAPTER 10

'Very Gallant in Every Way'

Early Losses

It was during 1915 that the British public began to realise the scale of the losses the nation was suffering on the Western Front. The casualties at Neuve Chapelle between 10 and 17 March were 11,200; at Second Ypres between 22 April and 25 May they were 70,000; at Loos between 25 September and 14 October they were 50,000. On 25 September 1915, the first day of the Battle of Loos, the roll of honour notices in *The Times* filled four columns. It was in 1915 that the first of our letter writers were killed. Three of the soldiers who are leading figures in this book, Wilbert Spencer, Julian Grenfell and Yvo Charteris, were killed or died from wounds between March and October 1915. A fourth, Ernest Smith, died in the course of trench duty in December 1915.

The Battle of Neuve Chapelle was the first serious attempt to break through the German trenches in what was considered a weakly held sector. It taught the Allied Command some real lessons. The initial artillery barrage enabled an infantry attack which rapidly captured parts of the German line. Things then became much more difficult, since the defending German gunners knew the ground they were shelling.[1] Wilbert Spencer, approaching his eighteenth birthday, wrote home in reasonably good spirits on 8 March, two days before the attack was launched. A few days earlier Captain Rowe, commanding his company, had assured Wilbert's father that, though incredibly young for front-line service, he was a 'good subaltern officer' whom he would do his utmost to protect.

The 2nd Battalion of the Wiltshire Regiment was in the forefront of the assault on 10 March. The first telegram reporting Wilbert's death reached his father, an MP, on the 14th; a second one, from the King, followed on the 16th. Sydney Belsham, a subaltern colleague of Wilbert's, explained what happened. Soon after the Wiltshires had driven the Germans out of their trench and dug into it themselves, a German battery opened fire on them. Wilbert was killed instantaneously when a shell burst close to him, fragments striking his head and body. Four other men were killed by this same shell. Sydney spoke of the fearlessness Wilbert showed in action that day and of his 'cheerfulness and devotion to the men'. Some, he claimed, 'wept at his death'. He was leading a group of 'strong brave fellows' who had been commended for their 'courage and steadfastness'. Sydney returned Wilbert's gold watch to the family. Captain Rowe was wounded on the 10th, when the battle still raged at Neuve Chapelle. He wrote to the Spencer family when he had reached Guy's Hospital to have a shrapnel bullet removed from his shoulder. Though in his letters Wilbert had often been frankly depressed in his last weeks, in death he instantly became a hero, a born leader, his father was told. Rowe had 'often refused him permission to visit German lines at most dangerous times'.

Family grief often focused upon lack of information about proper burial. In the chaos of the battlefield rough and ready graves were dug for officers who were killed. Sydney Belsham and his colleagues said they knew exactly where Wilbert fell and a cross had been placed to mark the grave. Yet, in April 1915, Belsham confessed to the boy's father that they were not currently able to locate where Wilbert was buried. The grave was not in fact found so he is commemorated on the Le Touret memorial to 13,389 men for whom there is no known grave in the Pas de Calais prior to the Battle of Loos.[2]

The last weeks of Julian Grenfell's life are well documented. In February 1915 he started keeping a diary, showing a much gentler and more matter-of-fact attitude to the war than in his jaunty early letters to his mother which had been so full of bravado. His regiment, the diary records, moved closer and closer to the front line in the salient during the Second Battle of Ypres.[3] On 12 May the 6th Cavalry Brigade, which included Julian's Royal Dragoons, was in the second line of trenches, close to a small rise in the ground called Railway Hill. The Germans began a heavy bombardment of the trenches and the hill early on 13 May. The Royals were told to watch for a German advance round the flank of the hill. It was Julian, typically, who at noon went out and brought the news of the expected German advance. After carrying more messages he accompanied the General up the hill again. When a shell landed a few yards away both were hit by splinters from it.

Julian received a splinter from this shell in his head. Writing to his mother Ettie Desborough from the casualty clearing station on the 14th, he remained buoyant. 'I stopped a Jack Johnson with my head and my skull is slightly cracked but I am getting on splendidly.' Then, more anxiously, 'today I go down to hospital, shall you be there?' An X-ray at the hospital at Boulogne on the 16th showed that the wound was far more serious than had been supposed. There was damage to his brain. It was not clear whether an operation undertaken at once had been successful in saving his life. Early the next day his parents reached his bedside.

Julian was in a tiny room with two other badly wounded officers. His parents, in lodgings nearby, visited him twice daily but were not allowed to stay long. On the 20th, his brother Billy came to see him on his way to the Front with his battalion in the Rifle Brigade. When he left, Julian told him 'I'm glad there was no gap.' For a time he seemed to be getting better. But, on 23 May, the doctors discovered further inflammation on the brain and operated again immediately. From then on his parents and sister Monica were with Julian constantly. 'Hold my hand till I go,' he asked his mother. When he died on the 26th his parents had been there for nine days. There was time for the family to live with Julian's death and prepare for their grief. 'He died radiantly as he lived,' Ettie announced a fortnight afterwards; 'he seems very near to us.' 'Into Battle', Julian's sublime evocation of war, published in *The Times* on 27 May, was his fitting epitaph. The poem inspired many many people.[4]

During his five weeks in France, Yvo Charteris celebrated his nineteenth birthday. He told his mother how he enjoyed the marches which took the Grenadier Guards inland from St Omer, 'one's legs swung onwards by a thousand singing men'. They were heading right into the midst of the Battle of Loos which raged for weeks from 25 September 1915.[5] On the 29th, writing from Vermelles in 'bleak black mining country', Yvo told his sister Mary excitedly 'we have had Loos since Saturday, that's an advance of four to five miles'. On 6 October, reporting to his papa, he was still full of the battle, declaring 'we have got Loos (a terrible spectacle) and Hill 70 and consequently a distinct salient'. Yet he still could not get it out of his head that the German rockets were 'as good as any Roman Candles' he had seen at Fourth of June celebrations at Eton. Yvo was in denial that this was war. He confessed as much, telling his father that, on getting into the trenches, 'I found it difficult to persuade myself that a war was in progress and not a display of fireworks'.

Yvo's last letter to his mother spoke of their being ready 'to move up at an hour's notice'. So far he had not been close enough to the action to experience real danger. He had just heard that, as the postscript to this letter noted, 'our attack is progressing favourably and that we have taken the Hohenzollern Redoubt'. Yvo's commanding officer, Gerald Trotter, explained what happened when the 1st Battalion of the Grenadiers took over the front line on 14 October from a Territorial division. It was an 'unhealthy spot', within 140 yards of German trenches. They were ordered to try to bomb the Germans out of one of their trenches but were held up at a barricade.

Yvo's platoon supported the bombers who had moved forward. Men began to panic. 'I sent Yvo up to see what was wrong,' explained Captain Wakeman, who was commanding the attacking company, 'and get things going again.' Several times Yvo 'came back to report how things were progressing and went back up the sap quite disregarding the danger . . . the sap proved to be a very shallow trench . . . the Germans had machine-guns turned on it and I believe it was a bullet from one of these that hit him; death must have come at once and been quite painless.'

Gerald Trotter's letter to Yvo's father on 19 October confirmed this definitive account of his death two days previously. 'I am told he was very gallant in every way,' he commented, 'he was shaping so well as an officer.' Bernard Bates, Yvo's servant, writing to his mother was movingly direct about the platoon's care and respect for Yvo's body. They carried him to be buried at Sailly-Labourse, a village just behind the firing line (plate 31). A small wooden cross was erected with an inscription so that the grave could 'easily be found'. Bates concluded that 'there never was an officer so brave and fearless as Mr Charteris undoubtedly was and as a soldier I cannot but regret the death of a brave gentleman'. Sergeant Stagg, who had given him such support, wrote of how Yvo died 'a real noble soldier's death'. Stagg's last words to him that morning, tenderly recalled, had been 'Good luck, Sir.'[6]

The northern sector of the Western Front was comparatively quiet in the last weeks of 1915. Ernest Smith wrote home on 19 December about 'an eminently peaceful evening' in a nearby town with his friend Ford, 'during which we managed to get the war well out of our thoughts'. His leave was due. He expected to get away immediately after the next spell in the trenches that his battalion had by then been manning for some time. Ford wanted him to bring back an Aberdeen terrier from England and some gramophone records, and he had agreed to run these errands. He expected to reach Victoria about four o'clock on Boxing Day. His letter outlining these plans was in fact delivered after the telegram with the notification of his death.

Letters from his servant, his close friend Sergeant Mould and his colonel tell the story of how Ernest was killed. At 'stand to' on 22 December, 5.30 on a dark winter morning, he was spotted across no-man's-land. They 'put a shell at him and it bursted just in front of him and two of the pieces hit him, one in the head', Private Smith, Ernest's servant, explained. The stretcher-bearers bandaged him up and took him down to the dressing station when it was dark again. He was lapsing in and out of consciousness there and later at the casualty clearing station. He died during an operation lasting four hours to remove two pieces of shell which had penetrated the abdomen and which had fractured his skull. The surgeon, offering his mother what comfort he could, said that Ernest was very drowsy when he was admitted 'and certainly did not feel much pain'.

Ernest was buried in the Lijssenthoek military cemetery at Abeele. 'I could not believe it when they told me,' wrote his servant, who was 'along with him all the time', until it came to the operation. 'He was liked by every single man in his platoon and they were doing nothing else but talking about him all day,' Private Smith related. Sergeant Mould was very cut up. He believed the men loved Ernest. Personally, he wrote a month later, 'I have never felt the same since, I have tried but could not take any interest in my work since.' Testimony to Ernest's leadership was wholehearted, comforting a bereft mother with the knowledge that war had brought out the very best in her boy. The keynote was Mould's statement that 'anyone in difficulties he was first to lend a hand'. Edward Finch Hatton, his colonel, spoke sincerely of his great 'influence for good'.[7]

These early deaths of men whose patriotic commitment has shone through initial chapters of this book reminds us of the overall toll of lives, which, as we have seen, during 1915 grew rapidly. It shows us how the making of heroes began, as colleagues sought to comfort themselves about very young friends they had lost, using the best words they could find to celebrate the glory of soldiering lives which had been so quickly cut short. We shall return to Yvo Charteris's sacrifice of his schoolboy life as one of 'the best and choicest and unblemished' in Chapter 16. The construction of heroism was accomplished between 1914 and the 1920s, as we shall see, through words chosen during the mourning of thousands who had lost ones they loved.

CHAPTER 11

'Blighty, oh Blighty in about a Week'

Leave

Officers did much better than men in getting leave. They could expect it two or three times a year, while a single short trip home was the best the average Tommy could hope for. There was always a sense of unreality about going on leave. 'All he seemed to want was to be at home and rest . . . we did all we could to strengthen him up but the time was all too short . . . he felt parting keenly.' Robert Saunders's account described how he welcomed a son home from the Front in December 1915.[1] Letters home are often filled with men's excitement about and anticipation of leave. Some did talk when they got home. Members of the Liverpool Territorials, we are told, spoke much about their experience to families and friends at social and sporting clubs.[2] But how could they cross that chasm between life at the Front and in their homes, when so much about the war in France was simply unimaginable for their families? Overall, therefore, the actual experience of Blighty, the shock of suddenly being at home for a short time, is little documented in letters written during the war.

For officers who were single, leave meant family cosseting and catching up with the lives of brothers and sisters. Julian Grenfell was more privileged than most. Reaching the Front in October 1914, he twice enjoyed short trips back to his home at Taplow on the Chiltern Edge that winter. He was as predictably ecstatic about these leaves as he was about fighting. 'I've never loved three days better,' he told his mother in December, 'it was absolutely perfect and better from being so unexpected.' 'I did love my last leave,' he reiterated in February 1915. Then, projecting his own war fever onto his men, he declared, 'you should have seen our men setting out from here for the trenches – absolutely radiant with excitement and joy to be getting back to fight again.'[3]

Ernest Smith, with no premonition of how short his life was to be, announced his plans with suppressed excitement in June 1915. He would arrive at Victoria on the 25th and be leaving on the 29th. 'My idea is to have a quiet Sunday with you all at home,' he told his mother, 'and then bustle about on

Monday and fix up about my kit.' 'I cannot run about visiting,' he advised her, so he left it to her whom to ask on each spare day. He remained fussed about his kit, expressing his fears to his father that there would be 'no end of things to think of'. A friend had warned him how little spare time he had found there was 'but I expect he was rather more conscientious and minute than I shall be'. His leave turned out to be quite glorious, giving him renewed energy: 'it seemed to go in a flash, but at the same time I feel as if I am going to enter with zest into everything here'.

When his next leave came round Ernest had won his spurs in battle but was more worn down as a result. There was an even chance of the next week he announced on 2 October 1915: 'how I am looking forward to it!!' He ended a breathless note next day 'no more now as I can think of nothing but leave at the moment'. This time he worried that his men would lack his leadership while he was away. However, his right-hand man Sergeant Mould, he wrote later in a reassuring note, having arrived back after a comfortable journey, 'I find has not lost the platoon in my absence, or misbehaved himself in any way!'[4]

When Graham Greenwell published his letters home he set them out in chapters, divided by the five spells of leave he was granted over two years from November 1915 to October 1917. They bookmarked his time at the Front. Graham was pleased that his first leave gave him the chance to introduce his friend Conny, whose leave coincided with his, to the family in London. 'I shall clean up at the Grosvenor,' he promised, writing from Courcelles. Back in the 'rain and the gloom' ten days later, he reflected that already in early November 'the holiday seems like a distant and happy dream'. But the generosity of the officer leave rota at this period in the Oxfordshire and Buckinghamshire Light Infantry undoubtedly did much to keep men like Graham optimistic. There was no news, but 'the thought of seeing you all again next month keeps me cheerful and well', he wrote in mid-December 1915.

Graham's second leave, in February 1916, was marked by a bad return crossing: 'departures from the cabin though hasty were never too late . . . the sides of the boat were literally a mass of men groaning and swearing'. He was lucky to snatch a third ten-day leave in the run-up to the Somme, marred this time by a terrible sixteen-hour train journey back from Le Havre. It felt like a 'long martyrdom' when Graham's next leave was delayed until May 1917. But he was given three weeks then and another month that October, after Passchendaele. Many officers found this irregularity of leave as the war went on difficult to cope with. Tommies had no choice but to live with it.[5]

The officer rota for the East Surreys began three months after they landed at the end of October 1915. Billie Nevill started getting excited that his turn was coming in mid-November. In a letter to Mother, Elsie and Doff, to be sent on to Amy, Howard and Tom, he was at his most ebullient. 'I don't want to see any fodder out of a tin the whole time I'm home, twiggez-vous?' No peppermints or chocolates either, since he supposed he would be returning to them as staple fare all winter. 'Toast I should like and coffee, buckets of it . . . a nice fried lemon sole, some haddock! A chicken!, some fresh green vegetables (Stop it my tummy aches). And so on, ad lib.' A warning, he felt, was in order: 'I expect you'll find me a wee bit quick worded, but don't mind that.' As men contemplated getting home, they wondered if they would tell everything too fast or close up completely. Billie was generally verbose. He expected to be garrulous with his family.[6]

Billie's plan was to fill every minute. His brother Howard told sister Elsie in 1918, no doubt recalling Billie's attitude, that it was the change that counted: 'it does not matter if you do yourself to a frazzle as long as you have heaps of things to think of the next few months'. Billie's six days in December 1915 were hectic. It was 'topping' visiting his old school, Dover College and seeing how his brother Tom loved it there. He saw a new play in the West End called *Bric-a-Brac* and caught up with plenty of relations. He was pleased he did not spend too much money: 'yet we didn't exactly skimp, but, Mother, you paid a lot too much'. Don't let that occur again, please was Billie's reprimand. But Mrs Nevill's affectionate largesse for those few short days was totally understandable.[7]

His first leave made Billie more confident that the family were coping without him and would continue to do so. His letters became less frequent, and shorter: 'there doesn't seem the need to keep you disalarmed about me now . . . you know I am permanently alright'. Billie looked forward to his spring leave in 1916 immensely. He hoped for nine full days this time, warning 'don't let too many relations know'. The 6.15 from Amiens to Boulogne, then Folkestone, then Victoria. Billie set out the timetable in a hurried note on 26 April. 'Blighty,' he sighed in expectation, 'oh Blighty, in about a week.'

But Billie in fact enjoyed his spring leave less than he had done his winter one. His teeth had become a nightmare. The dentist's ministrations, completed in far too much of a hurry, had, it was believed, given the East Surreys a secret weapon. Billie's new death's head grimace when he smiled would, it was reckoned, finish off any Boche encountered in the enemy lines. Sadly his relationship, expected to turn into marriage, with Muff Schooling collapsed on this leave under the strain of separation. The best of it was his time with Howard, also on leave from the Front. They went off together to buy the footballs for the Big Push everyone knew was coming soon.[8]

Lance Spicer, like Billie, was jolted into constructive planning by the start of a rota in his regiment. The allocation of time, eight days in all – effectively six clear days in England – set his mind racing with plans for a dash to Edinburgh to see a brother and sister. 'I think I should go a burst and have a sleeper,' he decided, reckoning on saving travelling time to allow more social time. His good spirits when it was over suggest that Lance's leave was highly restorative. Of course 'the time was all too short', he wrote in February 1916. But he was emphatic about having 'enjoyed my leave enormously' and 'living on sweet memories'. An hour by hour account of the journey back was a necessary exercise in acclimatisation. In the weeks when the Somme battle raged, Lance yearned for another leave but he became philosophical about its not coming his way. Largely due to a shortage of officers, it was 'a complete and utter washout', he confessed in August 1916. He consoled himself by reflecting that fortunately he was then serving 'in a very quiet part of the line'.[9]

Those with small children had the profoundly moving experience of seeing how they had developed. They had to come to terms with the fact that they were missing this period in their young lives completely. Sometimes this made adjustment afterwards difficult. Charlie May reflected in his diary on ten days of 'utter unalloyed happiness' in February 1916 with his wife Maud and daughter Pauline. It was so soon over, 'like a dream'. The shelling he returned to seemed unreal. The contrast between trench conditions and his clean and comfortable home was almost unbearable. Four days back in the trenches he confessed to feeling that his leave had 'been with me awfully strongly till I have felt quite humpy and fed up'. He longed to see the 'bally war won'.[10]

Rowland Feilding was to and fro to France throughout the Great War, both because he kept sustaining minor injuries and on the regular leave he was permitted as a senior officer. He spent a few days with his family in August 1915 and again in September. After a period of heavy responsibility during the Battle of Loos he was again home, for a week this time, in late October. He hurried down to Devon to visit two of his daughters, Joan and Anita, at their boarding school in Sidmouth. In December, he was invalided home with a badly infected knee which kept him incapacitated until the following March. 'The sea was like glass,' he wrote to Edith, describing his journey back to the Front in April, 'the scene was very picturesque and rather spectral as our ship lay to, outside the great submarine net, waiting for darkness before setting out.'

Rowland had left Edith pregnant, and his fourth daughter was born in October 1916. It was his sister-in-law who found the time to send a full account of the baby. Joan, at twelve years old, was besotted, telling her father, in a 'delicious' letter, that 'so far she had only seen Pru with her eyes shut'. A week later, replying to her, he confessed he was 'simply pining' to see the new baby: 'what a lovely baby Prunella sounds from your description. I hope she will keep her blue eyes.' Three weeks later he was back home in Gordon Place, Kensington drinking in the sight of his new daughter. Another decent three-week period of leave followed in March 1917. A broken hand and fractured rib in a riding accident brought him home again in July for two months. Then he fell and dislocated his elbow when leading an attack in March 1918. He had chloroform twice before his elbow was put right in the field hospital, then needed weeks in a hospital in Park Lane, before returning for a final spell of active service in August 1918. Rowland's was an adventurous war. He was a great survivor.[11]

There were some senior officers who, utterly absorbed in their work, had real difficulty about taking leave. Ethel Hermon, pregnant and missing him, began pressing Robert to get home in August 1915. 'I will come as soon as I can,' he pleaded, 'of course all this is dependent on what the Boche does to us or we to him.' He felt tied by 'such an exceptionally good lot, both of officers and men', who 'so absolutely trust one and look up to me to do the right thing' that he was finding it hard to get away. Then Loos intervened. Robert decided to send his servant Buxton home in his place to reassure Ethel that he was 'fit and well'. He would tell her all the news and 'buck like steam': 'I wish I was in Buxton's shoes but it is quite impossible just now as I have so much doing ... believe about one eighth of what he tells you.' Buxton received credit from Ethel for not grousing, but he went beyond his appointed role by announcing the war would be over by Christmas 1915. 'I don't see how it can be,' Robert wrote, hastening to disabuse her. He suggested it could be May 1916 before the Germans 'came tumbling home very much faster than they went out'.

Robert was thinking about his wife's coming confinement and assumed they would have a second son. They agreed his name for the present should be Benjamin. He arranged for a fur coat to be sent from a London store, reckoning that if Ethel wore it at once 'both of you could benefit by it'. Their fifth child, who was a son, was born on 11 November but it was two days later that Robert heard the news. 'The glorious news dawned' on him when Buxton brought him a wire in the middle of mess dinner. 'The new moon is shining in an absolutely cloudless starlit sky and the whole world seems at peace,' Robert wrote, describing his mood that evening, 'there isn't a gun firing and if Ben wanted a better augury he couldn't possibly have it.' He was the happiest man in France and would be home in just a fortnight.

Meanwhile the children's reports poured in. Betsy said Benjamin had 'lots and lots of hair for his age' and 'it is a very dark baby'. But sometimes, she had heard, 'dark babies turn fair'. 'I expect they have nearly torn him to bits by now in their anxiety to hold him,' Robert told Ethel, adding 'I expect you are feeling as proud as an old Peahen' to have produced a fifth child. Even Tom Woolven, Robert's gardener at Brook Hill, sent a congratulatory letter. The mess became a distraction. Robert needed peace to communicate his deepest thoughts about women's bravery: 'not a word of all your pain and your nice cheery card a few hours afterwards'. His emotions were stirred and hard to handle. 'I am very tired of this life apart,' he had written earlier. But now there was more fruit from his loins; and another boy, too.[12]

Leave boats were now sailing from Le Havre to Southampton, a journey in darkness to avoid German submarines, which took thirty-six hours. The Hermons christened the child Kenneth Edward, not Benjamin, during that leave, so the baby shared his initials with Robert's regiment the King Edward's Horse. The Armistice on his third birthday, though they did not know it, still lay well off during that blissful period of family reunion in the Sussex country-side. Robert was devastated that his manly reserve broke down at his departure. He dared not open a note Ethel gave him containing a four-leafed clover, but thrust it straight in his pocket. He explained in a letter from Southampton 'I was sorry I was so stupid and just broke down for a minute . . . I couldn't have read a message from you and then said goodbye to the kids afterwards without breaking down.' 'You say it was hard going before,' he wrote, 'but this dearie beats anything.'

Two days later, Robert confessed to 'a large aching void, Lassie mine, which will take a lot of filling'. But he believed that his 'lovely time at home ending with Ben's nice little service' would last him some time. He had not yet got used to the name 'Kenneth'. Ethel scanned his letters for hints of depression. Emotionally he was at home, not in the mess at Vaudricourt that Christmas. He came clean in a letter on Christmas Day in 1915: 'I hardly dare think of your day at home and I can't write decently with other folk in the room.' Four days later Robert confessed: 'it has somehow been a bit of a job settling down again and it was really far easier going before than it was this time . . . I think if I had stayed for Xmas I should never have come back at all.'

When Ethel spoke of his next leave in March 1916 Robert read her a stern letter in duty. Sixty-one NCOs and men in the squadron had been 'out the whole time and not yet had leave'. He could not claim special stress to justify putting his need above theirs. 'I want to get the original men home if possible before one goes again,' he insisted. Yet by October he was ready to declare 'I am heartily sick of having been away so long . . . I am afraid dearie it will be many weary months before we can do things together once more . . . the end is not in sight.' He was both desperate to be back with her and the Chugs and could not bear the thought of another parting. Ethel had been writing about the possibility of a meeting in Paris. He dismissed her 'low mind' about this. He did get home for two weeks in October 1916. He agreed, presumably at Ethel's prompting, that they needed time for them to be just themselves. So they spent their last three days together in London, staying at the Berkeley Hotel. Ethel may have been suffering from premonitions of losing him.[13]

Leave was much associated in everyone's mind with sex, the most severe deprivation of military life, for many not easily resolved by available French country girls. Lieutenant General Hacking, inspecting the Royal Welch Fusiliers in 1916, 'chatted and chaffed', it was noted, 'pinched their arms and ears', as he passed along the line and asked 'how many children they had and if they could be doing with leave to get another'.[14] Reggie Trench, feeling increasingly sex starved in June 1917 after five months apart from Clare, told her that there was much talk of this in his mess. 'The great excuse we young married officers want to give is "sexual starvation" – this would pass as far as Brigade with endorsements in favour of leave I'm sure but I doubt if it would get past Division.' His campaign for leave had just begun in earnest, with his CO forwarding an application declaring 'that this "zealous and energetic officer" should have the rest that leave entails'.[15]

When Reggie started thinking about leave that May his mind ran on his daughter, now just eighteen months old: 'will she recognise me? and talk to me? . . . she must have a rocking horse soon mustn't she?' Once it became clear that he might get his leave while Clare and Delle were having their long summer spell on the south coast, it took shape in his mind, in terms of sea, sand, paddling and bathing. 'If the place is not too crowded we could bathe from some isolated cove along the shore,' he suggested; 'that would be much nicer than bathing with crowds of other people.' When he heard they were settled at Charmouth on 3 July, he declared 'it must be jolly' there, 'wishing there was a decent chance of getting down to you'.

Next day, leave seemed to be in the wind. 'I'll be in Blighty by Tuesday noon,' Reggie dreamed, 'and with you for night ops that night!!!' It was actually another ten days before Reggie was reunited with his family and then his mother joined them too in their lodgings at Charmouth. The photographs on the beach prove that this holiday was all they had dreamed about. When his leave was over, Clare travelled to London for their traumatic parting. Reggie was anxious till he had heard she was safely back in Dorset, where Delle's nurse had been tending the child.[16]

Clare's letters expressed disbelief that it was all over so quickly. 'Yes Darling,' he replied, 'I feel that I can hardly realise that I was ever lying on the beach with you and Delle or undressing with you on that grass under the cliff – its all a lovely dream. Never mind we did have the time and it will come again one day.' His great sorrow in his letters those next weeks was that Clare sent him no news of Delle welcoming a brother. He longed for a son. Another ten days' leave at Christmas in 1917 enabled Reggie to visit relatives in Berkshire and Warwickshire.

11. Reggie Trench's combined leave and railway ticket, 18 December 1917–1 January 1918, France to Twyford, Berks.

That Christmas leave he basked in his daughter's company: 'Delle is looking so awfully pretty now – and of course talking much more than she used to.' He sent his mother a little paper knife made by one of his pioneers, the handle from 'a Boche cartridge case', the blade from 'a piece of brass shell case'. He was thrilled with Clare's present of 'a ripping fur-lined "British Warm", that is a short coat reaching to the knees' with 'a fine big collar of opossum that turns up right over one's ears'. Trying for a son was a preoccupation during those precious days. Writing on the journey back, Reggie reflected, using the nickname Clare gave him, 'I think if we have a "Chennie" he will be quite fit as we are both so well – which is more than is always the case with men on leave'. But it was tough leaving home again. His account was clipped, concealing his massive emotions. 'I hated saying goodbye,' Reggie wrote, 'but we had a jolly time together. It gets harder every time to say goodbye.'[17]

The Sherwood Foresters endured a long, hard winter. Temporarily in command of the battalion in February, Reggie was very aware that many of his officers and men were well overdue for Blighty leave. Tension was mounting with the expectation of a major German offensive. Everything possible was being done to meet it effectively. An Amiens pass became the best to be hoped for in those winter days. This in itself was a taste of bliss, so there was much competition for these passes. Simply to walk up and down the main street of Amiens, 'a gay happy place untouched by the ravages of war, jostled by the throng on the Rue des Trois Cailloux, stopping here and there to look into picture shops or book shops, was a joy that made the long journey there in a dusty, bumpy lorry, a mere thing of no account', recorded the battalion history. 'I am sending officers and men in to Amiens every day,' Reggie reported, 'it does them good I think: any change is good for a man.'[18]

For two of our soldiers, falling in love and the pursuit of a love affair at home provided the emotional impetus to remain strong as a soldier at the Front. When Cyril Newman created the typescript version of his war correspondence he organised it around the 'fiery ordeal' of his initiation into trench warfare, his first leave in January 1916, the Somme, 'second Blighty leave' in July 1917 and the 'Great German Attack' from March to August 1918, when he eventually came home wounded. It was the sheer unbounded solace of his two periods of leave that made sense of his long war for Cyril.

Cyril used the diary he had kept during his 1916 leave to write the account he gave his children of the glorious week when, briefly at home, he was betrothed to their mother. Every detail of his excitement on the journey from Carnoy to Waterloo was still vivid in his memory many years later. It was strange walking in his uniform, leaving the station he knew well, passing city workers, on his way to visit his own workplace, the offices of the Official Receiver in Carey Street nearby. 'I felt exalted, superior. The passers-by knew not of trench life . . . of the degradation of living in mud and dirt . . . hurrying along on their apparently purposeless pursuit of the daily means of existence – earthbound – muckrakers, missing the glory – the crown of self-sacrifice . . . not one stopped to enquire – was I from the front?' Cyril's recollections encapsulate that mental gulf between the Home Front and the Western Front which historians are still trying to puzzle out.

It is much easier to understand the rising joy of Cyril's experiences as that day, 14 January 1916, went on, than his lonely walk from Waterloo to Carey Street. There was the office welcome, the friendly chat there, his City shave, shampoo and haircut, meeting Winnie who had been at her office, the bus journey to Muswell Hill, the reunions with his family and hers. Tea was mixed with tears of joy. Cyril could hardly eat at all those first days home, when he saw many friends he had missed for eighteen months and talked with his Sunday school boys. Visiting Winnie's home one morning, when she had obtained leave from her office job, he recorded that she 'sang to me "Wonderful Love", "Just the same" and "Rock of Ages"'.

Their betrothal was a formal matter. Cyril explained his prospects to Mr Blackburn with Winnie discreetly absenting herself. When her parents had agreed to the marriage, the couple knelt together in the Blackburns' front room for her father's prayer for God's blessing upon them. Next morning Cyril and Winnie did the round of City jewellers, finding a ring they were happy with at Bravingtons in Ludgate Hill. On the day of his departure it was Cyril who sang in the Newmans' front room. The hymns, which Winnie played as he sang them, were 'God be with you till we meet again' and 'Blest be the tie that binds our hearts in human love'.

Their letters to each other after the desperate emotions of their sad parting at Waterloo were exercises in establishing, for Cyril and Winnie, the self-control they needed and the acceptance that the war would go on. After the family kisses at the station, Cyril noticed the train was pulling out. 'Give me one more kiss,' he pleaded with Winnie, then he 'had to run to be pulled into the carriage'. Writing to Winnie's parents, Cyril confessed his 'natural aversion' to the whole way of life he was thrust back into, but he insisted that, at war, 'by living for God I am best endeavouring to live worthy of Winnie and her love'. The next Sunday afternoon Cyril managed to escape for a long quiet walk to Sailly-Laurette, where he sat on a cart in a field. He could cry there quietly to himself. He told Winnie about this in one of his green envelope letters.[19]

By January 1917 it seemed an age since the eyes of these lovers had met. It was tantalising knowing that, as a Tommy, you could not expect to hear about your leave till the day before you went. The dream of visiting Winnie's sister at school in Essex, on the next leave, was focused for Cyril upon the notion of having her to himself most of a whole day: 'we might have a carriage to ourselves both ways'. In April 1917, Cyril discovered he was about number thirty on his battalion list but he knew leave was often stopped, 'owing to our or the enemy's activity'. In May, he was dreaming of a holiday with Winnie at the seaside: 'what a ripping time we would have together . . . a daily swim in the morning – walks in the afternoon. And at least three times a day I should demand a kiss – morning, afternoon and evening'.

Winnie continued to badger him about when he would get this leave. Three men granted it in May 1917 had waited nineteen months, he reported. Then he heard: 15 to 25 July with nine clear days in Blighty. His diary is a blank on the details of how he spent his time but begins again with the return journey. It recaptures his feelings: 'the cruel heart-breaking leave train has just brought me to this cruel place – Folkestone Rest Camp. My heart is numbed and burning tears are kept back only by strong effort.'

Cyril's record of an incident during his return journey reveals the hierarchy of the BEF and how this came across to one poor Tommy. He and two others were seeking to find their way to the battalion, untidy and bedraggled, when two Lancers passed them, escorting none other than General Haig, immaculately dressed.[20] They saluted, he returned the salute. What a few words would have meant in that flat, bleak countryside, Cyril reflected, 'if he had asked us who we were and whither we were wandering . . . how that story would have spread . . . but he was too lofty – too aloof – too proud – to take any interest in three riflemen.'[21]

Jack Sweeney explained to his pen-friend Ivy before his leave in May 1916 how shy he would be. He had even talked of putting his gas helmet on when he knocked at her door, 'then you will not be able to see me blushing'. But she had sought to bolster his courage in advance: 'I am so glad you are going to let me be your boy while I am on leave,' Jack wrote on 2 May.

His leave was beyond Jack's wildest dreams. Ivy sought to put his mind at rest about his not being sufficiently educated for her. To his amazement, she 'told him it didn't make any difference whatsoever', as Ivy related years later. Ivy's father was more concerned about this issue than she was, 'but soon became as fond of him as my mother'. When she plucked up courage to ask her mother about their going out to a show together, she was not surprised, knowing the mores of that time, to be told 'you'll have to get Dad to take you'. So they went as a threesome to a variety show at the Coliseum. 'But we had walks together,' Ivy recalled, 'and I saw him off at Waterloo.' She gave him a kiss when they parted, 'though I also gave a kiss to another soldier he was with'.

Too shy to declare himself on this leave, Jack did so when back at the Front. 'Dear Ivy, I've fallen in love with you . . . I know if I cannot be your boy I will love you as a loving friend,' he wrote. For her this was the most treasured of all his letters. When she replied positively, his confidence increased. 'Well my Darling,' he wrote on 23 June, 'I am so glad that my letter did not offend you . . . but now I know and you have made me so happy I can fight out here now with a good heart knowing I am fighting for such a darling girl.'[22]

As Jack went through the Somme that year the correspondence blossomed. Towards the end of 1916, he was asserting 'I am sure I shall not be shy next time I am home.' He needed a month in Blighty, he insisted, but leave was a long time coming. 'You might ask Lloyd George,' he joked, 'or ring him up on the buzzer.' Ruefully, he noted that leave was coming round for his officers every three months but, with only six in his battalion going on leave each week, it was taking a year for Tommies to get a turn. 'I only wish you would come and fetch me.'[23] But then his luck did come up: he was sent on leave just before Passchendaele.

It was on this leave that Jack and Ivy became engaged. She had no hesitation at all in accepting, though they had spent just a few days together more than a year before. She felt she had really got to know him through their intense and incessant correspondence. Her parents fully approved, giving him the spare room as a mark of how they felt. The last evening, with the gramophone playing and Ivy's affectionate attention overwhelming him, made Jack sleep so well he almost missed the leave train. 'I am glad that you did not cry dear,' he reflected, dwelling on those last hours they had together, when he wrote from the Front, 'but I must tell you dear that I was crying myself that morning I came down-stairs past your room.' Propriety prevented him from opening her door, 'so I glanced into the drawing room at the spot where we sat the night before'. Just catching his train at Victoria, Jack 'felt it when I saw the other boys with their girls on the platform, but still I wiped my eyes and fancied that you were there'. Jack related the reception his pals had given him: 'some say lucky kid, others Poor Old Nobbler caught at last'. He guessed that what friendly Sergeant O'Brien would say when he saw him would be 'tres bon, when's the wedding?'[24]

It took some while for the BEF to organise proper leave rotas. After all, with leave for two million men to be administered, just one week's leave in the year required the movement of around 40,000 men daily. As we have seen, the notion of an annual entitlement was not enforceable for all. When it did come up, going on leave meant entering a kind of limbo where disciplinary regulations were relaxed. But there was always tension. Leave trains were specially desig-nated and famous for their missing doors and broken windows. There were canteens at the larger stations run by society women. At Folkestone men scram-bled for seats on the London train. At Victoria men often received cigarettes and chocolate handed out by waiting crowds who welcomed them home.[25]

Many found leave hardly credible. It was difficult to adjust to Blighty, to home life and rich civilian food. Above all, it was the strangeness of being back in England which disconcerted men, though this was something they could only put their finger on much later. Because men did not write letters when they were at home, it would be easy for us to miss a crucial point about the double identity into which the Great War forced volunteers. Patrick Campbell, in his memoir *In the Cannon's Mouth*, published in 1979, wrote a short chapter which articulated the experience of leave many years afterwards very much more revealingly than anything written at the time.

The strangeness, he recalled, 'began as soon as I was in the train at Folkestone'. He had been told that Ypres would seem like a bad dream when he got to London. But, on the contrary, 'it seemed to me that London was the dream, Ypres and Potijze Road the reality'. The Thames Valley was familiar, 'but for some reason it seemed less home-like now'. He was missing something. It was strange how much he thought about his friends whom he would not see for ten days. His parents harried him with questions; his sister laughed with him 'but did not ask me questions about the war'. He could not help dwelling on the others, 'wondering whose turn it was to go to the Observation Post and what the shelling had been like today'.

In an attempt to snap out of his identity crisis, Campbell took off his uniform and went into Oxford. But a corporal who knew him stopped to ask whether 'I did not want to be out there with all the other lads'. He had forgotten his reply when he told the story decades later, but 'a true answer would have been that I was already there, not here in the middle of Oxford'. His parents took him to Brighton, hoping he might forget the Front, but his pretty young cousin, who lived there, asked him what battle was like and if the Belgian girls were as pretty as English ones. 'But she did not really want to know the answers and I did not want to tell her.'[26]

Leave always had a bittersweet tang. Letters cited in this account have hinted at the powerful emotions it induced, at the suddenness with which it began and ended, at the sense that it was baffling and almost inevitably disappointing in some way or another. Yet we have also seen how much it meant to individual soldiers, the importance of the brief experience of loving care for men living away from home in such demanding circumstances. Leave could be, despite everything, a temporary source of pure joy and exaltation.

CHAPTER 12

'I Am Serene, Unafraid'
The Somme

The confidence of the British Expeditionary Force, still largely untrained in battle, on the eve of the Somme is fully attested in many letters.[1] Charlie May reflected in March 1916 that this was an 'unlovely war in detail yet there is something grand and inspiring about it – men's sober pluck and quiet good-heartedness contributes very largely to this'.[2] 'The time has come for us to show our best and I am glad of it, eager and longing for it,' wrote the artilleryman Richard Downing on 14 June 1916: 'we shall have our work cut out to smash the Germans, but we <u>can</u> do it.'[3] Charlie May's mood was on a rising tide. 'When we strike it will be with a most mighty blow,' he wrote. Receiving final orders for the Big Push, he declared 'it is the largest thing yet attempted and if it means our success I think it will be the beginning of the end.' 'It is marvellous this marshalling of power,' he noted on 16 June, 'the greatest battle in the world is on the eve of breaking.'[4]

'The spirit of the men is excellent and they will I feel sure render a good account of themselves', mused General Sir Henry Rawlinson on 24 June.[5] For sound strategic reasons, Gordon Corrigan has argued, there had to be an offensive somewhere on the Western Front in 1916: 'planning was exact and the staff work preparatory to July 1st was superb'.[6] Michael Howard has written of preparations which were 'meticulous, far reaching and clearly signalled'.[7] But, as Hew Strachan has argued, the planning was fatally flawed by compromise in the Higher Command.[8] General Haig believed the wire 'had never been so well cut, nor artillery preparations so thorough'. But many of the shells fired in the initial bombardment were duds; the German machine-gunners had dug themselves deep into the chalk hillside; when the barrage lifted the long lines of overloaded troops coming across the slopes towards them were slowly moving targets.[9] The excessive and foolish confidence drilled into thousands of soldiers just before the Big Push has become legendary. In a Channel 4 documentary in the 1980s, numerous veterans of that day testified to their belief in the story that the wire had been cut and their advance, walking not running as Rawlinson insisted, would be a walkover.[10]

Some of our letter writers were not in the initial advance. Lance Spicer only joined it from reserve late in the day. Rowland Feilding, commanding the 4th Battalion of the Coldstream Guards at Corbie, did not go into the attack himself. Graham Greenwell's Oxfordshire regiment was on the northern sector of the Somme front but he was in a reserve line.

Just given command of his company, Graham told his mother on 23 June 'I am enjoying the excitement.' Everyone was 'very busy' and 'on the "qui vive"'.[11] Thousands of soldiers ready and waiting on the twenty-five-mile stretch of the Western Front north of the river Somme could not miss the evidence of massive preparation, especially the concentration of artillery moving to the area.[12] Will Streets was in good spirits when he updated his mother on the 23rd. People could not understand, he reflected, 'us being so light and indifferent near death, but if they could see us half coated in mud, wading through about two feet of it up a wet and narrow trench, they might realise that without the relief of humour we should become prey to the demon of bad temper'.[13]

Everyone was impressed with the bombardment, a spectacle to behold, which was scheduled to last five days but in fact extended to seven when drizzle and fog prevented flying. It boosted morale wonderfully on the eve of battle. Rowland Feilding, invited to lunch at the Artillery Battle Headquarters at Bray, found the bombardment still in full swing on the 28th: 'the Germans must be having a horrible time I should think. All our valleys are thick with guns and howitzers.' Billie Nevill's letter to his family on the 26th was headed 'UP.UP.UP.' 'Still alive. Why? Ask me another,' he joked, 'we're having the time of our lives now'. History was in the making and here he was in the midst of the show. The Boche had been 'shelled hard now for forty-eight hours day and night. It's a wonderful sight.' 'Watch the papers and keep them,' Billie advised.

The East Surreys, holding the brigade front and chosen as an assaulting battalion, were as exposed as anyone during the bombardment. So Billie's ecstatic optimism may seem extraordinary. He confessed, in a long letter to his sister Elsie on the 27th, that he felt 'hammered by the sound'. But this letter also explains why his morale was high. German surrenders lifted his spirits: 'now and then Bosche jump out in broad daylight and rush over to our trenches . . . saying they cannot stand it any more'. One German officer had surrendered at Fricourt 'and we had two on our right this morning.'[14] Graham Greenwell, at the other end of the Somme front, shared Billie's optimism but narrated it more soberly. This was 'one of the biggest shows in the war', he declared, 'I really think it ought to be a great success this time'. He was not in the least surprised to find crowds of Hun prisoners coming in on the 30th, some even seeming 'glad to be caught'.[15]

In the 1920s nations came to accept, understand and even welcome the enormous blood sacrifice of the Somme, fought 'for a cause and to a greater nobler purpose', as William Philpott has argued. The battle has provoked decades of controversy. Unusually, this was a single battle that raged almost unceasingly for more than four months. The Allied casualties were 623,907 between 1 July and 18 November. Yet it is the first day of the Somme, when there were 57,470 casualties, with 19,240 killed or dying of wounds, that is notorious.[16] Two of our letter writers and also our single diarist were killed on this day.

'Little did I dream in those far off Morecambe days that I should rise to command a company', wrote Charlie May in his diary, as preparations for the battle reached their climax in the 7th Division. It was given the task of capturing the village of Mametz. On 25 June, Charlie watched the massive bombardment in progress. He spotted a huge column of smoke by Mametz Wood where a German arms dump had been struck. For him indeed, writing his diary with eyes on his own assignment, this was simply the 'Battle of Mametz'. The Manchester Pals were 'keen as mustard'. They had sung the old local songs heartily during the officers' final reunion: 'it was top-hole and we all loved each other'.

Yet *Dulce et decorum est* was also very much in Charlie's mind. He had asked his adjutant, Frank Earles, to care for Maud and Pauline if he was killed (plate 20). In a diary entry on 17 June, he expressed his ultimate thoughts on the sacrifice of his life, in words that reach out to us with his longing to survive: 'I do not want to die, not that I mind for myself. If it be that I am to go I am ready. But the thought that I may never see you or our darling baby again turns my bowels to water. I cannot think of it with even the semblance of equanimity.' 'My conscience is clear', he continued, 'that I have always tried to make life a joy to you.' It was the idea of their being 'cut off from each other which is so terrible, the babe not knowing me or me her'. Her upbringing was his wife's 'greatest charge', for 'she is the hope of life to me'. The two of them, she must know, 'are all the world to me. I pray that I may do my duty for I know, whatever that may entail, you would not have it otherwise.'

'Waiting is rotten', Charlie noted on 28 June. 'We are all agog with expectancy and strung to a pitch', he narrated the next day. This was 'the greatest thing the battalion or any of us have been in.' He wrote a long diary entry at 5.45 a.m. on 1 July. Fritz had strafed them as they marched up that night, causing 'some uneasiness and a few casualties'. It was broad daylight and there were two hours to go. No-man's-land was 'a tangled desert' in front of him. His front-line trench was battered by German armaments but they had not stopped the British machine guns, which, reassuringly, were 'popping off all along our parapet as I write'.

Arthur Bunting was Charlie's faithful servant. His wife forwarded a letter she had received from him to Maud May. It provides the best account we have of Charlie's death. The initial assault went well for the Manchesters, who quickly took the German trenches in front of Mametz and reached the outskirts of the village.[17] Arthur was 'not three yards' away when Charlie was hit. He heard the shell burst and his captain call. 'I nursed him best I could and tied his limbs together with my puttees poor fellow and while I was with him dear said my prayers over and over again.'

The assault swept on, leaving them in open ground. Arthur was convinced that their end had come. 'It was just a case of waiting your turn next please,' was how he described it, 'but it didn't come and here we are having our well deserved rest.' Arthur was able to care for Charlie's body when he died. 'I often told you girlie what nice fellows were in our section,' he explained to his wife. Now all the other poor lads – in other words, his officers – but one had 'gone west'. Thankfully, though the last weeks had 'shattered my nerves a little', Arthur was 'glad to say I am in the pink'. Charlie was buried in the British Cemetery at Mametz.[18]

Bunting was a friend of the family so it was obvious for Maud to seek news from him when her husband was killed in the attack. She wrote from her home in Wanstead in Essex on 11 July thanking him for his 'words of comfort and most of all for your faithfulness and the loving care that you gave my beloved husband'. Maud knew from his letters 'how much he loved his work and all the brave men who it was his fortune to command'. 'Will you promise never to let me lose sight of you – you did all a devoted servant and friend could do for him in his last extremity.' He was one of those survivors who could 'comfort all those desolated by this terrible war'. It must have been Bunting who brought home Charlie's diary with its poignant account of the days before 1 July 1916. It was discovered among his daughter Pauline's possessions after she died. After the war ended, Maud gave Bunting's wife an engraved carriage clock marking Arthur's devotion to duty, which his grandson now has in his home.[19]

Billie Nevill's East Surreys were in the 18th Division, next to Charlie May's 7th Division. Their objective was the capture of the western end of the fortified village of Montauban, just along the road from Mametz. Billie's B Company would lead the attack. Exhausted by recent front-line service, his 8th Battalion spent 28 and 29 June recovering on the grass and sleeping behind the lines. On the afternoon of the 30th they moved off to take up battle positions. Major Irwin, the commanding officer, was optimistic, recalling later 'I took it for granted that the wire would be cut, that we would massacre the Boche in their front line, get to our objective and then be told to do something else.' During the night, ammunition, grenades, sandbags, flares and twenty-four-hour rations were issued. Breakfast and the rum ration came up at 4.30 a.m. Visiting the HQ dugout just before dawn, Billie and his colleague Pearce were 'both absolutely radiant and declaring everything for the best'.

It had been misty but at 6.30 the mist lifted. At 7.27 a.m. Billie, with Bobby Soames his second in command, led B Company over the parapet into no-man's-land. 'One just heard a wild cheer,' the artillery officer Christian Carver who was nearby remembered, 'above the continuous roar, to tell one that the eighth East Surreys were on their way to get their own back at last.' The veteran Private L.S. Price told the historian Martin Middlebrook many years afterwards about how 'I saw an infantryman climb onto the parapet . . . beckoning others to follow. As he did so he kicked off a football; a good kick; the ball rose and travelled well towards the German line.' Price knew that this was the signal for the East Surreys to attack.

Billie's notion about the footballs was shrewd. His officers discussed Billie's plan for them to dribble these before them as they attacked across no-man's-land. It would keep men's minds occupied, he insisted, and properly focused. Major Irwin sanctioned purchasing the footballs in England. Billie believed that something so familiar would calm the men and help fulfil General Sir Henry Rawlinson's insistence that the attack be pursued at a walking pace. Rawlinson thought Kitchener's untried and untested New Army units would disintegrate if they were expected to make a rush attack. Billie's joke was to print on one of his footballs 'The Great European Cup-Tie Final: East Surreys versus Bavarians'.

Writing to Billie's sister Doff on 15 July, C. W. Alcock, a subaltern in the battalion, later described Billie's courageous death. Five minutes before zero hour, he explained, Billie had strolled up in his usual calm way and 'we shared a last joke before going over . . . we had to face a very heavy rifle and machine-gun fire and nearing the front German trench the lines slackened slightly'. Seeing this caused Billie to dash in front with a bomb in his hand. Immediately he was shot through the head, almost side by side with Soames and Sergeant Major Wells. 'Poor Nevill willingly and intentionally gave his life at the beginning,' Alcock judged, 'fearlessly urging on some men who were badly held up by the fire and wire.' He was buried in Carnoy Military Cemetery on the Somme.[20]

Alcock's account was written in the sorrow of a fortnight's retrospect on that murderous day, when the East Surreys had lost many of their best officers and NCOs. 'One realises,' he declared, 'the disgusting sordidness of modern war . . . but one must bear these losses silently, for it is the way that lies before us and the only way to victory. Not surprisingly, dealing with nearly 60,000 casualties on 1 July, the War Office took some while to inform next of kin. On the 6th, when the family still had no word, Doff wrote to Amy, nursing in France, that 'poor Mother is being so brave'. Amy by then had heard about their brother's probable death from wounded East Surreys who were at her hospital.

Soon Major Irwin's definitive story reached the anxious family in Twickenham. 'Dear Mrs Nevill,' his letter ran,

> I hardly know how to begin to write this letter at all . . . your son Captain Nevill led his company most gallantly and with the utmost coolness up to the German front line trench where he was shot. Death must have been absolutely instantaneous . . . he was loved and trusted by his men to such a degree that they would have followed him anywhere and did follow him that morning through an inferno of shell, rifle and machine-gun fire.

It hardly needed saying that Billie had been 'the life and soul of the mess'.

Irwin's tribute to Billie as a 'most capable and fearless soldier' is well attested by his own letters in the Imperial War Museum which have been used throughout this book. Irwin asked for the recovered football to be given by the family as a regimental trophy to commemorate Billie's gallantry. It remains on display, almost a hundred years later, in the Regimental Museum at Clandon Park. The *Illustrated London News* commissioned their most celebrated artist, R. Caton Woodville, to illustrate the football incident. His drawing, under the caption 'The Surreys Play the Game', appeared in the magazine. When it did so on 27 July the whole British public was amazed by the story.[21]

Will Streets wrote a long letter to his brother Ben on 20 June 1916 about publication of a volume of the poems he had written while he was serving on the Western Front. 'How precarious life is here,' he told Ben, who received the manuscript and the list of the poems Will wanted included. He hoped the *Poetry Review* would publish the volume, 'either edited by myself or someone after my death'. Ben could send copies to some local newspapers since Will was 'pleased to hear I am being recognised locally'. Will wanted the sonnet sequence to be called 'The Undying Splendour'. He explained to Ben: 'of course the undying splendour is youth, full of love, hope and aspiration, leaving it all for an idea – liberty – scorning death, proud, true to his race. And the sight is splendid and undying, as the sight of Calvary has always been splendid and its sublimity and influence are undying as those of Calvary are undying.'

Will's mood on the eve of the Battle of the Somme was resigned: 'I am serene, unafraid, I look death squarely in the face'. Yet he wanted so much to survive 'to inspire growing youth with the great things of life'. He clung to hopes that the war might end that autumn or the next summer. He dreamed of a Christmas at home: 'my Spartan heart grows soft at the thought, my keen brave eyes grow wet with the dream'. One further letter of his from those tense June days survives. It was written to his mother on 23 June, stressing the awful mud but assuring her he was keeping 'comparatively cheerful'.[22]

The 31st Division, which included the Sheffield Pals, faced one of the toughest assignments on the British line on 1 July. Coming through Luke and John Copses uphill, their objective was the heavily fortified German village of Serre, which never in fact fell in battle. Will's D Company was in the second wave of the attack . As a sergeant, he knew his duty was to keep the men going forward while he could. But he was wounded in no-man's-land and apparently made it back to his own lines to seek treatment. Hearing though that one of his platoon out there needed help, he went straight back to try to bring him in. He was never seen again.

Just over half this battalion of the York and Lancaster Regiment was lost. Will's body may have lain on that strewn battlefield for months. For it was only after the German retreat to the Hindenburg Line in February 1917 that the dead could be recovered from the Somme battlefield and buried. Even now, uncertainty remains. The gravestone in Euston Road cemetery bears the words 'believed to be buried in this cemetery'. The Commonwealth War Graves Commission was scrupulous in attempts at identification. Sometimes bodies were recovered but there was no way of telling who was really who.

It was not until 1 May 1917 that the family was officially notified that Sergeant Will Streets had been killed. In the same month, Erskine Macdonald Ltd published *The Undying Splendour*. The book contained two endorsements from officers in the 13th York and Lancasters. Major Plackett, Will's company commander since the war began, spoke of him as 'a thoroughly reliable NCO', whose reputation, gained in England and Egypt, 'was enhanced when we transferred to France'. Captain R.E.J. Moore, who too had worked closely with him, also made a contribution. 'Steady-eyed and rather stolid', he wrote, Will 'gave an impression of coolness even under extreme tension . . . he was not one of those who ignore danger; rather he faced it and found the cause more than sufficient compensation'.[23]

Will's Methodist upbringing and demanding life as a miner had given him exceptional strength of character. This shines through in the commentary he wrote on his motives in writing war poems:

I have tried to picture some thoughts that pass through a man's brain when he dies . . . we soldiers have our views of life to express, though the boom of death

is in our ears. We try to convey something of what we feel in this great
conflict to those who think of us, and sometimes, alas! mourn our loss. We
desire to let them know that in our keenest sadness for the joy of life we
leave behind, we go to meet death grim-lipped, clear-eyed and resolute-
hearted.

The book was warmly reviewed. *The Times* spoke of Will's 'heroic spirit'. The
Worksop Guardian called him a 'collier by occupation, a poet by right of genius
and inspiration'.[24]

There was no demoralisation on the Somme similar to that experienced by the
Regular army in 1914. Richard Downing was one of many who believed that
German casualties as the weeks went on were higher than British ones. Graham
Greenwell, seeing Hun prisoners on 'the verge of starvation and collapse' on 19
July, reckoned 'plenty of them are getting killed all right'. Moreover, he
pondered, BEF casualties were not so enormous, considering only one of its
four armies was engaged on the Somme.[25] 'The German infantry can't stand
what we are giving them', the machine-gunner Richard Williams told his
brother in the midst of the campaign, 'they give themselves up where they get
a safe opportunity.' German morale deteriorated rapidly from mid-July.[26] In the
second half of 1916, 40,207 Germans were captured, in contrast to a mere 1,101
in the first six months. This provided some compensation for the minimal
territorial gains and heavy British losses during the long battle. The censor
reviewing letters sent home commented in November that 'the spirit of confidence in the superiority over the enemy of our troops and of our artillery and
aircraft is everywhere noticeable'.[27]

Three of our subjects provide useful impressions of the ups and downs of
personal morale in July 1916 and after. Reflecting on the battle as 'a tremendous experience', Graham Greenwell was hopeful on 2 July. But he confessed
that his mess was 'not so optimistic' two days later. The very strong resistance
the attack had met north of the river Ancre was disconcerting. The following
week, Graham was not inclined to support the London betting he had heard of:
'six to four on the war being over before November 1st'. He expected at least
another year of fighting: 'we cannot hope to drive the Germans back at one
blow'.

Three weeks after this, Graham was still convinced he 'wouldn't have missed
it for anything'. Yet the Somme sobered him. 'I shall never look on warfare as
either fine or sporting again,' he told his mother in August, since shellfire
'reduces men to shivering beasts'.[28] The autumn remained tough going. 'Great
difficulties getting food and water, but still it's a wonderful war,' Graham

insisted in November. He enclosed a private note from his commanding officer, sympathising about his recent casualties, which ended 'Cheer up' – followed by his initials.[29]

For Lance Spicer the Somme left lifelong memories of what pitched battle was like. His account on 5 July carried the verdict, in the euphoria of survival for the previous four days, that he was 'fit and flourishing': it was 'the most marvellous show I've ever seen or had anything to do with'. Five days later, he still held the view that 'the show is I think being a success, a great success I believe and hope'. He had now had time to reflect on the absent faces and was trying to console himself by believing 'that these brave fellows gave their lives in a successful effort and not in a forlorn hope'.

After a brief rest cure in late July, Lance fought on not quite so convinced as he had been that the war was going well. By the end of August he was 'a little doubtful whether the Somme show is a success': 'we have obviously entirely altered our original plan . . . also the progress seems so dreadfully slow'. Lance was wounded by a bullet through his left arm, which 'came out below the shoulder', in the attack on Gueudecourt near Flers on 16 September. As a result of this injury, he was spared the whole of the next winter in the trenches while he recuperated in England.[30]

Rowland Feilding spent 1 July motoring behind the British lines. He felt 'rather a beast' seeing the battle as a sightseer but believed it was 'a wonderful day'. Yet much of what he saw in the next weeks sickened him. In this fraught period, Rowland found his transfer to the command of the New Army's 6th Battalion of the Connaught Rangers on 7 September exhilarating. Irishmen, he quickly decided, were difficult to drive but easy to lead. 'They are easily made happy,' he told Edith on 25 September, 'I feel the sincerest gratitude for the generous and open-hearted manner in which they have received me and the zeal with which they have supported me.'[31]

They, equally, had much to be grateful for to their new commanding officer. Rowland's first days leading the Connaught Rangers, a true baptism of fire, were triumphant ones in rallying men who were 'very tired'. He took over on 3 September, when the battalion with three others in the 47th Brigade, in its first attack, had captured the village of Guillemont. This was 'as hard a nut to crack as there has been in this battle so far', Rowland told Edith. He found them bivouacking near the ruins of the village of Carnoy four days later, having suffered the loss of 1,147 out of the 2,400 men who had fought in that attack, including their CO and second in command. So hectic was this latter stage of the Somme battle that his assignment was to take 250 men of the battalion, 'straight out of one exhausting attack and so punished as this one', into the attack on Ginchy the next day but one.

12. 'On the Somme', sketch by Rowland Feilding, 1916, no. 24 in his sketchbook.

Well might Rowland remember Ginchy. When he published his letters home in 1929, he included photographs of the ruins of Guillemont, where his men were in action on the 3rd, and of supporting troops moving up in the attack he led on the village of Ginchy six days later. His letters to Edith provided a candid and emotional account of this second engagement involving the Connaught Rangers. Ginchy, repeatedly assaulted from 8 to 10 September, now no more than a group of rubble heaps, did fall to the BEF on the 10th.[32] Rowland wrote about it after the march back following 'three practically sleepless nights under shell-fire': 'the scene was very weird as we picked our way back through the waste of shell-holes with their mournful contents, accompanied by our wounded, and preceded by a stretcher on which lay the body of Colonel Curzon'. He had commanded the 6th Battalion of the Royal Irish Regiment, which had been in the action, 'and who dined opposite me with the Brigadier four nights ago . . . I found myself following immediately behind his body.'[33]

On 12 September 1916, further north on the Western Front near Béthune, the Argyll and Sutherland Highlanders were in reserve. Peter McGregor had time to write a long letter to his wife Jen, actually more than 1,200 words in all. He confessed how homesick he was: 'oh to be in dear old Edinburgh – it's the loveliest place on this earth', and wished the end of the war would 'hurry up'. He had been on a ration fatigue and watched a stretcher pass by carrying 'one of our men caught by a sniper – he was standing at the entrance of his dug-out'. The letter struck a melancholy tone when reporting this, Peter noting that 'his passing didn't seem to cause much stir . . . we all of course came to attention as it passed . . . war is a terrible thing and so few realize it'.

It was almost as if Peter could see his own fate coming upon him the very next day. His captain, A.H. Miller related it. 'Your husband was working with several others in a reserve trench. Suddenly the Germans began to shell the trench and I very much regret to say that your husband was struck down . . . he was taken to the dressing station within a few minutes.' The chaplain's letter stated that Peter died within ten minutes of being hit. His brother-in-law was convinced that he suffered no pain; he was consoled to find the wounds were all on Peter's body, with 'no disfigurement of the face'.

His company commander, Major H.B. Murdoch, spoke of a 'simple but beautiful service at the graveside'. The Reverend B.D. Anderson's account of the burial was conventional but no less well meant for that: 'we gave thanks that your husband had heard and answered the call of duty and that God had seen him fit to lay down his life'. The most personal and moving testimony came from Private Charlie Holroyd, who was Peter's brother-in-law. It was a lovely evening, he assured Jen, with a beautiful rainbow: 'I placed a sprig of Scottish heather from his pocket book on the grave. Dear Jen, I feel as though I had not taken proper care of Pete and yet what could I do?' Peter McGregor is buried in the Maroc British Cemetery at Grenay. This was a front-line cemetery protected from German observation by a slight rise in the ground.

The letters Jen received convincingly painted Pete as the life and soul of his company. 'He was always so cheerful . . . and he always got a laugh from the men with his jokes and sayings,' testified his captain. The commanding officer remembered him as 'a centre of good humour.' The chaplain, recalling him as 'a great favourite, one of the best known men in his company', declared that 'after many a weary day he cheered his comrades and he always had a pleasant smile for the Padre'. The shy organist and choirmaster, once uncertain whether he could manage to go to war, had proved himself: he was sorely missed after September 1916 by his Scottish regiment.

Jen McGregor wrote seven last letters to Peter which he never read and were returned after his death. In microcosm these encapsulate that tragic poignancy of universal loss which dominates the history of the Great War. They express the trivia which helped wives to carry on and with which they tried to keep their hearts in check, as well showing the depth of loving concern between loved ones parted for months on end and then suddenly for ever. 'I always mean to say not to bother about not saying loving things in your letters,' Jen wrote on 1 September, 'I know they are there and that you are loving us more than ever. I could say more than I do, but I am afraid lest I make you more homesick than ever if I pour out too much of my loving feelings … I am longing for you to come and give me a hug.' Jen wrote again on the day Peter died, thanking him for his letter of the 8th. She was sorry he was 'back in the beastly trenches again'.

In these letters there was the usual news of the children – Bob 'getting to be a fine bold laddie'. Then there was the musing, 'sitting over the fire'. 'It seems terrible that you should be there in the midst of all that while I sit in peace and quiet comfort at home. I suppose it's just to let your wives and bairns do that that you are suffering like that.' Why did she not have to suffer at all 'except for the continual anxiety about you'? In Edinburgh, she found, 'one would never know that a war was going on at all'.

Bob McGregor, nine at the time, remembered very well the day the news of his father's death was broken to his mother. Away from home with relatives, 'my mother was in an upstairs room cleaning out the canary cage', Bob recorded. 'I was surprised to see Aunt Helen and Aunt Kitty walking up the terrace … I followed them upstairs and through the closed door heard them crying. It was a shattering blow … she had a breakdown and went to stay with a sister in London.' Bob looked after his mother, as he had promised Peter he would, till her death in 1946. He knew his father's letters were in a large suitcase and began reading them in 1968. He subsequently copied them out word for word into sixteen exercise books which are now in the Imperial War Museum. On to one page he pasted the scarlet pimpernel his father had picked to send them home from the Front.[34]

Alec Reader, in the 1/15th Battalion of the London Regiment, grew increasingly desperate about coping in August and early September 1916. He pinned his hopes on his father, who had recently joined up, being able to arrange a transfer for him. But the paperwork for this was delayed. Writing on 22 August, he admitted 'we are having rather a strenuous time but with a bit of luck it will soon be over'. Two days later, he declared 'a Blighty one is what one hopes for'. By 3 September he had become openly fatalistic. At church parade, Alec wrote on the 10th, they sang 'Nearer, my God, to Thee'. Field postcards, declaring he was fit, followed on 12 and 14 September.

Alec served in the prolonged battle of attrition on the Somme which brought the eventual capture of Mametz Wood, Delville Wood and Leuze Wood. The British front line, when the Civil Service Rifles reached High Wood in late August, ran across the southern half of the wood, which lay in the midst of a featureless wilderness with 'ragged stumps sticking up out of churned-up earth poisoned with fumes of high explosives'. The Allied offensive on 15 September, when the wood was captured, became known as the Battle of Flers-Courcelette.[35] Alec's battalion entered the wood on the evening of the 14th. An officer described the scene: 'it was almost dusk when we reached the dangerous gap through which all traffic to and from High Wood must pass . . . here on the threshold of dark tragedy all lightheartedness fled'. The men spent a quiet night with little or no sleep. Rum was issued at dawn. The objective of the Civil Service Rifles was to capture the wood and their allotted sections of the German switch trench, which extended through and to either side of the northern quarter of the wood. Moving forward at first light, the infantry met murderous fire from the enemy front line, with hand-to-hand fighting and scenes of carnage near the well-defended switch trench. One of those who fell, probably about 8.30 a.m., was Alec, still only eighteen years old. He had fought his way some distance across the wood.[36]

Alec Reader is commemorated, with 72,000 other British and South African soldiers killed in the prolonged Battle of the Somme, on the Thiepval Memorial which dominates the Somme countryside. The largest number of names comes from his regiment, the London Regiment, but few can have been as young. The Memorial was designed by Sir Edwin Lutyens and built between 1928 and 1932. Thiepval is a triumphal arch that has been multiplied. It calls for no excessive interpretation. Lutyens was a conventional patriot who brilliantly created an abstract space that is wholly appropriate for a 'Monument to the Missing'.

We have none of the letters about Alec's bravery written by senior officers that fill out other cases of death in battle described here. There is just that single and sad family photograph at Wandsworth, with Alec head and shoulders above his siblings. He was the one just old enough to go to war. We can only imagine the family's grief.[37]

The 1st of July 1916 is well known as the blackest day in the history of the British army. Instead of the immediate breakthrough that all longed for, 419,654 men died during the two and a half months of the Somme campaign. This effort won the Allies just 98 square miles of land. The Great War was still expanding in 1916: new nations became engaged and more resources were being committed to the conflict. There would have to be more war before there could be peace. But William Philpott has written of the Somme offensive as 'the point at which ideals changed and fortunes turned'. Henry Wilson commented, as military adviser to Lloyd George, on the year's fighting as 1917 arrived. This had been a year of indecisive struggle but 'on the whole victory inclining to us and the final decision brought nearer'.[38]

One subaltern, Lieutenant Waterhouse, wrote as early as August 1917 of his belief that the Somme had marked the 'turning point of the war', showing Germany for the first time that its opponents could break through. John Masefield later noted that this was where the 'driving back of the enemy began'. Philpott, assessing such material in his recent account, notes that, while the 'self-sacrifice of 1 July 1916 still hangs heavily on the nation, the disciplined, confident conquering army of November 1916 goes less remarked'. At a deep level, the very essence of this whole story – the lasting confidence in final victory – became established in the aftermath of the Somme.[39]

CHAPTER 13

'Capable of Finishing the Job'

Battles of 1917–1918

The German retreat to the Hindenburg Line in February and March 1917 was carefully conducted, slow and measured. General Ludendorff abandoned all the Somme battlefields, moving his forces back some twenty-five miles, destroying and burning villages in the process.[1] The excitement engendered by this was the main theme of Reggie Trench's letters as he marched his fresh troops across from Le Havre. 'It was very thrilling,' he told to his mother, when, on his first visit to the front line, he saw huge fires behind the German lines as the enemy laid waste to the territory they were abandoning. 'We knew something was up from the special patrol instructions that we got,' he explained; 'he's gone now and we have to trek after him.' This retreat proved that the attritional struggle of 1916 had achieved something, which was not to say there had yet been a breakthrough.[2]

The Sherwood Foresters read in the *Daily Mail* about the British advance on an eighty-mile section of the Western Front: 'I do not know where we shall go to but it's East, Hurrah!' was Reggie's euphoric summary. He wished he had been with a party of his colleagues who crossed no-man's-land to the German front line and 'couldn't find a Boche anywhere'. The evidence of forward movement was all around them, 'guns and ammunition moving up . . . an endless stream'. All this, Reggie was convinced, had 'a great moral effect on our men.'[3]

Rowland Feilding was continually impressed by 'the staying powers of the men.' He reflected in April 1917 on his seven months in command of the Connaught Rangers. He himself was now tired: 'the glamour and romance of war die away after a time and only the reek of it remains'. Duty had become for him 'the one and only incentive'. For two years life on the Western Front had 'interested and held' him, he told his wife, 'and I shall always look back on 1915 and 1916 as a time of extraordinary happiness'. As a huge battle was raging some miles away that week on Vimy Ridge he heard about the Americans coming in. He was sorry about this: 'we feel we are capable of finishing the job and we would prefer to do so by ourselves.'[4]

Returning to France after becoming a casualty on the Somme in April 1917, Lance Spicer could hardly believe the desolation of the previous year's battle-field through which he travelled to reach the new lines. 'The woods have been thinned down to mere ghosts . . . the few remaining trees are all blasted and cut down by shell fire . . . the villages in all cases are utterly ruined,' he reported. Lance's experience and obvious ability led to his taking on strenuous new battalion roles.[5] Men like him and Reggie were typical of the junior officers who bore the brunt of leadership in 1917 and 1918, sharing a cautiously posi-tive outlook based on the conviction that this was a war the Allies were now winning.

Sir Douglas Haig launched his strategy of attrition in the old battlefields of Flanders in June 1917 with the attack on Messines Ridge. This prolonged struggle has become known as the Third Battle of Ypres and it involved contin-uous fighting around the whole Ypres salient from 31 July until 6 November, when the Passchendaele ridge was taken.[6] Lance commented in August on how 'the Staff in their usual optimistic way still think the war is going to end this year'. But he had 'no such illusions – at any rate we cannot win the war this year'. 'We can win it in 1919 and not before,' he believed. A few weeks later he was admitting that, so far as the 10th Corps and Yorkshire Light Infantry was concerned, Third Ypres 'really has been a great success'.[7]

Reggie had enthused in June about how tanks were transforming the poten-tial for effective pursuit of attritional warfare. He had seen a demonstration of one in action: 'it was quite wonderful . . . barbed wire is no obstacle at all – it simply crushes anything in the path.' His letters to both his wife and mother were upbeat during this prolonged battle, when, as second in command of his battalion, he remained throughout in reserve. 'The Boche infantry is undoubt-edly done,' he wrote on 29 September, 'we've got him cooked – our lads had no trouble with him at all – it was "hands up" and he came in like a lamb – hundreds – they say 5000 prisoners in this last show.'[8]

Military historians have developed the theory of the 'learning curve' in their analysis of the Allied defeat of Germany in 1918. The key year was 1917, when in a series of set-piece battles the Allies began decisively to gain the upper hand despite huge casualty rates. The high morale in our letters reflects the course of this campaign. Arras and Vimy Ridge in April, Messines in June, then the trio of engagements led by General Sir Hubert Plumer at Menin Road, Polygon Wood and Broodseinde, reflected a dramatic series of tactical advances. The key features of these battles were very careful preparation, limited objectives and the effective use of the creeping barrage.[9]

Yet the cost of a year of gruelling fighting in terms of demoralisation and exhaustion became enormous. Morale in the ranks was undoubtedly low in the second half of the year. Nevertheless, the censors of letters home noted that basic confidence in British ability to win the war remained solid. The feeling even among the most war weary was that 'only one kind of peace is possible and that the time is not yet come'.[10]

By early October 1917, the British Expeditionary Force had demonstrated mastery of the set-piece, bite and hold offensive. But at Cambrai, just ten days after the last attack on the Passchendaele ridge, something more was attempted. On 20 November new artillery tactics focused on cutting the barbed wire as the infantry crossed the starting-line instead of providing a preliminary barrage, as on the Somme. For the first time, a massive punch was delivered by the BEF's tanks which soldiers like Reggie Trench had urged for months because of their potential to transform modern warfare.[11]

The cavalry attack at Cambrai was in fact abortive but this did not dampen Reggie's ecstatic enthusiasm about its role: 'I would have given something to have seen them cross our line' – the line he himself had patrolled as a captain in the 2/5th Sherwood Foresters in the summer. His mother must have seen the account in *The Times*, Reggie wrote on 24 November. 'It's very wonderful isn't it,' he declared, 'and you would marvel more if you had any vague idea of the arrangements needed before a show of that sort.'[12] The 2/5th Sherwoods' battalion history records the boost that Cambrai gave Tommy morale. The news on the 23rd 'was splendid'. 'The enemy had been taken completely by surprise . . . the war was over boys: well perhaps not quite but very nearly. We had them on the run at last.'[13]

As it turned out, it was just under a year after that day of optimistic euphoria at Cambrai until the Armistice was actually signed. In any case, the brief exaltation at the breakthrough at once turned to bitter disillusionment. The low point in public confidence at home, it should be noted, came between October 1917 and February 1918. This was when news of the bloodbath at Passchendaele sank in at home. Many in Britain at the turn of this year still saw an 'unending war'.[14]

Casualties in the major battles of 1917 and 1918 were enormous. People became accustomed to the mounting toll of war dead and huge numbers of injured: 158,000 were killed and wounded in the Battle of Arras between 9 April and 16 May 1917; there were around 244,897 casualties at Third Ypres between 31 July and 6 November. The German Spring Offensive in 1918, known as 'Operation Michael', brought another 239,8000 Allied casualties.[15] Two of our letter writers and leading characters were killed in action in these engagements.

The Battle of Arras was the second of three great attritional offensives which the British army launched in 1916 and 1917, coming, in April 1917, between the Somme and Passchendaele. It proved that strong German defensive positions could be captured by a well planned set-piece attack. The creeping barrage proved itself at Arras, where the artillery's targets moved steadily and systematically forward, with the infantry following close behind to exploit the disruption the artillery had caused. On the morning of 9 April the British and Canadian forces launched simultaneous offensives at Arras and Vimy Ridge.[16] At 5.30 a.m. Robert Hermon, as their commanding officer, led the men of the 24th Battalion of the Northumberland Fusiliers into the attack on the Hindenburg Line near Rollincourt, which was north of Arras.

In his last letter but one, Robert mused on national spirit. 'If you told me you could lay hands on every man you met in the street, clap a uniform on him and send him out into this and that he would behave like a stoic . . . I should have said the whole thing was absolutely idiotic . . . anyhow we have done it and one is proud that one is a member of a country that produces men like the

13. Four-leafed clover sent by his wife Ethel to Robert Hermon, 11 August 1916, found after his death in his breast pocket.

men out here.' His last letter was written from his billet in Arras on 7 April, when he felt revived by sleep after a strenuous three days in the line. Ethel's letters with news of the Chugs had been a 'pick me up'. Now the big assault lay ahead. 'I must store up what energy I can as I shall probably need it these next few days,' he ended, sending 'a kiss from Dad' to his children and his love to her 'and your dear old face to love'.

Robert was killed shortly after 6 a.m. on 9 April crossing open ground to follow up his troops. This time, unknown to Ethel who was worrying desperately, Buxton had given in to Robert's insistence on his staying behind. He was in good spirits in his determination on this, as Buxton explained afterwards: 'he thought it much better for me to stop in the dugout until he was settled down in the new line and then he would send for me to bring along the rations'. Maybe, above all, Robert needed to be sure his faithful batman would survive, and be able to testify to the outcome of the day.

This is exactly what happened. For it is Buckin's sorrowing letter to Ethel Hermon which provides the fullest evidence of her loss. He wrote on 12 April, pouring out his emotions at the start. 'I have prayed to God to comfort you. I have thought of you night and day since I found the poor dear Colonel, oh dear it is so awful, I feel so broken-hearted and I don't know how to write this letter.' There had been no proper parting: 'when he started he said nothing to me and I didn't like to say anything to him, now I wish I had, if it was only to grab his hand for one second.' It was just minutes later that Robert was shot through the heart, a bullet slicing through the papers in his top pocket, including family photographs close to the four-leaved clover Ethel had given him for good luck.

These papers included final orders issued by Brigadier General Trevor at 1.20 a.m. that day, with best wishes for 'you and your battalion'. Trevor supplied more detail to Ethel about how Robert came to be killed. 'A tank was caught up on the German front line and the Boches were firing at it,' he explained. The adjutant just behind Robert had told him Robert was caught by a rifle bullet intended for the occupants of this tank. He went down on his knees saying 'Go on' and died almost at once. The medical officer believed a large blood vessel just below the heart had been severed by the bullet.

Buckin took charge of Robert's body until the burial at Rollincourt. 'We had a nice little service,' he related, 'and after everybody had gone I lingered by the grave of my dear Master and friend. Oh dear Madam, my thoughts were of you, so far away it seemed so cruel to leave him there.' He took the gold chain Robert wore round his neck, assuming Ethel would like it and planning to bring it home. 'I have a lock of hair which I put inside his watch,' he wrote to her.

More intimately, Buckin described to his wife Marie how 'nobody touched him but me. I did him up in two groundsheets and made him look as nice as possible. I buried him in his uniform just as he died.' All the deference and class loyalty of Victorian and Edwardian society are summarised in this heavy-hearted account. Buckin's letter also illustrates the sheer misery of a man's loss of the officer to whom he was devoted. 'I had to have a good cry Marie love, I couldn't help it. Oh, everything seems so changed now, there seems nothing to work for.'

One of the letters of sympathy to Ethel from a fellow officer in King Edward's Horse was a remarkable tribute. 'The men just adored him,' Lieutenant MacKinnon wrote, 'he had an extraordinary influence over them which I have never seen another instance of.' He tried to explain this, seeing it as different and bigger than 'the kind of blind devotion' that one encountered 'among the regular Tommy class'. For in the squadron 'the majority were well-educated folk and mostly above the average age'. What these seasoned men recognised in Robert Hermon was a total lack of meanness, of the occasional spite towards others which was normal in soldiering. He helped all he commanded to rise above that 'and in this his spirit will never leave me, nor the rest of us'.

For Buckin there was a silver lining since, predictably, her husband's servant became Ethel's rock in the next months. It was he who tended the grave, ensuring that its place remained known so he could take her there. 'I shall never rest now till I've seen where he lies and I must go out after the war,' she told him. It was Buckin she corresponded with when she wanted to see that the family's horses, which Robert had taken to France, were cared for: 'I don't know that I could ever have them back, I feel I should never hunt again nor do I want to.' Buxton served abroad until the war ended.[17]

The key to Erich Ludendorff's offensive strategy to break the Allied line in March 1918 was effective integration of artillery bombardment and troop movements. The German attack was focused upon fifty miles of the Western Front, with 72 German divisions facing an outnumbered 26 British infantry divisions.[18] The 2/5th Sherwood Foresters were in the Battle Zone, between the forward and rear lines of British trenches at Noreuil.

The night of 20 March was fine, dry and moonlit with ground mist developing into dense fog towards morning. The bombardment, making heavy use of gas shells, began at 4.40 a.m. on the 21st. The battalion moved out at once to their 'stand to' positions, facing a barrage that one Tommy who survived the day later described as 'all hell let loose'. Reggie Trench sat down to write home just before seven, explaining that, deep in the headquarters dugout with blankets across its entrance he was safe from the gas, but his gas mask was in position just in case. He managed to joke about the ferocity of the barrage: 'whenever a big one lands on top of the dug-out it puts out one or more lights! Involving a large expenditure of matches.' It would be a 'bore' if the cookhouse just above him got a direct hit, doing in the mess stores. With the gas now dispersing outside, he ended 'I am going to have a shave while I can, ever your ownest Reg', adding the postscript 'many kisses for Delle and for you darling'.[19]

The German infantry assault, immediately after the bombardment ended at 9.40, broke upon battered and disorientated British troops. Within three minutes, Corporal Lambert in the 2/7th Sherwood Foresters in the forward line later testified, 'suddenly there was Gerry at the top of the dug-out with a rifle and bayonet pointing down the steps'. The 2/7th was quickly overcome, with 177 men killed.[20] Before 10 a.m. the 2/5th faced the full might of the German attack. Reggie, as second in command, led the British resistance, defending the battalion headquarters dugout. 'His death was very noble,' wrote Colonel Gadd to Clare. He explained that Reggie was wounded in two places by a shell. 'I saw him dressed and told him to go to the rear to the dressing station. He said he would prefer to stay with us and as the Germans continued to press us he again took part in the defence of the position.'

The fight for the Battle Zone on 21 March has been vividly described in Martin Middlebrook's account, which drew upon much testimony from surviving veterans in the 1970s.[21] The last hour or so of Reggie's life is remarkably well documented, because several soldiers gave evidence or wrote to Clare themselves about how he was killed. 'The Germans having taken the support line were in a position to enfilade with a machine gun,' Captain Greaves told Herbert Trench in a conversation many years later. Reggie 'took a box of Mills bombs, collected three men and started along a slip trench to try and get round the machine gun'. Greaves wrote to Clare in June 1918, as a prisoner of war, about Reggie's last stand which lasted for 'about an hour', after sustaining wounds in his left arm and shoulder blade.[22]

But the paradigmatic account of Reggie's stand was written by Drummer Field, for an officer in Derby who collected data for a battalion history in 1919.

'Jerry was all round us,' he explained, 'and we found that our ammunition was giving out . . . time after time I saw Major Trench bring up case after case, until finally he was wounded in the head and shoulder. The next time I saw him he was on top (which was certain death) with bandages round his head and a sling for his arm still bringing ammunition up . . . I think it was a brilliant death . . . it will certainly bring comfort to his people to know that he died like that.'

Private Borchat regarded the calm of Reggie's leadership, in bandages and his smoking his pipe under stress, as the epitome of courage. R.W. Lloyd, writing long after, remembered Reggie 'encouraging us all through the morning, even smoking a pipe.'[23]

Brigadier Stansfield took evidence from two privates who were with Reggie when he was killed. On the sunken road near Sydney Avenue, 'Major Trench came and got on the fire step', reported Private Crosby: 'he asked me whether it was the Boche advancing, I replied "Yes". I continued firing and the next thing I heard was a noise and I looked round and saw Major Trench on the ground.' He was 'bleeding from the back of the head ... he did not speak again ... a stretcher bearer came along and he confirmed my opinion he was dead.'

Captain Greaves sent Reggie's servant Lane with a message to Colonel Gadd. When he heard Reggie was badly wounded he hurried back along the slip trench finding him on the ground but still breathing. But he must have died within minutes of the stretcher-bearer's arrival. Lane was deeply upset that he had been called away from his master's side. 'I never felt so awful in my life,' he declared to Clare. He took charge of his master's body and 'carried him in at battalion headquarters'. He told Clare later he was convinced a machine-gun bullet just above his right ear had killed Reggie.

Colonel Gadd at once instructed Captain Greaves to take command. But further resistance by the Sherwoods was useless for, within fifteen minutes, a runner reported at the headquarters that the Boche 'were on top of us'. Gadd, Lane and others were taken prisoner. Corporal Bradley, who escaped, confirmed, as 'one of the last to leave the dug-out', that Reggie's body was made safe there 'from further shell fire'. Lane had just had time to recover Reggie's wristwatch, which he hid in the sole of his shoe and later returned to Clare. Leaving his master's body to the mercy of the German attackers, he told her, 'hurt me more than anything'. He found it devastating that he 'did not know the last of him.'[24]

In two letters Clare wrote to Reggie before she heard he had been killed, on 26 and 29 March, returned postmarked 4 April, she tried hard to conceal her worst fears. She had read the newspaper reports and knew very well where he was serving at the Front. 'Loss of territory is not everything,' she tried to persuade herself, 'if we can keep the bulk of our armies intact and put masses of them out of action.' Delle was flourishing, she assured him: 'she can really throw and catch quite well now.'[25] When definite news came that her beloved was not just missing but dead, she fled, overwhelmed by grief, to Reggie's mother Isabel Trench in Ireland. They were just one of the thousands of pairs of mothers and wives who sought to comfort each other in those war years.

Reggie's sociability had brought him many friends in the 2/5th Sherwoods. Several corresponded with his widow. Quartermaster Sergeant Wild recalled on 3 May how they had met when the battalion was training on the Curragh in

Ireland in 1916. He stressed how often he and Reggie had talked 'about home and the loved ones there' and then reflected on the tragedy in which they were all bound up. 'Sorrow,' he felt, 'makes us all one in a great and noble cause but it seems unfathomable somehow to lose one's best and dearest and leave but a noble memory behind.' In another letter, Wild remarked on how all D Company's officers were lost 'and the correspondence I have had since has been very sad'. It is hard to grasp how men coped with their battalion being almost wiped out, as happened to the 2/5th Sherwood Foresters on 21 March 1918.[26]

Tributes from Reggie's colleagues meant a great deal to Clare Trench. More than a page in the battalion history *The Green Triangle*, published in 1920, was devoted to Reggie's character and achievements. 'He was not a comfortable man with whom to share a dugout,' it noted, 'his personality was too big, his vitality and enthusiasm for work filled the atmosphere.' The book mentioned his 'enormous gifts for organization and great administrative ability'. 'With all his practicality,' it concluded, 'he had a mystic strain in him, probably due to his Irish origin.'[27]

Captain Barrows told Clare 'how delighted I was with his welcome when I joined the battalion and felt very raw and young'. Barrows commented on his 'marvellous way of taking a great personal interest in officers and men alike'. Captain Rossiter thanked Clare for taking him out to tea when he was home wounded after Le Verguier. He recalled serving with Reggie at Berkhamsted, 'where he was always considered the best officer and out in France he was far better'. 'I simply can't tell you what we thought of him,' he sighed, 'we all loved him.'

Major Pratt who served with Reggie in the Sherwoods, both 'in Ireland and out here', declared his admiration not only for his courage 'but also for his knowledge and fine handling of men'. Brigadier Stansfield wrote to Clare 'I must tell you I had the very greatest opinion of your husband and hoped that he would very soon get command of a battalion'. Captain Stebbing, perhaps Reggie's closest friend in the 2/5th from Ireland onwards, wrote 'had there been any of the 2/5th left I know no officer would be more missed'. He had 'never spared himself any amount of trouble to ensure that we were all looked after well'. Reggie's work as second in command of the battalion 'made him loved by us all in a way only a soldier can be'.[28]

Letters like these have often been quoted in the course of this book. They emphasise the searing grief of men at the Front at the loss of valued colleagues. Communicating with those who were nearest and dearest to the fallen at home, soldiers often wrote emotional letters of condolence. Naturally they focused on what those back home needed to know, especially on details about the manner of a man's death. Such letters presented the deaths of colleagues as specifically heroic. The constructions of patriotism and sacrifice, bravery and duty, with which this book began, became the core of creating the identity of the fallen, among the crowd of others who had gone equally courageously to war and had come safely home.

CHAPTER 14

'The Men Cannot Grasp It'

Armistice

Lance Spicer wrote reflectively to his father in February 1918 during the lull before the Germans launched their final offensive. He was expecting a massive assault and envisaged that it could 'make us withdraw a little'. But his concern was the need to keep up morale at home to match confidence among those at the Front. The fight was to uphold 'certain ideals and beliefs which we and our fathers before us have held for centuries'. Both sides were now war weary but there was nothing to be said for 'grousing and talking about peace'. He and his colleagues needed, on the contrary, to know that those at home were not 'worrying about our individual safety but are really keen to see us win and not come back till we really have finished the war properly'.[1] This was an expression of one young officer's fighting spirit. Lance was explicit that he loathed and hated the war. But he was in absolutely no doubt that 'we've got to fight on'.[2]

Conversations that soldiers had in early 1918, just before mobile warfare was reopened by the German March offensive, shed light on British morale. Cyril Newman recorded one such chat with his adjutant Captain Nichols, who was expecting 'a death or glory struggle'. He marvelled at how calm Cyril was when, just as they spoke, three shells exploded near them. 'They don't seem to affect you Newman,' he said. He recalled that Newman had also been cool in 1916, when they worked together in Leuze Wood on the Somme. It was the officer who had less confidence in this conversation than the Tommy. Cyril insisted they would 'come through the trial – that victory would ultimately be ours'. They talked for some time. 'You're wonderful Newman,' Nichols concluded. 'No, Sir,' he replied, 'but I do believe it and so say it.' Cyril knew that this conversation cheered them both, which is why he told Winnie about it.

Cyril remained optimistic through the gruelling next months. By July his confidence that the war was ending was such that he assured his mother it would do so. Winnie at once grilled him about what he really meant. Yes, he wrote on 3 August, he did believe the Allies would inflict a decisive defeat that year. In his view, the enemy was well aware that 'daily, hourly, our strength is growing and that the New Year can bring him nothing but loss'. 'Were I a German,' he opined, 'I should not be elated as I peered into the future.'[3]

This was when the young Bert Fereday from Wimbledon came into the war. Between May and August 1918, serving with the Civil Service Rifles, Bert's almost daily letters to his parents were usually cheerful. He much appreciated the letters he received from family, friends and members of his Scout troop. 'I certainly do not see where the "glory of war" comes in,' was his view as a late-comer to the action, 'except it be the wonderful courage and endurance our boys are daily manifesting.' On another occasion he commented, 'I am indifferent to the sadness of this war; naturally I am tired of it and long for home; but since I have to remain out here for some time to come to fulfil my share of the peacemaking, it behoves me to accept my lot in the most cheerful manner possible for in this way I shall better weather this stormy life.'[4]

Lance Spicer, kicking his heels in a staff job, did not see action until late April in 1918. Then he became a Brigade Major in the 64th Infantry Division south of Ypres and his life suddenly became 'extraordinarily hectic'. He lived through, on 24 and 25 April, what he called 'the most complete battle day I have ever spent'. Even if his work was once again 'very strenuous', he explained when writing home, 'I feel far happier here than I did at Army HQ which I left without one single tinge of regret.'[5] For Lance had rejoined the front line as the war began to enter 'its most intensive, climactic phase'. Ludendorff's bid for a decisive breakthrough on 21 March was seen to have failed. The British and French forces had not been separated, nor had their line been broken irrevocably. The objective had been to take Amiens but the Germans were halted ten miles short of the town. Sixteen days of battle had merely achieved a salient forty miles deep, at the cost of 250,000 German casualties. The Allies' 'dynamic rearguard action' had paid off, as the German infantry outran their supply lines and became increasingly short of food and ammunition.[6]

Between April and June 1918, the war assumed a new pattern: German attacks achieved initial success but then resistance stiffened and stalemate was restored. The strength of British morale was the key to a 'Forgotten Victory', as Gary Sheffield has called these great defensive actions on the Western Front. With the failure of the German attack on the Marne in July, the strategic initiative passed to the Allies. The watershed battle, achieved with complete surprise, was at Amiens on 8 August. A whole series of factors led to this turning point. The Australian and Canadian corps demonstrated skill and high morale, the Allied advantage in numbers was now overwhelming, British logistical support and domination of the air were important, the British Expeditionary Force's weapons system, especially its tanks and artillery, had become a battle winner. Ludendorff's resignation after Amiens reflected the huge psychological blow he had suffered. In the German High Command, confidence in a crushing victory over the Allies was lost for ever on that day. At best, Germany sought to hold out for some kind of compromise peace.[7]

A major new Allied offensive was launched following the Battle of Amiens. With the Battle of Albert on 21 August, Sir Douglas Haig became confident of victory before the year was out.[8] Returning to active service that month, Rowland Feilding was given command of the 15th Battalion of the London Regiment, the 1st Civil Service Rifles. 'We have been at it, hammer and tongs, the last few days,' he told Edith on 26 August, after four days and nights with hardly a break. 'Things have gone well,' he felt, 'and there is no doubt we are killing a lot of Germans . . . besides we are capturing large numbers of prisoners. I am with a splendid crowd. They are like lions – these London men.' They were so brave, he reckoned, that a good many others 'would look like shivering rabbits beside some of them'.

Rowland sent a long account of his battalion's role in the Battle of Albert, between 21 and 23 August, when the town fell to the 18th Division. The 15th Londons had sustained 389 casualties, killed, wounded and missing. But Rowland's tour of the battlefield revealed the damage the enemy had sustained: 'the dead lay thick, their packs opened and the contents scattered; their letters and little souvenirs they had carried, thrown out by the ghouls of the battlefield, littered the ground beside them'.[9]

The end of the Great War is often discussed in terms of the last hundred days, which began on 8 August. Our letter writers, now much diminished in numbers, afford little material on this stage of the war but other commentators writing home stand in for them. 'They were a wonderful last hundred days,' Second Lieutenant Poynting in the Royal Sussex Regiment wrote after Christmas, when it was all over.[10] There was a sense in August and September that the war was finally moving in the Allies' favour, though few began even to dream that Armistice would occur so soon. Colonel Bill Murray was serving in the border country south of Ypres, where the German withdrawal was slower than at the centre point of the Allied summer attack. 'We keep on pushing out our line bit by bit,' he wrote on 13 August, and 'it exasperates the Hun beyond words'. But he discovered that none of the prisoners he took knew what was happening further south. They were still being told they were over the Marne and advancing on Paris 'and simply won't believe they have been driven back'.

Now we have 'the Huns fairly on the run', Murray confirmed on 1 September. There was heady momentum, but the downside was sheer exhaustion. 'It is a very hard life compared to the war a year ago,' Captain Saunders of the Border Regiment told his wife on 5 September. They were all worried and tired: 'what is so bad is the continual moving over open country, both day and night, usually under shell fire. I wonder how long this kind of warfare will go on.'[11]

Rowland Feilding enjoyed the party atmosphere at Leslie Henson's concert and his Divisional 'Follies' in September. He related a joke that went down well with a front-line audience. 'What is a Patriot? Answer: A man who sheds *your* blood for *his* country.' But he found a rumour that his regiment was to be shifted to the Italian Front very disagreeable. He would be sorry to leave France just then. 'It is a cursed war,' he confessed to his wife, 'and I dislike the whole business as much as anybody. Yet I love it: it has been the breath of life to me and I shall always look back upon the time I have spent here with great happiness.'[12]

The outcome of the first fifty of the hundred days, from 8 August to 26 September, was that the German army was pushed back almost to its jumping-off point in March. The cost was higher in British casualties in September 1918 than it had been in September 1916. The Spanish flu was making an impact, besides the perils of attacking the retreating German army. On 31 August the 2nd Australian Division captured Mont St Quentin, the key to Péronne. Two days later, the Canadian Corps attacked and broke through the Hindenburg Line. In their first assault as an independent army, the Americans recovered the St Mihiel salient on 12 September. The Grand Offensive reached its climax in late September and early October. On 2 October, the British at last broke out of the Ypres salient. Four days later, the North Midland Division stormed the St Quentin Canal and the whole of the Hindenburg trench system, taking 4,000 prisoners. Overall this was an advance of about twenty-five miles on a front of forty miles. Casualties were still high, though much lower than on the Somme or at Passchendaele. Through constant pressure and effective mobile offensive warfare, the Allies steadily wore down German combat power and morale. The British Expeditionary Force had broken free of the trench systems and battlefields of 1915 to 1917: it was now fighting in open country.[13]

Germany requested an armistice on 4 October in the midst of domestic upheaval. There were many units that put up fierce resistance as the Allied armies pursued the rearguards across northern France and Belgium during that month; 185 German divisions remained in the field even if they were skeletons of their former selves. Yet, if the Allies were tired too, they knew they were marching to victory. Between August and October they took 385,500 prisoners and captured 6,615 guns. The BEF advanced some twenty miles in October and suffered 120,000 casualties. The Battle of the Sambre on 4 November, the last major battle of the war, is relatively well known because of the death that day of the poet Wilfred Owen.[14] But its immediate significance was that it finally dispelled any illusions among the German leadership that they could fight on. Armistice negotiations had been pursued for a month but the war now had to be terminated immediately.[15] The victory in the end was a coalition effort.[16]

For Rowland Feilding, pursuing the retreating Germans with the London Regiment across Belgium south of Ypres, it was the devastation of the landscape which formed the burden of his letters in the last weeks of the war. He found it 'very harrowing' watching women who had just returned to inspect the damage to their homes following the enemy's withdrawal. Rowland railed against the injustice of the fact that those 'responsible for these outrages' were being let off. He observed the wanton destruction of 'hundreds of square miles of territory, including endless villages, towns and cities'. Personally he rejoiced, stopping at Fontés on this march, in 'an extremely cheerful billet with electric light'.

The highlight of the month for the Londons was a triumphal march on 28 October through Lille. It was 'a truly wonderful experience', Rowland wrote: 'for miles we marched through decorated streets, through immense crowds of cheering citizens . . . I hear that the very morning the inhabitants awoke to find the enemy gone, women were to be seen running about the streets waving tricolours which had been hidden during the four years and more that Lille has been held in captivity'. Each battalion was headed by its band. Rowland's 'played English airs as we passed through the suburbs' and then burst into the Marseillaise, 'when we reached the more fashionable parts with electrical effect upon the people'. Rowland was on a huge charger at the head of the procession. When he asked a lady for a flag *'pour mes enfants'*, she rushed in and found him a bunch of hand-painted ones. He sent one to his eldest daughter Joan with a note, from 'your loving Daddy'.

On 5 November, billeted at Cornet, when armistice was rumoured, the Germans used heavy trench mortars against one of Rowland's advance posts. He was visited that day by Lieutenant Colonel Bernard Montgomery, a staff officer in the Division, who 'seemed a little nettled that the Germans should still be there'.[17] This was an early display of the typical impatience for which Monty became famous. Germany's allies had almost all agreed terms. On 8 November, German armistice negotiators arrived in France. Next day the Kaiser abdicated; the day after, the new Social Democratic republic was proclaimed.[18]

During these last days of war there was rising anticipation that peace was coming. Rowland Feilding reported a sweepstake in his mess on 7 November,

'on the hour when hostilities shall cease'. He found that he was already beginning 'to look back upon the last four and a half years as a sort of dream', in
which his wife's 'faithful patient figure' stood sentinel over his comings and
goings from their London home. Ironically, his battalion was detailed as
advanced guard for the capture of another town on the 11th. When news of the
signing of the Armistice, at 5 a.m., came through, effective at 11 a.m., his orders
were hastily countermanded.[19]

The last hours of the war were especially anxious for those still fighting or
within range of enemy guns. Captain T.H. Westmacott was spending his time
collecting prisoners, in his role as Deputy Assistant Provost Marshal to
the 24th Division. As he entered another liberated town with a Belgian interpreter a shell hit the mayor's house and a splinter passed close to him. He
thought what rotten luck it would be to be wounded just then. As the final
hours ticked away, the thoughts of Sergeant Robert Cude were the thoughts of
many: 'if only I can last out the remainder of the time and this is everyone's
prayer'. 'I am awfully sorry for those of our chaps who are killed this morning,'
Cude wrote in his diary, 'and there must be a decent few of them too, for
mines are still going up and will continue to take a price from us for months to
come yet.'

There was no great demonstration, Westmacott told those at home, when
eleven o'clock did come, 'I think because it was hard to realise that the war was
really over.' Just before the Armistice took effect, the artillery had fired a huge
barrage. 'I never heard such a roar.' It was, he explained, a 'great contrast to the
deathly silence which followed'. A diary entry by Captain Dartford summarises
the muted mood on his sector of the Front: 'so we have at last reached the day
and everybody is terribly pleased'. With troops being ordered to 'stand fast and
adopt normal precautions' there was a kind of paralysis. Nobody knew 'what
ought to be done really and existence seems pointless'. Yet there was at once
'much talk of how and when demobilisation will start'. The guns in the distance
had kept firing up to the last minute, noted Sergeant Robert McKay in his diary
on 11 November, then he simply noted 'great rejoicing'.[20] Despite requirements
for continued military discipline and lack of resources for partying on the front
line, Adrian Gregory argues, 'there was a degree of jubilation and high spirits'
at the Front.[21]

Apathy and scepticism are nevertheless entirely understandable. The war
had gone on too long for men to be able to envisage life without it.[22] Lance
Spicer's account, in an immediate letter home, expressed this sense of bewilderment. 'The men cannot grasp it,' he told his father, 'they have become so
used to this soldier life, so numbed to endurance that they find it hard to
believe they can live otherwise.' His men, he explained, under orders to halt

their march at eleven o'clock, did give three cheers 'but there is no enthusiasm'. 'Of course they are glad it is over,' was his shrewd comment, 'but they do not realise it.'[23]

In some cases ceremonies to mark the event were hastily arranged. Burgon Bickersteth was at the village of Leuze, where representatives from all the regiments in the vicinity were summoned and drawn up in an orderly manner in the square just before eleven o'clock struck. Every window, he recorded, had its onlookers. The trumpeters played 'Cease Fire'; the band crashed out 'God Save the King'; the Marseillaise and the Belgian national anthem followed. The mayor made a speech about the Allies' valiant defence of his country. The General and he wrung each other's hands.

The emotions of the day were also described by Philip Gibbs that morning as he entered Mons. 'All the way,' he wrote, 'there were columns of troops on the march, and their bands played ahead of them and almost every man had a flag on his rifle, the red, white and blue of France, the red, yellow and black of Belgium.' This area had only just been liberated. Crowds of people cheered the soldiers, showering them with chrysanthemums. 'Our men marched singing, with a smiling light in their eyes,' Gibbs noted.[24]

Rowland Feilding's account was written six days later when he had heard from Edith, who expressed bewilderment at the sudden and complete collapse of the German war effort. His response carries the authentic sense of a momentous day. 'The feeling among the soldiers here,' he explained, 'was rather one of awe and inability to appreciate the great relief that had so suddenly come to them. There was no visible change in their demeanour and I do not think many felt much inclined for jubilation.'

His reflections, though simply for his wife's eyes, stand the test of time. He felt bitter about the strikes in England, the bickering and muddles. Rowland's wisdom enabled him to take a long perspective. 'I cannot help hoping,' he declared, 'that in the excitement at home no English man or woman has failed to feel humbled by these terrific events or has forgotten to give proper thanks for the Empire's wonderful escape – indeed for the escape of all humanity.' He hoped especially that children – his children and all the children of Europe – 'may have had the duty of thanksgiving impressed upon them'.[25]

This immediate testimony shows the mixed feelings with which soldiers greeted the Armistice. Those who wrote about how they remembered it later retained the sense of huge relief that the fighting was over. But the memory of bewilderment remained uppermost in their minds. 'I tried to visualize the end of the war and my return home but there my imagination failed me,' recounted Fred Noakes in his memoir *The Distant Drum* published in 1952. 'It seemed as if only a miracle could make the military machine loose its hold on me'. His mind, he recalled, 'refused to envisage any more permanent release other than a wonderful vision of leave'.[26]

But, as time went on, post-war disenchantment predictably coloured such accounts. Charles Douie, publishing his recollections of life as a subaltern in 1929, stressed that the abiding memory of 11 November 1918 was of a silence free from gunfire. But Guy Chapman gave the impression in his memoir *A Passionate Prodigality* in 1933 that his comrades in the Royal Fusiliers managed to accept the Armistice with no more than a shrug: 'a blanket of fog covered the countryside ... the band played but there was very little singing ... we were very old, very tired and now very wise'.[27]

J.C. Dunn, chronicling the recollections and reflections of the 2nd Battalion of the Royal Welch Fusiliers, said the news was greeted with 'anticlimax relieved by spasmodic cheering'. An officer from whom he collected memories for his 1938 volume *The War the Infantry Knew* spoke of 'the uncanny silence that pervaded'. The confidence that the war was over, he said, grew only through the absence of the 'rumbling of guns, the staccato of machine guns, the roar of exploding dumps'. Stuart Dolden, writing in 1980 about hearing the news as he made breakfast for his company, remembered relief: 'frankly I had had enough and felt thoroughly weary and in that respect I was not alone'.[28]

It was very different in England on 11 November. In London euphoria was the keynote. Winston Churchill stood at the window of his room in the Hotel Metropole, looking up Northumberland Avenue towards Trafalgar Square. As Big Ben chimed, he watched streams of people pour out of all the buildings. The square was soon swarming. He wrote of how 'fifty-two months of gaunt distortion' of people's lives had ended. Soberly, he reflected on how 'the chains which held the world were broken', how, as he saw it, the 'links of imperative need, links of discipline, links of brute force, links of self-sacrifice, links of terror, links of honour' which had held the nation in chains were snapped upon 'a few strokes of the clock'. Excitement on the Home Front was, in these terms, entirely understandable.[29]

Servicemen at home who had access to alcohol and fireworks were best placed to demonstrate the joy they felt.[30] For thousands who had lost close relatives inconsolable grief made it impossible to give their minds fully, or even at all, to celebration. In close-knit town and village communities, the concern of those who had escaped personal bereavement for others who had not pervaded local relationships. Robert Saunders, a Sussex schoolmaster, put this well. Seeing tragedies in families all around him, people mourning for boys in whom he had instilled patriotism dead and wounded, he reflected in his diary 'it does not seem right that those who have escaped shall give themselves up to Joy days'. After all, he decided, 'I think most people feel that some time must elapse before we can properly celebrate peace, our feelings have been too much harassed and our sympathies too much called forth for the losses of our friends and neighbours.'[31]

Six of our sixteen letter writers survived the war and three of these were already home when the Armistice was signed. The most interesting, in terms of his emotional journey, was Herbert Trench. Invalided out with shell shock in October 1916, he eked out a precarious existence in London during 1917 and 1918, living on money from his mother and temporary jobs. His watch, cigarette case and fountain pen were all in pawn, he confessed to his younger sister Cesca at one point. 'They were charming people,' he declared sadly, regretting the collapse, 'through lack of petrol', of a motoring school that had briefly employed him. It was run by, among others, the young actress Yvonne Arnaud. Then he found new work in the Ministry of Shipping.

His elder sister Margot sent Herbert money for a Harley Street psychiatric consultation, so he felt obliged to give her an account of himself: 'In regard to nerves I think that mine are as right as they'll ever be – you see – I fancy with a normal person total recovery is only a matter of time – while with a hopelessly temperamental person like myself you can recover to a point and that is all.'[32] Herbert undoubtedly followed the story of Siegfried Sassoon's celebrated letter to his commanding officer, which was read in Parliament and published in the press in June 1917. It insisted that a war he had entered for 'defence and liberation' had become a 'war of aggression and conquest', prolonging men's suffering for ends, as Sassoon saw it, which were 'evil and unjust'. Instead of being court-martialled, Sassoon, with influential voices in his support, was sent to the Craiglockhart Hospital for neurasthenic officers in Edinburgh, though he later returned to the Front.[33]

Sassoon was in contact in 1917 with the tiny pacifist circle of Bertrand Russell and Lady Ottoline Morrell. These were people who swam bravely against a mighty tide. In August 1917, he published his moving poem 'To any Dead Officer (who left school for the army in 1914)' in the *Cambridge Magazine*. Herbert Trench, avid for poetry, certainly read it. Here was the discordant music that conveyed the ugly truth of trench warfare to an audience that had hitherto been lulled by patriotic propaganda. Most people, of course, were not yet receptive to Sassoon's account of the war. But for Herbert it was not so much the man's stand on principle, which shocked the patriotic nation, that struck a chord, as the similarity of his own fighting experience to Sassoon's tragic story. His hours in a French ditch in December 1914 must have come flooding back as he read Sassoon's account of an officer who went 'out patrolling in the dark', was caught and wounded 'beyond the wire', then left for dead in a shell hole 'moaning for water'. Herbert identified himself at once with the man who was able to express the kind of physical and mental agonies he himself had suffered. Sassoon used poetry of extraordinary power and grace in doing so.

When his brother Reggie was reported missing in April 1918, in desperation Herbert wandered the homes of his relatives in London. 'He feels it dreadfully,' Georgiana Steel reported to Clare. His Aunt Francie reported he was 'so broken-hearted'. 'Poor fellow,' she told his mother, 'it must be so hard for him.'[34] Sassoon's verse was still very much in his mind in August 1918 when, grieving for Reggie, Herbert went to stay with his cousins in Scotland. He took with him *Counter-Attack*, the anthology of thirty-eight of Sassoon's poems which had been published by Heinemann in May that year. Herbert was still deep in his own shell shock, and it is evident from his letter to his sister Cesca that month how lonely he was. The assertively patriotic and imperialist company of his Gore-Booth cousins was almost intolerable. So he found the family holiday, admittedly 'extraordinarily comfortable and pleasant', hard to take.

Knowing his Irish sister would understand, Herbert told Cesca of his real feelings, with the caustic comment on the family 'we all think the war and the soldiers "too splendid"'. He was sorely irritated by their jingoistic mother's constant 'harassing of our emotions', as he put it, with her stories of the heroism shown by army chaplains. 'You know our cousins do talk rather rot a lot of the time,' he confided to Cesca. Did she know Siegfried Sassoon's poems? In his letter he copied out for her the first and last verses of 'To any Dead Officer'. He was well aware that Sassoon's was still a voice in the wilderness. 'If it appeals to you let me know and I'll send you his latest book – *Counter Attack*,' he wrote, adding disarmingly, 'I think it's essentially for some folk and not for others.'

To Herbert Trench, in the sorrow of personal failure as a soldier, Sassoon's satires on the patriotic pretensions of the government spoke loud and clear. His family's overwhelming and simple commitment to the national cause was difficult to cope with when he was still oppressed by his own trench experience as well as mourning a dear brother. He needed quiet and time to meditate. 'You know what energetic folk Geordie and Ethel are, I've been on the move continually,' Herbert complained, uneasy with the mood of his relatives in Scotland.[35]

It was late in 1917 when Jack Sweeney obtained that most sought after form of release, a Blighty wound. Working with a crowd of conscripts and inexperienced young officers whom he found it hard to respect, he was now the oldest man in his company at twenty-nine. Lean faced with some of his hair turned white, he had done well to survive three full years in the firing line. In a sudden night-time raid on his trench he sustained a head wound, remembering only 'a horrible noise in my ears and blood running down my face', before 'reinforcements came up and cleared Fritz off'. He told Ivy all this from the hospital in Rouen, where 'the sisters are very nice and the beds are lovely'. The matron spoke up for him. Moreover, his long service counted when an ear specialist saw him 'and marked me for Blighty'.

After convalescence in a Devon hospital, Jack was passed fit for duty but his luck held. Taking into account his having been wounded five times, the commanding officer found him a job as a mess orderly in Britain. On leave in March 1918, Jack and Ivy were married. A devoted relationship found its maturity in lasting fidelity. Most of the letters he wrote to Ivy before his discharge from the army, in March 1919, were retained by her as 'private and personal love letters' when she sent the archive to the Imperial War Museum. One of those in the archived collection, from shortly after their marriage, ended typically with 'millions of kisses, tons of love, I am always your loving Old Bean, Jack'.

In November 1918, Jack was guarding prisoners of war at Cuckney in Nottinghamshire. When his unit heard news of the Armistice, he related on 12 November, the flag went up on the church and he gathered his pals for a victory peal. They rang the bells 'or at least made a terrible noise for an hour and then we went and had a drink'. Jack climbed on the roof of the prisoners' billet and stuck up a big flag. He found they were 'as excited as we were'.[36]

'I was wounded early this morning but as you see I am well and cheery,' wrote Cyril Newman from a casualty clearing station on 10 August 1918. He was laying telegraph lines as usual when 'ping' – he felt a machine-gun bullet just tip the edge of his hat and enter his shoulder. This surely, if anything, must be a Blighty one. But two days of hospital consultations followed, Cyril praying hard the doctor would 'mark me for Blighty'. 'I am eating my heart out for a sight of you,' he told Winnie on the 12th. Cyril's release came just three years and three months after he had first landed in France. Having made a good recovery in hospital at Torquay, he moved to billets at Shoreham in Sussex.[37]

Cyril's Armistice Day was at first very anticlimactic: 'nothing happening, no guns going off, no bells ringing' in the morning, he reported. But later some 5,000 men in his camp gathered to celebrate, with 'whistling, cheering, singing, shouting, caterwhauling, laughing and smoking'. Cyril's reflections were sober ones. He could hardly believe it: 'one has a sense of inward elation that one has been permitted to take part in such a struggle'. He was glad, in November 1918, that he had volunteered in 'the darkened days after the *Times* announcement on August 30th of the virtual destruction of the British Expeditionary Force at Mons'. Cyril recalled emotionally the huge losses the nation had sustained in the years that followed, feeling 'those responsible should be brought to justice'. He saw the Armistice terms as not too hard at all on Germany.[38]

Cyril Newman went up to London for his demobilisation at Crystal Palace on 10 January 1919. He had to stand in a queue for about half an hour until his name was called out; then he went forward to the table where a War Office official gave him various papers to sign. He took the bus to Muswell Hill, noting succinctly in his diary 'I was free: saw Winnie'. A few days later, Cyril talked to his boys in the Bible class about his experiences. The keynote was autobiographical: King Arthur's advice to his knights on the path in life they should take: 'love one maiden only, cleave to her and worship her by years of noble deeds until they win her'. This was the spirit in which Cyril had fought his war. He and Winnie were married at the Baptist Church in Muswell Hill on 21 August 1919. In June he had withdrawn £205 from the Post Office savings account, which he had kept since he was a child, for the costs of his approaching marriage.[39]

Demobilisation had been worked out on paper by the army well in advance. The plan was to break up the British Expeditionary Force in a controlled way by individuals rather than by units, with priority going to men with long service, who had come from essential civilian jobs, or could show evidence from an employer that employment was waiting for them. The process began in December and was conducted with slow and deliberate military precision. Existing stocks of grade three cloth were at once requisitioned for demob suits. Uniforms and helmets could be retained. There were free rail warrants for the journey home. An unemployed man received 24 shillings a week for the first year, with supplements of 6 shillings for one child and 3 shillings for others.

There were some noisy rumblings of discontent from men whose discharge was delayed in late 1918 and early 1919. Winston Churchill, taking over the War Ministry, modified the system in favour of one based on age, length of service and combat experience. More rapid implementation prevented further disturbances. Nine hundred thousand men were retained to guard the Rhine bridgeheads and serve as a home force. A year after the Armistice only 125,000 eligible men were still awaiting release from military service.[40]

Graham Greenwell's Oxfordshire and Buckinghamshire Light Infantry had served in Italy since November 1917. 'Here there has been practically no excitement, only a period of most strenuous work,' he told his mother just after the Armistice. 'I have begun seriously to consider what I am going to do now that the war is over,' he wrote a few days later. Part of him yearned to stay in the army but he was in no doubt that his mother would not wish for that. He was in touch with one of his closest friends about entry to Oxford, noting that students seemed to be discriminated against, being class 43, the last but one, on the demobilisation list, while gentlemen were in class 37, 'so it would seem better to be a mere gentleman'.

Mrs Greenwell's letters strongly supported her son's university entry. Less than a month after the Armistice, Graham wrote to the Dean of Christ Church about the five years of delay the war had caused. His entering the college had been arranged in 1914, to follow a summer break after leaving Winchester. He suggested that his mother write to the Dean as well to confirm his intentions. His attitude, he confessed to her, was that 'after four years in the army it will do me good and will give me a rest'. But friends, many of them with the same plan, chided Graham when he spoke of getting to Oxford as quickly as the summer term of 1919. He would do no work, he was told. The banks of the Cherwell, far away and alluring, seemed a kind of Elysium from an officers' mess in Italy. 'But I am determined to get my long-neglected brain into order again,' Graham insisted, 'I shall read some history and try to take an honours degree in five terms'. He was demobilised in January 1919 and hurried up to Oxford.[41]

Rowland Feilding took rather longer to get home. In early December he was in Brussels. He went, he explained to his daughter Joan, 'to look for traces of Uncle Wilfrid', his wife's brother, who had been killed near there very early in the war. 'I found all the inhabitants dancing and singing in the streets,' he related. The King of Belgium had just entered the town for the first time in over four years. Rowland also, a few days later, took an American army doctor to explore the Loos battlefield, which he knew so well from personal experience. He regretted this when the man became absorbed in souvenir collecting. It horrified Rowland 'to see this sacred ground desecrated' by scavenging. Already, almost instantaneously, the gulf was opening between the thoughts and memories of deeply scarred combatants and the attitude of the simple battlefield tourist.

It was 18 January before Rowland spoke of demobilisation, finding it in full swing then on his arrival at Ferfay in the Pas de Calais. He described the ritual: the demobilisation party – which that day consisted of an officer and twenty-six men – 'is paraded at 2.0 pm, when I say goodbye and shake hands with the men and the band plays them down the road'. Ten days later, the band played a demob draft away for the last time and was then itself demobilised. Rowland watched the intense disillusionment of his troops grow, as they became increasingly frustrated by waiting for their discharge. On 3 February he sent Edith another of his wise and thoughtful letters. Standing back from trench warfare and assessing what was positive about it as a human experience of collective living, he contrasted this with the picture that had grown in the minds of soldiers now impatient and given too much time to think: 'a heavenly picture of an England which does not exist, and never did exist and never will exist so long as men are human'.

Rowland Feilding perceptively saw what was coming. Disillusion would grow in 1919 and the 1920s as the war, it turned out, was not a magic key to open the door to an age of plenty for everyone. The national mood of the years from August 1914 to the end of 1918 was hugely fragile. In an unforeseen emergency, the British people had almost ignored the rigid and hierarchical class divisions of their society, or overlaid them with something powerful and inspiring: a resolute and absorbing patriotic commitment till the war was won, so that men of all sorts put everything else aside in their common purpose. In this book, we have seen how class was really there under the surface all the time. But there was a very good reason for unease and arbitrary standoffish-ness temporarily to be laid aside. Once the peace was made, it was as if the nation returned in puzzlement and haste to what people had left behind.

Feilding, predictably and like others no doubt, at once took refuge in nostalgia. In the 'old trench life', he wrote, the next meal was always 'as certain as the rising sun': the shells fell 'without favour on all alike'; rich and poor stood 'upon their individual merits, without discrimination'. In that life, where you got used to 'the taste of chloride of lime in tea', there was 'an atmosphere of selflessness and a spirit of camaraderie the like of which has probably not been seen in the world before, at least on so grand a scale'. Men were easily pleased in trench life, where 'even a shell when it had just missed you produced a sort of exultation'. Because there was no humbug in the trenches 'the better kind of men who have lived in them', Rowland felt confident, 'will look upon them hereafter with something like affection'.

After two months of kicking his heels, though, even Rowland became depressed. He hated the way demobilisation was managed, seeing 'officers and men slink to their homes one by one as if they had lost the war instead of won it'. But, when he and the last of his men eventually crossed the Channel in May, the homecoming he experienced revived his confidence in British warmth of heart. He had sometimes heard soldiers talk during the war of the people at home being callous and thoughtless about their sufferings. When the inhabit-ants of Felixstowe 'thronged the streets as we passed and cheered and waved their handkerchiefs', such imaginings were banished from his mind. This for his men was 'personal and first-hand recognition from their fellow-countrymen'. Rowland confessed he had 'not seen this side of England before': 'a tinge of sadness was mixed with the joy of homecoming as I looked on'.[42]

PART III

SACRIFICE

CHAPTER 15

'We Will Remember Them'

Remembrance and Commemoration

The poet Laurence Binyon was sitting on the cliffs of north Cornwall when in early September 1914 he wrote the seven stanzas of 'For the Fallen'.[1] The casualty rates among the British Expeditionary Force were growing day by day. The Battle of the Marne was foremost in people's minds when the poem was published in *The Times* on 21 September. 'They went with songs to the battle; they were young' runs the first line of the little-known third stanza of the poem. But it is the fourth stanza that we all know well: it is read year after year on 11 November at services throughout the land. It is also read at the Menin Gate in Belgium at eight o'clock every evening, usually by a British serviceman:

> *They shall grow not old, as we that are left grow old:*
> *Age shall not weary them, nor the years condemn.*
> *At the going down of the sun and in the morning.*
> *We will remember them.*

The Ode of Remembrance, as it is also known, has come to be claimed as a tribute to all casualties of war, regardless of state. It is often recited in Canada, Australia and New Zealand and has grown more and more famous as the decades since 1914 have passed. There is a stone plaque at the point where Laurence Binyon is believed to have been sitting when he wrote it, looking out to sea between Pentire Point and the Rumps promontory. But this was erected in 2001.[2]

The Armistice was both an ending and a beginning, bringing trench warfare and battle to a close, initiating a pattern of remembrance which now has a permanent and treasured place in British national life. Almost a hundred years on Remembrance has acquired a timeless quality. This is a national festival over several days, according to each year's November calendar. Its component parts were in fact assembled gradually during the period from 1918 to 1927. The sale of millions of poppies in the weeks before 11 November, the Albert Hall Festival of Remembrance, the Cenotaph service attended by the Royal Family and representatives of the Commonwealth and political parties, the Two Minute Silence, are events which appear, in the twenty-first century, to make up a seamless whole. It was not like this to begin with.

The pattern of Remembrance evolved at the instigation of the British people, as the government took account of expressed needs and desires. The stories of the creation of the Cenotaph in Whitehall and the establishment of the Two Minute Silence are intertwined. Sir Edwin Lutyens designed the Cenotaph, constructed from plaster, cloth and wood, as the centrepiece for a march past in Whitehall of the victorious armies and their leaders on 19 July 1919. The intention was to incorporate the dead in a celebration of military victory. Lutyens's exercise in the 'elemental mode' of commemorative art was seen as subsidiary to the main event that day, which was recognition of the glory of military achievement.[3]

By some magic though, Lutyens exactly caught the mood of collective bereavement following the Armistice. He used mathematical relationships as a language to express pantheist and unconventional religious beliefs. His work in New Delhi had strengthened his ecumenical outlook. In his first Cenotaph he captured, in an abstract architectural form and a minimalist manner, a whole people's bereavement. Lutyens's Cenotaph, Jay Winter has said, expressed existential truths, providing a focus 'for collective mourning of a kind unknown before or since in Britain'.

But, as his Cenotaph became laden with wreaths during the weeks after the victory parade, Lutyens quickly understood the British people's need for his work to remain in Whitehall, although he had designed it as a temporary war memorial. On 29 July 1919 he drafted a letter requesting this. So when the first anniversary of the Armistice came round, those present in Whitehall, as Jay Winter has put it, were able to 'contemplate the timeless, the eternal, the inexorable reality of death in war'. The Cenotaph as we know it was ready for Armistice in 1920. Lutyens's genius was to produce a monument to the dead 'which says so much because it says so little': 'it is a form on which anyone could inscribe his or her own thoughts, reveries, sadnesses'.[4]

The phenomenal appeal of the Cenotaph was cemented for thousands, most of whom had not yet seen it, when the government inaugurated the Two Minute Silence, led by the Prime Minister David Lloyd George, at this spot on 11 November 1919. This was sprung on the nation, causing almost as much of a surprise to the public as the Armistice had done the previous year. Just a week before, Sir Percy Fitzpatrick submitted, for the attention of the Cabinet, a memorandum suggesting this silent pause in the nation's life, which generations since have grown up to accept as a national institution.

Rather like bonfires on Guy Fawkes Day, this is a classic case of what historians call 'the invention of tradition'. Fitzpatrick was specific about the purpose and meaning of the ritual: 'it is not in mourning but in greeting that we should salute them on this day. When we are divided it may serve to remind us of the greater things we have in common. When we are gone it may help to bring home to those who come after us the meaning, the nobility and the unselfishness of the great sacrifice by which their freedom was assured.'

After the King had agreed to it, the request for the silence was published in all the British newspapers on 7 November. Remembering 'the world wide carnage of the four preceding years' and marking 'the victory of right and freedom', we shall all gladly, George V wrote, 'interrupt our business and pleasure ... and unite in this simple service of Silence and Remembrance'. Fitzpatrick had set out who the Silence was for: 'the women who have lost and suffered and borne so much', children for whom he intended it to be pedagogic, veterans for whom it was both a tribute and a reminder of their fallen colleagues.

The silence was signalled to the nation by maroons, artillery gunfire, harbour sirens and church bells. Many assembled at places where war memorials had already been created. Early in the morning, the King's wreath was placed at the foot of the Cenotaph. As eleven o'clock approached, ran the report in the *Daily Express*, 'few saw the Prime Minister, with bent white head, carrying a wreath of orchids and roses with a background of laurels . . . then the hush came . . . there is nothing under heaven so full of awe as the complete silence of a mighty crowd'.

The first silence struck people with irresistible force, sweeping them into a display of collective emotion that was public yet at the same time intensely private. This was the key to its lasting appeal. Everyone had to stop and pay their respects at eleven o'clock. Thus Armistice Day became, in the immediate aftermath of the Great War, an extraordinary display of national solidarity. Ordinary life came to a halt, as everywhere else, on the north British railway system: 'from Northumberland to Inverness', we are told, 'on mainlines and branches, in sheds and yards, passenger trains, goods trains and shunting engines stopped wherever they happened to be. Engine crews stood bare headed at their footplates, passengers sat silent in their compartments'. Armistice Day became crucial to the sustained and creative effort to bring meaning and purpose to mass death, at once so terrifying and in 1914 so unexpected.[5] British understanding of war had come a long way since those first months in the late summer of 1914 when Reggie Trench, awed by what had suddenly happened, euphemistically noted that one friend or another had been 'knocked out'.

Lutyens's stone Cenotaph, replacing the temporary one, was unveiled on 11 November 1920. Cyril Newman pasted a sepia postcard photograph of the unveiling into his family album.[6] That day, two years after the Armistice, the war dead were brought for all time into history through a special funeral. It was the Dean of Westminster who proposed that an unknown body from the battlefields of France and Flanders should be disinterred and then buried with full military honours in Westminster Abbey. On 9 November 1920, it was reported in the press that six bodies had been exhumed from Ypres, the Somme, Cambrai, the Aisne, the Marne and Arras. It was understood that the corpses were those of regular army members, not Kitchener volunteers or Territorials. A blindfolded officer then selected one of the coffins. On 11 November 1920 the reception and burial of the Unknown Warrior in Westminster Abbey, among the greatest in the land, showed the government's understanding of the general desire at that moment, especially by mourning women, for a place of pilgrimage.

The coffin of the Unknown Warrior was made from an oak tree at Hampton Court Palace. Admirals, field marshals and generals were the pall-bearers on the morning of 11 November. The congregation was composed primarily of widows and mothers who had lost sons. After the committal, the grave was filled with sandbags of earth from all the main battlefields. A slab of Tournai marble, given by the Belgian people, was placed on top inscribed simply 'An Unknown Warrior'. The nation was touched by this event, Adrian Gregory has argued, 'in a way that few other events have ever done'.[7] The *Daily Mirror* reported that on 15 November there was still a seven-mile queue of people waiting to lay wreaths at the newly unveiled Cenotaph. It is recorded that 100,000 wreaths were laid there by those who had visited the grave of the Unknown Warrior.

The tomb of the Unknown Warrior fulfilled a need that the Cenotaph, from the Greek for an 'empty tomb', could not. For all Lutyens's abstraction and his avoidance of Christian symbolism, it did carry, as Adrian Gregory has noted, 'a coded Christian message in its very name'. The Cenotaph became the subsidiary monument in November 1920, because the need to have some contact with what could at least be imagined to be the real body of a lost son or husband overwhelmed those who did not know the fate of a loved one. Veterans probably never acquired the same attachment to the tomb as families with a missing relative, because it required too much suspension of disbelief for those who had seen unknown bodies litter a battlefield. Yet the power of the grave of the Unknown Warrior also rested on his being nameless: his was a surrogate body for the mourning of thousands.

The war memorials created after the Great War across the British landscape display a variety of symbolism. Two motifs predominate: war as noble and uplifting and war as tragic and unendurably sad. The impetus in the early 1920s came from the drive to list and commemorate by name the local war dead. In those first years after the war, a town or village memorial was a living monument: the populace passed it and studied it day by day, remembering the faces and personalities of the fallen from their own community. The business of commemoration in those years drew on the energies of men who had known their lost friends well. As Jay Winter has emphasised, 'they were built as places where people could mourn and be seen to mourn'. If the names of those who had died were inscribed, these were also the names of the families who mourned. Thus a village war memorial both commemorated the dead and identified those who needed help in the aftermath of war.[8]

Inauguration of war memorials usually involved a procession, either on 11 November or another day hallowed by a great battle, that of the Somme on 1 July. Ilfracombe's memorial, for example, was unveiled on 11 November 1920 before a huge assembly including veterans, VAD nurses and coastguards in the village church. The service opened with Kipling's 'Recessional', which includes the refrain 'Lest we forget'. In 1921 memorials at Macclesfield and Dartford were among those unveiled. On the Macclesfield one were inscribed names of men from the local Pals battalion. The bereaved who looked up saw a gassed, soldier and a grieving woman standing in the attitude of sad but stoic sorrow holding in her hand a wreath of remembrance. At Dartford, the mayor in a stirring speech asked the living 'to reap the harvest so prodigal in the sowing, before the forces of evil once more capture the citadel of human intelligence and set men warring against their fellows'. The Two Minute Silence was observed during the dedication of the Llandudno memorial in 1922. Wreaths were placed by relatives of those killed and others. The hymn 'O God, our help in ages past' followed the silence at the unveiling of the Sheffield memorial in 1925. Buglers from the Sheffield Pals regiment sounded the last post and reveille.[9]

Some individuals commissioned leading architects and sculptors to create memorials to sons they had lost in war. Thus, at Mells in Somerset, Frances Horner paid £1,000 to Sir Edwin Lutyens and Alfred Munnings for the base for the statue to her son Edward on horseback. She wanted to put it 'under the tower riding up the church'. When she found the churchwardens were 'rather alarmed at the idea of a horse being put in church', the Horners managed to squeeze it into their family chapel.[10] Anthony Powell has called it 'the bare-headed saintly young horseman, an Arthurian knight from the pages of Tennyson, riding out on his charger'.[11]

Gentry families worked closely with their villagers on the placing of community memorials. The Horners called a meeting at Mells about what the village would prefer: 'was it something useful – such as seats, or a village fountain, or a playground or a garden, and they said it was something to look at', which would attract attention from passers-by. Lutyens, who came to stay for a weekend, 'found a perfect site in the centre of the village, which no one else had found, or thought of, and with a little tact and patience it was carried by the village with acclamation'. A copy was made of a statue of St George in Westminster Abbey for the top of the column that Lutyens designed. The village paid over £400 for the whole memorial, using Portland stone for the base, steps and column. Mells was proud of its men who had gone to war.[12] At Stanway in Gloucestershire Mary Wemyss planned and commissioned the remarkable memorial to the 'Men of Stanway' who did not return, including her two sons Ego and Yvo. Alexander Fisher created an outstandingly fine bronze of St George and the Dragon, with strong lettering by Eric Gill.[13] Thus the chivalric impulse, which we traced at the start of this book, found its embodiment in the personal memorialisation after the war of some of the young patriots from English country houses.

The American lawyer James Beck and his English companion H.E. Brittain toured the Somme late in 1916 to boost their campaign for US intervention in the war. 'We are standing on ground which will forever be regarded as holy,' they wrote in the preface to their report. Inspecting the captured Fricourt defences, looking towards Mametz Wood, they understood how 'martyrdom hallows'. This, they believed, was a 'spot that must be for ever sacred'. The poet John Masefield was there in May 1917. His journey evoked personal confusion and despair. Some parts of the charred battlefield, so recently the scene of mass slaughter, he told his wife Constance, he found 'romantic, some strange, some unearthly, some savage'. Lieutenant McInnes, an early sightseer that April, found that 'fine wooden crosses' had already been erected in memory of particular brigades and divisions.[14]

Over 150,000 graves of British soldiers in France and Belgium had been marked by the Imperial War Graves Commission by the summer of 1917. It was Fabian Ware who began this work, taking a Red Cross unit to France in September 1914. His initiative, energy and tact enabled him to set the seal, at an early date, on policy regarding burial of the national dead. No bodies would be returned to England. He was convinced that the democratic spirit of the trenches should be reflected in the design of graveyards, and made no distinction between the officers and men who lay together in the same cemetery. The landscape of the Western Front, visited today by tourists in their thousands, shows his wisdom and vision. The decision about design of headstones, after a rumpus in parliament in 1920, was the logical outcome of Ware's approach. In January 1918 *The Times* supported him, declaring 'all from General to Private . . . should receive equal honour' in memorials expressing 'a common symbol of their comradeship and the cause for which they died'.

The first cemeteries were somewhat chaotic, though by 1917 many of them were being planted with shrubs and flowers. From that year soldiers employed by the Commission were looking after them. The artist William Orpen visiting the Somme battlefield in 1917 found 'white daisies, red poppies and a blue flower great masses of them . . . like an enchanted land but in place of fairies there were thousands of little white crosses'. Lutyens was moved by 'ribbons of little crosses each touching each across a cemetery – set in a wilderness of annuals – oh so pathetic'.[15]

It took time to bring order into these landscapes of death. Countless scattered and isolated graves posed an immense challenge for the War Graves Commission. After much debate in 1919 and 1920, the standard tablet-shaped plain headstone won the day. In a letter read out in parliament, Rudyard Kipling remonstrated about the dissension, reminding MPs 'how more than fortunate they are to have a name on a headstone in a known place'. His son John was posted as wounded and missing but they never found his body or grave.

Lutyens's Stone of Remembrance, inscribed with words chosen by Kipling 'Their name liveth for evermore' and Reginald Bloomfield's Christian Cross of Sacrifice, it was decided, would be placed in every cemetery. Again, as at Thiepval, Lutyens's choice was minimalist and geometric, ecumenical rather than specifically abstract. It was conceded that families could add their own inscriptions of not more than three lines. This convention has made touring the cemeteries in the twenty-first century a wonderful exercise in exploring the patriotic rhetoric of an earlier age.[16] By February 1920, 300 of the 1,500 British burial grounds in France had been acquired by the War Graves Commission, but only three of the new war cemeteries with which we have now become familiar had been constructed.[17]

Pat Jalland has told the remarkable story of the Bickersteth family's search for the grave of their missing son Morris, killed on 1 July 1916. His two brothers, who had served with him on the Somme, Burgon and Julian, played a large part in this search. On 24 August 1916, Ella Bickersteth wrote sadly, 'our Morris's body has not been found nor will it be'. Yet, on their sacred pilgrimage in 1919, Julian's intimate knowledge of the battlefield enabled him to find Morris's wooden cross, which had been broken at the base. He fixed it firmly in the ground and said a short prayer.[18]

Many widows and mothers went to find the graves of their lost husbands and sons, once permission to visit the battlefields was given in the summer of 1919. Frances Horner, looking for the graves of her son Edward and son-in-law Raymond Asquith, found villages that had disappeared, 'only a signpost pointing to them as if they still existed, the trees all black sticks holding their leafless limbs up'. Mary Wemyss brought Yvo's wooden grave marker back to Stanway once his permanent headstone was in place (plate 31).[19]

There was a long agony for Clare Trench before she heard whether Reggie had been properly buried. A normal mourning process seemed impossible when the location and condition of the body remained uncertain. In July 1918, Clare had received confirmation from the Red Cross in Geneva and then the War Office that Reggie was named in an official German list of dead. He had been buried as decently as possible 'at the side of the road from the Noreuil to Ecoust St Nein'.[20] It helped her to find some peace to go there with her brother Walter and with Reggie's brother Herbert, a year later.

'We found Noreuil – a sad heap of ruins – and Battalion Headquarters', Clare wrote to her mother-in-law, 'as Reg described to me . . . with a shelter for the cookhouse and stores on the top and the deep dug-out below with unusually low and easy steps leading down – very deep and well-timbered walls – it was so strange seeing it all.' The site remains unexcavated, but it is easily spotted, where the lane from Noreuil to Ecoust becomes a sunken road. The French farmers have not ploughed close to the buried dugout which Reggie's wife inspected, when it was still open to the sky, nearly a hundred years ago.[21]

Herbert Trench wrote vividly about what they saw on that trip. 'There are no words to describe', he told his sister, 'the utter chaos of a country now devoid of the order of either peace or war, desolate beyond man's desolation.' He found a landscape, eight months after the Armistice, still strewn with tanks, guns, ammunition and barbed wire. Herbert's impression was of 'a land utterly forsaken and abandoned – a graveyard across half a continent, smeared with the legend of a world's despair'. It was hard to find the words, but it was necessary to attempt them, 'to identify such one time famous and for ever immortal villages as Bullecourt, Noreuil etc. – where a slight unevenness in the ground is all that is left – happily much overgrown with poppies and other wild flowers'.[22] Pilgrimages to the war cemeteries in the next years brought much consolation to many of the bereaved.

They continue to this day. For the family of Alec Reader the pilgrimage was very long delayed. Alec's mother received a letter saying that his body had been found at the edge of the wood and properly buried. In 1923 the War Graves Commission told his parents that the area had been searched but the last resting place of Private B.A. Reader had not been identified.[23] Nothing further happened until 1983, when his seventy-seven letters home came into the possession of his nephew Roger Goodman, his little sister Minnie's child. It was Roger and his brother Doug who zealously pursued the proper commemoration of young Alec. Gradually, they pieced the story together. They gained access to High Wood with the help of a local historian, and found the remains of the German switch trench which was the focus of the final slaughter of many of the Civil Service Rifles. This, they finally believed, was the spot where Alec was killed. Alec's immediate descendants, led since Roger Goodman's death by his brother Doug, gathered to place a small cross in his memory on 15 September 1991; they will do so again on the same day in 2016.[24]

The immense personal prestige of Sir Douglas Haig assisted the unification of organisations of ex-servicemen achieved by the creation of the British Legion in 1921. It quickly adopted the idea, first implemented in America and France, of the production of poppies to be worn at the time of Remembrance. The response throughout the country was immediate. The first poppy appeal raised £106,000. It was hailed in the *Yorkshire Post* as adding to the general symbolism of a day of 'remembrance, gratitude and sympathy'. In the first years, poppy sales in London led the provinces, increasing from 55,000 in 1923 to almost 86,000 in 1928, but provincial regions gradually caught up. The British Legion set out to establish a monopoly of manufacture in its own factory employing disabled ex-servicemen.[25]

During the 1920s there was tension between celebrating Britain's victory and mourning the dead. Socially exclusive Armistice balls at London hotels seemed to mock the loss of loved ones and show disrespect for the dead. Debate raged in the press. A fancy-dress ball, declared the Reverend Dick Sheppard in 1925, seemed an indecent way to remember deliverance from 'the unspeakable agony of 1914 to 1918'. A growing sense of propriety led to the balls being cancelled.

Veterans varied enormously in how they felt in the inter-war years about their experience between 1914 and 1918. Some wanted to recreate the camaraderie and mark their survival; others wanted to put the whole thing aside. The Festival of Remembrance, which was Sheppard's idea and began in 1927, answered the first need in a sober manner. 'Keep the home fires burning' and 'Abide with me', sung in the Albert Hall, were among the more respectable wartime songs which brought memories and emotions flooding back. Dan Todman has noted the process through which, by the end of the 1920s, the rituals of Armistice Day became 'much more codified, consistent and regulated'. A restrained ceremonial, with a validation of heroic death as redemptive sacrifice, proved to be what most British people really wanted. Commemoration of the dead and celebration of victory began to be seen as not incompatible.

This was how the writer of a letter to *The Times* in 1925 put it: 'many people regard Armistice Day as one of universal thanksgiving. One ventures to think the fallen are like-minded. They were not melancholy people and many of us celebrate as they did when they were home on leave.'[26]

But it is on the battlefields themselves that the cult of Remembrance is now most fully realised and practised. The Somme has naturally become pre-eminent as the Great War's main field of memory for the British Empire. Here 250 of the Commonwealth Graves Commission cemeteries, with their 150,000 identified and unidentified burials, are tended and visited weekly by thousands in search of the graves of family members.

As early as 1919, Michelin began to publish its famous illustrated guides to the Western Front. Soon there were railway excursions from Paris to Albert, with transfer to the 'pilgrimage train' which steamed up the Ancre valley to Authuille, Beaucourt and Miraumont. Traces of the actual battle lines remained for a good while. When Martin Middlebrook published his book *The First Day on the Somme* in 1971, he commented that, with the fields ploughed and sown every year since the battle, there were by then few signs of the war. But one could still see 'especially after the winter frosts, the distinct white lines in the earth', which showed 'where the old trenches had been dug into the earth beneath'.[27] This footprint of the Great War is still visible as these meandering scars etched upon the Somme landscape, but it now needs the expertise of military historians to read the chalk lines and interpret them in terms of the battle lines of long ago.

It is the imposing national memorials that now dominate this landscape. The Thiepval Memorial to the Missing of 1916 is another work by Sir Edwin Lutyens. A red-brick ziggurat, which displays a pleasing symmetry, it was built atop the ruins of the promontory village which it cost the British army dear to capture. The Memorial was inaugurated by Edward, Prince of Wales on 1 August 1932, amidst a throng of Somme veterans, widows and orphans. There was a crowd of 5,000, more than seventy years later on 1 July 2006, when the Prince of Wales led the mourners at a memorial service to commemorate the passing of ninety years since the battle.

Of the other memorials, Newfoundland Park had come first in 1925, followed by South Africa's National Monument in 1926. Australia's Memorial to the Missing was inaugurated in 1938. The Ulster Tower commemorates glory won by the 36 Ulster Division on 1 July 1916. The Sheffield Memorial Park, consecrated in 1936, is less conspicuous, in the copse where remains of the trenches can still be seen which were manned on 1 July until the 7.30 a.m. advance by the Yorkshire Pals battalions.[28]

In the 1920s and '30s charabancs began to navigate the narrow lanes joining the villages fought over in 1916. Visitor centres and rest stops for a multitude of tourists have taken over the Somme. Ocean Villas Tea Room, memorialising the name of the village of Auchonvillers popularised by the Tommies, is now usually thronged. But it was not always thus. For several decades after the Second World War there was a lull before the explosion of massive popular interest in the battlefield that more than any other epitomises the struggle of 1914 to 1918.

'There are few visitors to the Somme now,' Martin Middlebrook wrote in 1971. The more isolated cemeteries, he had found, when doing his research on the battle, sometimes did not see an English visitor in a whole year. Denis Winter, working on his book on soldiers of the Great War a few years later, noted that at Delville Wood cemetery only 170 people signed the visitors' book in 1973, and that visitors to the whole area still came 'in small groups'. He did not predict what has happened, that, as the ranks of veterans finally thinned in the 1990s, interest in perpetuating the memory of those who fought on the Western Front, and in celebrating their valour, would start increasing. Perhaps it is because they are all now gone that we remember them more energetically today. The need to cling to the past is accompanied, more forcibly than ever, by the need to try to understand.

When Martin Middlebrook interviewed veterans, his survivors were growing old but were still numerous. There was one in particular who had found his own way of commemorating his release from life in the trenches at the Armistice. Private H.C. Bloor, of the Accrington Pals, first returned to the Somme on a motorbike in 1935. By 1971, he had been back twelve times. 'I try to be there on July 1,' he told Middlebrook, 'I go out and at 7.30 a.m. I stand at the exact spot where we went over the top in 1916.' [29] He and others could not grasp it at first when the guns fell silent two years later. Stories of men who fought in this patriotic war can help us to do so almost a hundred years later.

CHAPTER 16

'All the Best and Choicest and Unblemished'
War Heroes

In his famous Queen's Hall speech on 19 September 1914, David Lloyd George claimed that he saw 'honour, duty, patriotism, and clad in glittering white the great pinnacle of sacrifice, pointing like a rugged finger to Heaven'.[1] It was ironic that, while other leaders – Asquith, Bonar Law and John Redmond – lost a close family member, Lloyd George did not himself make an ultimate sacrifice of that kind. But no one spoke the language of sacrifice like Lloyd George. Yet he merely dramatised a new national mood which had become established with almost lightning speed over six weeks or so. Already, when Lloyd George spoke, the kingdom was united in defence of Belgium, taking to heart idealistic war aims such as freedom, liberty and justice. There was a new moral order based upon volunteering, self-sacrifice and equality of sacrifice. It was a mood that remained intact through more than four years of personal heartbreak in families across the land.[2]

We cannot, for the most part, match the accounts given in earlier chapters of letter writers at the Front celebrating the heroism of colleagues there with detail on how each of them was mourned with pride at home. But we can catch the atmosphere of intense mourning that pervaded a few family circles. The archives reveal rich detail of the grief suffered in the Charteris, Grenfell and Horner and Trench families. This intimate and rare material illustrates immediate commemoration. The elevated public language of sacrifice never rang hollow at home, as thousands of families came to terms privately with their searing grief.

Mary Wemyss's diary recorded her journey from Gosford, her Scottish estate, to London on 14 October 1915. She had been receiving letters from her son Yvo there and was getting them typed out to pass round the family. She could not account for a mood of deep sorrow three days later: 'have felt very depressed since I got to London ... everything seems to get worse and worse'. The whole page of her diary for 19 October is then crossed through in red pencil with the single word 'Yvo'. She was out much of the day. Coming in, 'I went up and found Cynthia in tears . . . I guessed of course . . . a wire Yvo'. Her nephew Evan Charteris had received a telegram from the War Office; her daughter Cynthia brought it to Cadogan Square, their London home. The family gathered rapidly, some arriving, Mary noted, in the midst of dinner.

On the 21st, Mary finalised plans for a memorial service at Stanway, the Wemyss estate in Gloucestershire. Letters from senior officers in the Grenadiers arrived, confirming how Yvo had died. 'Felt thankful it was swift,' she wrote. Yvo's sister Mary, engaged to a fellow officer of his brother Ego, was on the way to Egypt. The depleted family travelled to Gloucestershire on 22 October. 'Stanway bathed in moonlight unendurable homecoming . . . we felt Yvo's near-ness,' runs Mary Wemyss's diary entry. Yvo's sister Bibs, just fourteen, very close to her mother, 'helped me so'.[3]

It poured all day on Sunday the 24th. 'Stanway was weeping,' wrote Cynthia Asquith in her diary. Every inch of the house reminded her of her youngest brother that weekend, 'sometimes as a child, sometimes as a youth'. Yet in a way, she reflected, the atmosphere was healing. It was only a few steps across the courtyard to the village church at six that evening: 'a lovely service for Yvo . . . letters stream in every post'. An empty bier stood in the chancel with a Union Jack spread over it and a laurel wreath leaning against it. Yvo's grandmother, Grace Wemyss, wrote in her diary about the service. 'It was very simple and impressive and Mr Allen preached such a pathetic little sermon about him.' For the aged Grace, Yvo was 'the very incarnation of youth and strength'.[4]

Mary treasured the sermon and had it printed to send to friends unable to come.[5] In effect this was a service of thanksgiving more than memorialisation. It was led by the local vicar Hubert Allen, an unconventional clergyman said to have had 'no beliefs or dogmas whatever'. But he rose to this occasion.[6] They gathered, he declared, in 'affection, grief and gratitude' for Yvo's sacrifice of 'his life for us'. They sought to comfort the family and to claim him as their own, in that little corner of Gloucestershire, with 'ties that bind him to us'. Above all they came to give thanks for the manner of Yvo's death.

Yvo, quite explicitly if perhaps unconsciously, the preacher argued, prepared himself for death. So he was able to 'go forth pure in heart and clear in the eyes of others, outwardly and inwardly clean'. His sister Mary, less than a year older and his dearly loved childhood companion, knew the depth of this when she read that sermon later. For she remembered the last walk they had together in Scotland just before Yvo left for the Front. 'We walked with arms round each other and said little but thought the more of what the future might hold. He went gladly, but with full realisation of what he might be asked to give. He said to me with his little tender whimsical smile "You know I may not come back" – and I never saw him again.' Yet she did see him in a vision once. Sleeping alone at Stanway, she dreamed of him 'standing before me'. 'He put his arms round me and kissed me and I felt an uplifting surge of happiness and love and peace.'

Three times in 1915, Yvo had been in touch with Hubert Allen on visits home. In January, he brought with him to read 'some Greek author and he chose the masterpiece upon the doctrine of the immortality of the soul', showing clearly the thought he had already given to the subject. In March, he came to be confirmed at Stanway among those of his own village. He was inspired by the Bishop of Gloucester's appeal to the young men present to 'fight for God by fighting for their country'. Then he was back for his first communion before rejoining his regiment. Yvo knelt in the little church on a bright morning beside his mother and sister to pray.

The law of sacrifice, Hubert Allen asserted, agreed across all religions that 'all the best and choicest and unblemished' are sought first. He preached on the text 'Heaviness may endure for a night, but joy cometh in the morning', with a message to hold the Charteris family in awe. 'The splendour of a death like this,' he declared lifting them above their Cotswold fields and woods, 'is too brilliant to be long obscured by the night-mists of heaviness . . . for the memory of those who fall, as he has done, can never fade away: it will be treasured as a possession for ever that shall be handed on from generation to generation, as a thing for those that come after to tell.'[7]

No one could have been less suited to a soldiering life than Yvo, which makes the eagerness with which he grasped it the more ironic. He was the very opposite of Julian Grenfell, grudging time spent playing games. 'We had in common a deep love of nature, animals, birds-nesting and adoration of our home,' wrote Mary Charteris in an appreciation of her lost brother. Horace his pet mouse was a constant companion in Yvo's teenage years. When she was trying to absorb the sad news of his death in October 1915 sailing across the Mediterranean, it was apposite that Mary suddenly saw 'a darling little grey wagtail on deck'. This reminded her of how they used to walk through the fields to the stream below the house 'to look for the grey wagtail's nest'. Yvo, she remembered, 'loved thunderstorms and eventually converted me to them'. On walks through the estate when thunder clapped he 'gloried in the elemental raging of nature'. Their childhood together was 'full of beauty and magic'.[8] Yvo Charteris was killed before he had learnt anything of the difference between episodes of shelling that he saw as stunning firework displays and the realities of prolonged trench service. He was the most innocent of the leading figures in this book. He was given no time to grow up.

Parents, siblings and friends clung together as the roll of honour grew between the summer of 1915 and the end of 1917. In an intimate group of the aristocracy and gentry, the Grenfells, Charteris and Horner families, members of the 'Coterie', children of the 'Souls' whose parties were legendary, the procession of death in battle did not cease: Julian Grenfell went first on 26 May 1915, his brother Billy next on 31 July, Yvo Charteris on 17 October, Ego Charteris on 23 April 1916 and Edward Horner on 21 November 1917.[9] Katharine Horner's husband, Raymond Asquith, eldest son of the Prime Minister, brother-in-law to Cynthia Charteris, was killed on the Somme on 15 September 1916.[10]

'Juju would not wish us to grieve', wrote his seventeen-year-old brother Yvo Grenfell to his father on 28 May 1915, 'but only to think of him in his peace and great glory, if we could only live and die like him how beautiful a place the world would be'. A few weeks later, when Nancy Astor had sent him her condolences, Billy Grenfell wrote: 'how could a man end his life better than in the full tide of strength and glory . . . Julian has outsoared the darkness of our night and passed on to a wider life. I feel no shadow of grief for him, only thankfulness for his bright and brave example'. His mother Ettie clung to her daughter Cassie, writing, when she was back nursing at Wimereux: 'I could not have lived through these weeks without you; all your lovely help to him; and the revelation of strength and tenderness you poured out'.[11]

Ettie Desborough accepted the loss of Julian with extraordinary serenity. Cynthia's empathy came easily as the daughter of her very close friend Mary Wemyss when she wrote about his death on 30 May 1915. 'Nothing human could possibly have been more wonderful,' she assured Ettie, 'than just to have been his mother and to have given and had such a perfect love'. 'You were able to ensure him a supremely happy childhood and youth,' she declared, 'and – in spite of the aching loneliness – it must be wonderful to think of him and all his glamour as so utterly unassailable – to know that he "carries back bright to the Coiner the mintage of man" and yet to feel that he had already found time to fulfil himself as the perfect Happy Warrior'. For Cynthia, looking around in dismay after ten months of war, Julian was a rare interpreter, who helped her to 'make the war bearable to the spectators'. The lines of the poem the nation had read in *The Times* following his death inspired her that week: 'How lovely his poem is . . . I think his is one of the deaths that must confirm one's belief in immortality'.[12]

Mary Wemyss herself visited Ettie at Taplow on 12 June 1915, finding her 'wonderfully calm and upheld by a sense of Julian's continued presence and love'. 'She deserves the reward of her courage and faith,' Mary declared: 'even if the uplifting or sustaining power seems to wane as the slow days go by it is never quite forgotten'. Billy Grenfell's death, coming so soon after, on 30 July, was a shattering second blow which rocked London society. Lord Kitchener's private secretary recorded that 'almost the only time' he was known to break down in the office 'was when the news of Billy's death at Hooge came through; he had to leave off work for an hour to recover himself'.[13]

It was two months later that Ettie returned Mary's visit in the first days of her grief about Yvo. 'I loved seeing her,' Mary noted, 'but my heart ached to see all that she had gone through graven on her face – she is brave and triumphant.' 'You and I have prayed that this might not be,' wrote Ettie to Arthur Balfour, Mary's closest platonic male friend, 'not little Yvo. And yet now the single glory of his life and death will hold all up, it seems to already.' Mary's 'lion heart' would carry her through even this and 'prove her indestructible'.[14] But there was more to come for Mary too.

Ettie and Yvo had travelled back to London in the train together after a Stanway weekend in the spring of 1915. 'It amused him and me to discover,' she wrote in a note for Mary about that journey, 'that we both used to go . . . to the ramshackle loft over the Poetry Bookshop, where the coming poets read their works aloud . . . he produced several books, like a conjuror as he had no bag with him, and read aloud most delightfully, both prose and poetry, with shining eyes and flushing cheeks . . . his face was fascinating: very striking in repose, like a portrait of a boy by Raeburn; and as he read or talked, his thoughts and emotions streamed through it, and became actually visible'. 'There surely can never have been a greater disappearance of the living principle in the death of one human being,' Ettie insisted to Mary.[15]

Ego Charteris took his wife Letty with him when he sailed for Egypt in 1915, leaving their two little boys, David and Martin, with their grandparents at Stanway. When the Gloucestershire Hussars moved on to Gallipoli in August, Ego was left to spend a miserable winter in charge of the depot at Cairo. On 25 April 1916, Mary Wemyss read in the papers that there had been a fight at Katia, east of the Suez Canal; next day Letty sent a cable reporting that Ego was a prisoner and had been 'slightly wounded in the shoulder'. The strain of worrying about Ego had told on her: he had ridden off with his Hussars from Hunstanton on 7 April 1915. During this year the loss of Yvo had already almost shattered Mary. Ego's death in the battle at Katia was not confirmed in England until 1 July 1916.[16]

Later in life, Mary Wemyss recounted what had clearly been a psychological collapse, in terms of a 'dream-vision' she experienced at Stanway during the night of 22 April 1916. The news in the papers three days later made her jump to the awful conclusion that she had lost both her sons on active service. Mary's vision counterpointed the war with the heroic figure of her firstborn: 'the atmosphere of the room seemed to quiver with excitement – I saw, as if thrown on a magic-lantern sheet, a confused mass of black smoke, splashed with crimson flame.' Mary was dreaming she was in the war while actually lying in her bed. 'It was like a child's picture of a battle or explosion,' she wrote. In front of her was Ego 'standing straight and tall': 'I saw him in profile, his dark eyebrows and his moustache made his face look very pale. I got the impression he was exercising all his forces with all his might and main. Round his chest was wrapped a golden banner, its colour very beautiful, it swathed his body in spiral folds and seemed to protect him as he stood there with his face set and stern'.

The function of this powerful dream of a soldier's last stand was to release Mary from unbearable anxiety about her son. She was emphatic that the dream did this. She mentioned it to Cynthia at breakfast the next day, which was Easter morning, but 'I seemed unable to talk about it ... I felt something had happened, but I knew not what ... I was not anxious nor worried but stunned ... I knew, without actually realising that Ego was dead and through all the day that followed ... this vision had a strangely quieting influence, it helped me to wait and keep outwardly calm.' Mary Wemyss had received a premonition about her son's death, for he was killed outright by an exploding shell at Katia that Easter Day. There is a convincing psychic explanation of this premonition, which Michael Roper has set out, in terms of understandable mental defence against loss: 'Ego is not just unimpaired in body, but wrapped in the banner of salvation, as if like Christ he is risen again. Manic defences are mobilised when the anxiety about a loved object feels intolerable as it did for Mary.'[17]

The death of their eldest son may have brought Mary and her husband Hugo closer together than they had been for years. 'I think Ego was the greatest darling that ever lived,' Hugo wrote to Mary when the news finally came through that he had been killed, after twice being wounded and encouraging his men to the last. 'We must try and face it without him,' Hugo told Mary in that letter, 'I know you will and I will try to help you and we must see him again in those darling boys.'[18] It also bound together Mary Wemyss and Ettie Desborough with hoops of steel, for now both of them had lost two of their three boys. On 3 July 1916, Ettie wrote to her friend Evelyn de Vesci, Mary's sister-in-law, that 'the thought of Mary is like a sword, I would have given my soul out of my body to have saved her this – one knows it too well, the long, long pain, the crushing of the second blow'. She had always loved Ego 'and now they are together in the shining company', she declared, 'but it is just the thought of Mary that cannot be endured'.

Ettie attended Ego's memorial service at Stanway on 23 July 1916, when Hubert Allen preached again about sacrifice. 'Dearest brave Ettie with two swords in her heart,' exclaimed Mary to Evelyn de Vesci afterwards, had been such a comfort that day because she 'knew and cared and understood'.[19] The two mothers continued in the next years to find consolation in each other. 'As the agonising days go on,' one of Ettie's letters to Mary declared, 'one can almost feel glad that Ego and Yvo and Julian and Billy are safe in the dream of peace.' The women of Great Britain became inured to suffering as the war went on and on.

Frances Horner and Mary Wemyss were old friends who had enjoyed house parties together from the late 1880s onwards. Their families gradually became entangled by their children's marriages with members of the Asquith family: after a protracted courtship, Katharine Horner married Raymond Asquith, the eldest son of the leader of the Liberal Party, in 1907; Cynthia Charteris married Beb Asquith, his younger son, in 1909. Tragedy did not reach the household at Mells in Somerset until 1916, when Raymond was killed on the Somme. Katharine was clever but diffident and lacked confidence. She told her brother Edward once in her youth 'I feel it is years since I spoke to anyone who understood me or whom I could understand.' But once she and Raymond were married, society saw them as a perfect couple and she began to feel safe.

Diana Manners has been seen as 'a focus for all the interlocking friendships of the Coterie'.[20] In the summer of 1916, in addition to nursing some of the wounded brought home to London, she was giving emotional support to her sister Letty, who was devastated by the loss of her husband Ego. When she heard the news that Raymond had fallen, she hurried down to Mells on 14 September. 'Before I went I was frightened for Katharine,' she wrote to Patrick Shaw Stewart, another of the Coterie and now in Salonika, 'her energy even when stimulated by Raysie was so slender a thread held by him; he taught her to breathe and articulate'. 'I found her crouched in a dark room over the fire,' she related, 'too dead a thing to seek death . . . poor angel. Thank God I felt competent and strong. I tried hard to sink my misery and think only of holding K up as we all must.'

Katharine Asquith believed in the next months that she would never cope with life without Raymond. 'I thought that if this supreme misery fell on one that nothing would help and one must push everyone away and bear it or not bear it alone and it isn't so,' she told Diana Manners; 'you and Edward and Mother do help me and I cling to you.' Katharine found solace working as a nurse in the Duchess of Sutherland's hospital, then settled down at Mells to bring up her son, christened Julian but nicknamed Trimalchio, soon shortened to Trim. A few years later she converted to Roman Catholicism.[21]

The last one to go in this procession of death was Katharine's brother Edward Horner. This left Katharine as the heir to the Manor House at Mells.

Edward had been one of the closest friends of Julian Grenfell at Eton and then at Balliol but did not sweep through his young life with the same abandon. Active service, it has been said, 'suited his uncertain and dependent temperament': 'it provided a framework of purpose for his wayward impulses', as he was never clean of debt. Edward was seriously wounded in early May 1915 and found himself in the hospital where Julian was to die on 26 May, though Julian was not well enough even to hear that his school friend was in another ward.[22] Having lost a kidney, he stayed at Gosford, the Wemyss mansion, for his convalescence in a miserable state of mind, managing when he went shooting with Hugo Wemyss to pink a keeper in the ear. In September 1917 Edward was back in France. Frances Horner did her best to cheer him up there, sending a constant supply of cakes, jam, biscuits and books. It was very peaceful in the pretty farm where he was billeted, Edward wrote on the 23rd, 'but I think longingly of the Mells Sunday luncheon with its divine food and merry atmosphere and love surrounding me'.

On the second day of the Battle of Cambrai, Edward and his cavalry squadron were sent to Noyelles where he commanded a Lewis gun, stopping German troops from coming into the village. He was hit in the groin close to his old wound and died that night. It was a crushing blow, especially to his ageing parents. 'It went to one's heart,' wrote Cynthia Asquith when she saw them two months later: 'the poor old boy looked bowed down and stupefied with grief'.[23] Frances Horner wrote to Mary Wemyss about Edward's death: 'we know each other's lives and what it has all been. I don't feel unhappy about Edward as we had such a heavenly fortnight with him and he seems hardly to have let go his hand. He went off radiant and I seem to hear nothing but love and praise round his name.'[24]

The war had been going on for more than three years and its toll rose day by day. There was a kind of resignation in these words of Frances Horner's. It was almost as if she expected to join her friends, Ettie Desborough and Mary Wemyss, as another of the nation's mourning mothers sooner or later. Julian, Billy, Yvo, Ego, Raymond and Edward: all these young men, grew up, it has been suggested, 'in a society which was half in love with death and for all their promise they were afflicted by the romantic fatalism that characterised their apocalyptic age'.[25]

The telegram reporting that Reggie Trench was missing reached Orpington post office on 1 April 1918. Its fading envelope reveals that the boy was directed to take it to the hospital in the village, where Clare was nursing. Just five days later, Clare received the letters sent by Brigadier Stansfield and Captain Clifford breaking the news that Reggie had been killed. Clare at once decided to give up her hospital work and take full charge of her daughter Delle. Though it had been nice 'to be doing something directly for the men who are doing everything for us', she told her childhood friend Florrie Holman, she felt this was the right thing to do now.[26]

When the news of the massive German advance on 21 March reached Ireland, Reggie's sister Cesca was preparing for her wedding on 17 April to Dermot Coffey. She comforted herself with Dermot's assurance that 'Commanding Officers are usually bound to be in less direct danger except from specially directed shells aren't they?' 'You simply must get leave to come over . . . do please', she had written to Reggie on 24 March, 'I want you most awfully badly. It's simply divine here like summer and all the daffs are out.' There was supreme sadness in the fact that this letter was returned to Dublin while Clare was there, with 'deceased' scrawled in pencil on the envelope by Reggie's colleague Captain Clifford. In the same post, Isabel Trench's pathetic final missive to 'my own Reggie' came back to her: 'it is agonising to think of all you are enduring at this awful time: the surroundings must be terrible and I do not forget you for a moment; my precious son – always the best of sons to me and infinitely dear . . . we are in sunshine and flowers and you are fighting for our safety and freedom . . . God protect and keep you and bring you home to us.'[27]

Clare's preoccupation while in Ireland, where she received the formal notification of Reggie's death, became what she should say to the world about her husband. There were two kinds of heroism explicit in the letters from colleagues for which she wanted Reggie remembered. 'His first thoughts', Clifford had written, 'were always for his officers and men.' 'He died', Clifford continued, 'a soldier's death facing fearlessly overwhelming odds.'[28] The announcements in the *Irish Times* on 13 April, *The Times* on 15 April and the *St Mary Cray and Orpington Times* on the 19th all carried these sentences in full. It was 'glorious to read' those words about overwhelming odds, a friend Joyce Shipley wrote to Clare.[29] But before that, the news that Reggie had been killed went round Clare's neighbourhood. The story was circulated first in the Orpington households by the family doctor on his rounds. The key sentences from Stansfield and Clifford's letters went from mouth to mouth: 'I heard how splendidly he went on fighting and then fell', Dr Battiscombe told Clare in his letter of sympathy on 8 April.[30]

Back at Orpington, Clare received Reggie's own last message, a three-page letter left with the bank 'to be forwarded only in the case of my death'. He had known the night they met at her coming-out dance in 1911, he told her, 'that there was only one girl in the world for me'. He left no instructions about Delle, saying simply 'I know you will bring her up as few children have been brought up'. His final words were moving and timeless: 'well the war is over for me and will I hope soon be over for everyone. It's a bad business for the whole world.' Clare tried to read this letter to her daughter in the 1920s when Delle was about eight years old, but she broke down after the first page. It was never read again until I inherited Reggie and Clare's archive in 1989 and began, in the next years, to share its most intimate items with my family, particularly my mother Delle.[31]

Those who wrote condolence letters to Clare and Isabel Trench about Reggie represented a remarkable cross-section of English and Irish society. They are a microcosm of how the British people were feeling, as the decimation of their countrymen continued in this climactic year of the Great War. Clare heard from forty-seven friends and relatives, including sixteen relatives through her marriage to Reggie. Many of them wrote twice, on hearing the news that he was missing and then again when his death was confirmed. Isabel heard from forty-one friends and relatives, the majority in Ireland, but some from the clerical circles of her earlier married life. This archive, revealing the specific thinking of one particular community of mourning, exemplifies the glorification of sacrificial death which had become such a marked feature of British culture at the height of Empire.[32]

In the depths of grief Clare herself hardly put pen to paper. But, just once, we glimpse a hint of her state of mind. Her closest friend was Joyce Pollock, whose husband Charlie had encouraged her secret love affair with Reggie in 1912. The couples lived together at Berkhamsted in 1915. Both dreaded losing their men from the moment they went to France. When Clare heard first that Reggie was missing, Joyce wrote of 'gnawing hope' replacing the 'blank anxiety'. Then, she related, a few days later, Charlie's letters were being returned and he was being reported missing too. In shock on 2 April 1918, before certainty arrived with Brigadier Stansfield's letter, Joyce was the one person to whom Clare felt able to confess the depth of her despair. 'Yes, you are right we've certainly had heaven on earth,' Joyce replied, 'but it does make such blows doubly hard to bear.' 'We suffer but the help is that they do not . . . be brave', she wrote when Clare finally had her loss confirmed.[33]

Letters from people already coping with personal grief were particularly heartfelt. Lilian Morris, a village friend of Clare's, reflected, 'having lost three brothers I realize a little what you must be suffering'. Maud Mead's boys had been close friends of Reggie's at Charterhouse, where, as she recalled, there was great affection for 'Chennie', as he was known there. She had lost one boy, Christopher, who died of enteric fever in Egypt. Two more of her boys were fighting in France. Maud asked Clare for a 'soldier photo' of Reggie, which she would 'much prize'. 'What a fearful time it is for the whole nation to live through,' declared Laura Pollock on hearing Reggie was missing, 'it is as if the whole world were throbbing with agony.' Her godson was missing too and the War Office said they 'feared the worst'.[34]

Each writer had their own personal perspective. Reggie had taken his girl-friend Primrose Barstow to a Merton Commemoration Ball, where she met a friend in college, Geoffrey Cheshire, in 1908. She subsequently married him. She lost a brother in Mesopotamia, then gave birth to Leonard Cheshire, the future Second World War ace, in 1917. She had memories of happy times with Reggie, whom she had known as a teenager when their families were in Switzerland.[35] 'I cannot say how shocked I am,' she told Isabel Trench, recalling him as 'a splendid companion'. Margaret Sheepshanks, a friend of Isabel's, had been through the agonies of a son missing, then reported killed, the previous year. 'I feel that my boy is not really dead, but we just long to see them again,' wrote Lady Violet Ashtown, commiserating as mother to mother. Frederick Trench, heir to the family's Irish estates, had been killed in 1916.[36]

The youngest of ten, Clare had a large family which rallied round. The men and women struck different notes. Her sister Ida, a close companion on climbing holidays in their youth, simply regretted how little she could say 'to comfort in a sorrow like this'. Her short note was to convey 'my very dear love and sympathy'. 'I do feel tremendously that his life was so tremendously worth-while,' wrote her sister Violet emotionally from East Africa. 'Our very best are taken in this awful war,' Dorothy Howard lamented. 'Your dear one is safe now, safe on the other side and perhaps he has been spared the worse to come' but, having lost a brother herself, she knew the 'ache' and the 'dreadful loss'. Of all the forms of consolation people offered the bereaved, religion was the most important. Yet Delle, 'the image of her father too', would also be some comfort, Dorothy insisted, suggesting that Clare should spend time together with her children at the seaside that summer.[37]

Her brother Walter, more matter-of-fact, had 'always thought Reggie a splendid fellow and felt privileged by his friendship'. 'If ever I have any sons,' he avowed, 'I shall be well satisfied if they can in a small degree model themselves on him.' On 8 April, he was able to corroborate details Clare had received, following conversation with a stretcher-bearer in the battalion's C Company, whose injuries were being tended in hospital at Warwick. For Reggie's sake, Walter knew she would do her best to 'buck up and carry on'. But it was her brothers Stanley and Edgar who most passionately denounced the German enemy. Edgar hoped the tide would soon turn, 'when we shall hear no more of the Hun and his vile acts'. More strident, Stanley wrote 'God damn every man, woman and child who bears the Prussian stamp – final extermination is the only thing possible for the whole of that race, who brought all this misery to England.' He had always been immensely fond of Clare: 'of course you will be splendid all through this agony period. I know your grit. You will go on working at the Hospital and if you can't stick that you will volunteer for work in France.' 'Take Reggie's place for the Homeland,' Stanley urged, 'wherever you think you are most fitted – I am sure this is what he would have had you do.'[38]

Clare found herself in the midst of an outpouring of family love. There were many figures in her life – her governess, the chauffeur, the gardener, servants at Bark Hart in Orpington – who had cared for her in the tranquil Edwardian days before war clouds gathered. Their words now meant much. 'Do not write dear Clare,' declared her boarding school headmistress Emily Ismay, 'until you are feeling able – this blow must have almost stunned you at first.' Her grief indeed was both so stunning and so disorientating, Clare confessed to Florrie Holman, that 'it seemed so hard to believe and understand what had really happened'. The Trenches and Reggie's brother Arthur's new family had taken Clare to their hearts. This is the testimony of letters from numerous aunts and cousins by marriage. 'You have been so brave all along and will not fail now,' insisted Aunt Francie. She had sustained Clare on visits to her London home over the months when she was missing Reggie, away at the Front. The thought of his 'high character and conviction' would help her now.

'Reggie has lived so gloriously and died so gloriously,' wrote Ethel Gore-Booth, childhood playmate of Reggie's in Scotland, 'the world will be the poorer for his going on – for just now we need his sort so much.' Ethel related meeting a Sherwood Forester in some hospital work the previous year. He knew Reggie by repute 'and how much they all thought of him'. The blank was hard to bear, but his 'beautiful, upright, loyal character' would remain as a most precious memory for them both.[39] To understand what Reggie meant to others as a man, the best testimony comes from Merton friends, who were plunged into the war like him. A good many fell with him, as the college memorial records, including a flatmate from bachelor days in London. But one of the closest, Edward Burney, remained in touch with Clare until the 1960s and they saw each other occasionally. Burney's two letters to Clare and Isabel, written as a Royal Flying Corps instructor, in the depths of immediate grief on 9 and 10 April 1918, are among the most touching. 'You know that I loved him as one of my best and dearest friends,' he told her, 'a man as loyal and straight and true as ever lived.'

'He is not one of those who have to die to be praised,' declared Burney to Isabel Trench; 'not even the few at Merton who constituted themselves on occasions his critics, ever dared to suggest that his conduct was anything but perfectly straightforward and honourable'. Reggie's seriousness about life was softened, Burney had learnt, by 'a charm in him which made us all love him, and kept him quite safe from being a prig'. Most of them got third-class degrees, and Reggie was never much of an athlete, Edward Burney told Clare forty-five years after the war ended, but 'a fine man was something rarer and bigger'.[40] His Merton companions Walter Wood, his best man, and Guy Beech wrote about Reggie in the same strain. Wood, seeing him as his ideal of a Christian gentleman, praised the strength of character which 'must have helped directly and indirectly hundreds of young men' at the Front. Later when he himself had been ordained, Beech wrote of Reggie as 'one of the pure in heart on whom Our Lord pronounced this blessing: upright and sincere, with a profound sense of duty, righteous in all his ways'.[41]

The manner of Reggie's death, this Merton circle were saying, was exactly what they expected of him. They were all of the generation in which the language of sacrifice, drawing upon classical, chivalric and religious models, reached its apogee. Condolence letters during 1918, predictably, just as those written in 1915, often drew upon images of sacrifice. For the act of dying in battle marked a man out as one of the best. 'What light! What joy!' wrote Reggie's godfather who had performed the marriage ceremony in 1915, reflecting to Clare on her husband's 'glorious end'. Reginald Copleston's tribute encapsulated all the certainty of this patriotic war. 'He seems to have been called away,' he wrote, 'in the supreme moment of re-dedication of himself, just returned – was he not? – after the dressing of his wound to the high places of the field. What could be nobler?' Reggie's death, his godfather believed, came 'in the very moment of reconsecration'. His uncle Benny, a London stockbroker, had also taken an interest in his career. He was deeply affected, as he told his sister Isabel, at Reggie's chucking 'a soft job which he could have retained with honour to make the greatest sacrifice a man can make in response to the conscious call of duty'. It was an inner nobility which came out, as Benny saw it, 'when with wounded arm he sought the Front again to die a hero's death'.

'One knows instinctively that his death was a glorious one,' wrote Noel Hunter, a cousin serving in the 37th Division. It was not of course a condition in dying a hero's death that reports had actually come in of a courageous last stand, such as Reggie's, or of bold and fearless action, such as Julian Grenfell's. But it mattered very much to Clare exactly how Reggie had given his life. For she understood the mood of the whole of British society. The cadences of grief were shared by all, young and old, rich and poor. 'I cannot say how sorry I am that poor Captain Trench as got killed,' wrote a servant girl who had worked in the household, 'it is a terrible time for everyone, there is hardly a home without some trouble.'[42] Clare could immerse herself in the universal public mood, confident in pride in her husband.[43]

Condolence became inspirational and didactic. The words of Horace *Dulce et decorum est pro patria mori*, we have seen, were the national banner of Britain's patriotic spirit. Obituaries, such as the one for Wilbert Spencer in 1915 which appeared in his school's Old Boys' newsletter, sometimes drew upon the classical tradition. Spencer's alluded to the epitaph for the 300 at Thermopylae: 'Go tell my country those that passeth by / That here obedient to her call I lie'. Harold Dehry, writing to Wilbert's father in March 1915, noted how at Weymouth Wilbert had been an 'example of splendid cheerfulness and efficiency. May we all follow the example of the friend of whom we are so proud.'[44]

So the Trench archive reveals in rich detail the extensive dialogue of comfort which the Great War created between correspondents, sometimes previously unacquainted, for whom bereavement was their bond. 'Personally we are entire strangers, and yet in a sort of kinship of trouble we do not quite feel that to be so,' William Swan wrote to Clare. His son Willie, a captain in the Sherwoods, had been good friends with Reggie. He had sent them a letter, 'which we appreciated very much', giving them extra information about Willie's death in December 1917. William Swan's younger son meanwhile, also an officer, was back from France with shell shock. 'The price we are all paying,' he reflected, 'is a heavy one indeed.'

'I have lost two sons in this hideous war,' Isabelle Davis informed Clare, writing out of the blue when she saw Reggie's death announced in *The Times*. She had been moved that Reggie had written to her in sympathy about her second boy, when he realised no one else in authority was available to explain his death to her family. She grieved that Clare too 'had been called upon to suffer'. Isabelle's strong faith enabled her to claim that, though it seemed to her 'that the finest and best have been taken', they had 'proved themselves worthy of a nobler work and that God needs them'.

Clare had been in correspondence since 1917 with Maud Alliban, the mother of Reggie's dedicated subaltern William who was killed at Malakoff Farm. Maud was one of those who wrote quickly when Reggie's death was confirmed, since she felt they had a powerful bond through Reggie's attempts to recover her son's body after the battle. Still suffering the agony of uncertainty about whether William himself had died quickly or lain wounded, she was glad to think Reggie's end had been instantaneous. 'He loved my boy now they are together again,' Maud declared. She had arranged a special communion in her Derbyshire village on hearing the news, with the hymns 'God moves in a mysterious way' and Tennyson's 'Crossing the Bar'. She cried often, she confessed, looking at the picture Clare had sent to her of Delle with her father.[45]

At times in these Trench condolence letters, one catches something of the depth of national humility which the Great War imposed. 'We can never be worthy of all this sacrifice of the very best,' Ethel Gore-Booth told Clare. Edward Burney wondered if it was to be his 'honour to join Reggie and other brave and noble spirits in the world beyond' or 'my heavy task to live in a manner worthy of them'. The village revered Reggie's memory, George Fearn declared after the prayers at Orpington church on 8 April 1918, for his passing 'in the great cause of righteousness'. She should take comfort, as his widow, that it was 'wholly a Christlike thing to suffer and die for others'.[46]

There was a sense in early 1918 that the titanic struggle might sweep up many more before the war was over. The Godsal family, friends of Isabel Trench's brother Benny having lost one boy and then two more at the Front, remained confident of final victory. But, as Edward Godsal confessed to Benny, 'this continual passing of all that is freshest and brightest and best is making this present world of ours a sad place for some of us old ones'. A national community of mourning held its breath in 1918. The fallen, their numbers still mounting week by week, were coming to be seen, in a sense, as the chosen ones. Returning letters about Reggie's last stand, an Irishwoman Josie Carson told his mother Isabel about how her heart should be filled with thankfulness 'that to your son was given the high honour of acting as a hero and leaving footsteps in the sands of time'.[47]

The ideological framework of sacrifice within which the war was fought, evident in all these letters, is explicable in terms of the reverence of the British people in 1914–1918. This was a legacy of spiritual habits of thought and unspoken assumptions in Victorian and Edwardian England, going far beyond statistics of church attendance. A study of popular religion in the London borough of Southwark in this period has portrayed it as cultural system in its own right.[48] Sunday school attendance formed the war generation, leaving its mark though many never attended church or chapel as adults. Salvation Army bands played outside pubs. Hymn tunes were adapted for popular wartime songs. 'The bells of hell' even ended with an adaptation of the biblical injunction 'Oh death where is thy sting a-ling, oh grave thy victory?'

If resistance to religious authority was deeply rooted in Britain, so was the vitality of a certain residual belief in God and in an afterlife. The wartime language of sacrifice was a constant bulwark to patriotism, carrying in its wake centuries of evangelism, which had made the British both an independent people and at the same time a deeply Christian one. It was a small step, in the national crisis of the Great War, to imagine the purchase of a better world through the blood of the nation's soldiers. Thus the idea of redemptive sacrifice, so powerfully expressed in all the letters quoted in this chapter, became in the long run the hallmark of the British war effort.[49]

CHAPTER 17

'Among the Happiest Years I Have Ever Spent'

Survivors

Our six soldiers who survived lived through the events of the 1920s and 1930s. They saw another world war begin and end. Rowland Feilding, by far the oldest, died in 1945. The next officers to die were Graham Greenwell in 1970 and Herbert Trench in 1971. Lance Spicer lived until 1980. The two Tommies, Jack Sweeney and Cyril Newman, died in 1961 and 1978 respectively. We know very little about what these men thought of their war experience in the long retrospect of their later years. This chapter gathers the shreds of evidence on their lives as they grew older and the Great War receded in time and in their minds.

Three of the six men published their letters. Rowland was the first to do so. He worked on the large bundles of letters Edith had kept carefully, with all their Field Post Office numbers, adding information from his diaries about places and units omitted as sensitive. In 1929 he bowed to pressure from friends to make a substantial part of the collection, which he knew was of outstanding importance, publicly available through the Medici Society. He was braving a climate that he knew had become hostile to this kind of objective material on the war.

The Medici Society volume was presented with a narrative structure in the form of page-by-page headlines. These both indicated the chronology of Rowland's long service and drew attention to incidents in his life at the Front. The endpaper maps showed many of the villages which had meant so much to 'Snowball': Festubert, Givenchy and Cuinchy, Mametz, Carnoy, Maricourt and Hardecourt for example. In a Preface Rowland explained that in case anyone thought he had defied the censorship he wanted to say that 'place names and other indiscretions' had been added from his diary. The book was illustrated by an impressive series of photographs of the devastated French landscape held by the Imperial War Museum, some of which have been little reproduced since.

Among the most striking is a photograph of the British attack on the Hohenzollern Redoubt on 13 October 1915, showing three stunted trees and the lines of the British trenches before it, traced by the piles of chalk which had been excavated to make them.

There are poignant images too of the ruined high street at Ginchy, of soldiers in the destroyed village of Wytschaete on 8 June 1917 and of the 'battered stumps' of Delville Wood (plates 26, 27). These illustrated Rowland's evocative accounts of desecration. The letters were written, his Preface stressed, 'while the events described were fresh in mind'. 'That is their claim to interest,' he declared, 'coupled with the extraordinary luck which permitted an individual to survive so long in the front line.' Rowland was deeply aware of the privilege of this experience, 'allowed by Fate to very few'.

An Introduction to these letters by his first commanding officer, Major General Sir John Ponsonby, praised Rowland as 'an officer in whom all ranks had the greatest confidence'. His command of the 6th Battalion of the Connaught Rangers, Ponsonby explained, reflected belief at HQ that his age, ability and experience fitted him for a command in Kitchener's New Army. Few men, Ponsonby believed, had left the testimony of letters 'so full of interest, so free from criticism of his senior officers, so free from exaggeration and so modest and unassuming'.[1] No wonder, with a public hungry for accounts of the war and fed by the literature of disenchantment, that Rowland's book *War Letters to a Wife* was an instant success. It went through three impressions before the end of 1929.[2] Pleased with excellent reviews Rowland was content thereafter to retire and devote himself to family life.

Copies of this Medici Society edition are rare. Rowland's letters are much better known through the 2001 edition by Jonathan Walker, who provided full biographical and background notes. He was given much help by members of the family and was able to reproduce several of the sketches Rowland made in the French fields and woods. There were also letters he wrote to his eldest daughter Joan, which did not appear in the original edition. It is the 2001 edition which I have used in writing this book. Rowland enjoyed old age at Stoke House, a small early Victorian mansion of yellow brick, at Stoke Poges in Buckinghamshire. Living through the Second World War, he had long survived those he called the 'dearest and best' of his generation.[3] Two of his children married military men, and his four daughters between them brought him a crowd of grandchildren.[4]

After his degree course at Oxford, begun in 1919, Graham Greenwell joined the London Stock Exchange. He married and settled at Goring-on-Thames in Oxfordshire, where he brought up three children. It was in 1935, six years after

Rowland's edition of his letters had been well received, that Graham found a publisher for the letters he wrote to his mother during the war. He was a career stockbroker, alert to the mood of a time when much was said 'of the attitude of the younger generation towards war in general and towards the next war – if it ever comes – in particular'. He felt that through the reactions in 1914–18, faithfully portrayed in his book, of a normal schoolboy to the sudden imposition on him of responsibilities as an army officer he had something to offer the public. Readers of *An Infant in Arms* would have little difficulty, he surmised, in tracing his development from 'immature subaltern' to the veteran of the later years of the war.

To his delight, the book sold well. For Graham knew he was striking a new note, while the 'horrors' and 'miseries' of the war dominated the current literature so completely. There was something a little provocative in his stance. Now just forty, he had the confidence to speak out, confessing he saw the war 'as among the happiest years I have ever spent'. There were certainly 'moments of boredom and depression, of sorrow for the loss of friends and of alarm for my personal safety', but the great compensations were being 'perfectly fit', living 'among pleasant companions', having 'responsibility and a clearly defined job'. These were things that mattered 'when one is very young'. The comradeship Graham had enjoyed on the Western Front shines through a reading of his letters, which he presented as an authentic record of youthful adventure.

It gave Graham even more delight that the book was warmly received, although it came out of the blue as a rebuttal of the post-war mood, which was summarised in books such as C.E. Montague's *Disenchantment* (1922), Robert Graves's *Goodbye to All That* (1929) and Max Plowman's *A Subaltern on the Somme* (1928). The poets too from as early as 1917 had begun to fix in the public mind the myths of idealism turning to disillusion, futility, the squalor of the trenches and the obscenity of battlefield death. Graham's letters, striking a different note, were transparent and uninhibited, youthfully naïve and compellingly persuasive.

Some reviewers, baffled, retreated behind the barriers of the modish antimilitarism of the time. How could these have been 'the happiest years' he had spent puzzled the *Listener's* reviewer, absorbing the story of mud and rain, of the deaths of the author's friends and the destruction of the group of men he commanded. The letters did not seem to this reviewer to communicate happiness. But Charles Carrington, aged seventeen in 1914 while Graham was eighteen, also spoke for young subalterns who, by the 1930s, felt frustrated at the negative image of the war that dominated the public mind. Perhaps he was more fully articulate about what their youth meant to them than Graham was.

Carrington's *A Subaltern's War*, published interestingly enough under a pseudo-
nym in 1929, had actually made Graham's case for him in advance.

Carrington insisted he had experienced no corrupt sergeant majors or
incompetent colonels. 'The generation of young men who were soldiers before
their characters had been formed, who were under twenty-five in 1914,' he
stated, understood the mental barrier separating them from those who had
been too old or too young to fight. For 'the war made them what they are'. They
were still in the process of growing up, as the letters used in this book have so
amply illustrated. It was simply a legend that these men 'went gaily to fight in
the mood of Rupert Brooke and Julian Grenfell, lost their faith amidst the
horrors of the trenches and returned in a mood of anger and despair'. The
whole literary myth of disenchantment, Carrington insisted, was false. Young
men liked adventures. They rejoiced in the special bond of comradeship 'richer,
stronger in war than we have ever known since'.[5] These young men, as they
moved through middle and old age from the 1930s to 1960s, were keen partici-
pants in regimental dinners marked by sober and less than sober reminiscences
of days in the trenches. Unfortunately for the most part we do not have a record
of these occasions.

'It is not honest,' wrote Carrington in 1929, 'to deny the existence of happiness which was actually derived from the war by men who knew how to make
the best of a bad job.' He and Graham Greenwell, at different times, were lone
voices resisting the tide of disenchantment. Thus John Terraine, in his
Introduction to the 1972 edition of *An Infant in Arms*, was right to insist that
his book 'takes its place in a stream of literature and is not to be admired simply
as an isolated product, some sort of freak'. Graham Greenwell's testimony is as
crucial as any to the cumulative argument about our understanding of the
experience of fighting on the Western Front that this book has set out.[6]

Lance Spicer relates in the Preface to his published letters that he was not even
aware that, during the war, his mother had asked the family to pass all the
letters he sent them to her for safe keeping. They were given back to him when
she died in 1934. More than thirty-five years later, his three surviving sisters,
Gwen, Olga and Ursula, encouraged him to publish them. Then eighty-six,
he sought assistance in editing his letters from Brian Bond, the military
historian.

Tragically, Lance's only son Roger was killed in the Second World War. But
he enjoyed a long and successful professional life in the family firm, Spicers
Ltd, which was Britain's largest paper merchant. Founded in 1796, it finally
became part of the Reed Paper Group in 1959. Lance was its final chairman,
holding office from 1950 to 1959. He retired at sixty-six. His hands-on

management style led him to make a world tour in 1957, covering 30,000 miles, to meet staff in his far-flung paper empire in Aden, India, Australia, Singapore, Thailand, Hong Kong and Canada. He stood as a parliamentary Liberal candidate in 1945, was a prominent prison welfare visitor and a keen honorary treasurer of the Commonwealth Society for the Blind. He was faithful as a free churchman to the family's Nonconformist business roots. Fighting on the Western Front was thus, for Lance Spicer, just the first act of a long and enormously fulfilling life.

Lance came from a cohesive family of eleven. In his sixty years as a Great War veteran, he kept in touch with many of the colleagues in his regiment, the King's Own Yorkshire Light Infantry. He recalled some of them by name in a postscript to the letters, written in 1977. Harold Yeo had died in 1957, Basil Liddell Hart in 1970 and George Ellenberger in 1975.[7] He was then still in touch with one colleague from his work at Brigade HQ in 1917, V.H. Wells Cole. But of his group of close friends, he recorded, 'I alone remain'. His strongest memories in his eighties, wrote Lance, were of the Somme offensive, where he had displayed brave leadership, and of the German attack in March 1918. He recalled most clearly, as well as winters in trenches full of mud and water, trivial things like lilies of the valley 'growing wild in their thousands' in Champagne and asparagus waiting to be picked in quantities sufficient to feed a battalion.

Three of Lance's descendants remember him from their youth as a man of great personal warmth who was very good with younger people. His great-nephew Nicholas has boyhood memories of him as 'a thoroughly decent man with a boyish sense of humour'. A great-niece Susanna confirms his 'wicked sense of humour'. Another great-nephew, David Young, recalled Lance's kindness to him as a boy, remarking that he must have found it easy to transfer the leadership qualities he honed in the trenches to the energetic and caring management he displayed in the family's famous paper manufacturing company.[8]

Jack and Ivy Sweeney, wartime sweethearts by correspondence, found great personal happiness after the war, bringing up four boys and two girls in the hard times of the 1920s. 'He was always so gentle and kind,' declared Ivy after Jack's death in 1961, 'a wonderful father and I loved him dearly.' Their eldest daughter Doris had early memories of standing with her father in the dole queue. She grew up in the Walthamstow streets among families that were poorly fed and clothed. Ivy was forced to take shorthand typing jobs.

But it was cooking that was in Jack's blood. 'Private Sweeney is an excellent officers' cook,' ran a scribbled recommendation by one of his captains in the

Lincolnshires. He was resourceful in making nourishing dishes using cheap foodstuffs for his straitened family in the 1920s and '30s. He rented a stall in Leather Lane market in Holborn, where he sold sweets and toffees he made himself from his father's recipes. A friend who lost everything in the Blitz wrote to Jack, now nearly fifty, in September 1940, proposing that they set up together using the sugar and glucose permits he possessed and could transfer for their joint use. But nothing came of this. Jack served as an ARP warden for the rest of the war. Doris recalled how her father's acute ear for the sound of bombs saved her when he pulled her into a shelter just in the nick of time.

Pride in his regiment always came high in Jack's priorities. He was a regular attender at the Cenotaph parades. Throughout the 1920s and 1930s, he missed very few of the annual dinners of the Lincolnshire Regiment's Old Comrades' Association. These were nostalgic and emotional occasions when Jack found himself lifted out of his East End life, as he joined in the toasts led by veterans who had been his officers and leaders. The list was a traditional one: The King, the Memory of Those who Fell in the Great War, Our Regiment, Our Guests, Absent Comrades and the Old Comrades' Association Committee. The list of the regiment's battle honours on his treasured menu cards reinforced his identification with a proud national past. They ran from Blenheim and Oudenarde to Neuve Chapelle, Ypres, Delville Wood, Kemmel and the Hindenburg Line. 'Nothing is more binding than the friendship of companions in arms,' a programme note reminded those attending these dinners.

The local celebrations of Great War veterans probably meant as much or more to Jack as these grand regimental occasions. In January 1957, four years before he died, Jack was present at the annual dinner dance and cabaret of the Walthamstow 'Old Contemptibles', the name the survivors of the regular army gave themselves. The menu was roast chicken, chipolatas and game chips. The veterans gathered to exchange their increasingly confused memories, but what counted was the nostalgia for past experience, as they observed their accustomed one minute of silence 'for chums who have passed on'.

Doris Finch, Jack's eldest daughter, gave all his memorabilia, together with the enormous bulk of his wartime letters, to the Imperial War Museum in the 1970s. Ivy had kept the letters in Jack's army chest in her bedroom at her flat in Leytonstone. This was not far from the house in Maude Terrace where they first met, that day in 1916 when she had walked in the door to find a stranger in uniform sitting with her mother.[9]

Cyril Newman was one of the fortunate men who had a secure job to return to. He had kept in close touch with some of his seniors at the Official Receivers' Office in Victoria Street, London and was warmly welcomed back. His was a model career, pursued with unimpeachable professionalism over almost forty years until his retirement in 1958. In the 1940s he worked for four years in the Bristol office, returning to London as Senior Official Receiver for the South London District in 1950. The youngest of his three sons, David, remembers how hard his father had to work when the children were young, often late into the night, at their Surrey home.

His experience on the Western Front was never far from Cyril's mind. In a series of photograph albums he meticulously recorded the dinners of the Queen Victoria's Rifles that he attended, and he was at their annual camp at Shorncliffe as late as 1974, four years before he died. In 1925 he attended the tenth annual dinner commemorating the departure of the regiment on 4 November 1915 for France. He was often at thanksgiving and memorial services for colleagues in the regiment.

But Cyril's special concern was the record of the Signals Section of the Queen Victoria's Rifles, of which he was a proud member. In the press notice of his wedding his achievement of the Military Medal was recorded, 'for gallantly laying telephone lines under heavy artillery fire'. The most moving item in all his albums is the picture of Cyril's fellow signallers, with the dates of their deaths written in his neat hand beside their names. In 1957 Cyril noted the death, at the age of eighty-nine, of the last of those who had served as officers in the QVR. By the time he died himself, in 1978, he was one of the oldest of all the survivors in the regiment.

The most stirring occasions of his later life, for Cyril as for so many others, must have been the trips to the battlefields. His first one to Ypres in 1929 cost three guineas all in, for four days across the Channel. He went again the next year, in a party which included his wartime friend and later brother-in-law Reg Noakes. They travelled to the Somme, exploring the Carnoy cemetery and Leuze Wood, or Lousy Wood as it was etched into their minds.[10]

For a soldier who had suffered shell shock and been invalided home the post-war years carried a particular burden of recovery from trauma. Reintegration into British society was an immense challenge. Herbert Trench was fortunate in his extraordinarily happy marriage to Marjorie Bell and in the birth of two daughters, Robina and Valerie, in the late 1920s. For almost fifty years he basked in a happy family life. Herbert spoke little to his children about his war experiences. It must have helped him to come to terms with lying abandoned in that roadside ditch to have an elder brother, Arthur, who had served successfully in Mesopotamia. They saw each other regularly until Arthur's death in 1968. In the Second World War, Herbert served in the Ministry of Shipping in Whitehall.[11]

Herbert's most moving experience in relation to the war occurred in 1930, when he had tea with H.R. Greaves, the trench mortar officer whom he believed was the last man to see his brother Reggie alive on 21 March 1918. Greaves was taken prisoner that day. This tea party, described in a letter Herbert wrote to his sister Margot, was also attended by the brother of Padre Judd, killed just after Reggie. There was little new to Herbert in the oral account Greaves gave him, except for one rather shocking particular which no one, naturally, had spoken of before. This concerned the conduct of the commanding officer H.R. Gadd who in the final crisis, according to Greaves, 'got cold feet and would give no orders whatever'. When he told Colonel Gadd that his second in command was 'knocked out', Greaves said, he 'remained inactive and eventually surrendered in his dugout'. 'It is strange hearing so full a story after so long a time as twelve years,' Herbert reflected, 'and I do not suppose we are ever likely to hear further details.'[12]

All this was more than twenty years before I first met my Uncle Herbert as a schoolboy in the 1950s. There was no apparent trace in him then of how he had suffered from shell shock. I was not even aware he had fought in 1914–18. Perhaps I thought he had been too young but I did not actually do the arithmetic. I remember a caring and considerate man who showed great interest in my youthful doings. No doubt the inner scars remained, but it seems that breakdown in the trenches had fostered a quality of empathy in Herbert, a sensitivity to others, which I could not comprehend at that time but which makes entire sense now. He had been through fire and emerged a deeper and more compassionate human being. Yet, so far as I was concerned, Herbert was also a particularly friendly and approachable uncle.

Three other survivors are closely involved in our story: Albert Lane, Gordon Buxton and Arthur Bunting, the batmen who worked with Reggie Trench, Robert Hermon and Charlie May, respectively, all mourned when they were killed in action. A brief account of how their families have preserved the loyalties created in war tells us something of legacies of 1914–18 which are with us today. Remembrance is about gratitude and the emotions this carries with it.

Clare Trench first learnt of how steadfast Lane's loyalty was when she received the letter he wrote to her as a prisoner in Germany written on 18 May 1918. This told her some things she had not gathered from others about how Reggie died, and, more crucially, explained his difficulties in taking the photos in Reggie's pocket, his ring and his watch, when the Germans were almost on top of the last defenders of the Sherwood Foresters' HQ dugout. He only managed to save the watch, which he hid in his shoe for months. 'I will see you get that as soon as I get back to England,' he promised.[13] A few days later, Clare heard from Mrs Lane that he had felt his master's loss very much. Clare at once began a correspondence with the Lanes which lasted all the rest of Albert's life.[14] On 14 August, Lane wrote stoically about POW conditions: 'I am not the man I was; we cannot help ourselves like we could in the old cookhouse but I don't think it will be long.'[15] Meanwhile Clare began sending Mrs Lane money.[16] It was December, not long after the Armistice, when Lane wrote to Clare from his home in Croft near Leicester, pleased that he was 'able to write to you again in dear old England'.[17] This was where I eventually visited their home and met Albert Lane, hearing the story he tells in this book for the first time, around 1970.

For sixty years, from Reggie's death until his own death in 1980, Clare sent Albert Lane money and a letter at Christmas. They met several times when the Lanes were on holiday near her home at Hastings. 'I am delighted you still have the watch,' he wrote to Clare in 1961, 'just fancy it must be about 43 years. It must be a good one. Of course I had permission from Colonel Gadd that anything that I thought you would like I could take it for you.' It still preyed on his mind then that he had been stopped by a RAMC corporal and the burial party from taking off Reggie's ring. Albert Lane mentioned this again when he met Delle shortly before he died.[18] His son Ron, writing to Clare, spoke of the feelings of his siblings and children at seeing the spray of flowers he bought on her behalf at his father's funeral in 1980. He remembered Albert relating to him, 'as a small boy', his pride in the time they served together. Ron thanked her for 'your extreme generosity over the past sixty years'.[19]

Arthur Bunting sadly never got home. Seized by a German raiding party in March 1917, he remained a prisoner of war until after the Armistice and died in early December 1918. So we are left with the puzzle of how Charlie May's wonderful diary reached the hands of his wife Maud. Arthur must often have seen him writing it. The clue comes in a letter to him in which Maud thanked him for returning her husband's belongings, including his wedding ring and correspondence. We can take it that it was normal, in the regimental welfare system, for this kind of responsibility to be passed to the man who had given an officer faithful service in time of war. It is appropriate that, in the making of this book nearly a hundred years later, we owe something special to Arthur Bunting in ensuring that Charlie's moving testimony of his patriotism has become available to us.[20]

After Ethel's death, Gordon Buxton worked for Robert's daughter Betty and her family until well after the Second World War. They had six sons and then at last a daughter, Jessica, for whom the church bells at Cowfold in Sussex, it is said, rang in celebration. When he died, Robert's daughter Mary wrote to tell Buxton's widow Marie that he had been 'a very great friend and counsellor to me all my life'. Buxton's passing, she reflected, 'seems to have severed the last link with my old home, my parents and my childhood'.[21] But it has not turned out like that. For, in working on her edition of Robert Hermon's huge archive, Anne Nason, his granddaughter, made contact with Jessica Hawes, who had inherited her father Gordon Buxton's diary and letters from the Front. Jessica remembers her father telling her how he quickly decided to accept Robert Hermon's offer in 1914 of service as his batman and never regretted it.[22] The link, continued to this day, between the Hermon and Buxton families encapsulates the patriotic family loyalties which were created by the Great War.

Another such link, between the May and Bunting families, was revived in 2005 when Gerry Harrison, Charlie May's great-nephew made contact with Lieutenant Colonel Adrian Bunting, Arthur Bunting's grandson. This brought to light their comradeship during the training of the Manchester Pals for the Western Front.[23] Thus the story of the survivors of the war links seamlessly with the commemorative efforts, through preservation and use of archives of soldiers who fought in France, of men and families who were part of this great struggle.

The stories of our survivors provide some insight into the huge variety of men's attitudes to the war as they lived out their subsequent lives. Thousands of veterans never spoke about the Western Front outside their families. It never crossed their minds to engage in debate or controversy. Cyril Newman, a meticulous man living a well-ordered life, predictably left a typescript version of his story, with instructions to his children on how they could learn from it about his devotion to their mother. He never seems to have contemplated any self-advertisement. Nor, to be sure, did Jack Sweeney, who was far too busy keeping his own and his family's bodies and souls together to imagine anyone was interested in his humble trench experience. Our three letter writers who allowed the public to read their personal stories no doubt felt they had done all or more than they needed to justify their personal war records. The availability of such rich documentation for the war lives of men like Jack, Cyril and Herbert is due to the loyalty to their memory which has been shown by each of their families. The making of this book owes a great deal in particular to my six survivors, as well as to the eleven others who gave their lives for their country. As it turned out, the ultimate sacrifice was not asked of six of our soldiers or the three batmen mentioned here. But theirs was also a very considerable youthful sacrifice, of some of their best years. Who are we to measure one man's performance of duty against another's?

Epilogue

The Great War in Perspective

Henri Barbusse's novel *Le Feu* was given a rapturous reception when it was published in January 1916. It takes the form of a memoir written by a French poilu soldier, much of it in dialogue. It offered a moral condemnation of war as a radical evil, and in its first year sold 200,000 copies in French. It has been called by Jay Winter 'the first in a long line of war novels which told the world about the war from the inside'. It expresses, he declares, a kind of moral witness which lives on after publication in the midst of war, because Barbusse was a 'truth-teller, with a story to tell and re-tell'.

Barbusse had served as a stretcher-bearer on the Western Front for seventeen months, was cited twice for bravery, contracted a lung condition and was invalided out of the front line. One of the book's first French readers told Henri Barbusse in March 1917 that he had written 'a masterpiece: it is perfectly observed . . . it is a document which will remain as a witness to this war, a war unique in the history of humanity'. The first English translation of the book, *Under Fire*, offering the story told by the peasants of the French squad in an Edwardian high diction that now seems dated, was reviewed with acclamation in the *Manchester Guardian* in November 1917.[1] 'I had long been wanting to buy it,' Reggie Trench told Clare that month, 'I saw it reviewed in some paper.' He found a copy while on his short leave in Paris. He consumed it avidly, reading it in two days from cover to cover.

In two letters on 5 November, to his wife and to his mother, Reggie was full of the book he had found. He knew it was 'considered wonderfully true to life'. Perhaps it exaggerated the conditions under which the French poilus lived, which seemed 'very much worse than our own soldiers', but 'one can see the book is written by a master writer'. *Under Fire* was a quite 'wonderful book', he assured his mother; 'it tells the truth about the war in all its beastliness, nothing kept back, the real thing in print'. But this was not a book for any single woman to read. 'It is dreadful in places and you will not read it my love as I would not like you to do so please,' he warned Clare.

This stern patriarchal reaction to the possibility that his wife might read *Under Fire*, startlingly reveals Reggie's masculine as well as his chivalrous nature. *Under Fire* was to be a novel whose echoes were heard throughout the inter-war years and beyond. Penguin published a new translation in 2003. That Reggie forbade his wife to read it is a reminder that it comes from an altogether different world, one in which masculinity was a performance, which every man knew he must attempt and in which he realised he could not afford to fail. Reggie's impulsive reaction, his bid to shield Clare from the real world he understood, reminds us of how the soldiers I have written about in this book gave their utmost to the trial of their manhood, which they saw as the very essence of their patriotic duty. Never has the upper lip been so stiff as in this husband's command to his wife in November 1917.

In his account to Isabel, Reggie picked out one particular incident. It seemed to him to sum up the struggle in which he was engaged and the cause for which he would shortly give his life. 'There is a fine story in it,' he narrated, 'of an aviator who before a great battle flew over the lines and saw men formed up in the front Boche trench and the front French trench . . . flying lower he saw that in each trench there was a church service going on. Flying lower still he heard the words at the same moment from each side "God be with us".' Reggie felt this scene was somewhat implausible, since it was normally too dangerous to collect many men together in that way. 'But still,' he reflected, 'in parts of the line it might be done.' 'Anyhow,' he concluded, 'it shows clearly the spirit that is to be found in both nations each thinking it is striving for the right. What can be the end of it? That is the cry of the book.'[2] All the patriotic enthusiasm with which, since those August days in 1914, he had taken up arms came flooding into Reggie's mind as he told his mother about the book he had been reading. And never far from the front of his mind, in that brief stretch of Paris relaxation, must have been that precept *Dulce et decorum est* . . .

Only a tiny minority of those who fought felt moved to seek publishers for their memoirs. These were often constructed from the diaries or piles of letters kept by the veterans. Moreover the spate of memoirs took time in coming. Then it was largely officers, with more access to publication than Tommies, who spoke to the world. Temporary soldiers needed some years after 1918 to assimilate their experience, to recover physically, to establish themselves in civilian life. Many of them, after all, had been incredibly young in 1914. Adulthood thrust upon them by trench warfare had hit them like a blunderbuss. They may often have felt, as Graham Greenwell and Charles Carrington certainly did, that they had been misunderstood, that people had no grasp of what they personally had endured. This was one motive for setting the personal record straight.

When memoirs did flow, between 1927 and 1938, they proved the rich variety of trench experience and of the interpretation and meaning men drew from this experience. For the difference between these works and the editions of letters used in this book is that memoirs were constructed accounts of going to war, which by the act of selection and emphasis were bound to convey an argument. Authors needed a strong egoistic streak to make a success of establishing their own significance in a junior officer role. Some of course wanted to make some money from their personal stories, others to protest and explain how the war had induced in them a pacifist stance.[3]

There were men who wrote to escape the overwhelming spell exerted on them by their war experience. Robert Graves was polemical in saying goodbye to 'all that'.[4] The problem of their dual identity as civilians and soldiers came back to haunt two men in particular. Charles Carrington and Guy Chapman each published a second memoir, in 1965 and 1975 respectively. Unable to escape a kind of enthralment to both their lost and their surviving colleagues, writing helped them to keep reliving the war. They recollected their past obsessively, in terms of what they believed they could never really replace, once they were back in Blighty.[5]

Carrington never forgot the special bond of comradeship he had enjoyed.[6] In fact, he became increasingly obsessed with it, recalling his war years when in the company of other ex-soldiers as 'their own special world and theirs alone'. Brian Bond has written that for Carrington the trenches became 'a sort of mental internment camp or a soldiers' home'. His reflective and elegantly written second memoir, Soldier from the Wars Returning, established a distinction that was clear to him between winning the war and the general disappointment with its political legacy. It was a distinction, he believed, that has often not been understood.[7]

Chapman felt the need to write soon after his long service with the 13th Battalion of the Royal Fusiliers ended in 1918. It had been an overwhelming emotional experience. Once he began, he was inspired and his story told itself. The first pages of his book A Passionate Prodigality, completed in 1930, were extraordinarily candid. 'For a long time,' he stated, 'I used to think of myself as part of a battalion and not as an individual. During all that time the war, the forms and colours of that experience, possessed a part of my senses. My life was involved with the lives of other men, a few living, some dead.' Fear was at the start his dominant emotion: 'I was loath to go . . . I was not eager or resigned to self-sacrifice and my heart gave back no answering throb to the thought of England. In fact I was very much afraid and . . . anxious lest I should show it.'

Twenty-five in 1914, Chapman trained at Berkhamsted and the Staff College. He was in the thick of the Somme and Third Ypres. By November 1917 his battalion was in shreds: even in the final advance of August 1918 its casualty figures were high. He was *A Kind of Survivor*, the title of his second memoir, which was published posthumously in 1975. Chapman admired and revered the senior officers and fellow subalterns he worked with. Senior NCOs in his narrative were like mythical heroes. Such men were 'the salt of the earth, the backbone of the human race, men to whom duty is an inalienable part of their nature'. Late in life, he could read a platoon roll and conjure up faces, habits, nicknames and the men's aitch-less way of speaking. He believed passionately into old age that it was these ordinary soldiers who had won the war.

Few have written of the compelling fascination of war as Guy Chapman did in *A Passionate Prodigality*:

> once you have lain in her arms you can admit no other mistress. You may loathe, you may execrate, but you cannot deny her . . . no wine gives fiercer intoxication, no drug more vivid exaltation . . . even those who hate her most are prisoners to her spell. They rise from her embraces, pillaged, soiled, it may be ashamed, but they are still hers.

His widow, the novelist Storm Jameson, testified to Chapman's total absorption in the identity he wrought for himself in France in 1915–1918. She had to live with it. 'Nothing before or after that war gave him as keen a sensual and spiritual satisfaction,' she wrote. Over the war years and the years of peace that followed, in losing the companions of the trenches, she declared, he lost 'an integral part of himself'.[8]

It was possible to live with the Great War for as long as sixty years and then write about it with an intensity of feeling, freshness and vividness that can astonish the modern reader. Patrick Campbell achieved this in his two books *The Ebb and Flow of Battle* (1977) and *In the Cannon's Mouth* (1979). He was able to trace the roots of his patriotism to his love of the English countryside just as convincingly as Siegfried Sassoon or Rupert Brooke had done in 1914.[9] A passage in which he describes serving behind the lines at Ypres, shortly before the Passchendaele offensive was launched in October 1917, is paradigmatic. His servant, Campbell remembered, put his letters on the table at breakfast after a night's raiding party. His fourteen-year-old sister described in one of them bicycling out of Oxford to the village of Islip. 'I was back in England as I read,' he recalled, 'I could smell the reeds at the side of the river and see forget-me-nots and purple loosestrife on the banks.'

We have seen how disorientating it was for Campbell when he first went on leave in September 1917. Returning to his battalion was confusing too: 'I did not say I was glad to be back, I did not know whether I was. But at any rate it was a relief to be only one person again, just a part of the British Expeditionary Force, no longer a mixture of two quite different people.' He could still in the 1970s remember distinctly his feelings during a snowball fight between officers and servants at New Year's Eve in 1917. 'For as long as the war lasted,' Campbell knew, 'this was where I belonged. At first I had just been an individual, now I was part of the battery, the battery was part of the Brigade and the Brigade was part of the B.E.F. All my friends were in France and all the men in France were my friends.'[10]

Patrick Campbell was writing on the edge of that period, in the final two decades of the twentieth century and the first years of this new century, when the Great War was becoming reduced to a single set of easily communicated myths. These were the years when the last survivors dominated the public scene. They were naturally proud of being the survivors of so momentous an historical event, but they could not really remember very much. So the dominant mythology easily affected what they spoke of in public, as they sought to fit themselves into the way the war was being talked about by those around them. These veterans were not straightforward truth tellers. It would give them no respect to pretend that they were.

The problem of the reliability of the testimony of ageing veterans had become apparent as early as the 1960s when the BBC Television series *The Great War* brought veterans into the foreground. In 1964, just over eight million people watched each episode of the twenty-six-part series which Michael Redgrave narrated in mellifluous but mournful style. The taped interviews collected were preserved in the Imperial War Museum's sound archive. They were used by Max Arthur in his 2002 book *Forgotten Voices of the Great War*. Yet these are not so much forgotten voices as the voices of men managed by their interviewers, at a particular time fifty years after the war had ended. They tell us about the concerns of these interviewers in the 1960s but their words hardly provide material useful to historians seeking to reach a balanced view of the war as a whole. There is much about mud and horror. A surprisingly high number of veterans recalled executions. The veterans were speaking to a script dominated by myths which were, by the 1960s, fully established. They appeared to have become the permanent story. At the same time, these veterans played a crucial role in perpetuating and strengthening these same myths.

It was the end of this decade, with the availability of cheap portable audio-tape recorders, which saw the development of an oral history movement bent on capturing the participation of ordinary people in great events. This chimed neatly with the growth of interest in individual experience of the past. From the 1970s onwards there were pioneers in research with veterans who did very thorough and worthwhile work, confronting the methodological problems inherent in historical study of this kind. But they may not all, it can be suggested, have thought enough about the impact of an interviewer's questions, attitudes and responses in putting together the material they gathered.[11]

Martin Middlebrook meticulously researched the battles he worked upon and made notes with his witnesses, instead of using a tape recorder. Middlebrook was always aware of the range in the veterans' attitudes to what they had been through. Both his books, *The First Day on the Somme* and *The Kaiser's Battle*, describing 21 March 1918, were accurate, well written, analytical accounts which conveyed what battle had been like for those who could remember something about being there. Yet it is no coincidence that Middlebrook selected days of disaster for these studies, for he was driven by the wish to illustrate patriotism, courage and self-sacrifice. He did not question the now standard myths of mud, blood and incompetent leadership.

Lyn Macdonald was a BBC reporter and producer who took a group of veterans to the battlefields in 1972. Between 1978 and 1998 she produced a remarkable series of books which were essentially compilations of veteran testimonies set in a narrative framework.[12] She identified with the veterans, arguing that her aim was always 'to stand in their boots, to see things through their eyes, to try to understand and above all not to be judgmental'. Occasionally, Macdonald was caught out by a piece of skilful fabrication.[13] But her achievement in finding so many veterans willing to talk and in stimulating popular interest in the Western Front was extraordinary. She took understanding of the Great War to a much deeper level than that achieved by the BBC in the 1960s. Between 1972 and 1998 she probably got to know more veterans better than anyone else in the field. It is interesting that, in her last book, Macdonald noted they had never spoken with her of 'horror', which was she said too 'glib an appraisal', though many had recounted experiences that were indeed horrific.[14]

Interpretation of the Great War has gone through many phases since 1918. I have sought to add another layer to it in this book by a precise focus on a particular kind of source material. I have, by and large, observed a self-denying ordinance about drawing upon remembered stories of life at the Front which were written down after 1918. When I have introduced material from memoirs it has been to support and fill out arguments that are based upon pieces of authentic first-hand reporting in letters to relatives. My interest is in what it felt like to be there and, in many cases, to grow up there, told in accounts written under the stress of trench service and in the immediate aftermath of battle. My stories of living and dying, of shellfire in the front line and football and concerts behind it, have sought to capture the struggle as a few men lived it. I see telling these personal stories as a contribution to the long and continuing historical project of coming to terms with four of the most momentous years in our national history.

Notes

Abbreviations

CCH	Clare Cecily Howard
CCT	Clare Chenevix Trench
CT	Cesca Chevenix Trench
HCT	Herbert Chenevix Trench
ICT	Isabel Chenevix Trench
IWM	Imperial War Museum
MCT	Margot Chenevix Trench
NA	National Archives
NLI	National Library of Ireland
ODNB	*Oxford Dictionary of National Biography*
RCT	Reginald Chenevix Trench

Prologue

1. For an account of the love affair and marriage of my grandparents in 1911 to 1915 see my *Growing Up in England*, pp. 345–50.
2. DeGroot, *Blighty*, pp. 174–96.
3. Meyer, *Men of War*, p. 14.
4. Roper, *Secret Battle*, pp. 47–71.
5. Ibid., pp. 71–2.
6. Smith, *Letters sent from France*, pp. 103–6.
7. IWM, Newman Letters, pp. 416–17, 468.
8. Trench Archive, RCT to CCT, 14, 18 April 1917, RCT to ICT, 13 April 1917.
9. Philpott, *Bloody Victory*, p. 13.

1 'Quiet Earnest Faces': The National Cause

1. *ODNB*, H.C.G. Matthew, Henry Herbert Asquith.
2. Jenkins, *Asquith*, pp. 360–5; Howard, *First World War*, pp. 15–26; Gilbert, *First World War*, pp. 1–34.
3. Trench Archive, RCT to CCH, 30 July 1914.
4. Ferguson, *Pity of War*, pp. 161–3; Sheffield, *Forgotten Victory*, pp. 42–9.
5. *ODNB*, Jane Ridley and Clayre Percy, Mary Charteris, Countess of Wemyss; Ruddock Mackay and H.C.G. Matthew, Arthur James Balfour.
6. Stanway Archive, Mary Wemyss diary, 2–5 August 1914; Jenkins, *Asquith*, pp. 365–70; *ODNB*, Kenneth O. Morgan, David Lloyd George.
7. Ferguson, *Pity of War*, pp. 174–7.
8. Gregory, *Last Great War*, pp. 13–16.

9. Pennell, *A Kingdom United*, esp. pp. 1–41.
10. Stanway Archive, Mary Wemyss diary, 3 August 1914.
11. Citations from Pennell, *A Kingdom United*, pp. 42–3.
12. Gregory, *Last Great War*, pp. 9–11.
13. Pennell, *A Kingdom United*, p. 36; Trench Archive, RCT to CCT, 1 August 1914, CCT to RCT, 2 August 1914.
14. *ODNB*, Jane Ridley and Clayre Percy, Ethel Anne Priscilla Grenfell, Lady Desborough; Davenport-Hines, *Ettie*, pp. 183–4.
15. Gregory, *Last Great War*, pp. 25–7.
16. Stanway Archive, Mary Wemyss diary, 6–15 August 1914; Wemyss, *A Family Record*, p. 41; Davenport-Hines, *Ettie*, pp. 179–80; Dakers, *Countryside at War*, p. 26.
17. Gregory, *Last Great War*, pp. 33–4.
18. Trench Archive, *The Times*, 7 August 1914, p. 7.
19. Pennell, *A Kingdom United*, pp. 44–5.
20. Cited in Gregory, *Last Great War*, p. 33.
21. Brooke, *1914 and Other Poems*, p. 11.
22. Scott quoted in Pennell, *A Kingdom United*, pp. 72–6.
23. Ibid., p. 118; Gilbert, *First World War*, p. 55.
24. Trench Archive, CCH to RCT, 24 August 1914.
25. Wemyss, *A Family Record*, p. 249.
26. Pennell, *A Kingdom United*, pp. 79–83.
27. His work there is discussed in Chapter 3, pp. 69–71.
28. Trench Archive, CCH to RCT, 6 August 1914.
29. Trench Archive, CCH to RCT, 19, 23 December 1914; for Sir John French in these months see Gilbert, *First World War*, pp. 55–123.
30. Trench Archive, CCH to RCT, 13, 14, 15 August, 19 October 1914.
31. See below, pp. 37–9.
32. Trench Archive, CCH to RCT, 19 August 1914, RCT to CCH, 13, 19 August 1914.
33. Trench Archive, RCT to CCH, 24 August 1914, CCH to RCT, 25 August 1914. For shell shock see below pp. 106–18.
34. Trench Archive, RCT to CCH, 4, 14 October 1914, Edward Burney to RCT, 27 October 1914.
35. Trench Archive, RCT to CCH, 2 November 1914.
36. For Herbert's enlistment see below, p. 38.
37. Herbert Trench Archive, HCT to RCT, 18 November 1914; see below pp. 107–11.
38. Trench Archive, CCH to RCT, 13 November, 16 December 1914, RCT to CCH, 14 October, 2, 7 December 1914.
39. Trench Archive, RCT to CCH, 9, 16 November 1914.
40. Ibid., CCH to RCT, 6, 18, 20 October 1914. Gilbert, *First World War*, pp. 42–3, 81.
41. For Clare's upbringing see my *Growing Up in England*, pp. 78–9, 147–8, 242–3, 257–8, 345–50.
42. Trench Archive, CCH to RCT, 21, 23, 24 October 1914.
43. Trench Archive, CCH to RCT, 2, 3, 6, 13, 23 November, 8 December 1914.
44. Trench Archive, CCH to RCT, 5, 8, 19 November, 10, 12, 24 December 1914.
45. Trench Archive, RCT to CCH, 1, 3, 9, 11, 20 September 1914.
46. Trench Archive, CCH to RCT, 14 August 1914.
47. Gregory, *Last Great War*, pp. 18–24; Pennell, *A Kingdom United*, p. 162.
48. Corrigan, *Mud, Blood and Poppycock*, pp. 46–8.
49. Gilbert, *First World War*, pp. 55–77.
50. Violet Bonham Carter, cited in Simkins, *Kitchener's Army*, p. 35; *ODNB*, Keith Neilson, Horatio Herbert Kitchener, Earl Kitchener of Khartoum.
51. Davenport-Hines, *Ettie*, p. 111.
52. Thompson, ed., *Julian Grenfell*, pp. 212–13; Davenport-Hines, *Ettie*, pp. 184–5.
53. Simkins, *Kitchener's Army*, pp. 31–78.

54. Sheffield, *Leadership in the Trenches*, pp. 29–35.
55. Trench Archive, RCT to CCH, 4 August 1914.
56. Sheffield, *Leadership in the Trenches*, pp. 34–7; Simkins, *Kitchener's Army*, pp. 221–5.
57. R.C. Sherriff, 'The English Public Schools in the War', in Panichas, ed., *Promise of Greatness*, pp. 134–54.
58. Pennell, *A Kingdom United*, pp. 147–56.
59. Cited in Simkins, *Kitchener's Army*, p. 72.
60. Gregory, *Last Great War*, pp. 30–9; Watson, *Enduring the Great War*, pp. 49–51.
61. *ODNB*, Thomas Pinney, Rudyard Kipling.
62. Pennell, *A Kingdom United*, pp. 57–67.
63. Cited in Fuller, *Troop Morale and Popular Culture*, p. 33.
64. Citations from Pennell, *A Kingdom United*, p. 66.
65. Ibid., pp. 67–8. *ODNB*, Alan Bishop, Vera Mary Brittain.
66. Pennell, *A Kingdom United*, pp. 67–71, 92–107; David French, 'Spy Fever in Britain, 1900–1915', *Historical Journal*, 21, no. 2 (1978), pp. 335–70.
67. Pennell, *A Kingdom United*, pp. 108–17.
68. McCartney, *Citizen Soldiers*, p. 202.
69. Gilbert, *First World War*, pp. 55–99; Pennell, *A Kingdom United*, p. 118.
70. Trench Archive, CCH to RCT, 11, 26, 30 November, 15 December 1914; Pennell, *A Kingdom United*, pp. 106–10, 121–2.
71. Citations from Pennell, *A Kingdom United*, pp. 12–24.
72. Van Emden and Humphries, *All Quiet on the Home Front*, pp. 35–50.
73. Gilbert, *First World War*, p. 110.
74. Pennell, *A Kingdom United*, pp. 131–3.
75. Gregory, *Last Great War*, p. 60.
76. Sanders and Taylor, *British Propaganda during the First World War* cited in Gregory, *Last Great War*, pp. 40–69.
77. Pennell, *A Kingdom United*, pp. 130–1.
78. Trench Archive, CCH to RCT, 9 September 1914, RCT to CCH 15 September 1914.
79. Citations in Pennell, *A Kingdom United*, pp. 198–205.
80. Trench Archive, CCH to RCT, 22 December 1914.
81. Wemyss, *A Family Record*, p. 304.
82. Gregory, *The Last Great War*, pp. 142–50.
83. Cited in Pennell, *A Kingdom United*, p. 211.
84. Cited in ibid., p. 215.
85. Strachan, *Oxford History of the First World War*, p. 215.
86. Pennell, *A Kingdom United*, pp. 221–6.

2 'Glad to Go': Patriotic Idealism

1. Bond, *Survivors of a Kind*, p. 14.
2. *ODNB*, H.C.G. Matthew, Harold Macmillan. Citation from Winter, *Death's Men*, p. 32.
3. Carrington, *Soldier from the Wars Returning*, pp. 259–61.
4. Housman, ed., *War Letters of Fallen Englishmen*, pp. 291–2.
5. Brooke, *1914 and Other Poems*, pp. 11, 15; *ODNB*: Rupert Brooke. Carrington, *Soldier from the Wars Returning*, p. 260.
6. *ODNB*, Paul Addison, Sir Winston Leonard Spencer Churchill.
7. Hassall, *Rupert Brooke*, pp. 452–8.
8. Lehmann, *Rupert Brooke*, pp. 118–19; MacKenzie, *Children of the Souls*, p. 154.
9. MacKenzie, *Children of the Souls*, p. 174.
10. Hassall, *Rupert Brooke*, pp. 458–85, 515.
11. MacKenzie, *Children of the Souls*, p. 176.
12. Cited in Girouard, *The Return to Camelot: Chivalry and the English Gentleman*, p. 286.
13. Brooke, *1914 and Other Poems*, p.15; *ODNB*: Rupert Brooke.
14. Copies in Trench Archive, inscribed 29 July 1915 and Xmas 1916.

15. *ODNB*, Adrian Caesar, Rupert Chawner Brooke.
16. Arlington Court archives. I am grateful to the National Trust for permission to consult these papers.
17. *ODNB*, Richard Percival Graves, Robert von Ranke Graves.
18. Thompson, ed., *Julian Grenfell*, pp. 212–23: Davenport-Hines, *Ettie*, pp. 184–5.
19. *ODNB*, Mark Pottle, Julian Henry Francis Grenfell.
20. IWM, Sweeney Letters; Moynihan, *Greater Love*, pp. 63–5.
21. Feilding, *War Letters to a Wife*, pp. xi–xii.
22. Nason, ed., *For Love and Courage*, pp. xi–3.
23. I am very grateful to Gordon Buxton's daughter Jessica Hawes for showing me this letter.
24. Nason, ed., *For Love and Courage*, pp. 4–5.
25. I am grateful to Nicola Kent for this account.
26. IWM, Spencer Letters, Wilbert Spencer to his father, 14 August.
27. I am grateful to Nicola Kent for this information.
28. IWM, Spencer Letters, Wilbert Spencer to his father, 20, 25 November 1914; to his mother, 1 December 1914.
29. Spicer, *Letters from France*, pp. vii–xiii.
30. Greenwell, *An Infant in Arms*, pp. 1–3.
31. Harris, *Billie*, p. 15.
32. Ridley and Percy, eds, *Letters of Arthur Balfour and Lady Elcho*, pp. 311–12.
33. *ODNB*, Raymond Mackenzie, Lady Cynthia Mary Evelyn Asquith; Beauman, *Cynthia Asquith*; for Beb see Jenkins, *Asquith*, pp. 55, 59, 195, 424; MacKenzie, *Children of the Souls*, p. 203.
34. Wemyss, *A Family Record*, pp. 46–60, 194–262: Stanway Archive, YVO 1.02; Dakers, *Countryside at War*, pp. 25–30
35. NA, War Office Papers: Herbert Trench; NLI, Coffey and Chenevix Trench Archive, MS 46318/2.
36. Trench Archive, RCT to CCH, 20 July 1914.
37. Pyle, *Cesca's Diary*, p. 127
38. Trench Archive, HCT to CCT, undated August 1914; RCT to CCH, 19 August 1914; A.J. Fletcher, 'Between the Lines', *History Today*, November 2009.
39. Trench Archive, RCT to CCH, 26 August 1914; G. Goold Walker, *The Honourable Artillery Company 1537–1926*, p. 268.
40. NA, War Office Papers WO 339/27123.
41. Trench Archive, RCT to CCH, 18 September 1914.
42. Trench Archive, HCT to ICT, 19 September 1914.
43. Simkins, *Kitchener's Army*, pp. 79–103; McCartney, *Citizen Soldiers*, pp. 25–88.
44. Piuk, *Dream within the Dark*, pp. 18–23.
45. Ibid., pp. 15–18.
46. IWM Newman Letters.
47. IWM, Newman Letters, pp. 2, 464.
48. Moynihan, ed., *God on Our Side*, pp. 140–1.
49. Thompson, ed., *Julian Grenfell*, pp. 223–303; Mosley, *Julian Grenfell*, pp. 236–57.
50. Parker, *The Old Lie*, pp. 125–34; *ODNB*, rev. Richard Ingrams, Malcolm Muggeridge.
51. J. Springhall, 'Building Character in the British Boy: The Attempt to Extend Christian Manliness to Working-class Adolescents, 1880–1914', in Mangan and Walvin, *Manliness and Morality*, pp. 52–74.
52. *ODNB*, Allen Warren, Robert Stephenson Smyth Baden-Powell.
53. Parker, *The Old Lie*, pp. 145–7; DeGroot, *Blighty*, pp. 36–42.
54. *ODNB*, Peter Newbolt, George Alfred Henty; Girouard, *Return to Camelot*, pp. 253–66.
55. *ODNB*, David Gervais, Sir Henry John Newbolt.
56. Parker, *The Old Lie*, pp. 56–8; Girouard, *Return to Camelot*, pp. 169–73, 233.
57. Mangan, *Athleticism in the Victorian and Edwardian Public School*, pp. 179–206.
58. Trench Archive, RCT to CCH, 29 July 1912.

59. Girouard, *Return to Camelot*, pp. 283, 285; Trench Archive, CCH to RCT, 9 September 1914.
60. Trench Archive, RCT to CCH, 23 December 1912; Kipling, *Rewards and Fairies*, pp. 175–6; H. Ricketts, *The Unforgiving Minute*, pp. 293–4.
61. Trench Archive, RCT to CCH, 19 March 1914.
62. Carrington, *Rudyard Kipling*, Preface, pp. 446–7; Sheffield, *Leadership in the Trenches*, pp. 48–9.
63. Cited in Mangan, *Athleticism in the Victorian and Edwardian Public School*, p. 203.
64. Nason, ed., *For Love and Courage*, pp. 172–3, 177.
65. Housman, ed., *War Letters of Fallen Englishmen*, pp. 168–70.
66. Girouard, *Return to Camelot*, p. 281.
67. Cited in MacKenzie, *Children of the Souls*, p. 150.
68. Trench Archive, RCT to CCH, 15 December 1913; *History Today*, 54 (August 2004), pp. 31–2.
69. IWM, CC May Diary, 7 December 1915, 19 January, 19 March 1916.
70. IWM, Newman Letters, pp. 388, 464.
71. Watson, *Enduring the Great War*, p. 53.
72. Housman, ed., *War Letters of Fallen Englishmen*, pp. 221–5.
73. Cited in Dakers, *Countryside at War*, p. 11.
74. Trench Archive, RCT to CCT 20 July 1914, 18 November 1917.
75. Nason, ed., *For Love and Courage*, pp. 61, 161.
76. Harris, *Billie*, pp. 127–8.
77. Thompson, ed., *Julian Grenfell*, p. 275.
78. Housman, ed., *War Letters of Fallen Englishmen*, pp. 67–8.
79. IWM, Streets Letters, Will Streets to his mother, 12 July 1915.
80. Nason, ed., *For Love and Courage*, p. 6; Cited in Winter, *Death's Men*, p. 32.
81. Citations in Winter, *Death's Men*, pp. 32–3.
82. Housman, ed., *War Letters of Fallen Englishmen*, pp. 106–7, 128–32, 156–7, 177–81, 217–18, 275–9.

3 'Ready to Go': Training

1. Simkins, *Kitchener's Army*, pp. 296–300.
2. Piuk, *A Dream within the Dark*, pp. 35–42.
3. Winter, *Death's Men*, pp. 35–44 may overstate this.
4. McCartney, *Citizen Soldiers*, pp. 1–3.
5. Trench Archive, CCH to RCT, 24 August, 4, 18 September 1914, RCT to CCH, 17 September.
6. Greenwell, *An Infant in Arms*, pp. 1–2.
7. IWM, Newman Letters, pp. 32–3.
8. Cited in Simkins, *Kitchener's Army*, p. 302.
9. Greenwell, *An Infant in Arms*, p. 3.
10. IWM, Newman Letters, pp. 24, 26, 50.
11. Piuk, *A Dream within the Dark*, pp. 22–31.
12. Harris, *Billie*, pp. 17–30.
13. Moynihan, ed., *Greater Love*, pp. 3–9.
14. Hanson, *The Unknown Soldier*, pp. 45–51.
15. IWM, Reader Letters, 1–4.
16. Harris, *Billie*, p. 17; Greenwell, *An Infant in Arms*, pp. 4–6.
17. I am grateful to Gerry Harrison for much valuable information about Charlie May.
18. IWM, May diary, pp. 1–2.
19. Wemyss, *A Family Record*, pp. 282–91, 303.
20. Ibid., pp. 46–60, 194–262: Stanway Archive, YVO 1.02; Dakers, *Countryside at War*, pp. 25–30.
21. Wemyss, *A Family Record*, pp. 302–7, 314.

22. Smith, *Letters Sent from France*, p. 3; H.A.R. May, *Memories of the Artists' Rifles*.
23. IWM, Spencer Letters, W.B.P Spencer to his mother, 1 December 1914.
24. IWM, Spencer Letters, W.B.P. Spencer to his father 20, 25 November 1914.
25. IWM, Reader Letters, 6–13.
26. Moynihan, ed., *Greater Love*, pp. 4–15.
27. IWM, Streets Letters, Will Streets to his mother 12 July, 25 October 1915.
28. Harris, *Billie*, p. 28.
29. Thompson, ed., *Julian Grenfell*, pp. 222–3.
30. Smith, *Letters Sent from France*, pp. 1–3.
31. IWM, Spencer Letters, W.P.B. Spencer to his father, 1 December 1914.
32. Nason, ed., *For Love and Courage*, p. 7; Feilding, *War Letters to a Wife*, p. 1.
33. IWM, Newman Letters, p. 104.
34. Greenwell, *An Infant in Arms*, pp. 8–9.
35. Harris, *Billie*, pp. 43–5.
36. IWM, Reader Letters, 14–15; Hanson, *Unknown Soldier*, pp. 53–6.
37. Vaughan, *Some Desperate Glory*, pp. viii, 1–2.
38. Spicer, *Letters from France*, pp. 2–3; Gilbert, *First World War*, pp. 197–201.
39. Trench Archive, Western Front letters 1–21.
40. Greenwell, *An Infant in Arms*, pp. 10–11.
41. Moynihan, ed., *Greater Love*, pp. 17–18.
42. Feilding, *War Letters to a Wife*, pp. 1–2.
43. Nason, ed., *For Love and Courage*, pp. 7–11.
44. Trench Archive, RCT to CCT, 5 March 1917.
45. IWM, Newman Letters, p. 106.
46. Corrigan, *Mud, Blood and Poppycock*, pp. 79–85.
47. Edmonds, *A Subaltern's War*, pp. 120–1; Bond, *Survivors of a Kind*, p. 20.
48. Corrigan, *Mud, Blood and Poppycock*, pp. 90–1.
49. Greenwell, *An Infant in Arms*, pp. 12–14.
50. Wemyss, *A Family Record*, pp. 315–17.
51. Smith, *Letters Sent from France*, pp. 22–3, 29, 33, 43, 62–74.
52. IWM, Reader Letters, 18–21; Hanson, *Unknown Soldier*, pp. 56–66.
53. IWM, Nevill Letters, 19–27; Harris, *Billie*, pp. 45–54.
54. Greenwell, *An Infant in Arms*, pp. 12–17, 80.
55. Harris, *Billie*, pp. 72–3.
56. Trench Archive, RCT to CCH, 4–24 September 1914.
57. Roper, *Secret Battle*, pp. 130–7, 167–70.
58. Trench Archive, CCH to RCT, 9 December 1914.
59. Trench Archive, RCT to CCH, 13 October–23 December 1914. A.J. Willmer to RCT, 3 January 1915; F.H.L. Errington, *The Inns of Court Officers Training Corps*, pp. 13–30, 49–65.

4 'Write as Often as You Can': Letters and Parcels

1. IWM, McGregor Letters, 10 June 1916.
2. Feilding, *War Letters to a Wife*, pp. 3, 10, 36, 43, 61, 77, 100, 125, 128.
3. Moynihan, ed., *Greater Love*, pp. 1–33; IWM, McGregor Letters, 30 June, 7 July.
4. Nason, ed., *For Love and Courage*, pp. 32, 61, 63, 74–5, 115, 174, 185, 246–7.
5. Trench Archive, RCT to ICT, 31 March 1917.
6. Particularly transparent examples are Trench Archive, RCT to CCT, 20 March and 24 October 1917.
7. Trench Archive, RCT to CCT, 1 May, 4 July, 3, 8 August, 21 September, 16 October 1917.
8. Trench Archive, RCT to CCT, 19 March, 18, 20, 23 April, 19 August 1917.

9. IWM, Newman Letters, pp. 125, 361, 378, 381, 413; *History Today*, 59 (November 2009), pp. 49–50.
10. IWM, Sweeney Letters. Volumes 1 and 5 contain much miscellaneous material on his career before the Great War and after it; volumes 2 to 4 contain letters from the Front, mostly with their envelopes, in chronological order.
11. Thompson, ed., *Julian Grenfell*, pp. xix, 322–31.
12. Greenwell, *An Infant in Arms*, pp. 130–1.
13. Trench Archive, HCT to ICT, September 1914, 16 July 1915.
14. Harris, *Billie*, pp. 1–11, 116; Roper, *Secret Battle*, p. 59.
15. Spicer, *Letters from France*, pp. vii, 8–9, 19–20.
16. Wemyss, *A Family Record*, pp. 315–30.
17. Smith, *Letters Sent from France*, pp. 11–21, 37–8, 96–9, 119–20.
18. IWM, Spencer Letters, 8–31.
19. Harris, *Billie*, p. 5; IWM, Streets papers, Will Streets to Ben, 20 June 1916.
20. IWM, Reader Letters, 30.
21. IWM, Reader Letters, 15–77.
22. IWM, Newman Letters, p. 469.
23. IWM, McGregor Letters, 27 July, 29 August 1916.
24. Bourke, *Dismembering the Male*, p. 22.
25. Feilding, *War Letters to a Wife*, p. 134.
26. Nason, ed., *For Love and Courage*, pp. 183, 213–14.
27. IWM, Streets Papers, undated 1916.
28. Smith, *Letters Sent from France*, p. 100.
29. Trench Archive, RCT to CCT, 20 March, 17 October 1917.
30. IWM, Newman Letters, p. 422.
31. Trench Archive, RCT to ICT, 16 April, 5 May, 2, 13 June 1917, 14 February 1918; *History Today* 54 (August 2004), pp. 35, 59; (November 2009), p. 48.
32. IWM, Newman Letters, pp. 327–52, 408.
33. Greenwell, *An Infant in Arms*, pp. 89–90.
34. Harris, *Billie*, pp. 95, 112–15.
35. Roper, *Secret Battle*, p. 64.
36. Smith, *Letters Sent from France*, pp. 126–7.
37. IWM, Reader Letters, 12–72; Meyer, *Men of War*, pp. 22–3, 26.
38. IWM, Sweeney Letters, 10 September 1916; Moynihan, ed., *Greater Love*, pp. 63–85.
39. Feilding, *War Letters to a Wife*, p. 108.
40. IWM, McGregor Letters, 30 June 1916; Moynihan, ed., *Greater Love*, p. 19.
41. IWM, Spencer Letters, 3 January 1915; Roper, *Secret Battle*, p. 66.
42. Smith, *Letters Sent from France*, pp. 79–82; Roper, *Secret Battle*, p. 66.
43. I am grateful to Michael Roper for skilful analysis of this letter in 'Maternal Relations: Moral Manliness and Emotional Survival in Letters Home during the First World War', in S. Dudink, K. Hagermann and J. Tosh, eds, *Masculinity in Politics and War* (2004), pp. 295–315.
44. Trench Archive, RCT to CCT, 5–25 April 1917; RCT to ICT, 16 April 1917.
45. Nason, ed., *For Love and Courage*, pp. 159–61, 317–18.
46. IWM, Reader Letters, 30, 44.
47. IWM, Reader Letters, 18; Feilding, *War Letters to a Wife*, p. 10; Moynihan, ed., *Greater Love*, p. 26.
48. IWM, Charlie May Diary, 7, 22, 31 December 1915, 19 March, 13 April, 7 May 1916; above.
49. Trench Archive, RCT to CCT, 29 May, 5, 19 September, 15 November 1917.
50. Trench Archive, RCT to CCT, 22, 29 January, 5 February 1918.
51. Trench Archive, RCT to CCT, 14, 18, 23 April, 1 September 1917, RCT to ICT, 13 April 1917.
52. IWM, Spencer Letters, 17, 19.

5 'Sticking it Out': Fear and Shell Shock

1. Showalter, *Female Malady*, p. 169.
2. Roper, *Journal of British Studies* (*JBS*) 44 (2005), pp. 350–2; Sheffield, *Leadership in the Trenches*, pp. 140–1.
3. Roper, *Secret Battle*, p. 20.
4. Ibid., p. 17; Piuk, *A Dream within the Dark*, p. 59.
5. IWM, Newman Letters, 1–4 August 1916.
6. Piuk, *A Dream within the Dark*, p. 55.
7. Hankey, *A Student in Arms*, pp. 32–3.
8. Roper, *JBS* 44 (2005), pp. 351–5.
9. *ODNB*, R.R.H. Lovell, Charles McMoran Wilson, first Baron Moran.
10. Moran, *Anatomy of Courage*, pp. 27–9, 125–41.
11. Roper, *JBS* 44 (2005), pp. 356–8; Moran, *Anatomy of Courage*, pp. 41–74; Keith Simpson in Cecil and Liddle, eds, *Facing Armageddon*, p. 577.
12. Winter, *Death's Men*, pp. 115–20; McCartney, *Citizen Soldiers*, p. 200.
13. Cited in Winter, *Death's Men*, pp. 118–19.
14. Middlebrook, ed., *Diaries of Private Bruckshaw*, p. 153.
15. Cited in Roper, *Secret Battle*, p. 17.
16. Thompson, ed., *Julian Grenfell*, pp. 241–3; Mosley, *Julian Grenfell*, pp. 240–3.
17. IWM, Newman Letters, 24 May 1915, 24 March 1918; Meyer, *Men of War*, p. 21.
18. Greenwell, *An Infant in Arms*, pp. 24, 63, 79; Roper, *Secret Battle*, p. 17.
19. Harris, *Billie*, pp. 55, 66, 95.
20. Housman, ed., *War Letters of Fallen Englishmen*, pp. 295–300.
21. Roper, *Secret Battle*, pp. 263–6.
22. IWM, Reader Letters 24, 31, 36; Meyer, *Men of War*, pp. 18, 21.
23. Moynihan, ed., *Greater Love*, pp. 18–19.
24. Moynihan, ed., *God on Our Side*, p. 123.
25. Trench Archive, RCT to CCT, 13 April 1917.
26. IWM, Spencer Letters, 14.
27. IWM, Spencer Letters, 9.
28. Greenwell, *An Infant in Arms*, pp. 52–3.
29. Harris, *Billie*, p. 103.
30. Vaughan, *Some Desperate Glory*, p. 192.
31. Cited in Roper, *Secret Battle*, p. 255.
32. Moynihan, ed., *Greater Love*, p. 72.
33. IWM, May Diary, 27 March 1916.
34. Piuk, *A Dream within the Dark*, p. 49.
35. Campbell, *In the Cannon's Mouth*, pp. 1–39.
36. *ODNB*, F.C. Bartlett, rev. Hugh Series, Charles Myers.
37. Showalter, *Female Malady*, p. 174.
38. Roper, *Secret Battle*, p. 31.
39. Shephard, *A War of Nerves*, pp. 21–32.
40. Stryker, 'Mental Cases: British Shellshock and the Politics of Interpretation', p. 161.
41. Herbert Trench Archive, HCT to Cesca CT, 26 September 1914, CCH to RCT, 3 October 1914.
42. Herbert Trench Archive, HCT to Cesca CT, undated October 1914.
43. Herbert Trench Archive, HCT to MCT, 29 October 1914.
44. Trench Archive, RCT to CCH, 8 November 1914.
45. Herbert Trench Archive, HCT to MCT, 15 November 1914.
46. Herbert Trench Archive, typescript copy of postcard from HCT to Sheelah Trench, with manuscript note by Benjamin Bloomfield Trench; HCT to RCT, 18 November 1914.
47. Pyle, *Cesca's Diary*, p. 176.
48. Herbert Trench Archive, HCT to Cesca CT, 14/20 December 1914.
49. NA, War Office Papers WO339/27123
50. Pyle, *Cesca's Diary*, pp. 183–6.

51. Herbert Trench Archive, HCT to MCT, 15 November 1914.
52. Herbert Trench Archive, HCT to ICT, 16 July 1915; NA, War Office Papers WO339/22227123.
53. *ODNB*, rev. Wilder Penfield, Sir Gordon Morgan Holmes.
54. Babington, *Shellshock*, pp. 75–103; Shepherd, *A War of Nerves*, pp. 30–2; A.D. Macleod, 'Shellshock, Gordon Holmes and the Great War', *Journal of the Royal Society of Medicine*, 97 (2004), pp. 86–9; Gilbert, *First World War*, pp. 357–8.
55. McCartney, *Citizen Soldiers*, pp. 137–9.
56. Brown, *IWM Book of the Western Front*, p. 157.
57. Marks, *The Laughter Goes from Life*, p. 67.
58. *ODNB*, Richard A. Storey, Max Plowman.
59. [Plowman], *A Subaltern on the Somme*, pp. 52–4; Bond, *Survivors of a Kind*, p. 108.
60. Keith Simpson, 'Dr James Dunn and Shellshock', in Cecil and Liddle, eds, *Facing Armageddon*, pp. 502–20.
61. Greenwell, *An Infant in Arms*, pp. 56, 61–3, 129; Roper, *Secret Battle*, p. 247.
62. Brown, *IWM Book of the Western Front*, pp. 161–5.
63. http://web.mala.bc.ca/davies/letters.images/Fereday/Fereday.collection.htm, Canadian Letters and Images Project. I am grateful to Malcolm Kitch for this reference.
64. Cited in Meyer, *Men of War*, p. 22.
65. Brown, *IWM Book of the Western Front*, pp. 156–7.
66. Spicer, *Letters from France*, pp. 68–9.
67. Nason, ed., *For Love and Courage*, pp. 276–81.
68. Carrington, *Soldier from the Wars Returning*, pp. 191–7; Bond, *Survivors of a Kind*, pp. 21–3.
69. Trench Archive, HCT to Cesca CT, 30 September 1915.
70. NLI, Coffey and Chenevix Trench Archive, 46323/6.
71. Trench Archive, HCT to Cesca CT, 20 February 1916.
72. NLI, Coffey and Chenevix Trench Archive, 46323/8.
73. Trench Archive, HCT to MCT, 19 September 1916.
74. NA, War Office Papers WO339/27123; NLI, Coffey and Chenevix Trench Archive, 46323/12; Trench Archive, RCT to CCT, 12 May 1917, 3 February 1918.
75. Trench Archive, RCT to CCT, 13 September 1917; RCT to ICT, 27 February 1918.
76. Stryker, 'Mental Cases', pp. 163–8.
77. Roper, *JBS* 44 (2005), pp. 350–3.

6 'A Certain Sense of Safety with Him': Leadership

1. Trench Archive, RCT to ICT, 13 May 1917; RCT to CCT, 30 April 1917.
2. Smith, *Letters Sent from France*, p. 75.
3. Trench Archive, RCT to ICT, 5 July 1917.
4. Housman, ed., *War Letters of Fallen Englishmen*, pp. 279–82.
5. IWM, Charlie May Diary, 25 December 1915.
6. IWM, Newman Letters, pp. 468, 514–15.
7. Cited in Brown, *IWM Book of the Western Front*, p. 193.
8. Smith, *Letters Sent from France*, p. 78.
9. Cited in Sheffield, *Leadership in the Trenches*, p. 137.
10. Wemyss, *A Family Record*, p. 316; Greenwell, *An Infant in Arms*, p. 2; Roper, *Secret Battle*, p. 173.
11. IWM, Spencer Letters, 10; Greenwell, *An Infant in Arms*, pp. 9–16; Roper, *Secret Battle*, p. 175.
12. Wemyss, *A Family Record*, pp. 316, 333–4; Roper, *Secret Battle*, p. 176.
13. Smith, *Letters Sent from France*, pp. 96, 115, 142.
14. Housman, ed., *War Letters of Fallen Englishmen*, p. 240.
15. McCartney, *Citizen Soldiers*, pp. 31, 139–40.
16. Bracco, *Merchants of Hope*, pp. 155, 165.

17. IWM, Newman Letters, pp. 352, 461.
18. IWM, Sweeney Letters, pp. 223–9.
19. Panichas, ed., *Promise of Greatness*, pp. 133–54; Middlebrook, ed., *Diaries of Private Bruckshaw*, p. 165.
20. Nason, ed., *For Love and Courage*, p. 15.
21. Harris, *Billie*, p. 127.
22. Trench Archive, RCT to ICT, 2 June 1917.
23. IWM, Newman Letters, p. 158.
24. Trench Archive, RCT to CCT, 13 May, 25 June, 8, 10, 12 August 1917.
25. Greenwell, *An Infant in Arms*, pp. 25, 73, 83, 106, 120–1.
26. Spicer, *Letters from France*, pp. 22, 95–6.
27. Harris, *Billie*, pp. 60, 136, 155–6.
28. Trench Archive, RCT to CCT, 14, 24 November 1917.
29. IWM, Charlie May Diary, p. 24.
30. Greenwell, *An Infant in Arms*, p. 182.
31. Trench Archive, RCT to ICT, 2 June 1916; Roper, *Secret Battle*, pp. 166–7.
32. IWM, Charlie May Diary, 18 December 1915, 30 January 1916.
33. Cited in Holmes, *Tommy*, p. 170.
34. Spicer, *Letters from France*, p. 5.
35. Greenwell, *An Infant in Arms*, p. 51.
36. Holmes, *Tommy*, pp. 359–62.
37. Nason, ed., *For Love and Courage*, pp. 3, 8.
38. Ibid., p. 119.
39. Ibid., p. 351.
40. I am grateful to Lieutenant Colonel Adrian Bunting for information about this relationship.
41. Trench Archive, RCT to CCT, 23 April, 19 May 1917.
42. Trench Archive, RCT to CCT, 8 March 1918; Roper, *Secret Battle*, p. 145.
43. Trench Archive, Albert Lane to CCT, undated 1950s.
44. Roper, *Secret Battle*, pp. 137–8, 157.
45. Smith, *Letters Sent from France*, p. 132.
46. Greenwell, *An Infant in Arms*, pp. 51–4; Roper, *Secret Battle*, pp. 138–42.
47. Moynihan, ed., *Greater Love*, pp. 68–70; IWM, Sweeney Letters, 17 December 1915.
48. Harris, *Billie*, pp. 118–19, 168.
49. Spicer, *Letters from France*, pp. 72, 114–15.
50. Nason, ed., *For Love and Courage*, pp. 262, 362.
51. Feilding, *War Letters to a Wife*, p. 59.
52. IWM, Reader Letters, 21.
53. Middlebrook, ed., *Diaries of Private Bruckshaw*, pp. xxii–xxiii, 150.
54. IWM, Newman Letters, pp. 148, 178.
55. Smith, *Letters Sent from France*, p. 82
56. IWM, Charlie May Diary, 4–6 December 1915.
57. Greenwell, *An Infant in Arms*, pp. 107, 119–20.
58. Sherwood Foresters Regimental Museum, Operation Orders 27–30, 2/5th Battalion.
59. Trench Archive, RCT to CCT, 11, 13 October 1917.
60. Greenwell, *An Infant in Arms*, p. 59.
61. Trench Archive, RCT to ICT, 24 November 1917.
62. IWM, Charlie May Diary, 29 February, 8 March 1916.
63. IWM, Spencer Letters 9.
64. Harris, *Billie*, pp. 117–18.
65. Spicer, *Letters Sent from France*, pp. 3–6.
66. Spicer, ibid., p. 55 has a map showing the regiment's positions at 7.30 a.m. and at nightfall on 1 July.
67. Spicer, *Letters from France*, pp. 74–127.
68. Nason, ed., *For Love and Courage*, pp. 101–7, 260, 275–86.

69. Feilding, *War Letters to a Wife*, pp. 38–51, 69–73, 112–17, 159–60.
70. Gilbert, *First World War*, pp. 308–9.
71. Trench Archive, RCT to CCT, 5 April 1917, RCT to ICT, 13 April 1917; Sherwood Foresters Regimental Museum, 2/5th Battalion diary of events 23/2/17–3/8/18; Hall, *Green Triangle*, pp. 57–75; *History Today*, 54 (August 2004), pp. 35–6.
72. Trench Archive, RCT to CCT, 3, 7 May 1917; RCT to ICT, 3, 10 May 1917; Hall, *Green Triangle*, pp. 79–87.

7 'Such a Helpless Lot of Babes': Care for the Men

1. Winter, *Death's Men*, pp. 95–8.
2. Trench Archive, RCT to ICT, 13 April 1917; Roper, *Secret Battle*, pp. 122–3.
3. Smith, *Letters Sent from France*, p. 66.
4. Trench Archive, RCT to CCT, 19 May 1917.
5. Griffith quoted in Sheffield, *Leadership in the Trenches*, pp. 81–2.
6. Roper, *Secret Battle*, p. 165.
7. Smith, *Letters Sent from France*, p. 130.
8. Harris, *Billie*, p. 47.
9. Trench Archive, RCT to CCT, 28 February, 2 March 1917.
10. IWM, Spencer Letters, 8.
11. Meyer, *Men of War*, p. 51.
12. IWM, Newman Letters, pp. 109, 130; Roper, *Secret Battle*, pp. 124–5.
13. IWM, Newman Letters, pp. 388, 391, 445; Meyer, *Men of War*, p. 32.
14. Cited in Duffett, 'A War Unimagined: Food and the Rank and File Soldier of the First World War', in Meyer, ed., *British Popular Culture and the First World War*, p. 50.
15. Corrigan, *Mud, Blood and Poppycock*, pp. 96–8.
16. Holmes, *Tommy*, pp. 314–15, citing Dolden.
17. Trench Archive, RCT to CCT, 21 September 1917; RCT to ICT, 24 October 1917.
18. Corrigan, *Mud, Blood and Poppycock*, p. 97; Fuller, *Troop Morale and Popular Culture*, p. 59.
19. Cited in Holmes, *Tommy*, pp. 320–1; Thompson, ed., *Julian Grenfell*, pp. 227–8.
20. Trench Archive, RCT to ICT, 13, 22 May 1917; Roper, *Secret Battle*, p. 112.
21. *History Today*, 54 (August 2004), p. 34.
22. Hall, *Green Triangle*, p. 153.
23. Ibid.
24. Meyer, ed., *British Popular Culture and the First World War*, pp. 53–4.
25. Trench Archive, RCT to CCT, 23 August 1917.
26. Trench Archive, RCT to ICT, 19 August, 5, 9 September 1917.
27. Trench Archive, RCT to CCT, 3 February 1918.
28. Fuller, *Troop Morale and Popular Culture*, pp. 82–3; Bowman, *Irish Regiments in the Great War*, pp. 26–7.
29. IWM, Charlie May Diary, 16 March 1916.
30. Dunn, *The War the Infantry Knew*, pp. 184, 203–5.
31. Nason, ed., *For Love and Courage*, pp. 188–90.
32. Spicer, *Letters from France*, pp. 42–3, 52–3.
33. Trench Archive, RCT to ICT, 5, 9 September 1917; RCT to CCT, 29 August, 10 September 1917.
34. Trench Archive, RCT to CCT, 7, 9, 30 October 1917, 15 February 1918, RCT to ICT, 14 February 1918; Hall, *Green Triangle*, pp. 120–30; Roper, *Secret Battle*, pp. 132–3.
35. Trench Archive, RCT to CCT, 23 March, 18 April 1917.
36. Dunn, *The War the Infantry Knew*, p. 287; Roper, *Secret Battle*, p. 134.
37. Trench Archive, 9 November 1917.
38. Spicer, *Letters from France*, p. 2.
39. Thompson, ed., *Julian Grenfell*, pp. 233, 244, 253, 261; Davenport-Hines, *Ettie*, p. 189.
40. Cited in Sheffield, *Leadership in the Trenches*, p. 82.

41. Roper, *Secret Battle*, pp. 133–4.
42. Smith, *Letters Sent from France*, pp. 105, 121, 125; Roper, *Secret Battle*, pp. 130–1.
43. Harris, *Billie*, pp. 69, 183–4; Winter, *Death's Men*, pp. 146–7.
44. Trench Archive, RCT to CCT, 5, 9, 10 March 1917, RCT to ICT, 3 March 1917; Roper, *Secret Battle*, p. 121.
45. *History Today*, 54 (August 2004), pp. 34–5.
46. Harris, *Billie*, p. 77.
47. Greenwell, *An Infant in Arms*, pp. 44, 56.
48. Harris, *Billie*, p. 74.
49. Trench Archive, RCT to ICT, 26 January 1918.
50. Winter, *Death's Men*, pp. 155–6; Holmes, *Tommy*, p. 604; Fuller, *Troop Morale and Popular Culture*, p. 91.
51. Thompson, ed., *Julian Grenfell*, p. 268.
52. Cited in Fuller, *Troop Morale and Popular Culture*, p. 88.
53. Ibid., pp. 88–9, 94; Hall, *Green Triangle*, p. 98.
54. IWM, Newman Letters, pp. 366, 439.
55. IWM, Charlie May Diary, 22 April 1916.
56. Smith, *Letters Sent from France*, p. 132.
57. Thompson, ed., *Julian Grenfell*, p. 255.
58. Hall, *Green Triangle*, pp. 94–6.
59. Fuller, *Troop Morale and Popular Culture*, p. 91.
60. Trench Archive, RCT to CCT, 1 June, 30 July, 7, 20 August, 18 September 1917, 3 February 1918; RCT to ICT, 19 August 1917; *History* 60 (2005), pp. 533–4, 542.
61. Feilding, *War Letters to a Wife*, pp. 106–7, 128–9.
62. For this argument see Roper, *Secret Battle*, esp. pp. 159–63.
63. Cited in Holmes, *Tommy*, pp. 577–8; Roper, *Secret Battle*, pp. 164–5.
64. Smith, *Letters Sent from France*, pp. 112–18,
65. Spicer, *Letters from France*, p. 16.
66. Harris, *Billie*, pp. 56, 62.
67. *Burgoyne Diaries*, p. 85.
68. Trench Archive, RCT to CCT, 27 February 1917.
69. Trench Archive, RCT to CCT, 27 February, 11 April 1917.
70. Bond, *Survivors of a Kind*, p. 108.
71. [Plowman], *A Subaltern on the Somme*, pp. 63–4.
72. *Burgoyne Diaries*, p. 77.
73. Trench Archive, RCT to CCT, 7, 10 March 1917; RCT to ICT, 24 October 1917.
74. Trench Archive, RCT to CCT, 4 January 1918.
75. Harris, *Billie*, p. 140.
76. Holmes, *Tommy*, pp. 604–10.
77. Smith, *Letters Sent from France*, pp. 77–8, 132.
78. Holmes, *Tommy*, pp. 602–3; Fuller, *Troop Morale and Popular Culture*, pp. 94–110, 186–93.
79. IWM, Charlie May Diary, 20 April 1916.
80. Dunn, *The War the Infantry Knew*, pp. 185–6.
81. *ODNB*, rev. Eric Midwinter, Stanley Augustus Holloway.
82. *ODNB*, Eric Shorter, Leslie Henson.
83. Feilding, *War Letters to a Wife*, pp. 79, 184.
84. *ODNB*, Frank M. Scheide, Sir Charles Spencer Chaplin.
85. Feilding, *War Letters to a Wife*, pp. 133–4; Fuller, *Troop Morale and Popular Culture*, pp. 110–13.
86. Hall, *Green Triangle*, p. 95; Trench Archive, RCT to CCT, 23 September 1917.
87. Holmes, *Tommy*, pp. 503–24; Corrigan, *Mud, Blood and Poppycock*, pp. 100–4.
88. I am grateful to Dr Edward Madigan for these figures.
89. Trench Archive, *The Times*, 3 June 1963; Blackburne, *This Also Happened on the Western Front*.

90. Feilding, *War Letters to a Wife*, pp. 18, 75, 85–7, 109–10, 135–6.
91. Ibid., p. 174.
92. Chapman, *Passionate Prodigality*, p. 117; Holmes, *Tommy*, pp. 514–15.
93. Nason, ed., *For Love and Courage*, p. 216.
94. Trench Archive, RCT to CCT, 14 April, 5, 23 August 1917.
95. Trench Archive, letter from Rev. H.P. Greaves to the *Evening Standard*, undated; Hall, *Green Triangle*, p. 155.
96. Moynihan, ed., *God on Our Side*, pp. 116–43.
97. Ibid., pp. 144–73.
98. IWM, Newman Letters, pp. 331, 370, 375, 445.
99. Corrigan, *Mud, Blood and Poppycock*, pp. 99–104.
100. Fuller, *Troop Morale and Popular Culture*, pp. 26–7.

8 'Drops of his Blood on my Hand': Horror and Endurance

1. Todman, *The Great War*, pp. 1–26.
2. Gilbert, *First World War*, pp. 199–201.
3. Feilding, *War Letters to a Wife*, pp. 20–8, 52–4.
4. Nason, ed., *For Love and Courage*, pp. 102–7.
5. Ibid., pp. 279–81.
6. See, for this repression, Roper, *Secret Battle*, pp. 247–51.
7. Spicer, *Letters from France*, pp. xiv, 3–6. See above pp. 136–7.
8. Harris, ed., *Billie*, p. 145
9. Greenwell, *An Infant in Arms*, pp. 61–3, 125–6.
10. Trench Archive, RCT to CCT, 6, 13 December 1917, RCT to ICT, 8, 22 December 1917.
11. Moynihan, ed., *Greater Love*, p. 21.
12. Brown, *IWM Book of the Western Front*, pp. 246–7.
13. Moynihan, ed., *Greater Love*, pp. 74, 81–3, 86–8.
14. Housman, ed., *War Letters of Fallen Englishmen*, pp. 279–82.
15. Cited in Todman, *The Great War*, pp. 46–7.
16. McCartney, *Citizen Soldiers*, p. 200.
17. Trench Archive, RCT to CCT, 18 April, 9 October 1917, 14 February 1918.
18. IWM, Newman Letters, pp. 417–19, 424–5, 466–8, 477.
19. Moran, *Anatomy of Courage*, pp. 42, 128.
20. IWM, Charlie May Diary, 6 April, 24 June 1916; Meyer, *Men of War*, pp. 57–60.
21. Harris, *Billie*, pp. 98–9, 120, 170.
22. Feilding, *War Letters to a Wife*, pp. 73, 75–6, 79, 100, 127. For Ginchy see above pp. 219–20.
23. Trench Archive, RCT to CCT, 29, 30 April, 1, 2, 7 May 1917; RCT to ICT, 16 April, 3, 10 May 1917.
24. Trench Archive, RCT to CCT, 9, 12 May 1917; RCT to ICT, 22 May 1917; *History Today* 59(November 2009), p. 49.
25. Trench Archive, RCT to CCT, 9 October, 2 December 1917, 9 March 1918.
26. Greenwell, *An Infant in Arms*, pp. 9, 15, 17–18, 89, 131.
27. Nason, ed., *For Love and Courage*, pp. 160–4.
28. IWM, Charlie May Diary, 21.
29. Feilding, *War Letters to a Wife*, pp. 9–10.
30. For spiritualism see Winter, *Sites of Memory, Sites of Mourning*, pp. 5, 54–77
31. Trench Archive, RCT to CCT, 3, 29 July, 10, 25 August, 24, 28 November 1917: Hall, *Green Triangle*, pp. 91–2
32. Middlebrook, ed., *Diaries of Private Bruckshaw*, pp. 153–4; Moynihan, ed., *Greater Love*, p. 25.
33. Harris, *Billie*, p. 135.
34. Smith, *Letters Sent from France*, pp. 59, 77–87.
35. Trench Archive, RCT to CCT, 30 April 1917.
36. Trench Archive, RCT to CCT, 11 February 1917.

9 'I Merely Did my Duty': Discipline and Morale

1. Watson, *Enduring the Great War*, pp. 56–8, 140–1.
2. Bowman, *Irish Regiments in the Great War*, p. 21.
3. Carrington, *Soldier from the Wars Returning*, p. 172.
4. Babington, *For the Sake of Example*; Putkowski and Sykes, *Shot at Dawn*; McCartney, *Citizen Soldiers*, pp. 162–3.
5. Smith, *Letters Sent from France*, p. 93; Sheffield, *Leadership in the Trenches*, pp. 66–7; Roper, *Secret Battle*, pp. 160, 166.
6. See the table on p. 173 of McCartney, *Citizen Soldiers*.
7. Watson, *Enduring the Great War*, p. 59.
8. Sheffield, *Leadership in the Trenches*, pp. 63–4; Holmes, *Tommy*, p. 558.
9. Bourke, *Dismembering the Male*, pp. 99–101.
10. Citations from Sheffield, *Leadership in the Trenches*, pp. 64–5.
11. Citations from Holmes, *Tommy*, p. 559.
12. MacArthur, *For King and Country*, pp. 175–6.
13. Feilding, *War Letters to a Wife*, pp. 108–9.
14. McCartney, *Citizen Soldiers*, pp. 163–7.
15. Watson, *Enduring the Great War*, p. 39.
16. McCartney, *Citizen Soldiers*, pp. 172–5, citing Moran, *Anatomy of Courage*, p. 69.
17. Trench Archive, RCT to CCT, 5 June 1917.
18. McCartney, *Citizen Soldiers*, pp. 167–8.
19. Smith, *Letters Sent from France*, pp. 88–9, 114; Roper, *Secret Battle*, pp. 158–9.
20. [Plowman], *A Subaltern on the Somme*, pp. 84–5, 87–9.
21. McCartney, *Citizen Soldiers*, pp. 168–71, 173.
22. Watson, *Enduring the Great War*, p. 40.
23. [Plowman], *A Subaltern on the Somme*, pp. 189–91, 198–9.
24. IWM, Charlie May Diary, 16, 23–27 December 1915, 19 January 1916.
25. Ibid., 28–29 March, 23 April 1916.
26. Citations from Holmes, *Tommy*, p. 556; Watson, *Enduring the Great War*, p. 61.
27. For rules and procedure see Corrigan, *Mud, Blood and Poppycock*, pp. 221–7.
28. Middlebrook, ed., *Diaries of Private Bruckshaw*, p. 173.
29. Greenwell, *An Infant in Arms*, p. 152.
30. Trench Archive, RCT to CCT, 26 August 1917, 22 January 1918, RCT to ICT, 5 January 1918. For this incident see p. 166.
31. Watson, *Enduring the Great War*, pp. 56–9.
32. Trench Archive, RCT to CCT, 25–30 July 1917.
33. Trench Archive, RCT to CCT, 29, 31 July, 11 September 1917, 20 February 1918.
34. Spicer, *Letters from France*, pp. 55–9, 74–127.
35. IWM, Streets Papers; Piuk, *A Dream within the Dark*, pp. 27–8, 58, 63.
36. IWM, Newman Letters, pp. 438–44, 508–9.
37. Watson, *Enduring the Great War*, p. 64.
38. Citations ibid., p. 63; Feilding, *War Letters to a Wife*, p. 111.
39. Simkins, *Kitchener's Army*, pp. 79–103; Watson, *Enduring the Great War*, pp. 64–5.
40. Trench Archive, RCT to CCT, 22 August, 1, 12, 21 September, 2 October, 15 November 1917, RCT to ICT, 16 September 1917.
41. Feilding, *War Letters to a Wife*, p. 75.
42. Trench Archive, RCT to CCT, 9 October 1917; Hall, *Green Triangle*, facing p. 99.
43. Housman, ed., *War Letters of Fallen Englishmen*, pp. 248–9
44. Moran, *Anatomy of Courage*, p. 16.
45. Watson, *Enduring the Great War*, pp. 70–1.
46. Moynihan, ed., *God on Our Side*, p. 133.
47. Ferguson, *Pity of War*, pp. 357–66; Winter, *Death's Men*, pp. 210–11.
48. Fraser-Tytler, *Field Guns in France*, pp. 51, 255.
49. Fitzwilliams, *Letters from a Gunner*, pp. 16–17, 69, 72, 245–53, 299.
50. Nason, ed., *For Love and Courage*, p. 111.

51. IWM, Newman Letters, p. 165; cited in Meyer, *Men of War*, p. 19.
52. Trench Archive, RCT to CCT, 11 May 1917.
53. Watson, *Enduring the Great War*, pp. 73–84.
54. Trench Archive, RCT to CCT, 24 October 1917.
55. Cited in Holmes, *Tommy*, p. 545.
56. Feilding, *War Letters to a Wife*, pp. 130–1.
57. MacArthur, ed., *For King and Country*, pp. 82–5.
58. IWM, Charlie May Diary, 21 March 1916.
59. Spicer, *Letters from France*, pp. 12–13.
60. Ashworth, *Trench Warfare*, p. 19.
61. Feilding, *War Letters to a Wife*, pp. 16–17.
62. Housman, ed., *War Letters of Fallen Englishmen*, p. 241.
63. Greenwell, *An Infant in Arms*, p. 136.
64. Feilding, *War Letters to a Wife*, p. 55.
65. Smith, *Letters Sent from France*, p. 86.
66. For this argument see Watson, *Enduring the Great War*, pp. 141–7.
67. Gilbert, *First World War*, pp. 115–17.
68. Captain Liddell Hart cited in Ashworth, *Trench Warfare*, p. 25.
69. Ibid., pp. 24–7.
70. Gilbert, *First World War*, pp. 117–19; Brown, *IWM Book of the Western Front*, pp. 52–5; Holmes, *Tommy*, pp. 544–6.
71. Winter, *Death's Men*, pp. 220–2; Ashworth, *Trench Warfare*, pp. 27–39; McCartney, *Citizen Soldiers*, pp. 178–9.
72. Feilding, *War Letters to a Wife*, pp. 98–9.
73. Watson, *Enduring the Great War*, p. 149.
74. Sheffield and Todman, eds, *Command and Control on the Western Front*, pp. 6–8.
75. Greenwell, *An Infant in Arms*, pp. 12–79, esp. pp. 40–1.
76. Spicer, *Letters from France*, pp. 3–30, esp. 15–16.
77. Feilding, *War Letters to a Wife*, pp. 20–8. For a narrative of the battle see Gilbert, *First World War*, pp. 196–201.
78. Simkins, *Kitchener's Army*, pp. 316–17.
79. Sheffield, *Forgotten Victory*, pp. 154–7.

10 'Very Gallant in Every Way': Early Losses

1. Sheffield, *Forgotten Victory*, pp. 122–3; Gilbert, *First World War*, pp. 132–3.
2. IWM, Spencer Letters 31 and condolence letters.
3. Sheffield, *Forgotten Victory*, p. 124.
4. Thompson, ed., *Julian Grenfell*, pp. 287–99; Mosley, *Julian Grenfell*, pp. 252–67; Davenport-Hines, *Ettie*, pp. 191–4; Gilbert, *First World War*, p. 161.
5. Gilbert, *First World War*, pp. 197–204.
6. Wemyss, *A Family Record*, pp. 314–34.
7. Smith, *Letters Sent from France*, pp. 136–44.

11 'Blighty, oh Blighty in about a Week': Leave

1. Moynihan, ed., *Greater Love*, pp. 157–8, 181–3.
2. McCartney, *Citizen Soldiers*, p. 101.
3. Thompson, ed., *Julian Grenfell*, pp. 247–59.
4. Smith, *Letters Sent from France*, pp. 58, 65, 73, 101–2, 107.
5. Greenwell, *An Infant in Arms*, pp. 64–5, 84, 104, 181, 196.
6. Harris, *Billie*, pp. 120, 126.
7. Ibid., p. 134.
8. Ibid., pp. 142, 182–6.
9. Spicer, *Letters from France*, pp. 27–32, 71.

10. IWM, Charlie May Diary, 3–17 February 1916.
11. Feilding, *War Letters to a Wife*, pp. 16–172.
12. Nason, ed., *For Love and Courage*, pp. 83, 91, 127–40.
13. Ibid., pp. 141–50, 194, 297–8.
14. Dunn, *The War the Infantry Knew*, p. 185.
15. Trench Archive, RCT to CCT, 10, 12 June 1917.
16. Trench Archive, RCT to CCT, 29 May, 23 June, 4, 25 July 1917.
17. Trench Archive, RCT to CCT, 2 August 1917, 1 January 1918; RCT to ICT, 22 December 1917.
18. Trench Archive, RCT to CCT, 20 February 1918; Hall, *Green Triangle*, pp. 139–48.
19. IWM, Newman Letters, pp. 222–32.
20. *ODNB*, Robin Prior and Trevor Wilson, Douglas Haig, First Earl Haig.
21. IWM, Newman Letters, pp. 387, 413, 418–19, 427–8.
22. Moynihan, ed., *Greater Love*, pp. 73–6; IWM, Sweeney Letters, 2 May, 23 June 1916.
23. IWM, Sweeney Letters, 19 November, 8 December 1916.
24. Moynihan, ed., *Greater Love*, pp. 85–6.
25. Winter, *Death's Men*, pp. 165–9.
26. Campbell, *In the Cannon's Mouth*, pp. 96–8; Holmes, *Tommy*, pp. 610–12.

12 'I Am Serene, Unafraid': The Somme

1. For the planning of the battle and preparations between January and June 1916 see Philpott, *Bloody Victory*, pp. 88–171; Howard, *First World War*, pp. 64–5.
2. IWM, Charlie May Diary, 1 March 1916.
3. Watson, *Enduring the Great War*, p. 150.
4. IWM, Charlie May Diary, 14 May, 15, 16 June 1916.
5. Cited in Philpott, *Bloody Victory*, p. 171.
6. Corrigan, *Mud, Blood and Poppycock*, p. 276.
7. Howard, *First World War*, pp.64–5.
8. Strachan, *The First World War*, pp. 186–8; Holmes, *The Western Front*, pp. 124–6.
9. Gilbert, *The First World War*, pp.256–60
10. I am grateful to the producer of the film *Lions Led by Donkeys*, Brian Harding, for lending me a DVD of the film he made.
11. Greenwell, *An Infant in Arms*, p. 107.
12. For the plan and preparations see Middlebrook, *The First Day on the Somme*, pp. 53–106.
13. Piuk, *A Dream within the Dark*, p. 63.
14. Feilding, *War Letters to a Wife*, p. 50; Harris, *Billie*, pp. 190–2.
15. Greenwell, *An Infant in Arms*, pp. 108–9.
16. Philpott, *Bloody Victory*, pp. 8–9, 600–1.
17. Middlebrook, *First Day on the Somme*, p. 210; for Mametz see Philpott, *Bloody Victory*, pp. 184–7.
18. IWM, Charlie May Diary 17 June–1 July; correspondence between Maud May and Arthur Bunting.
19. I am grateful to Lieutenant Colonel Adrian Bunting for this information.
20. Middlebrook, *First Day on the Somme*, p. 124; *ODNB*, Roger T. Stearn, Wilfrid Percy Nevill; for Montauban see Philpott, *Bloody Victory*, pp. 172–84.
21. Harris, *Billie*, pp. 195–206.
22. IWM, Streets Papers, letters to Ben Streets 20 June 1916, his mother 23 June 1916.
23. J.W. Streets, *The Undying Splendour*, ed. H.W. Streets, pp. 6–10.
24. Piuk, *A Dream within the Dark*, pp. 65–78; Gilbert, *The First World War*, p. 261; for Serre see Philpott, *Bloody Victory*, pp. 187–92.
25. Greenwell, *An Infant in Arms*, p. 115.
26. Philpott, *Bloody Victory*, pp. 276–9.
27. Citations in this paragraph from Watson, *Enduring the Great War*, pp. 150–1.

28. The best short account of the battle in July and August is Philpott, *Bloody Victory*, pp. 209–82.
29. Greenwell, *An Infant in Arms*, pp. 110–49.
30. Spicer, *War Letters from France*, pp. 55–75.
31. Feilding, *War Letters to a Wife*, pp. 50–75.
32. Philpott, *Bloody Victory*, pp. 348–9.
33. Feilding, *War Letters to a Wife*, pp. 69–73; see above p. 140.
34. IWM, McGregor Papers; Moynihan, ed., *Greater Love*, pp. 26–34.
35. Philpott, *Bloody Victory*, pp. 359–66.
36. For a full account of the battle see Hanson, *Unknown Soldier*, pp. 165–88.
37. IWM, Reader Letters, 68–77; Winter, *Sites of Memory, Sites of Mourning*, pp. 105–8; Philpott, *Bloody Victory*, pp. 538–40.
38. Cited in Philpott, *Bloody Victory*, p. 433.
39. Ibid., pp. 434–45.

13 'Capable of Finishing the Job': Battles of 1917–1918

1. Howard, *First World War*, pp. 81–2; Gilbert, *First World War*, pp. 308–9.
2. Strachan, *First World War*, p. 192.
3. Trench Archive, RCT to ICT, 17 March 1917, RCT to CCT, 18, 20 March 1917.
4. Feilding, *War Letters to a Wife*, pp. 104–5.
5. Spicer, *Letters from France*, pp. 81–2, 93–6.
6. Howard, *First World War*, pp. 88–90; Gilbert, *First World War*, pp. 361–5.
7. Spicer, *Letters from France*, pp. 93–7.
8. Trench Archive, RCT to ICT, 20 June, 29 September 1917.
9. Sheffield, *Forgotten Victory*, pp. 190–216; Gilbert, *First World War*, pp. 319–23, 336–8, 361–5, 377–83; Howard, *First World War*, pp. 81–5, 88–90.
10. Cited in Watson, *Enduring the Great War*, pp. 153–5.
11. Sheffield, *Forgotten Victory*, pp. 216–20.
12. Trench Archive, RCT to CCT, 21 November 1917, RCT to ICT, 24 November 1917.
13. Hall, *Green Triangle*, pp. 129–30; Gilbert, *First World War*, pp. 378–83; Howard, *First World War*, p. 90; Sheffield, *Forgotten Victory*, pp. 216–20.
14. Gregory, *Last Great War*, p. 213; Brown, *IWM Book of 1918: Year of Victory*, pp. 1–18.
15. Gilbert, *First World War*, p. 365.
16. Sheffield, *Forgotten Victory*, pp. 190–6; Gilbert, *First World War*, pp. 319–21.
17. For the whole story see Nason, ed., *For Love and Courage*, pp. 352–5.
18. Howard, *First World War*, pp. 99–101; Gilbert, *First World War*, pp. 406–7; Strachan, *First World War*, pp. 282–9.
19. Trench Archive, RCT to CCT, 21 March 1918.
20. Middlebrook, *The Kaiser's Battle*, pp. 146–222: Philpott, *Bloody Victory*, pp. 497–8.
21. Middlebrook, *The Kaiser's Battle*, pp. 223–260.
22. Trench Archive, Captain H.J. Greaves to Mrs Trench, 30 June 1918.
23. Trench Archive, Drummer Field to Colonel Stepney, 28 January 1919; Private Borchat to Mrs Trench, 1 January 1919; R.W. Lloyd to Mrs Trench, 28 April 1930.
24. Trench Archive, A.J. Lane to Mrs Trench, 12 May 1918; Brigadier T.W. Stansfield to Mrs Trench, with enclosures, 11 April 1918; schedule of questions sent to A.J. Lane by CCT and his replies.
25. Trench Archive, CCT to RCT, 26, 29 March 1918.
26. Trench Archive, C.Q.M.S. Wild to Mrs Trench, 3, 29 May 1918.
27. Hall, *Green Triangle*, pp. 152–3.
28. Trench Archive, Captain Barrows to Mrs Trench, 27 April 1918, Lieutenant Rossiter to Mrs Trench, 16 January 1919, Brigadier Stansfield to Mrs Trench, 27 March 1918; Major Pratt to Mrs Trench, 9 April 1918, Captain Stebbing to Mrs Trench, 20 April 1918.

14 'The Men Cannot Grasp It': Armistice

1. Spicer, *Letters from France*, pp. 107–9.
2. Ibid.
3. IWM, Newman Letters, pp. 498, 538–9.
4. http://web.mala.bc.ca/davies/letters.images/Fereday/Fereday.collection.htm,Canadian Letters and Images Project. I am grateful to Malcolm Kitch for this reference.
5. Spicer, *Letters from France*, pp. 110–15.
6. Philpott, *Bloody Victory*, pp. 503–15; Gilbert, *First World War*, pp. 406–19; Howard, *First World War*, pp. 101–2.
7. Sheffield, *Forgotten Victory*, pp. 221–42; Philpott, *Bloody Victory*, pp. 519–27; Howard, *First World War*, pp. 105–6.
8. Cited in Gilbert, *First World War*, p. 455.
9. Feilding, *War Letters to a Wife*, pp. 172–82.
10. Cited in Brown, *IWM Book of the Western Front*, p. 323.
11. Ibid., pp. 323–31.
12. Feilding, *War Letters to a Wife*, pp. 184–6.
13. Sheffield, *Forgotten Victory*, pp. 242–51; Gilbert, *First World War*, pp. 454–71; Philpott, *Bloody Victory*, pp. 527–32.
14. *ODNB* Jon Stallworthy, Wilfred Edward Salter Owen.
15. Sheffield, *Forgotten Victory*, p. 257.
16. Philpott, *Bloody Victory*, pp. 532–3; Howard, *First World War*, pp. 107–12; Gilbert, *First World War*, pp. 469–500.
17. Feilding, *War Letters to a Wife*, pp. 189–98.
18. Gilbert, *First World War*, pp. 494–8.
19. Feilding, *War Letters to a Wife*, pp. 198–202.
20. Brown, *IWM Book of the Western Front*, pp. 339–44.
21. Gregory, *Silence of Memory*, p. 64.
22. Winter, *Death's Men*, pp. 235–7.
23. Spicer, *Letters from France*, pp. 124–5.
24. MacArthur, ed., *For King and Country*, pp. 400–2.
25. Feilding, *War Letters to a Wife*, pp. 203–4.
26. Cited in Winter, *Death's Men*, p. 237.
27. Bond, *Survivors of a Kind*, pp. 27–35.
28. Holmes, *Tommy*, pp. 613–14.
29. MacArthur, ed., *For King and Country*, pp. 402–4.
30. Todman, *The Great War*, pp. 49–50.
31. Cited ibid., p. 50.
32. Herbert Trench Archive, HCT to MCT, 1 February 1917; HCT to Cesca Trench, 12 April, 17 May 1917.
33. Gilbert, *First World War*, pp. 351–2.
34. Trench Archive, F.H. Chenevix Trench to ICT, 12 April 1918; Georgiana Steel to CCT, undated and 9 April 1918.
35. Herbert Trench Archive, HCT to Cesca Trench, 27 July 1918.
36. Moynihan, ed., *Greater Love*, pp. 88–92.
37. IWM, Newman Letters, pp. 540–1.
38. Newman archive reflections November 1918.
39. Newman archive reflections 1919.
40. DeGroot, *Blighty*, pp. 253–7; Holmes, *Tommy*, pp. 617–22; Winter, *Death's Men*, pp. 238–43.
41. Greenwell, *An Infant in Arms*, pp. 248–51.
42. Feilding, *War Letters to a Wife*, pp. 205–10.

15 'We Will Remember Them': Remembrance and Commemoration

1. *ODNB*, John Hatcher, Laurence Binyon.

2. http:// www//en,Wikipedia.org/wiki/Ode of Remembrance.
3. Todman, *Great War*, pp. 50–1.
4. Winter, *Sites of Memory, Sites of Mourning*, pp. 102–4.
5. Cannadine, 'War and Death, Grief and Mourning in Modern Britain', in Whaley, ed., *Mirrors of Mortality*, pp. 187–252.
6. Newman archive.
7. These paragraphs draw heavily upon Gregory, *Silence of Memory*, pp. 8–50.
8. Winter, *Sites of Memory, Sites of Mourning*, pp. 78–98.
9. Gregory, *Silence of Memory*, pp. 28–9; Winter, *Sites of Memory, Sites of Mourning*, pp. 95–7.
10. Winter, *Sites of Memory, Sites of Mourning*, p. 107.
11. Cited in Dakers, *Countryside at War*, p. 210.
12. Ibid., p. 209.
13. Pevsner, *Gloucestershire*, p. 632.
14. Philpott, *Bloody Victory*, pp. 311–12, 539–44.
15. Winter, *Sites of Memory, Sites of Mourning*, pp. 106–7.
16. Citations from Dakers, *Countryside at War*, pp. 185–6: Jalland, *Death in War and Peace*, pp. 50, 61–3.
17. Jalland, *Death in War and Peace*, p. 69.
18. Ibid., pp. 63–77.
19. Dakers, *Countryside at War*, illustrations between pages 192 and 193, p. 187.
20. Trench Archive, correspondence between CCT, the Red Cross and the War Office, June 1918–September 1919.
21. *History Today*, 54 (August 2004) with a recent photograph of the site, p. 37.
22. Trench Archive, HCT to MCT, 2 August 1919.
23. Imperial War Graves Commission to H. Reader, 7 August 1923. I am grateful to Doug Goodman for sight of this letter.
24. I am grateful to Doug Goodman for conversations about the family's acts of remembrance.
25. Gregory, *Silence of Memory*, pp. 98–108.
26. Ibid., pp. 34–41: Todman, *Great War*, pp. 51–6.
27. Middlebrook, *The First Day on the Somme*, p. 314.
28. Philpott, *Bloody Victory*, pp. 544–8.
29. Middlebrook, *The First Day on the Somme*, p. 314.

16 'All the Best and Choicest and Unblemished': War Heroes

1. Gregory, *Last Great War*, cites this from Lloyd George's own pamphlet, *Through Terror to Triumph* (1914) but many versions of the speech were circulated.
2. Pennell, *A Kingdom United*, pp. 57–91.
3. Stanway Archive, Melcho MFD4, Diary 2–24 October 1915.
4. Cynthia Asquith, *Diaries 1915–1918*, p. 62; Dakers, *Countryside at War*, p. 88.
5. Stanway Archive, YVO6.
6. Peter Warlock, *The Life of Philip Heseltine* (1994), p. 38. I am grateful to the Earl of Wemyss for this reference and for advice about Hubert Allen.
7. Wemyss, *A Family Record*, pp. 337, 339–42.
8. Ibid., pp. 335–6.
9. MacKenzie, *Children of the Souls*, pp. 180–262.
10. Jenkins, *Asquith*, pp. 464–6.
11. Davenport-Hines, *Ettie*, pp. 194–7.
12. Cited ibid., p. 196.
13. Citations ibid., pp. 197, 199.
14. For Mary and Balfour see Ridley and Percy, eds, *Letters of Arthur Balfour and Lady Elcho*.
15. Wemyss, *A Family Record*, pp. 337–8.

16. Ibid., pp. 263–4, 372–405.
17. Ibid., p. 372; Roper, *Secret Battle*, pp. 231–2.
18. Wemyss, *A Family Record*, pp. 404–5.
19. Davenport-Hines, *Ettie*, pp. 208–9.
20. MacKenzie, *Children of the Souls*, p. 189.
21. Ibid., pp. 4–22, 223–4, 231–42.
22. Davenport-Hines, *Ettie*, p. 192.
23. MacKenzie, *Children of the Souls*, pp. 242–58.
24. Stanway Archive, Melcho ME5, Frances Horner to Mary Wemyss, 3 December 1917.
25. MacKenzie, *Children of the Souls*, p. 262.
26. Trench Archive, Maud Tennyson Smith to CCT, 20 April 1918.
27. Trench Archive, ICT to RCT, 24 March 1918, CCT to RCT, 24 March 1918.
28. Trench Archive, Brigadier Stansfield to Mrs Trench, 27 March 1918; Captain Clifford to Mrs Trench, 30 March 1918.
29. Trench Archive, Joyce Shipley to CCT, 15 April 1918.
30. Trench Archive, Dr Battiscombe to CCT, 8 April 1918.
31. Trench Archive, RCT to CCT, 18 November 1917.
32. D. Cannadine, 'War and Death, Grief and Mourning in Modern Britain', in Whaley, ed., *Mirrors of Mortality*, pp. 195–6.
33. Trench Archive, Joyce Pollock to CCT, 3, 8, 14, 18 April 1918.
34. Trench Archive, Laura Pollock to CCT, 2 April 1918; Maud Mead to Mrs Trench, 15 April 1918; Lilian Morris to CCT, 16 April 1918.
35. *ODNB*, F.H. Lawson, rev. Peter North, Geoffrey Chevalier Cheshire; Christopher Foxley-Norris, Geoffrey Leonard Cheshire.
36. Trench Archive, Primrose Cheshire to ICT, 16 April 1918; Margaret Sheepshanks to ICT, 15 April 1918; Violet Ashtown to ICT, 5 May 1918.
37. Trench Archive, Sister Ida to CCT, 9 April 1918, Dorothy Howard to CCT, 10, 17 April 1918.
38. Ibid., Walter, Edgar and Stanley Howard to CCT, 7, 8 April 1918.
39. Ibid., Emily Ismay to CCT, 20 April 1918; F.H. Chenevix Trench to CCT, 4 April 1918; Ethel Gore-Booth to CCT, 12 April 1918.
40. Ibid., Edward Burney to CCT, 9, 23 April 1918, 30 January 1919, 18 May 1963; Edward Burney to ICT, 10 April 1918.
41. Ibid., Walter Wood to ICT, 12 January 1919; Guy Beech to ICT, 16 May 1918.
42. Ibid., Mary Holgate to CCT, n.d.
43. For comment on the manner of Reggie's death see Meyer, *Men of War*, pp. 93–5.
44. IWM, Spencer Archive, *Glasgow High School Magazine*, Harold Dehry to Mr Spencer, 21 March 1915.
45. Trench Archive, William Swan to CCT, 3 May 1918; Isabelle Davis to CCT, 3 May 1918; Maud Alliban to CCT, 4, 12 April 1918.
46. Trench Archive, Ethel Gore-Booth to CCT, 12 April 1918; Edward Burney to CCT, 23 April 1918; George Fearn to CCT, 8 April 1918.
47. Trench Archive, P.T. Godsal to Benny Trench, 13 April 1918; Edward Godsal to Benny Trench, 15 April; Josie Carson to ICT, 4 May 1918; Meyer, *Men of War*, p. 93.
48. Williams, *Religious Belief and Popular Culture in Southwark*.
49. Gregory, *Last Great War*, pp. 152–86.

17 'Among the Happiest Years I Have Ever Spent': Survivors

1. Cited in Feilding, *War Letters to a Wife*, Introduction.
2. Ibid., pp. xiii–xiv and illustrations.
3. Pevsner, *Buckinghamshire*, p. 248.
4. Feilding, *War Letters to a Wife*, p. ix, Introduction.
5. Edmonds [Carrington], *A Subaltern's War*, pp. 192–5.
6. Greenwell, *An Infant in Arms*, pp. ix–xix; Bond, *Survivors of a Kind*, pp. 13–17.
7. *ODNB*, Brian Holden Reid, Sir Basil Henry Liddell Hart.

8. Spicer, *Letters from France*, pp. vii–viii, 131. I am grateful to Sir Nicholas Spicer, Susanna Spicer and David Young for reminiscences.
9. Moynihan, ed., *Greater Love*, pp. 90–1; IWM, Sweeney Letters. See above p.
10. I am grateful to David Newman for making available the albums and papers from his family archive on which these paragraphs are based.
11. I am grateful to Robina Lockyer and Valerie Kerslake for conversations about their father.
12. Trench Archive, HCT to MCT, 11 February 1930.
13. Trench Archive, Albert Lane to CCT, 15 May 1918.
14. Trench Archive, Mrs Lane to CCT, 23 May 1918.
15. Trench Archive, Albert Lane to CCT, 14 August 1918.
16. Trench Archive, Mrs Lane to CCT, 13 October 1918.
17. Trench Archive, Albert Lane to CCT, 17 December 1918.
18. Trench Archive, Albert Lane to CCT, 27 January 1961; Delle Fletcher to John Fletcher, 14 August 1977.
19. Trench Archive, Ron Lane to CCT, 25 September 1980; Roper, *Secret Battle*, pp. 145–6.
20. Nason, ed., *For Love and Courage*, pp. 262, 362.
21. Ibid.
22. I am grateful to Jessica Hawes for telling me this story.
23. See above, pp. 130–1.

Epilogue: The Great War in Perspective

1. Barbusse, *Under Fire*, introduction by Jay Winter, pp. vii–xv.
2. Trench Archive, RCT to ICT and to CCT, 5 November 1917.
3. Bond, *Survivors of a Kind*, pp. 93–112.
4. Ibid., pp. 1–11.
5. Ibid., pp. xiii–xvi, 13–44.
6. Edmonds [Carrington], *A Subaltern's War*, pp. 192–5.
7. Carrington, *Soldier from the Wars Returning*, pp. 259–61; Bond, *Survivors of a Kind*, pp. 13–26
8. Bond, *Survivors of a Kind*, pp. 27–34; Jameson, wife of Chapman, *A Passionate Prodigality*, pp. 8–9.
9. Dakers, *Countryside at War*, pp. 11–19.
10. Campbell, *In the Cannon's Mouth*, pp. 41, 99, 143.
11. See the comments by Dan Todman in *The Great War*, pp. 200–1.
12. L. Macdonald, *They Called it Passchendale; Somme; 1914; 1914–1918: Voices and Images of the Great War; 1915: The Death of Innocence; To The Last Man: Spring 1918.*
13. Holmes, *Tommy*, p. 441.
14. These paragraphs owe much to Dan Todman's exploration of myth and memory in *The Great War*, pp. 187–219.

Bibliography

Manuscript Collections

National

Imperial War Museum

P. McGregor Letters 87/56/1
C.C. [Charlie] May Diary 91/23/1
W.P. Nevill Letters 66/140/1 and 1A and Con Shelf
C. T. Newman Letters 03/5/1
B. A. Reader Letters 83/3/1
W.B.P. Spencer Letters 86/56/1
J.W. Streets Letters 67/117/2
D.J. Sweeney Letters 76/226/1 and 1A and Con Shelf

National Archives

War Office Papers

National Library of Ireland

Coffey and Chenevix Trench Archive

National Trust

Arlington Court Archives

Local

Merton College, Oxford: Chenevix Trench Archive
Sherwood Foresters Regimental Museum: 2/5th Battalion, Operation Orders, Diary of Events 1917–1918

In private hands

Herbert Trench Archive
Newman Archive
Stanway Archive

Printed Primary Sources

Asquith, C., *Diaries 1915–1918* (1968)
Barbusse, H., *Under Fire* (2003)
Blackburne, H.W., *This Also Happened on the Western Front* (1920)
Brooke, R., *1914 and Other Poems* (1915)
Campbell, P.J., *In the Cannon's Mouth* (1979)
Carrington, C., *Soldier from the Wars Returning* (2006)
Chapman, G., *A Passionate Prodigality* (1933)
Edmonds, C. [C. Carrington], *A Subaltern's War* (1929)
Feilding, R., *War Letters to a Wife*, ed. J. Walker (2001)
Fitzwilliams, J., *Letters from a Gunner* (1935)
Fraser-Tytler, N., *Field Guns in France* (1922)
Greenwell, G.H., *An Infant in Arms: War Letters of a Company Officer 1914–1918* (1972)
Hankey, D., *A Student in Arms, Second Series* (1916/17)
Housman, L. (ed.), *War Letters of Fallen Englishmen* (1930)
Kipling, R., *Rewards and Fairies* (1911)
Marks, T.P., *The Laughter Goes from Life: In the Trenches of the First World War* (1977)
Middlebrook, M. (ed.), *Diaries of Private Harold Bruckshaw 1915–1916* (1979)
Moran, Lord C.M. Wilson (Lord Moran), *Anatomy of Courage: The Classic WWI Account of the Psychological Effects of War* (2007)
Moynihan, M. (ed.), *Greater Love: Letters Home 1914–1918* (1980)
Nason, A. (ed.), *For Love and Courage: The Letters of Lieutenant Colonel E.W. Hermon from the Western Front 1914–1917* (2008)
[Plowman, M.], *A Subaltern on the Somme* (1928)
Ridley, J. and Percy, C. (eds), *The Letters of Arthur Balfour and Lady Elcho 1885–1917* (1992)
Smith, E.K., *Letters Sent from France: Service with the Artists' Rifles and the Buffs December 1914 to December 1915* (1994)
Spicer, L.D., *Letters from France 1915–1918* (1979)
Streets, J.W., *The Undying Splendour*, ed. H.W. Streets (2002)
Thompson K. (ed.), *Julian Grenfell, Soldier and Poet: Letters and Diaries 1910–1915* (2004)
Vaughan, E.C., *Some Desperate Glory: The World War I Diary of a British Officer 1917* (1981)
Wemyss, M., *A Family Record* (1935)

Printed Secondary Sources

Ashworth, T., *Trench Warfare 1914–1918: The Live and Let Live System* (1980)
Babington, A., *For the Sake of Example: Capital Courts Martial 1914–1920* (1997)
Beauman, N., *Cynthia Asquith* (1987)
Bond, B., *Survivors of a Kind: Memoirs of the Western Front* (2008)
Bourke, J., *Dismembering the Male: Men's Bodies, Britain and the Great War* (1996)
Bowman, T., *The Irish Regiments in the Great War: Discipline and Morale* (2003)
Bracco, R.M., *Merchants of Hope: British Middlebrow Writers and the First World War 1919–1939* (1993)
Brown, M., *The Imperial War Museum Book of the Western Front* (1993)
—— *The Imperial War Museum Book of 1918: Year of Victory* (1998)
Carrington, C., *Rudyard Kipling: His Life and Work* (1970)
Cecil, H. and Liddle, P.H. (eds), *Facing Armageddon* (1996)
Corrigan, G., *Mud, Blood and Poppycock* (2003)
Dakers, C., *The Countryside at War 1914–1918* (1987)
Davenport-Hines, R., *Ettie: The Intimate Life and Dauntless Spirit of Lady Desborough* (2008)
DeGroot, G.J., *Blighty: British Society in the Era of the Great War* (1996)
Duffett, R., *The Stomach for Fighting: Food and the Soldiers of the Great War* (2012)
Dunn, J.C., *The War the Infantry Knew 1914–1919* (1938)
Errington, F.H.L., *The Inns of Court Officers Training Corps* (2009)
Ferguson, N., *The Pity of War* (1998)

Fletcher, A.J., *Growing Up in England: The Experience of Childhood 1600–1914* (2008)

Fuller, J.G., *Troop Morale and Popular Culture in the British and Dominion Armies 1914–1918* (1990)

Gilbert, M., *The First World War* (1995)

Girouard, M., *The Return to Camelot: Chivalry and the English Gentleman* (1981)

Goold Walker, G., *The Honourable Artillery Company 1537–1926* (1926)

Gregory, A., *The Silence of Memory: Armistice Day 1919–1946* (1994)

—— *The Last Great War: British Society and the First World War* (2008)

Hall, W.G., *The Green Triangle, Being the History of the 2/5th Battalion The Sherwood Foresters (Notts and Derby Regiment) in the Great European War 1914–1918*

Hanson, N., *The Unknown Soldier: The Story of the Missing of the Great War* (2007)

Harris, R.E., *Billie: The Nevill Letters 1914–1916* (2003)

Hassall, C., *Rupert Brooke: A Biography* (1964)

Holmes, R., *The Western Front* (1999)

—— *Tommy: The British Soldier on the Western Front 1914–1918* (2004)

Howard, M., *The First World War: A Very Short Introduction* (2002)

Jalland, P., *Death in War and Peace: Loss and Grief in England 1914–1970* (2010)

Jenkins, R., *Asquith* (1964)

Lehmann, J., *Rupert Brooke: His Life and his Legend* (1980)

MacArthur, B. (ed.), *For King and Country: Voices from the First World War* (2008)

McCartney, H.B., *Citizen Soldiers: The Liverpool Territorials in the First World War* (2005)

Macdonald, L., *They Called it Passchendale* (1978)

—— *Somme* (1983)

—— *1914* (1987)

—— *1914–1918: Voices and Images of the Great War* (1988)

—— *1915: The Death of Innocence* (1993)

—— *To the Last Man: Spring 1918* (1998)

MacKenzie, J., *The Children of the Souls: A Tragedy of the First World War* (1986)

Mangan, J.A., *Athleticism in the Victorian and Edwardian Public School* (2000)

—— and Walvin, J., *Manliness and Morality: Middle-Class Masculinity in Britain and America, 1800–1940* (1987)

May, H.A.R., *Memories of the Artists' Rifles* (1929)

Meyer, J. (ed.), *British Popular Culture and the First World War* (2008)

—— *Men of War: Masculinity and the First World War in Britain* (2009)

Middlebrook, M., *The Kaiser's Battle* (1983)

Mosley, N., *Julian Grenfell: His Life and the Times of his Death 1888–1915* (1976)

Moynihan, M. (ed.), *God on Our Side* (1983)

Panichas, G.A. (ed.), *Promise of Greatness* (1968)

Parker, P., *The Old Lie: The Great War and the Public School Ethos* (1987)

Pennell, C., *A Kingdom United: British Responses to the Outbreak of the First World War in Britain and Ireland* (2012)

Philpott, W., *Bloody Victory: The Sacrifice on the Somme* (2009)

Piuk, V., *A Dream within the Dark: A Derbyshire Poet in the Trenches* (2003)

Putowski, J. and Sykes, J., *Shot at Dawn: Executions in World War I by Authority of the British Army Act* (1998)

Pyle, H., *Cesca's Diary: Where Art and Nationalism Meet* (2006)

Ricketts, H., *The Unforgiving Minute: A Life of Rudyard Kipling* (2000)

Roper, M., *The Secret Battle: Emotional Survival in the Great War* (2009)

Sanders, M.L. and Taylor, P., *British Propaganda during the First World War* (1982)

Sheffield, G.D., *Leadership in the Trenches: Officer–Man Relations, Morale and Discipline in the British Army in the Era of the First World War* (2000)

—— *Forgotten Victory. The First World War: Myths and Realities* (2001)

—— and Todman, D. (eds), *Command and Control on the Western Front: The British Army's Experience 1914–1918* (2007)

Shephard, B. *A War of Nerves: Soldiers and Psychiatrists 1914–1994* (2000)

Showalter, E., *The Female Malady: Women, Madness and English Culture 1830–1980* (1987)

Simkins, P., *Kitchener's Army: The Raising of the New Armies 1914–1916* (1988)

Strachan, H., *The Oxford Illustrated History of the Great War* (1998)

—— *The Oxford History of the First World War*, Vol. I: *To Arms* (2000)

—— *The First World War: A New Illustrated History* (2003)

Todman, D., *The Great War: Myth and Memory* (2005)

Van Emden, R. and Humphries, S., *All Quiet on the Home Front: An Oral History of Life in Britain during the First World War* (2003)

Watson, A., *Enduring the Great War: Combat, Morale and Collapse in the German and British Armies 1914–1918* (2009)

Whaley, J. (ed.), *Mirrors of Mortality: Social Studies in the History of Death* (2011).

Wilkinson, A., *The Church of England and the First World War* (1978)

Williams, S.C., *Religious Belief and Political Culture in Southwark 1880–1939* (1999)

Winter, D., *Death's Men: Soldiers of the Great War* (1978)

Winter, J., *Sites of Memory, Sites of Mourning: The Great War in European Cultural History* (1995)

Articles and Essays

Cannadine, D., 'War and Death, Grief and Mourning in Modern Britain', in J. Whaley (ed.), *Mirrors of Mortality* (2011)

Duffett, R., 'A war unimagined: food and the rank and file soldier of the First World War', in J. Meyer (ed.), *British Popular Culture in the First World War* (2008)

Fletcher, A.J., 'An Officer on the Western Front', *History Today* 54 (August 2004)

Fletcher, A.J., 'Patriotism, Identity and Commemoration: New Light on the Great War from the Papers of Major Reggie Chenevix Trench', *History* 60 (2005)

Fletcher, A.J., 'Between the Lines', *History Today* 59 (November 2009)

Macleod, A.D., 'Shellshock, Gordon Holmes and the Great War', *Journal of the Royal Society of Medicine* 97 (2004)

Roper, M., 'Maternal Relations: moral manliness and emotional survival in letters home during the First World War', in S. Dudink, K. Hagermann and J. Tosh (eds), *Masculinity in Politics and War* (2004)

Roper, M., 'Between Manliness and Masculinity: the "War Generation" and the Psychology of Fear in Britain 1914–1970', *Journal of British Studies*, 44 no. 2 (2005)

Simpson, K., 'Dr James Dunn and Shellshock', in H. Cecil and P.H. Liddle (eds), *Facing Armageddon* (1996)

Springhall, J., ' Building character in the British boy: the attempt to extend Christian manliness to working-class adolescents', in J.A. Mangan and J. Walvin (eds), *Manliness and Morality* (1987)

Stryker, L., 'Mental Cases: British Shellshock and the Politics of Interpretation', in G. Braybon (ed.), *Evidence, History and the Great War* (2003).

Index